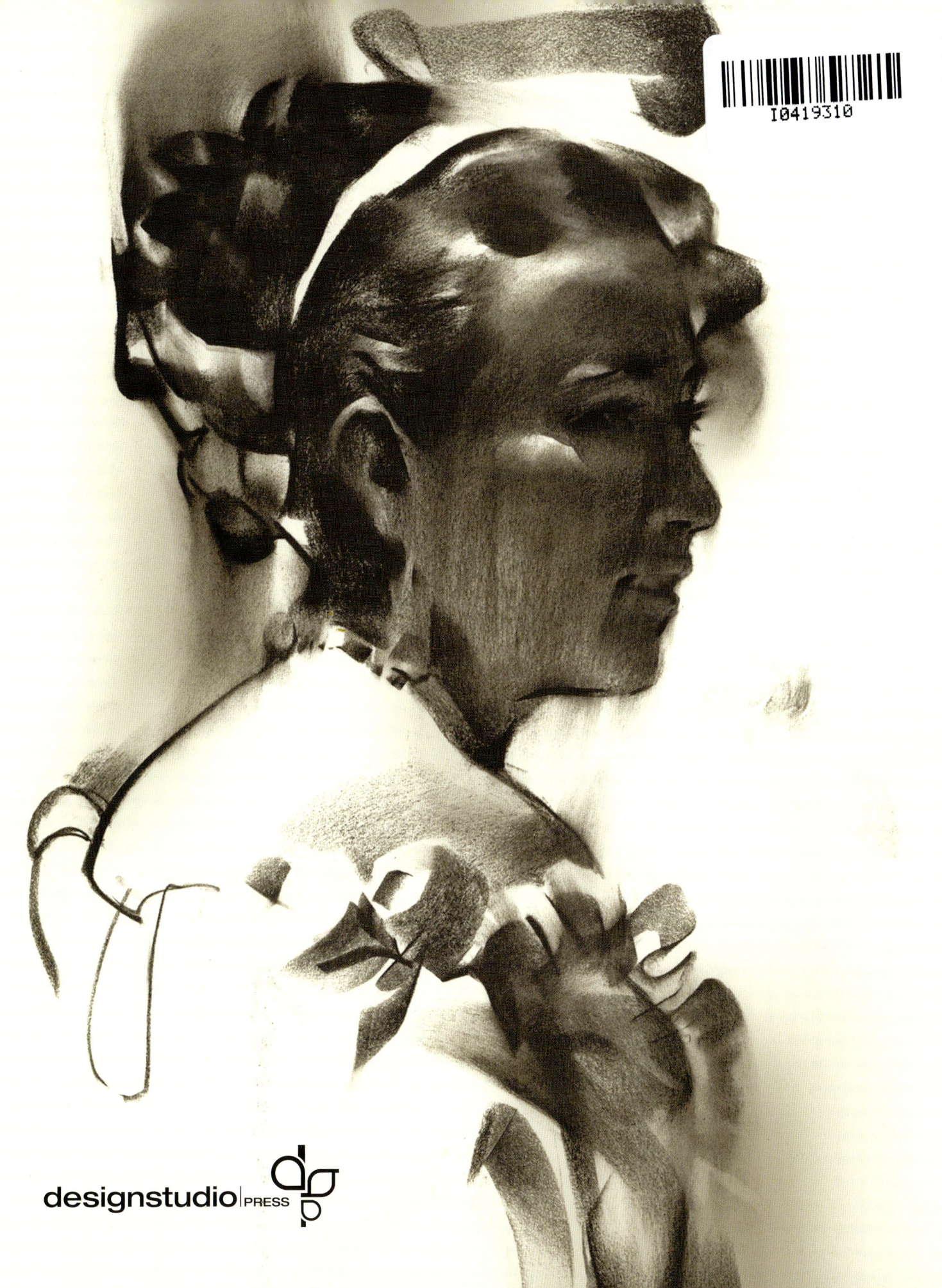

designstudio|PRESS

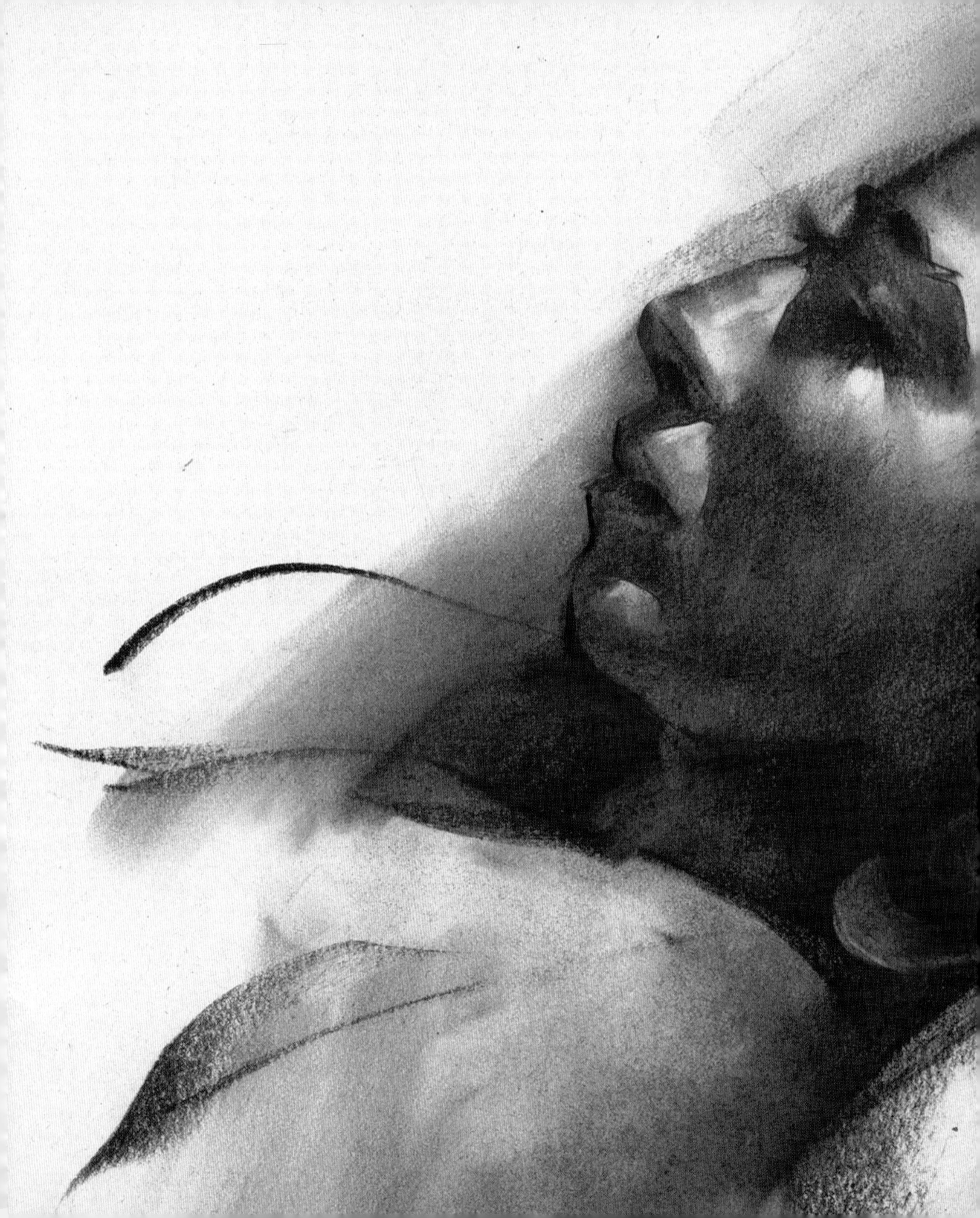

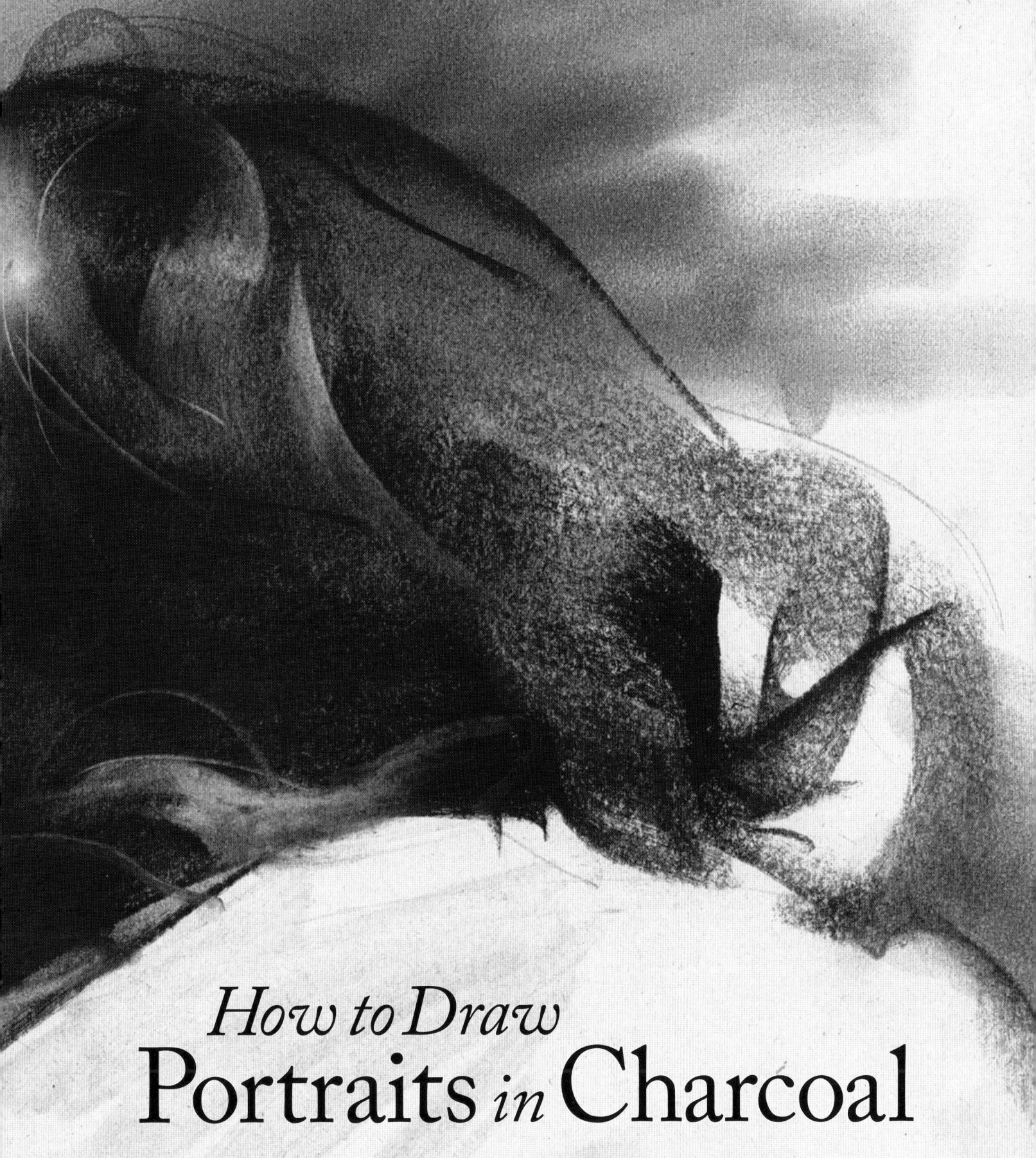

How to Draw
Portraits *in* Charcoal

by Nathan Fowkes

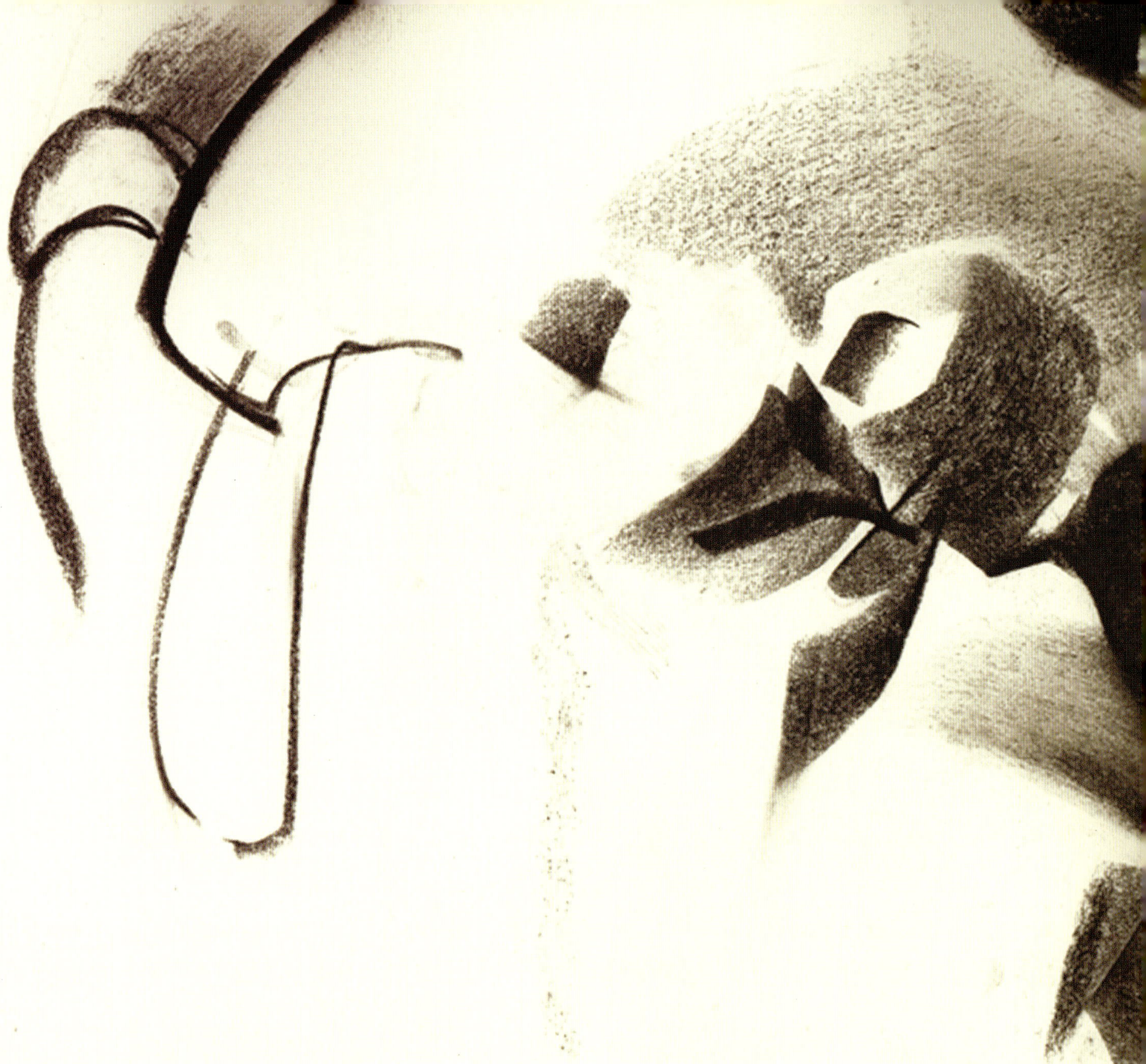

How to Draw
Portraits *in* Charcoal

Published by
Design Studio Press
Website: www.designstudiopress.com
Email: info@designstudiopress.com

Editor: Teena Apeles
Graphic Design: Alyssa Homan
Art Director: Scott Robertson

10 9 8 7 6 5 4
Printed in China
First edition, July 2016

Paperback ISBN: 9781624650314
Library of Congress Control Number: 2016941118

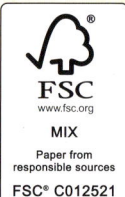

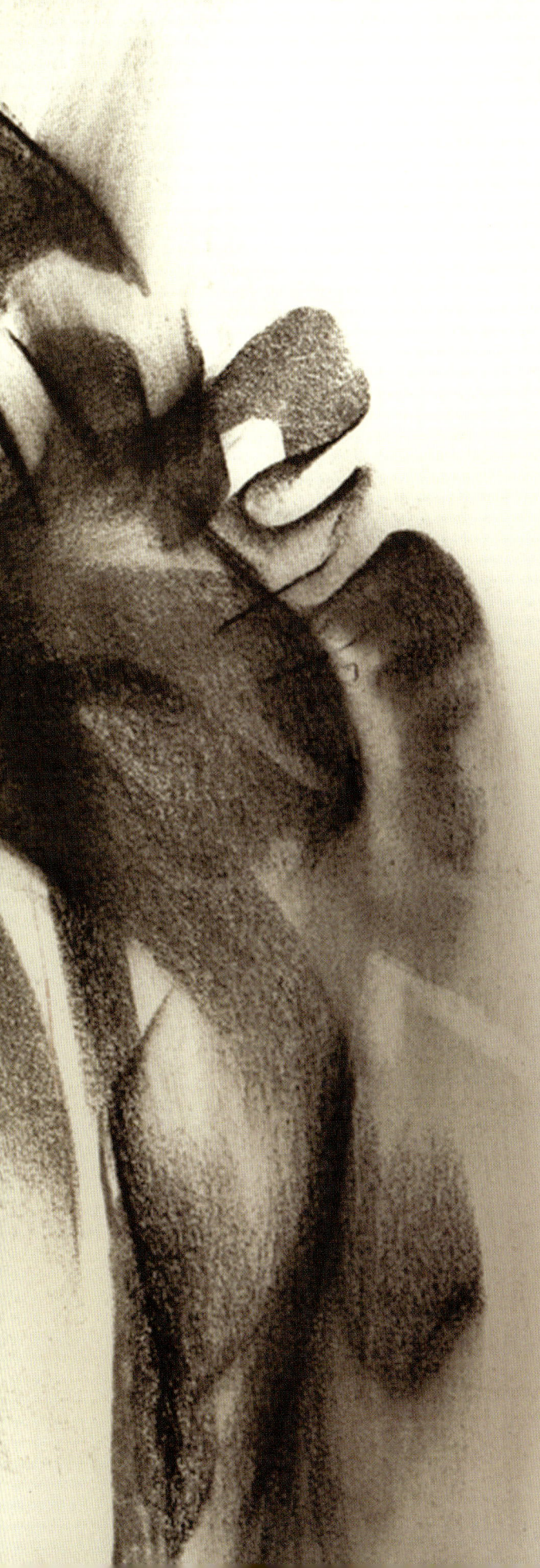

Table *of* Contents

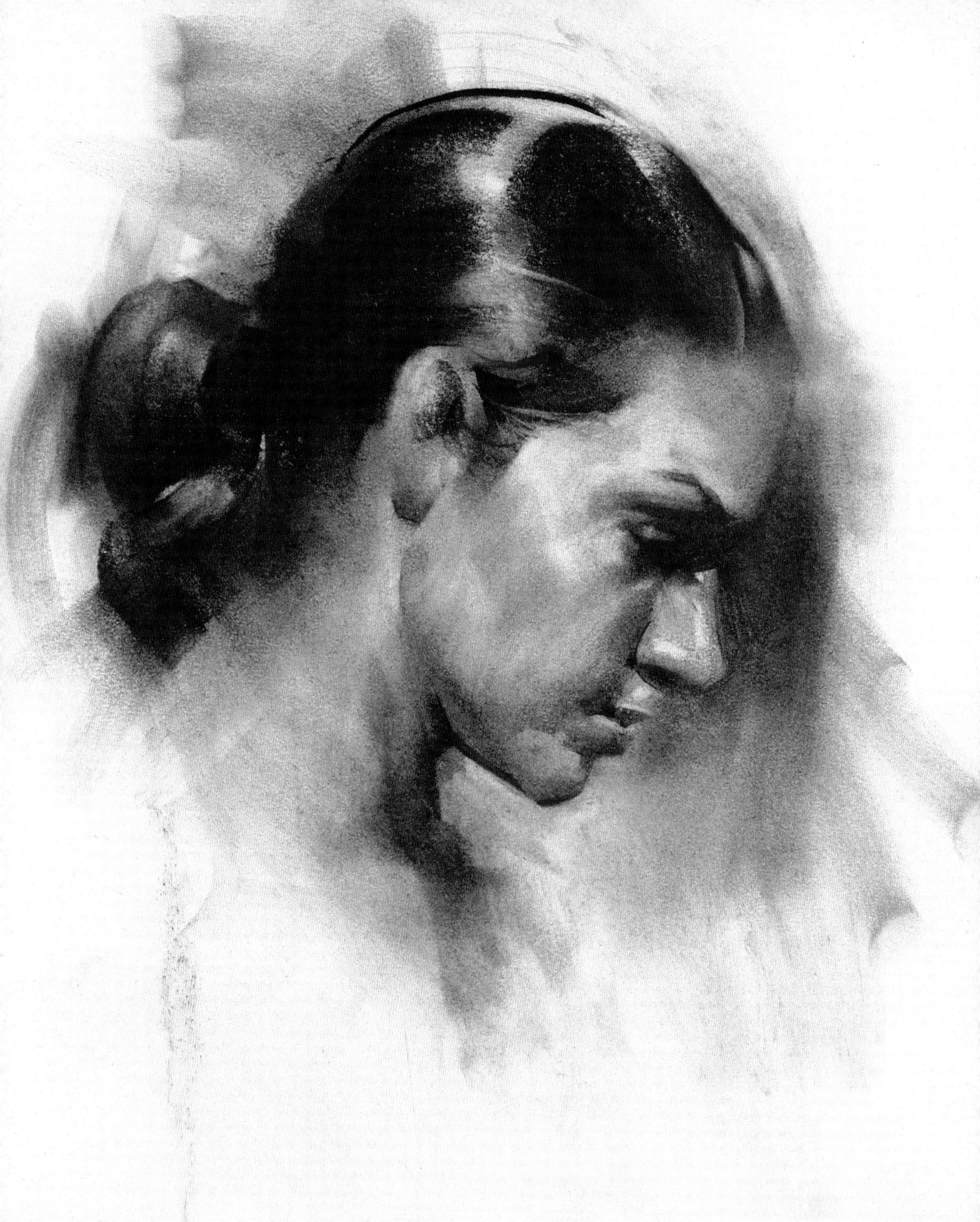

Foreword

Nathan Fowkes: Beyond the Surface

For those of us who have followed the art of Nathan Fowkes online, this book presents a welcome opportunity to study his dazzling charcoal portraits in beautiful detail.

Nathan's portraits overflow with virtuosity. Sweeping, energetic strokes dance across the page, as if animated by a master conjurer. The lighting is so brilliant that it seems to shine brighter than the paper. Shadows are soft and mysterious, concealing more than they reveal.

The student or fellow artist looking for the precise recipe will rejoice, for Nathan generously lists all the tools he uses and all the procedures he follows. There are plenty of step-by-step sequences showing how the drawings develop, and those process images are beautifully shot and printed.

If the book stopped there, it would still be a valuable contribution to a shelf of portrait drawing books. But it goes far beyond style and surface. Nathan delves deeply into the thought and planning that lies behind his drawings.

Beneath the painterly strokes lies a firm armature of line drawing, using an adaptation of the method taught by Frank Reilly (1906–1967), an instructor at the Art Students League. Having that diagrammatic foundation gives the drawings the structure that holds them together. The basic plan is: (1) a simple construction drawing; (2) simple masses of value to describe big forms; and (3) design hard and soft edges.

Nathan explains his principles of construction, lighting, planes, and edges. His insights are like gold: "I'm much more able to render complexity when I look for the simplest shapes first." A recurring theme is that drawing is not a literal representation, but rather an interpretation of what we see.

Although he is specific about his methods and principles, he is not dogmatic about them. He invites the reader to question. He doesn't want students to copy his outward style. Instead he encourages his reader to try out his way of drawing, and, if they wish, to apply it to their own work.

Nathan shows compassion for his subjects. They are not nameless models, but rather human beings. He is not just documenting someone's physiognomy, but rather creating probing studies of character. He tells the story of one of his models, Clark, who had a successful career as a performer until several tragic setbacks changed the course of his life. Nathan's drawings of Clark express both the dignity and resilience of the man.

This book will become a cherished classic of portrait drawing, and I can only hope that we'll see more books in the future that take a similar look at Nathan's observational painting and imaginative work.

James Gurney
Author of *Color and Light, Imaginative Realism,* and *Dinotopia*

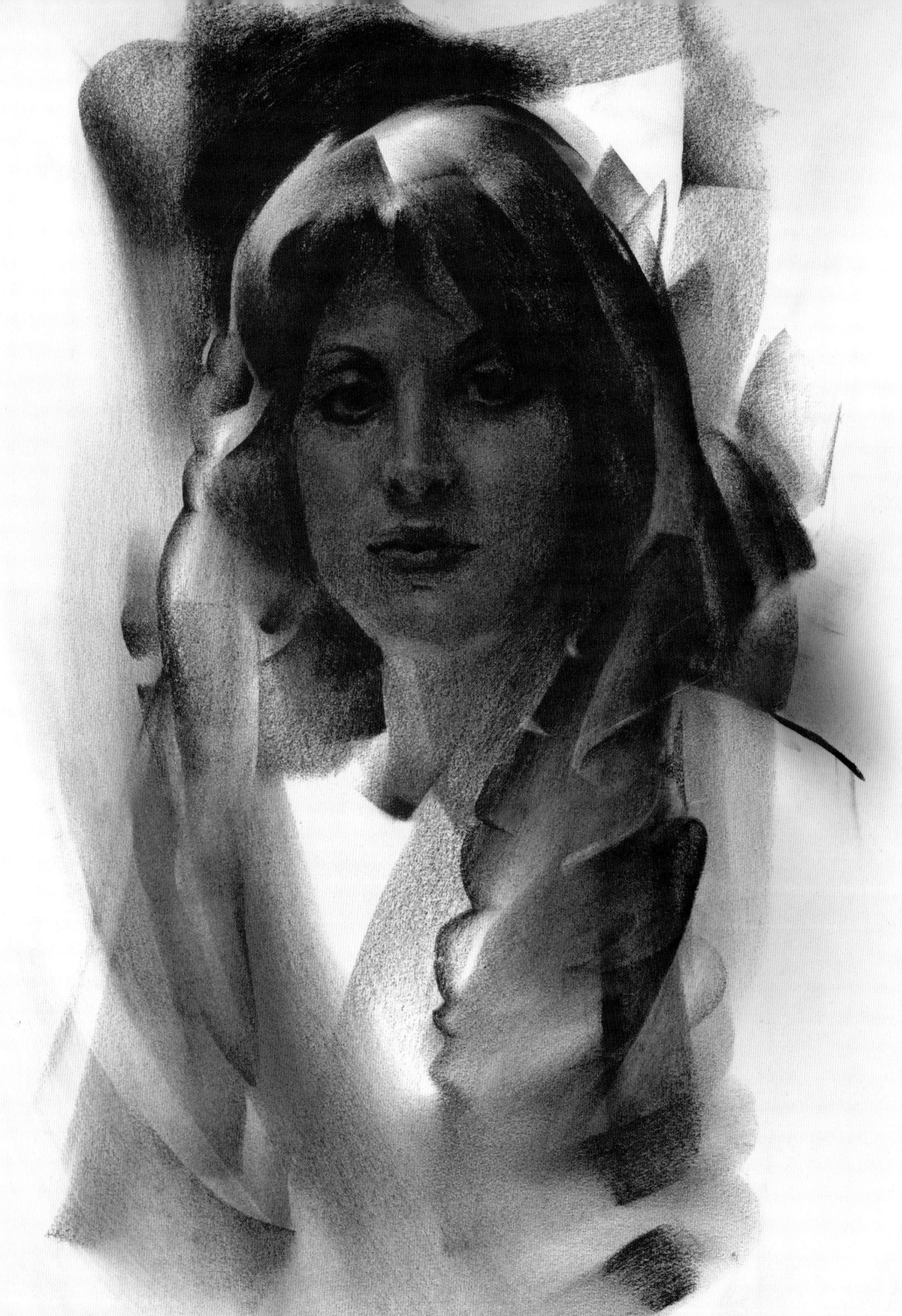

Introduction

Back in the year 2000, I was working as an artist on the DreamWorks Animation film *Spirit: Stallion of the Cimarron*. To launch the project we brought in a series of outside artists to do inspirational paintings, one of whom was Scott Burdick. I became familiar with Scott's personal work and was inspired by the quality of his portrait drawings and paintings. I couldn't help but pull him aside and ask how he got so gosh darn good at it. It was no secret; he said it was simply mileage and dedication. When he was studying at the Palette & Chisel Academy in Chicago, he studied consistently for three solid years. Each day started at 9 a.m. and he would draw until noon, take lunch, then come back and paint from the model until 4 p.m. After dinner he'd do another round of painting from 7 to 10 p.m. He did this consistently for three years.

Now mind you, I had been very serious about my own drawing for many years. I had pursued it as hard as I could throughout art school and continued to go to life drawing sessions on a regular basis. My drawings were coming along, but as the saying goes: "To be good is not enough when you dream of being great." So I went to studio management and arranged for a six-month break in my contract after we completed the current film. I was determined to take a sabbatical and keep the kind of schedule that Scott had described. I did exactly that and those six months have made all the difference. That time period is where this book begins; the portraits herein span from the year 2000 to the present, and I hope they bring to you some small amount of the value they've brought to me. Any modest success that I've enjoyed in my career has been built on a foundation of draftsmanship and a visual understanding of the world we live in. My hope is that this book will help bring those same benefits to your career as an artist. This book will lay out for you concepts, processes, and techniques to strengthen your own work and to build an understanding and appreciation for each face that passes your way.

As I continue to work in the animation and entertainment design industries, I've been a witness to a renewed appreciation for the traditional skill of rendering light and form through drawing. Artists who want to create imaginative visual storytelling are flocking to the life drawing classes to develop the skills that will bring a compelling believability to their artwork. They also do it as a refuge; putting pencil to paper is once again considered a great joy, and the handmade quality of a drawing is prized in the midst of a mass-produced digital world.

Best wishes and good luck!

Nathan Fowkes
Los Angeles, 2016

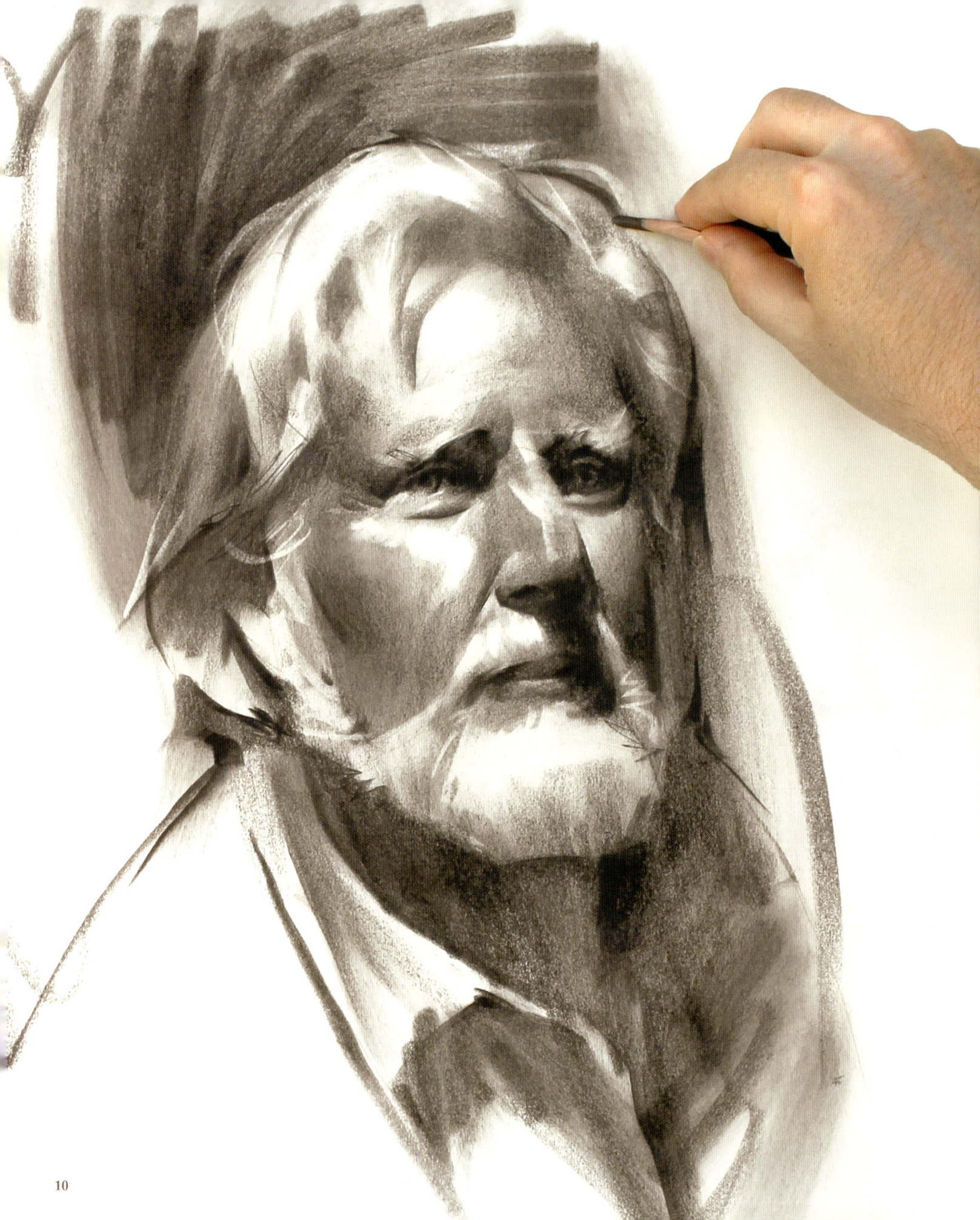

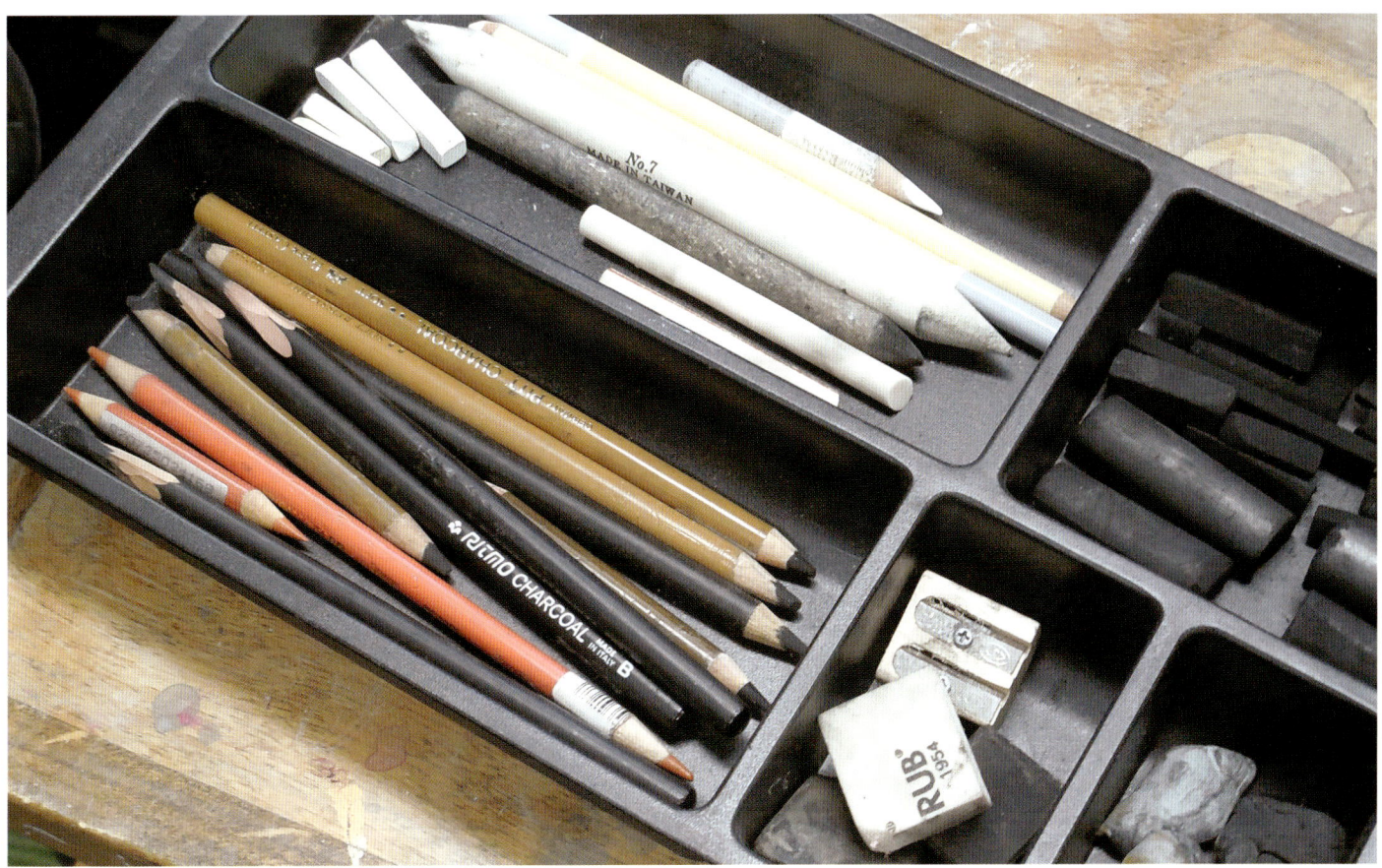

Chapter 1

Materials

Let me be very clear from the start: this is a principles book, not a technique book. Now don't get me wrong, I'm happy to show you every technique that I know, but techniques just don't mean much until they're driven by sound principles. That being said, let's start out by getting comfortable with our tools so when the time comes, we'll be ready to apply the principles to best effect.

And since we're talking tools, I have to say here that one of the great pleasures of being an artist is putting a beautiful piece of smooth charcoal to a well-made piece of paper and making a satisfying mark—there are few aspects of art that I enjoy more than that.

The following pages will show you the tools that I like, but I recommend experimentation. My materials are somewhat different than those my teachers used, and the way I draw is somewhat different as well. Your work will likely also evolve over time so any tool that gives you a full range of light to dark will be sufficient for the task ahead. And by the way, I don't mind a single bit if you start out by copying my approach. (I'll be quite flattered as a matter of fact.) But in the end you'll find that with dedicated practice, your own unique style will emerge as you draw the subjects you're most interested in.

> *"Techniques don't mean much until they're driven by sound principles."*

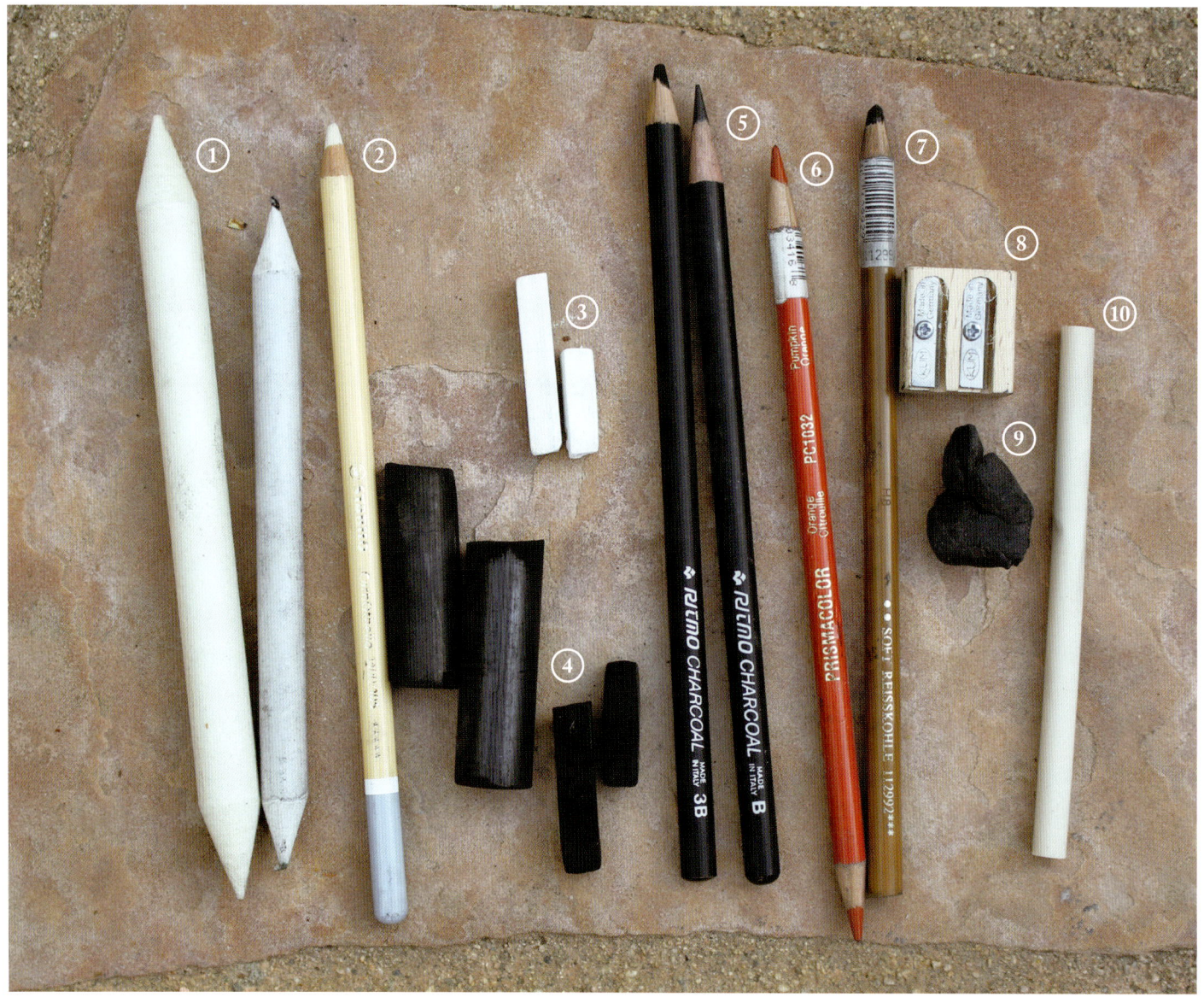

Suggested Materials

Blending stump ①

② CarbOthello pastel pencil, white or ivory

Prismacolor Nupastel, white or ivory ③
(any good pastel can work but I prefer this one)

④ Soft compressed charcoal, I prefer Alphacolor brand and
for my darkest tones I use Cretacolor Chunky Charcoal

Ritmo charcoal pencils, B and 3B softness ⑤

⑥ Prismacolor colored pencil, I prefer pumpkin orange

Pitt charcoal pencil, soft ⑦

⑧ Manual pencil sharpener

Kneaded eraser ⑨

⑩ Pen or stick eraser

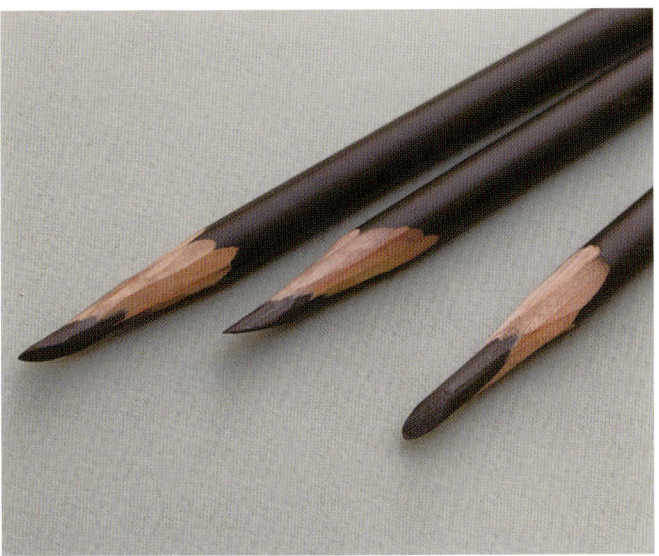

I often create a chisel tip on my pencils by manually sharpening them with an X-Acto knife and then flattening the edge with sandpaper. This is quite useful for quick and expressive drawing: the side of the chisel tip can create calligraphic thick and thin strokes, and the flat edge can create broad washes of tone. You'll see this technique used throughout my gallery of drawings.

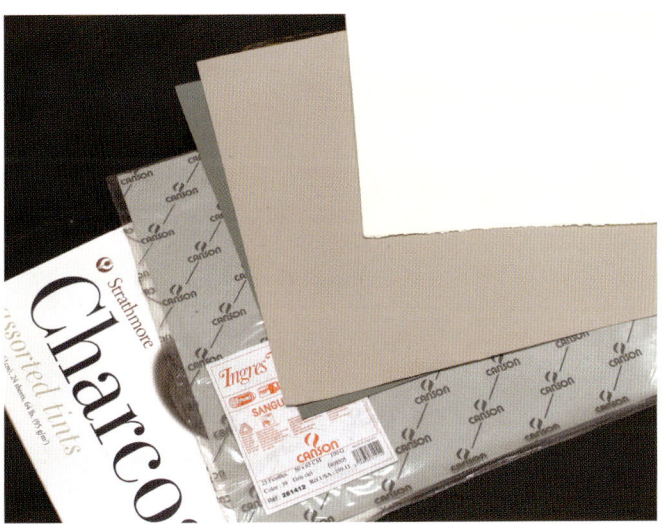

I love a good paper! When choosing paper, be sure to use only acid-free stock—the very best papers have high cotton content. You'll also want to experiment with surface textures to find the ones that work best for you. Here are a few of my favorites:

Rives lightweight paper, ivory or white
(I like the touch of warmth from the ivory)

Canson Ingres toned paper

Strathmore Charcoal paper

Newsprint (for practice only)

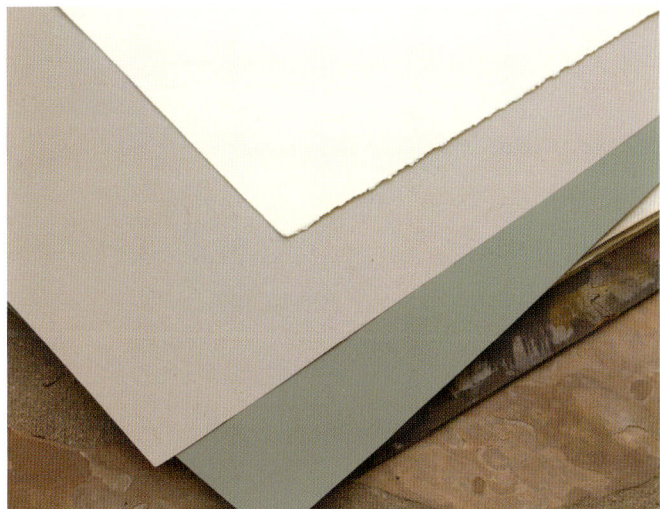

Sketching in pads of newsprint paper is good for practice, but keep in mind that newsprint is not archival and will yellow and deteriorate over time. But I always keep a pad of newsprint handy; I place my quality papers over a thickness of newsprint sheets so that when I draw, the surface has a little give rather than the hardness of a drawing board. I prefer to use rough newsprint rather than smooth, not because of the texture but because of thickness. Smooth newsprint tends to be so thin that it buckles and warps at any change of weather.

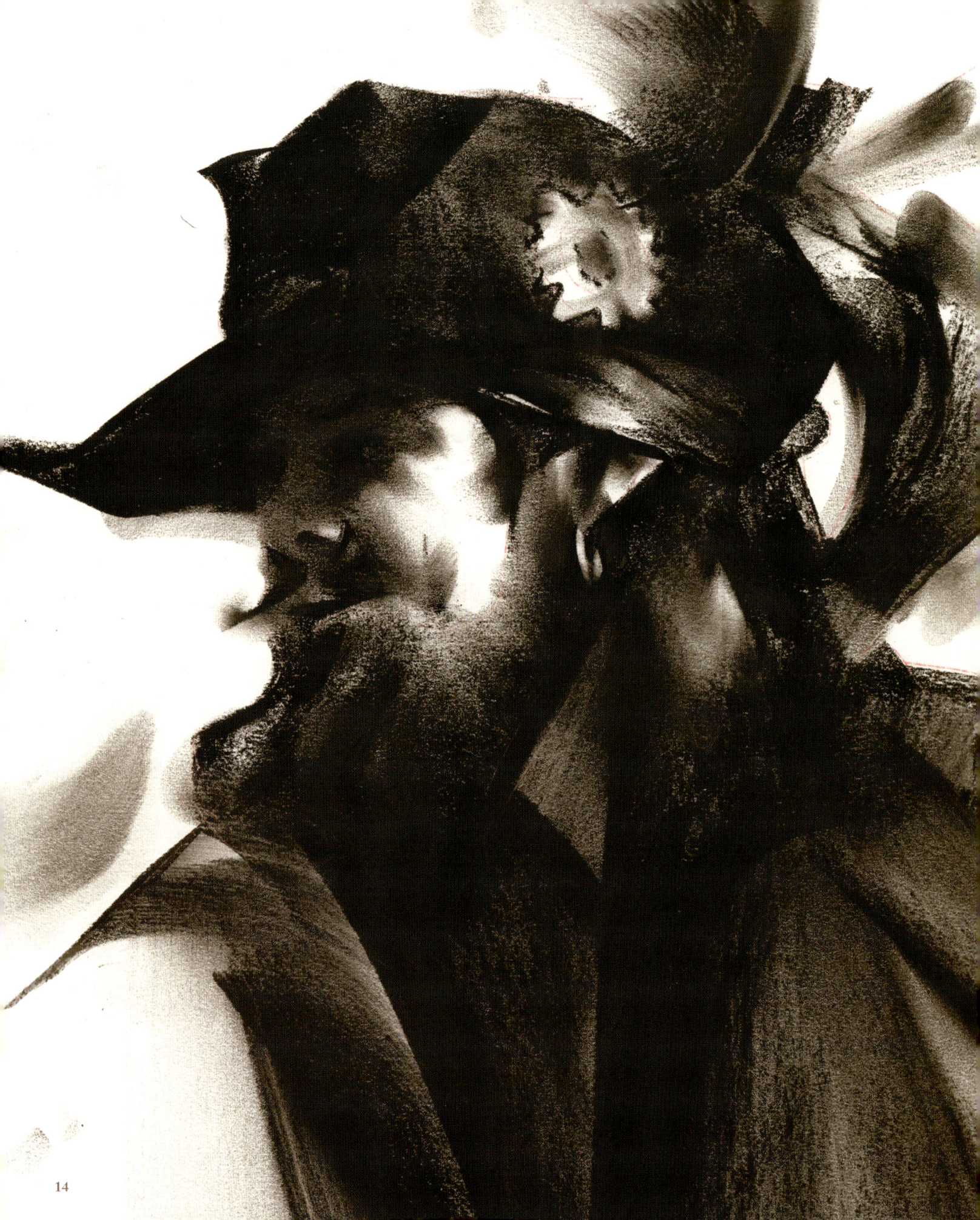

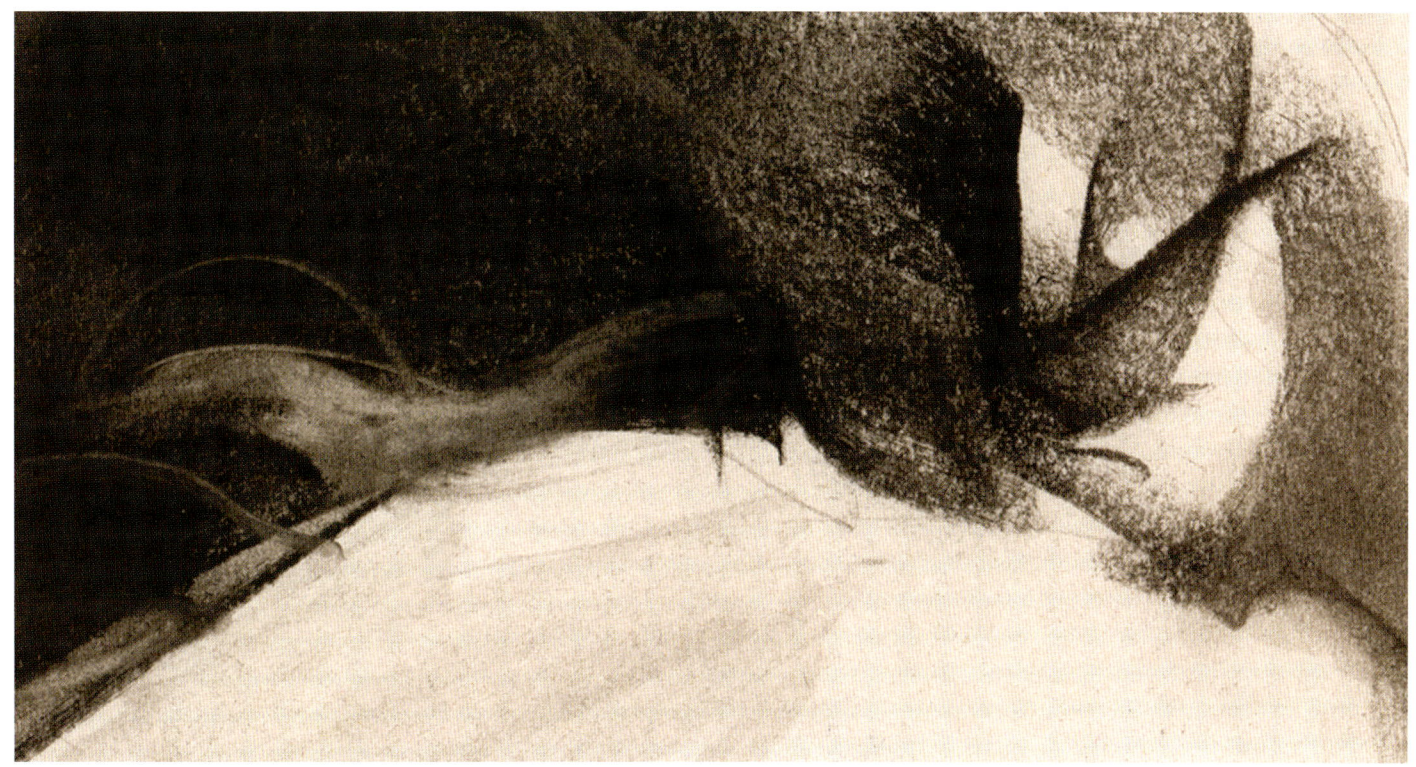

Using the Materials

So let's get right to it and get comfortable with our tools and materials. Keep in mind that this chapter will be specifically about mark making, and then we'll be ready to tackle the concepts that drive how we use the materials. This chapter will take you through five different drawing approaches:

① Using the charcoal pencil exclusively

② Using compressed charcoal in vignette

③ Using compressed charcoal in a full-page composition

④ Using toned paper and white pastel

⑤ Vine charcoal

"Using charcoal takes practice and can be frustrating but in time charcoal drawing will become your favorite pastime!"

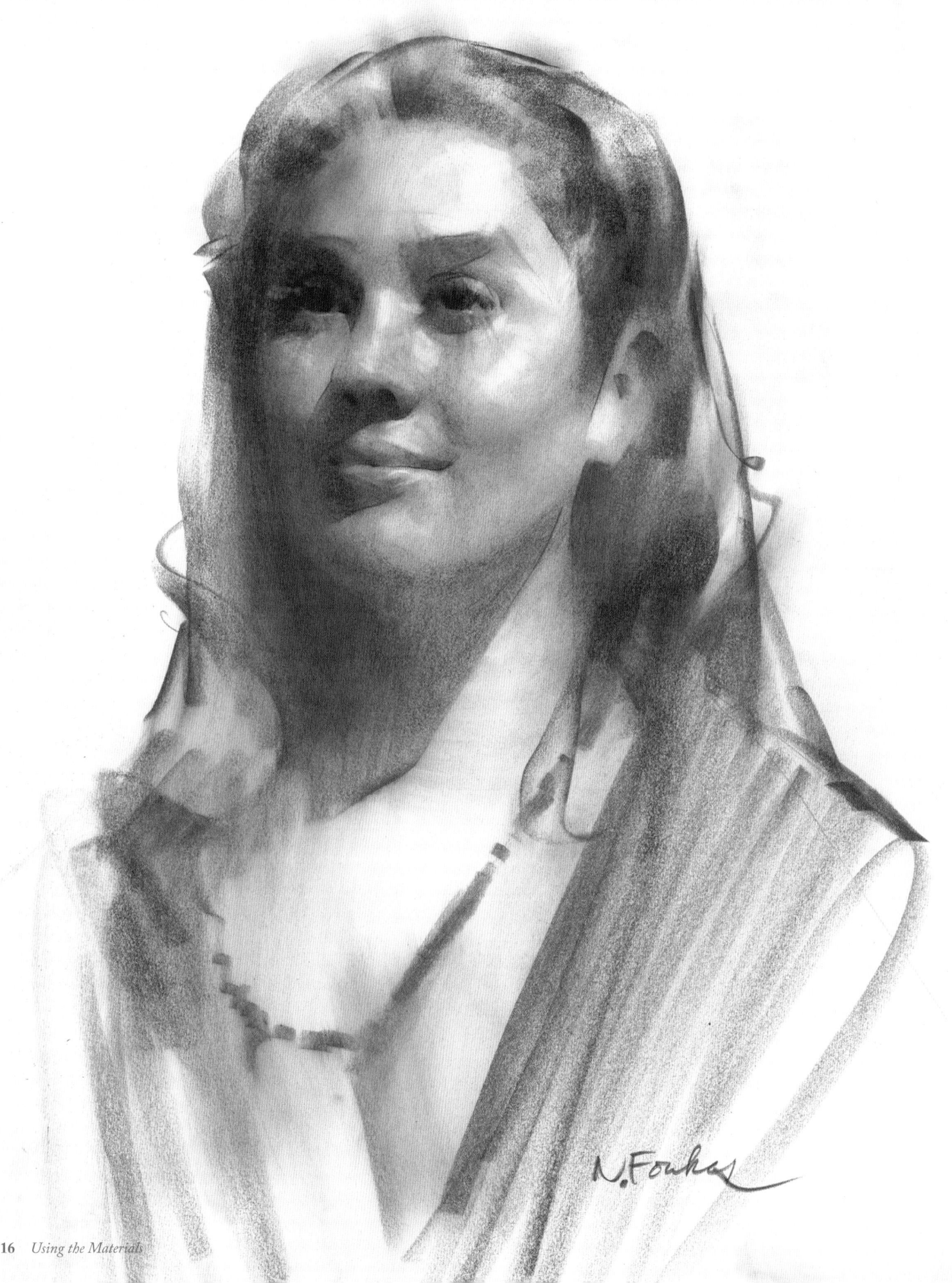

Approach 1: Ritmo Charcoal Pencil on Rives lightweight ivory paper

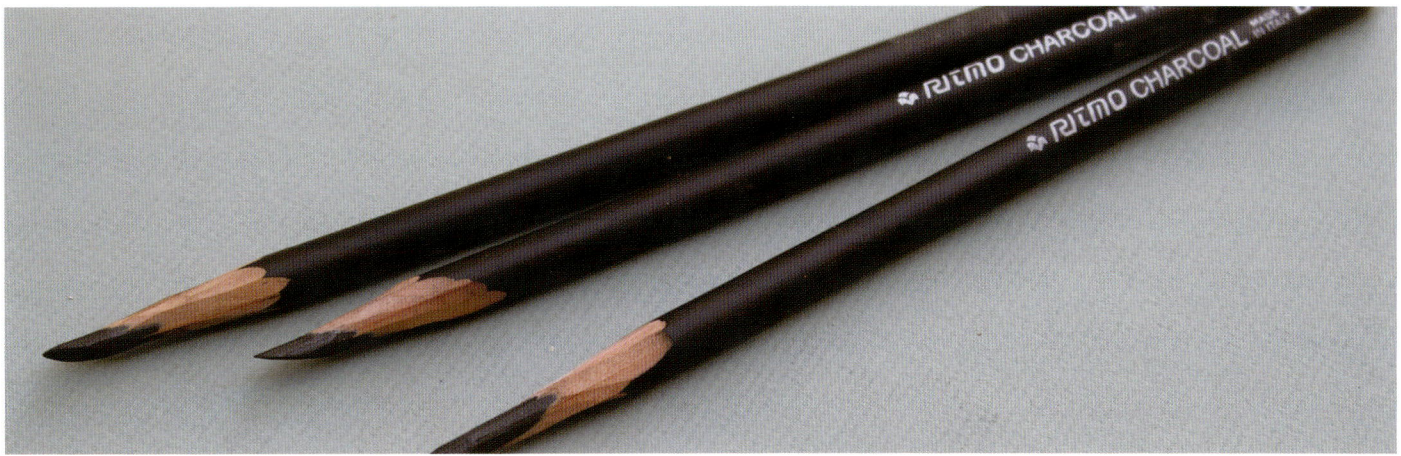

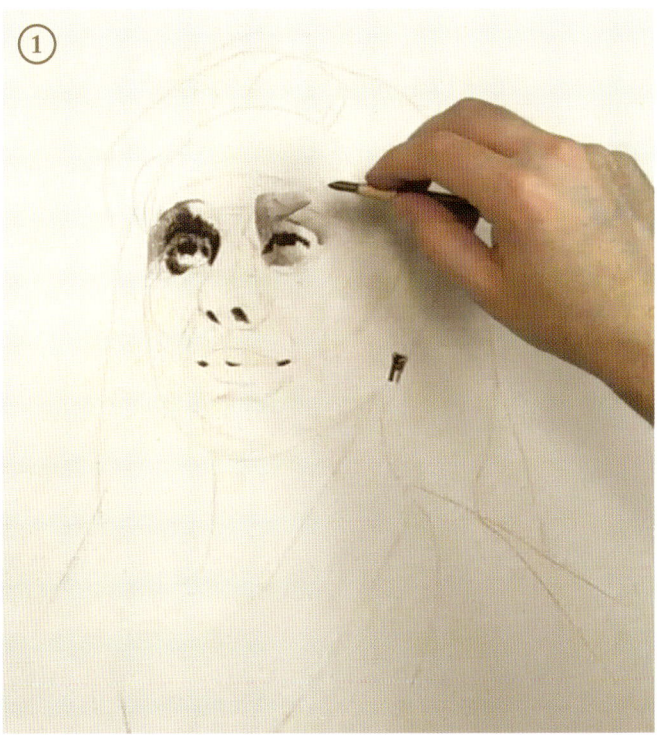

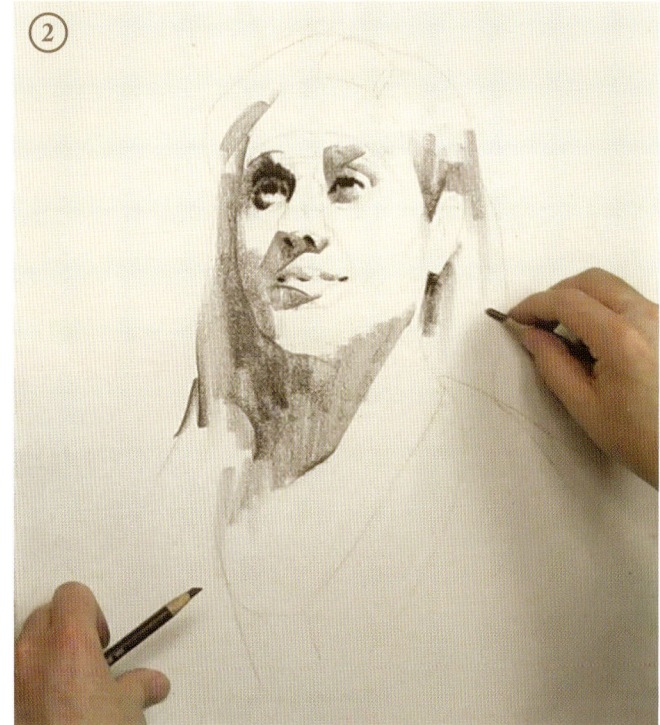

I lay down my initial line drawing very lightly. This is important because being too heavy-handed at this stage can score and mar your paper; I usually use a Ritmo B or a Prismacolor orange pencil. I've been using orange Prismacolor more and more because it makes a light line that remains visible throughout most of the drawing process; this way I'm less likely to lose my structural underdrawing as I continue to work over it. Once I'm confident in the accuracy of my drawing, I begin to find landmarks in the darks of the facial features using more pressure and committed strokes.

This is where the chisel tip comes in handy; I use the flat of the pencil tip to wash in broad shapes of tone and shadow. Sometimes I'll have my strokes follow the direction of the underlying forms to suggest three dimensionality as you can see in the hair and shirt of the finished drawing at far left. For the shadows my strokes are vertical to keep the shapes simple and to suggest the uprightness of the pose.

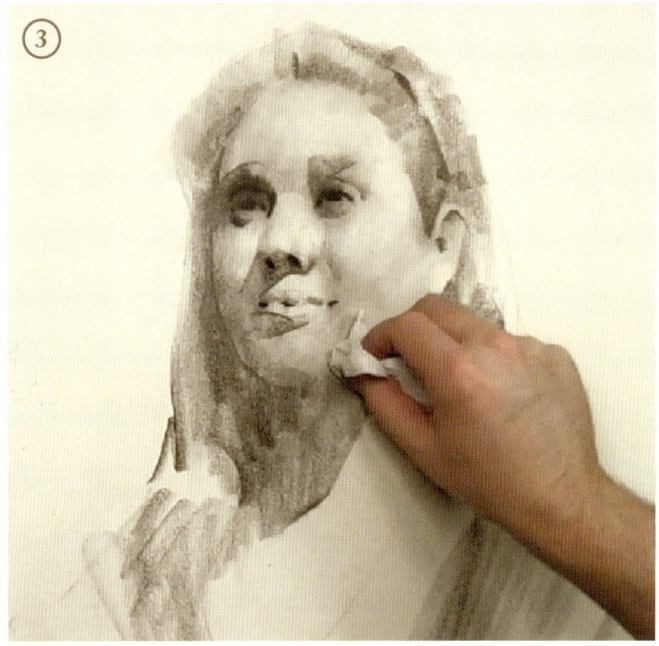

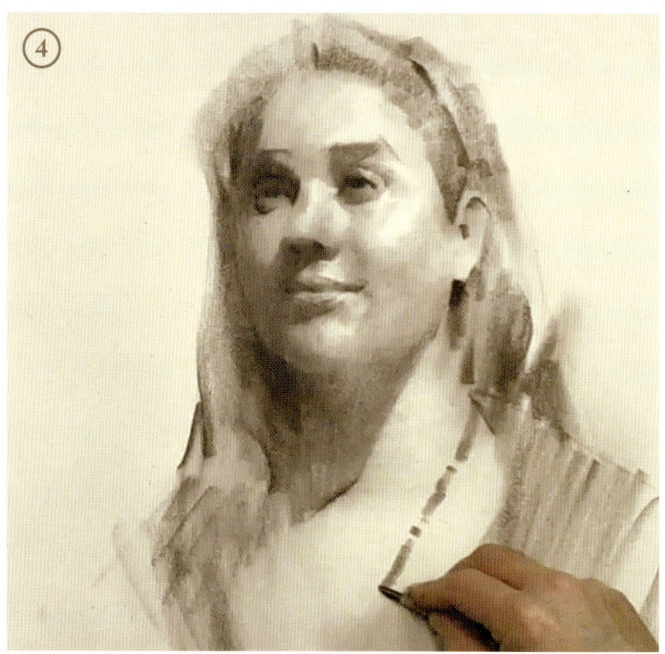

At this stage I use common tissue paper for blending. I very lightly smooth the shadow strokes and more firmly blend charcoal into the light areas. I also use my fingers for a lot of this type of blending; it gives me much more control and sensitivity. Just be sure to wash with soap first—the natural oils on your skin can mar the paper!

I'm now ready to use the kneaded eraser as a drawing tool; I use it to erase highlights out of the tones as you can see in the cheek, nose, etc. I favor creating highlights this way so I can put down my tone in broad strokes without having to carefully draw around the highlights. Next I add key details like the necklace with appropriate pencil strokes.

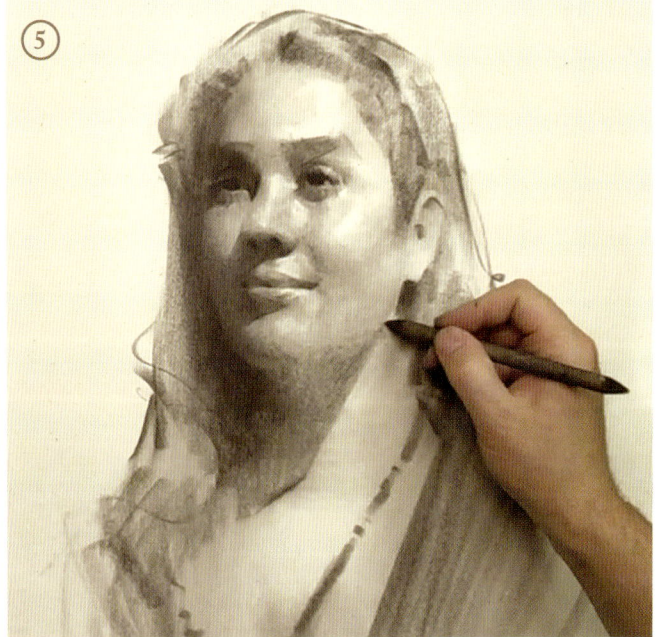

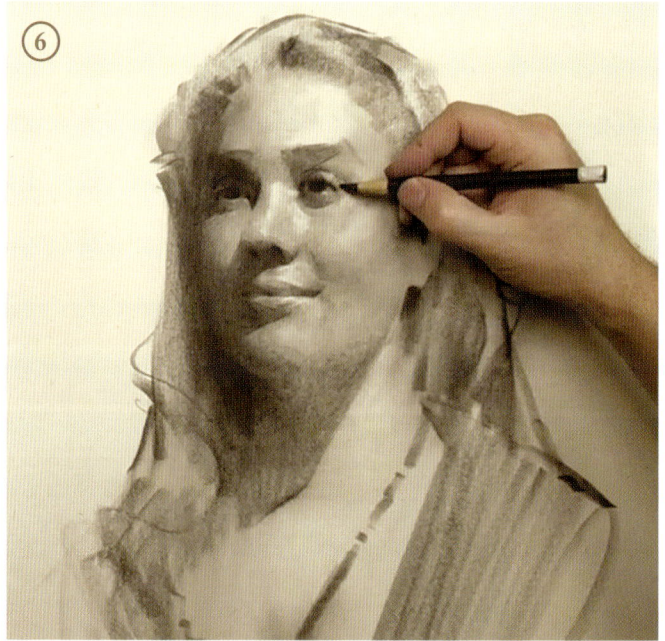

I continue refining the drawing area by area using the pencil, the kneaded eraser, and the blending stump. You can see the results in the detail at the upper right of the opposite page: the tissue and finger blending created the soft tones, the kneaded eraser for the highlight details, and the cast shadows from the eyelashes were created with the tip of the blending stump.

I lay down my final touches with the sharp end of the pencil. I'm primarily putting down final details and crisp edges where needed. And with that, it's a wrap!

Detail

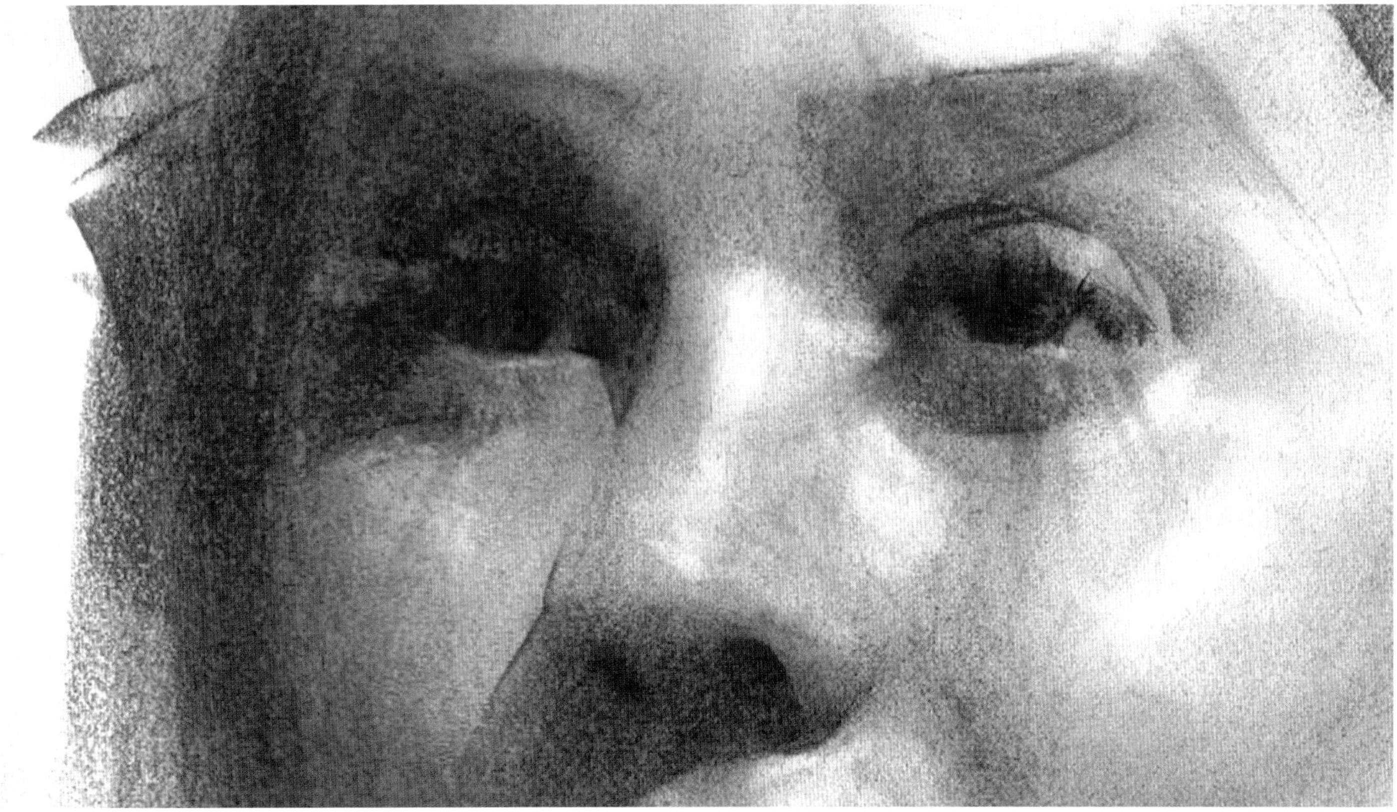

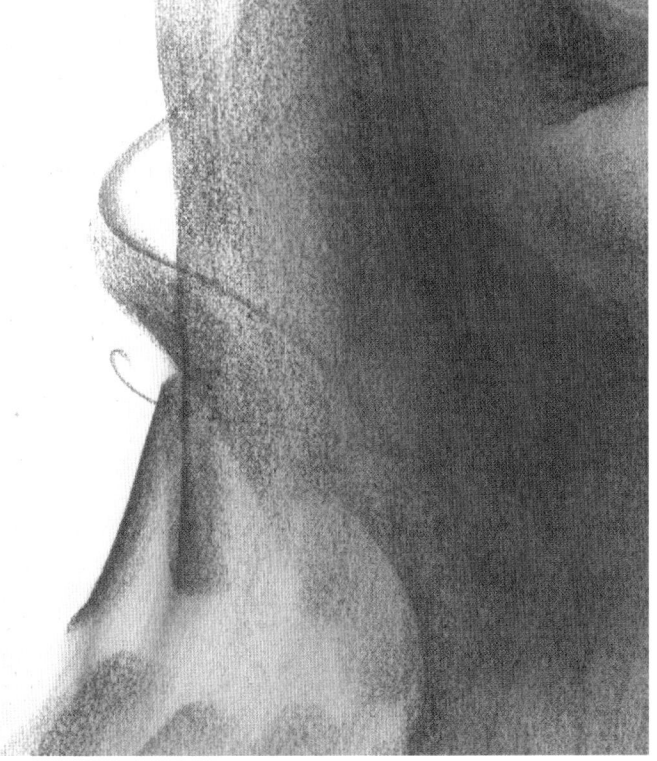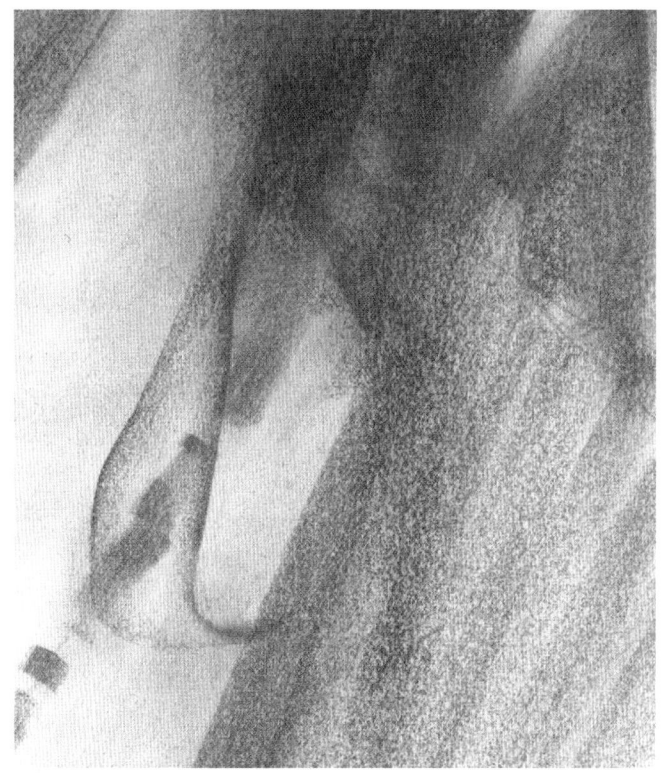

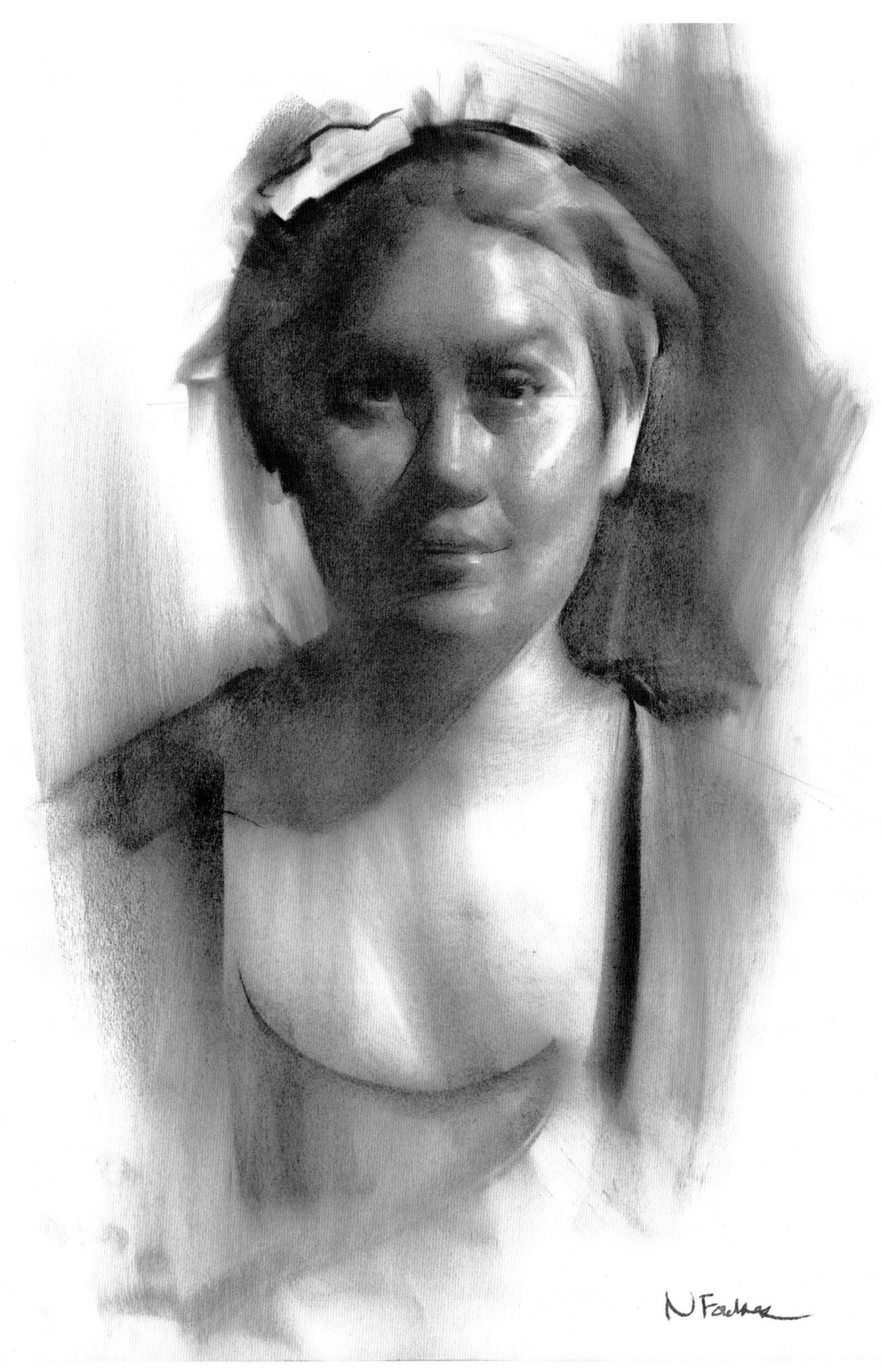

Approach 2: Compressed Charcoal Vignette on Rives lightweight ivory paper

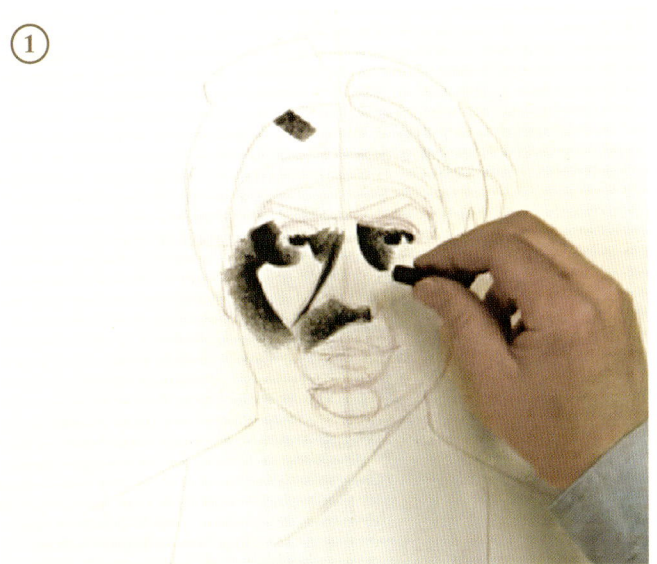

Compressed charcoal has a wonderful blending quality and is great for committed, dramatic shadows. It also turns into a big mess real fast so easy does it; using compressed charcoal requires serious practice. To begin I lay in an initial line drawing with pencil and then begin blocking in the shadow shapes with compressed charcoal. I always prepare my compressed charcoal stick by rubbing it on a piece of scratch paper to work away any rough edges.

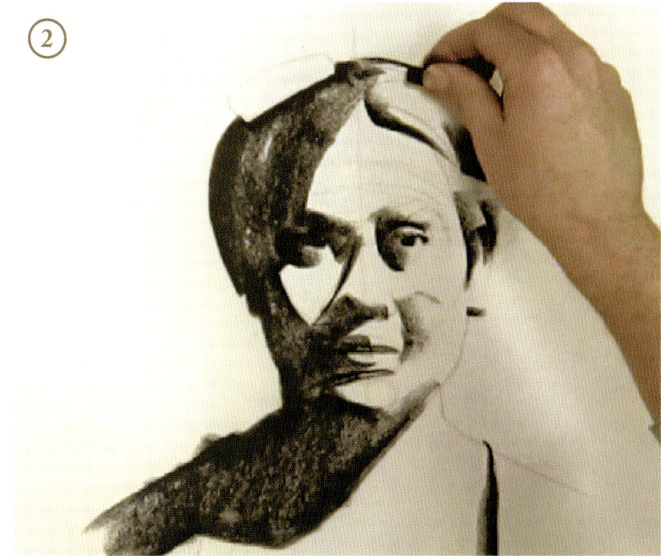

I continue laying in the darks with the compressed charcoal stick. I'm very careful to work only within the shadows; a good, soft charcoal stick is inherently black and is very difficult to erase out of the light areas.

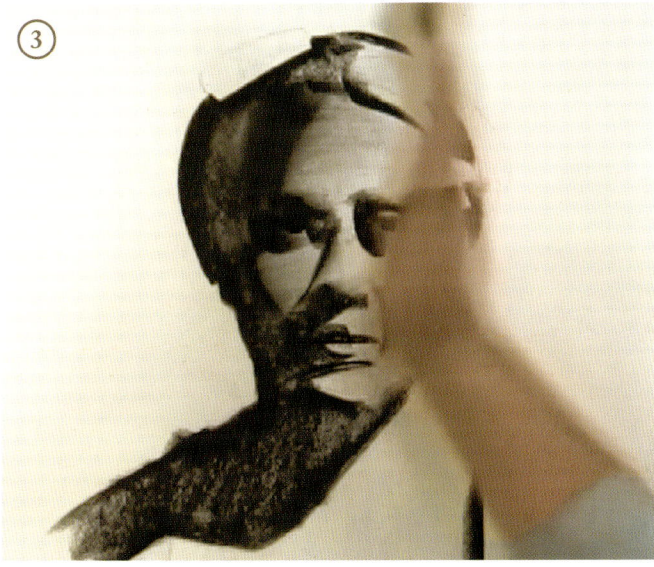

I'm now ready to blend tone into the light areas; I like to be very quick and direct about this. As you can see in the photo, I'm pressing the side of my hand directly into the shadow tone and dragging it over into the light. Two or three quick strokes is all it takes to get the tone to wrap around the whole form of the head!

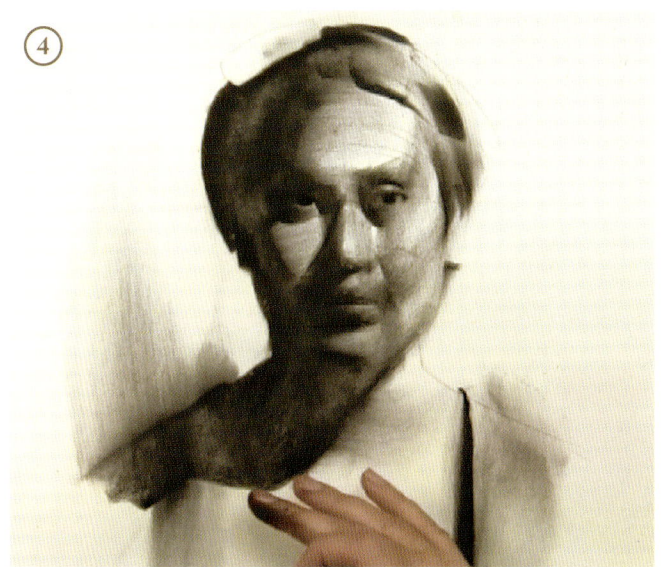

Now I use my finger for more detailed blending. I don't need to apply any new charcoal into the light areas with a pencil or charcoal stick; I simply grab charcoal that already exists in the shadow and pull it into the light areas. This helps give the illusion of light wrapping around form.

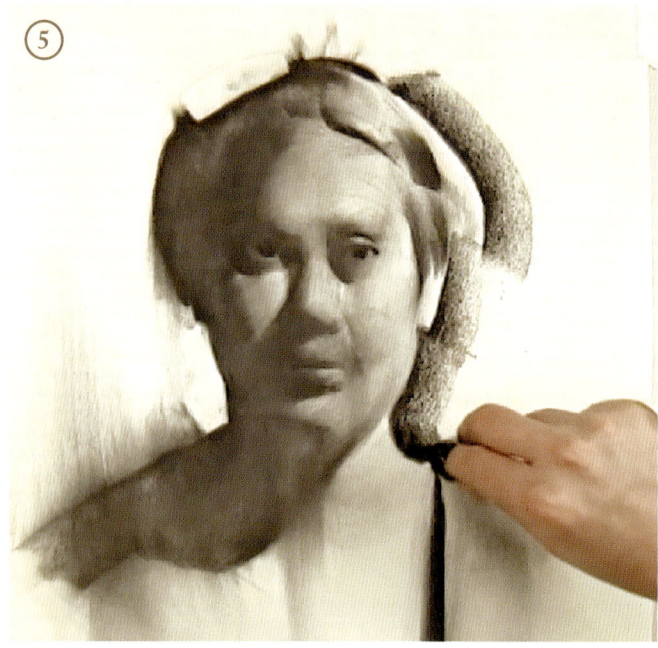

(5) Now I'm ready to lay in a backdrop and I feel that the light on the face will read best against a dark tone. It will also help strengthen the silhouette of the vignette head.

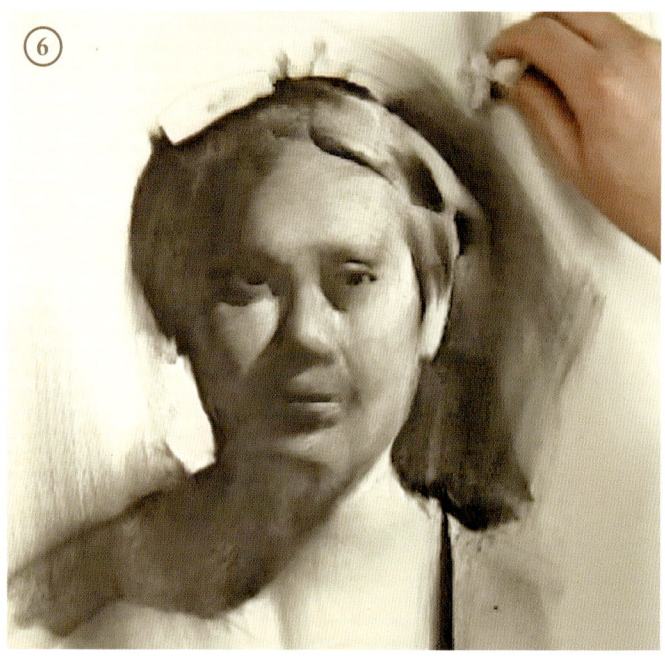

(6) Blending in the background is now in order so I reach for a tissue to soften those edges; this will strengthen the vignette by keeping attention on the face.

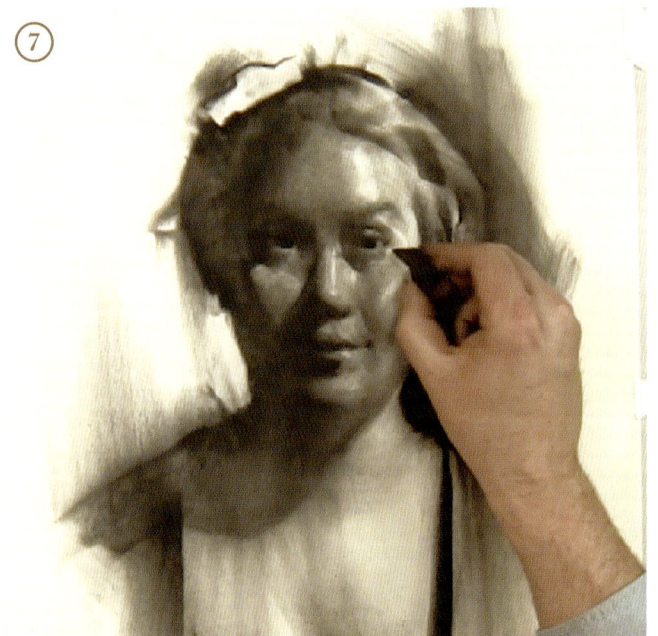

(7) I continue to pull tone from the shadow into the light until I'm satisfied there's a good transition from light to shadow. Now we're ready for the kneaded eraser: I use it to pull highlights out of the tone on the light side of the face.

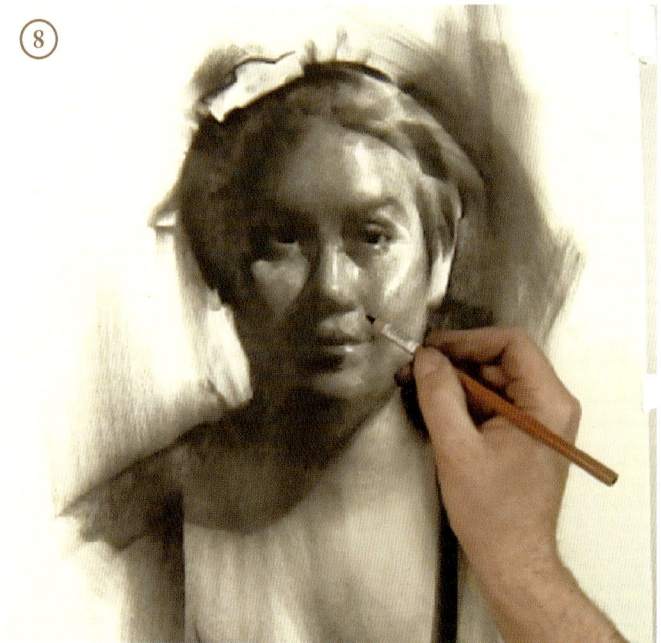

(8) Only at this point do I use a regular charcoal pencil for detail work. I'm using the Pitt charcoal pencil; it creates a much denser black than the Ritmo we used in the previous demonstration and is a good match for the dense quality of the compressed charcoal. And voila! Now we're done.

Detail

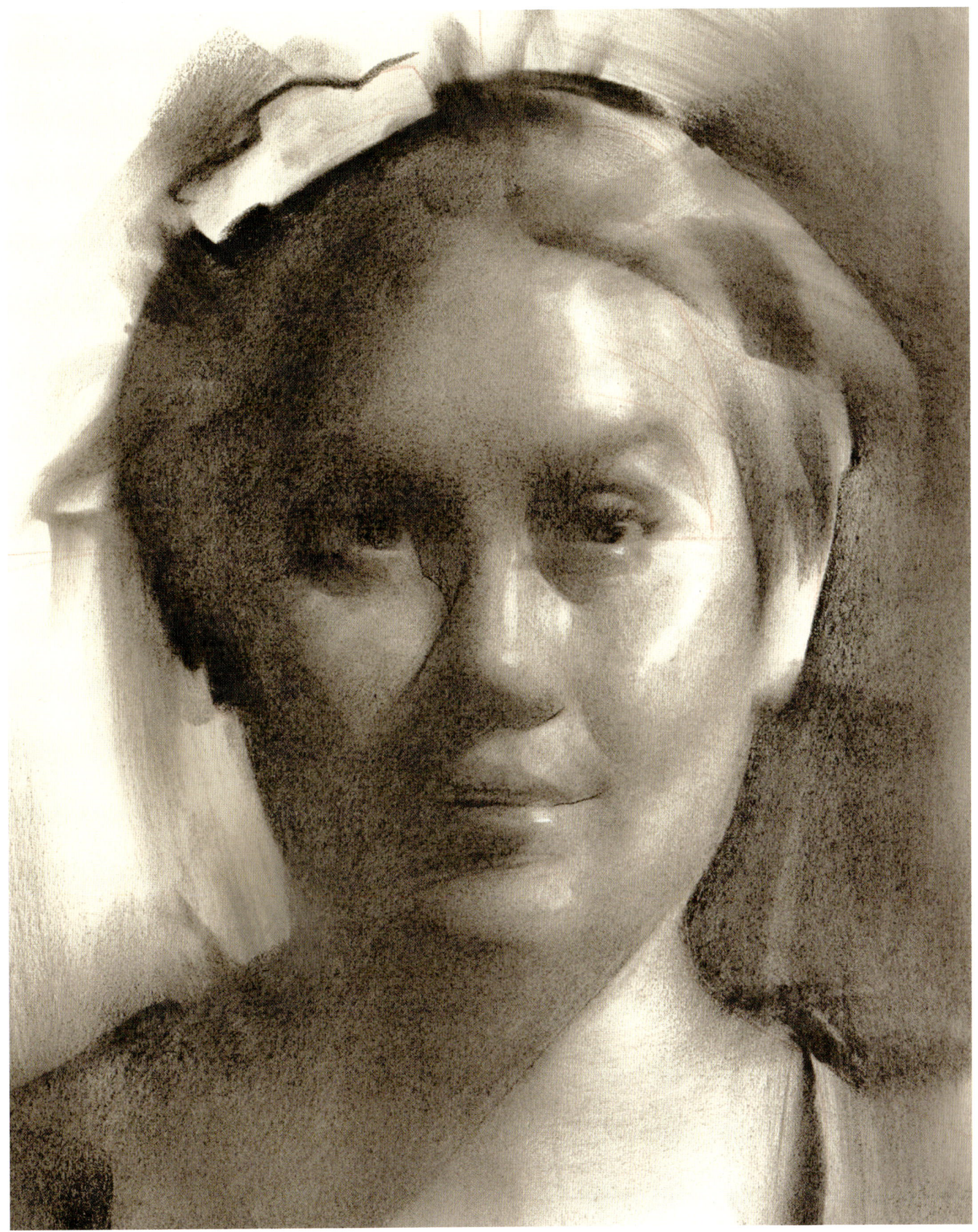

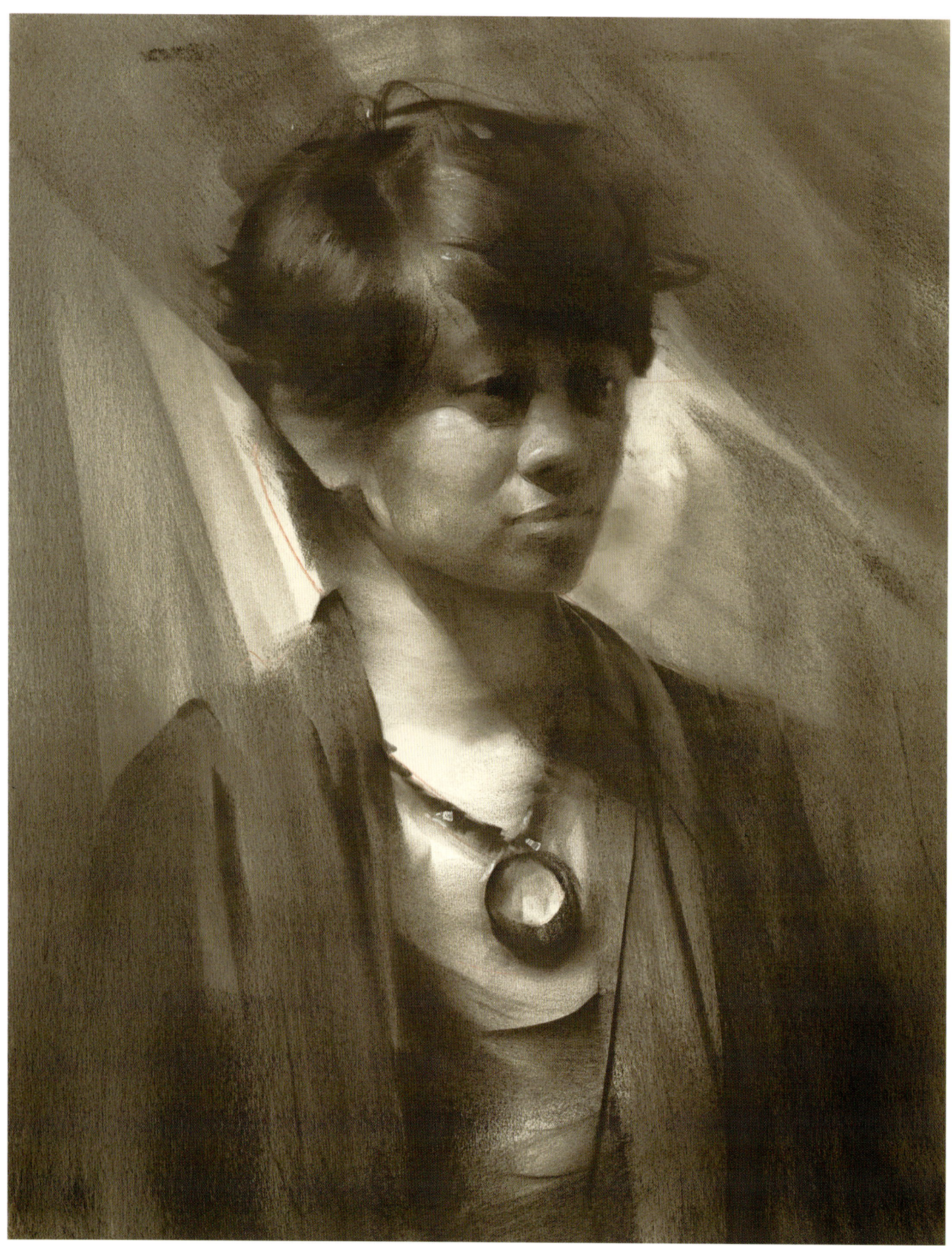

Approach 3: Compressed charcoal on Rives lightweight ivory paper

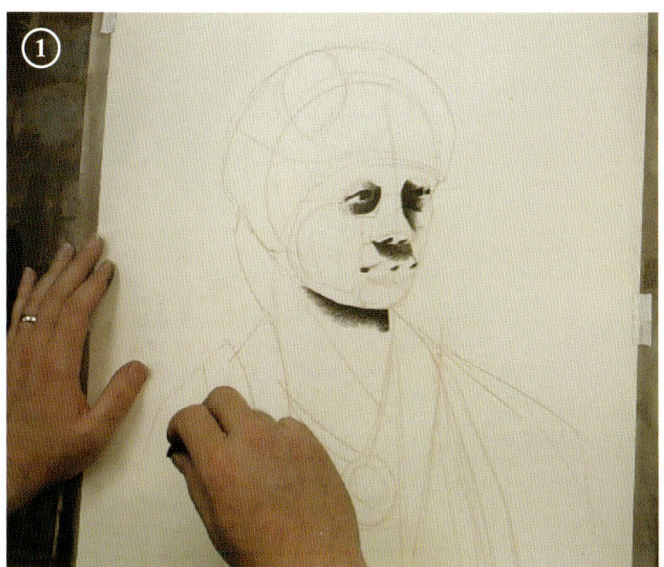

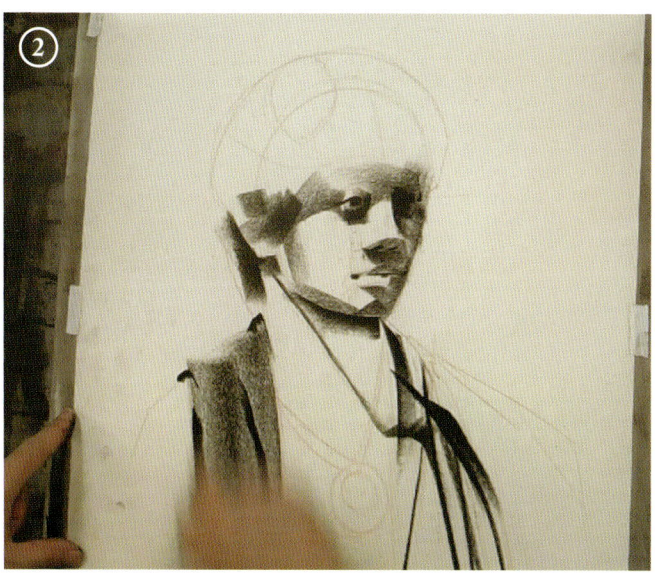

We're using the same paper and charcoal as the previous demonstration—this time for a full-page composition. To start I'm using my pumpkin orange Prismacolor for the lay in and taking time for accuracy. Once I'm confident in my drawing I dive in with compressed charcoal for the landmarks of the features and shadow shapes.

I'm careful to only place the compressed charcoal into the shadows and dark areas. I use the lengthwise corners of the charcoal stick to suggest folds in the fabric with calligraphic thick and thin strokes.

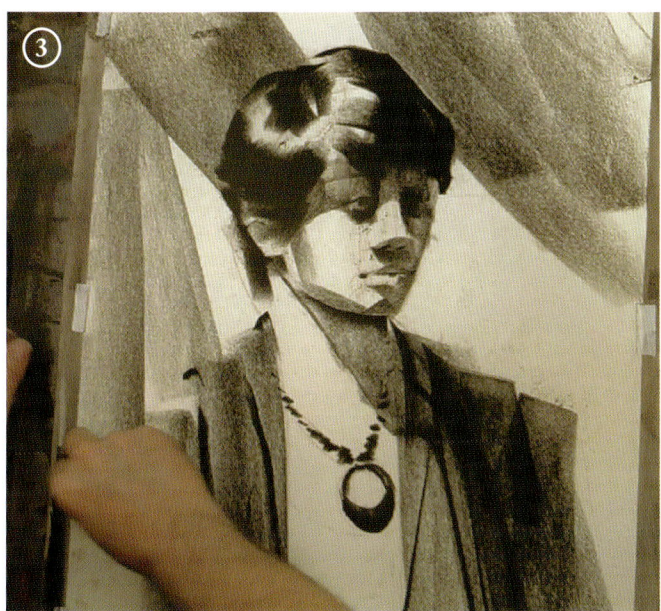

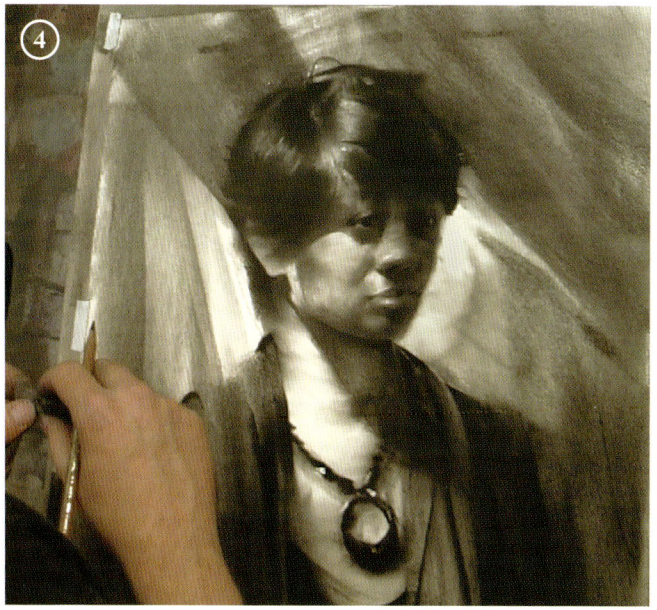

Since I want this portrait to be a full-page composition, the broad strokes I can get with the compressed charcoal stick are a huge advantage. I've seen students waste precious dozens of minutes of a portrait sitting by filling in broad areas of tone with a little, tiny pencil tip—ugh! The broad strokes in the background are also a big help compositionally; the model's gaze is reinforced by their direction.

I don't want the background to be visually active to the point of distraction so this is my big chance to break out my best blending tool, which is of course, the side of my hand. Then I do final detail work with a kneaded eraser and Pitt pencil to bring our composition to a finish. And then of course the washing of hands: heavy duty cleaners can leave hands badly chapped, so it's simple soap and water for me. My hands sometimes remain stained for days, and I wear it proudly.

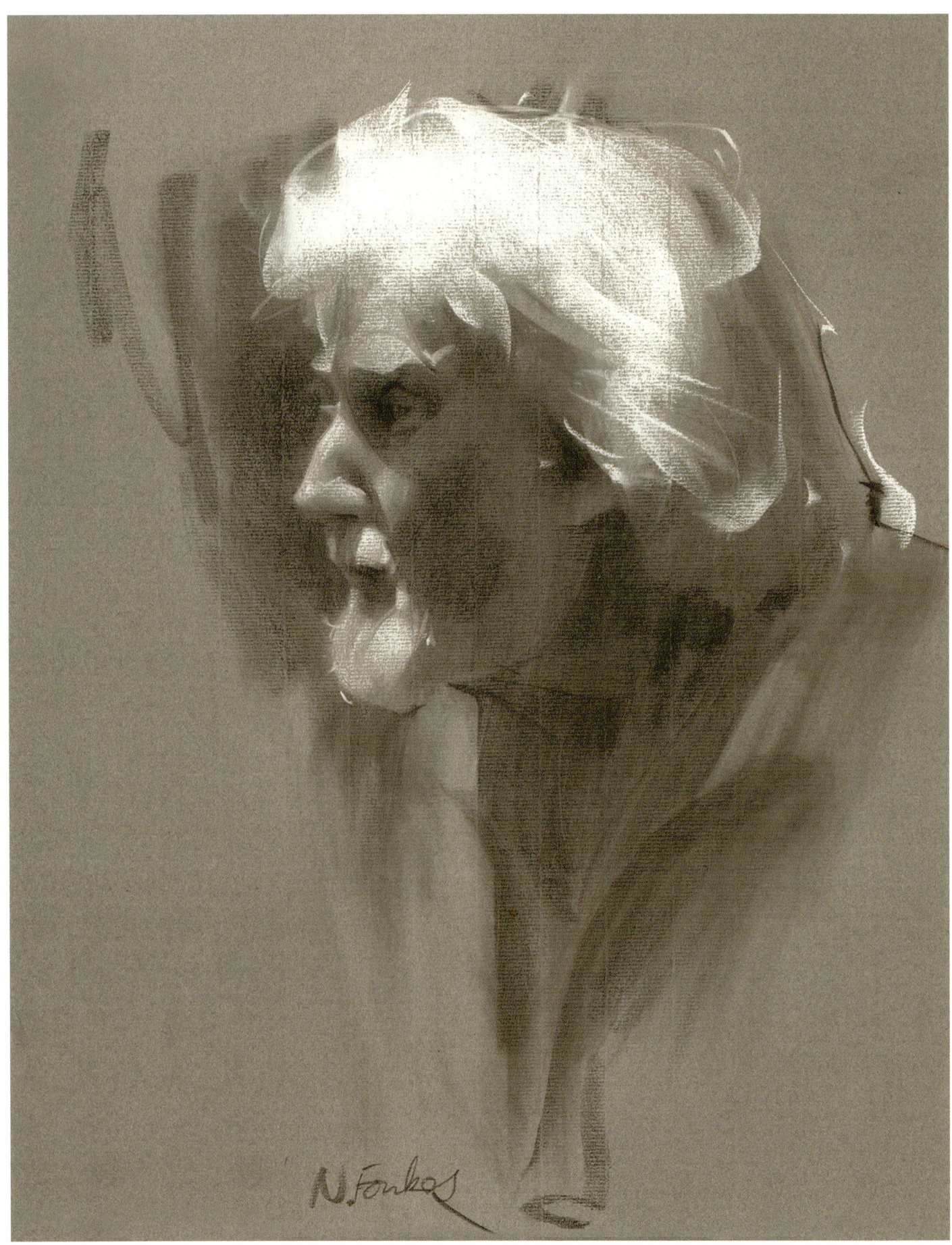

Approach 4: Ritmo charcoal pencils & white Nupastel on Canson Ingres steel grey paper

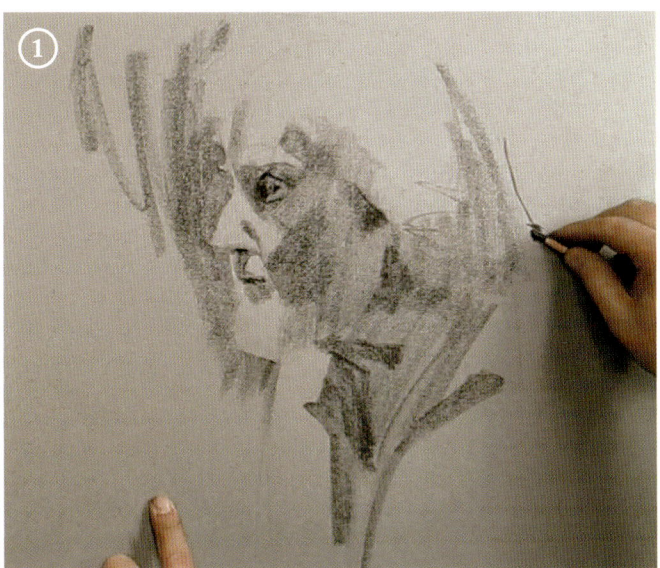

For this portrait I'm using Canson Ingres steel grey paper, Ritmo charcoal pencils, and white Nupastel. The toned paper lets me take best advantage of the lighting and the white of the hair and beard. You're very familiar with my initial steps by now so I'll dive right into the meat of the matter. I'm using the chisel style tip of my pencil to block in the big shapes of light and shadow.

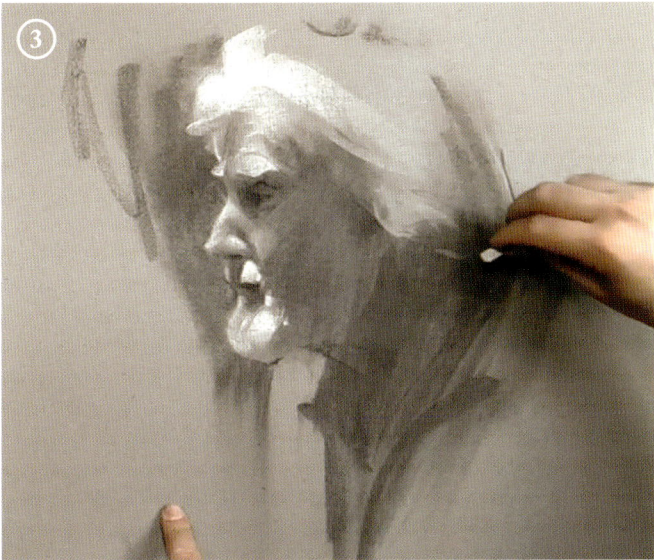

Next is the blending of the shadows; I want them to be somewhat smooth and soft so that the rougher textures of the light will be emphasized. I try to finish the charcoal portion of the drawing as much as possible at this stage because the white pastel will be delicate and will smear quite easily if I spend too much time reworking the drawing.

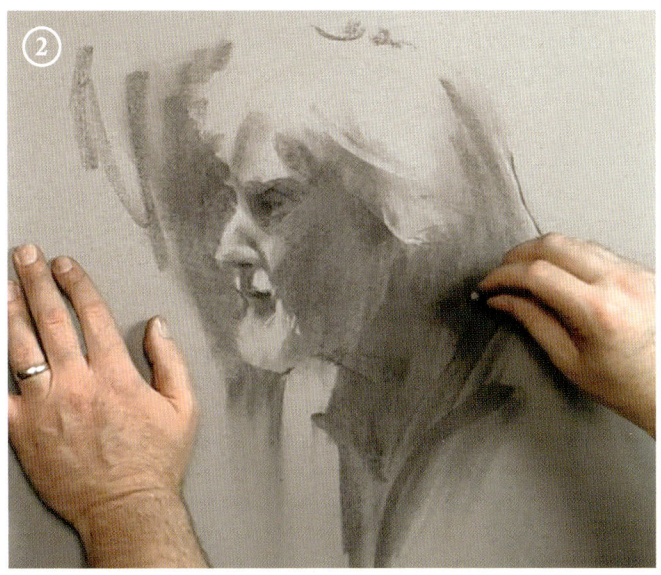

Now I'm ready to go to town! I lay in the big shapes of light with the pastel, making a point to follow the direction and form of the hair. I'm careful not to allow the strokes of chalk to overlap any charcoal, or, if I do, I limit it to a single stroke. Blending white chalk into black charcoal can create quite a mess. This is why the tone of the paper is so important for this technique; it bridges the gap between light and shadow.

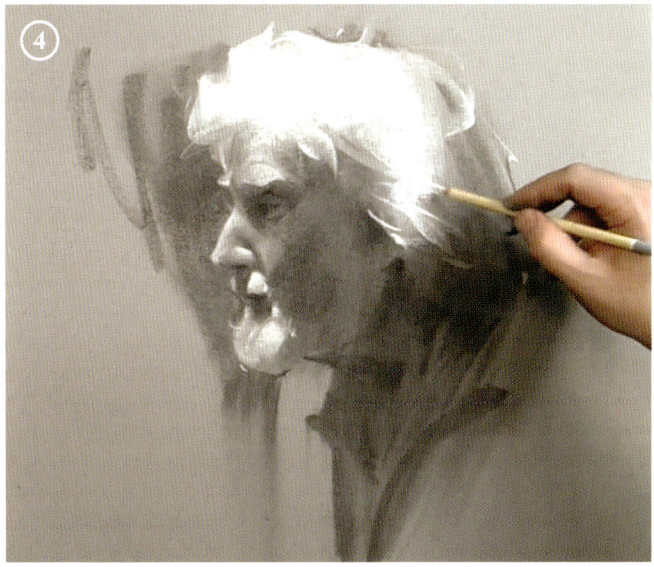

For any detail work in the light or for fine strands of hair, I employ the CarbOthello pencil. But easy does it; I want the lights to remain a nice strong group rather than a fractured bunch of details and marks. And as you can see in the full-page finish, we're already done and it's time to throw a signature on this bad boy!

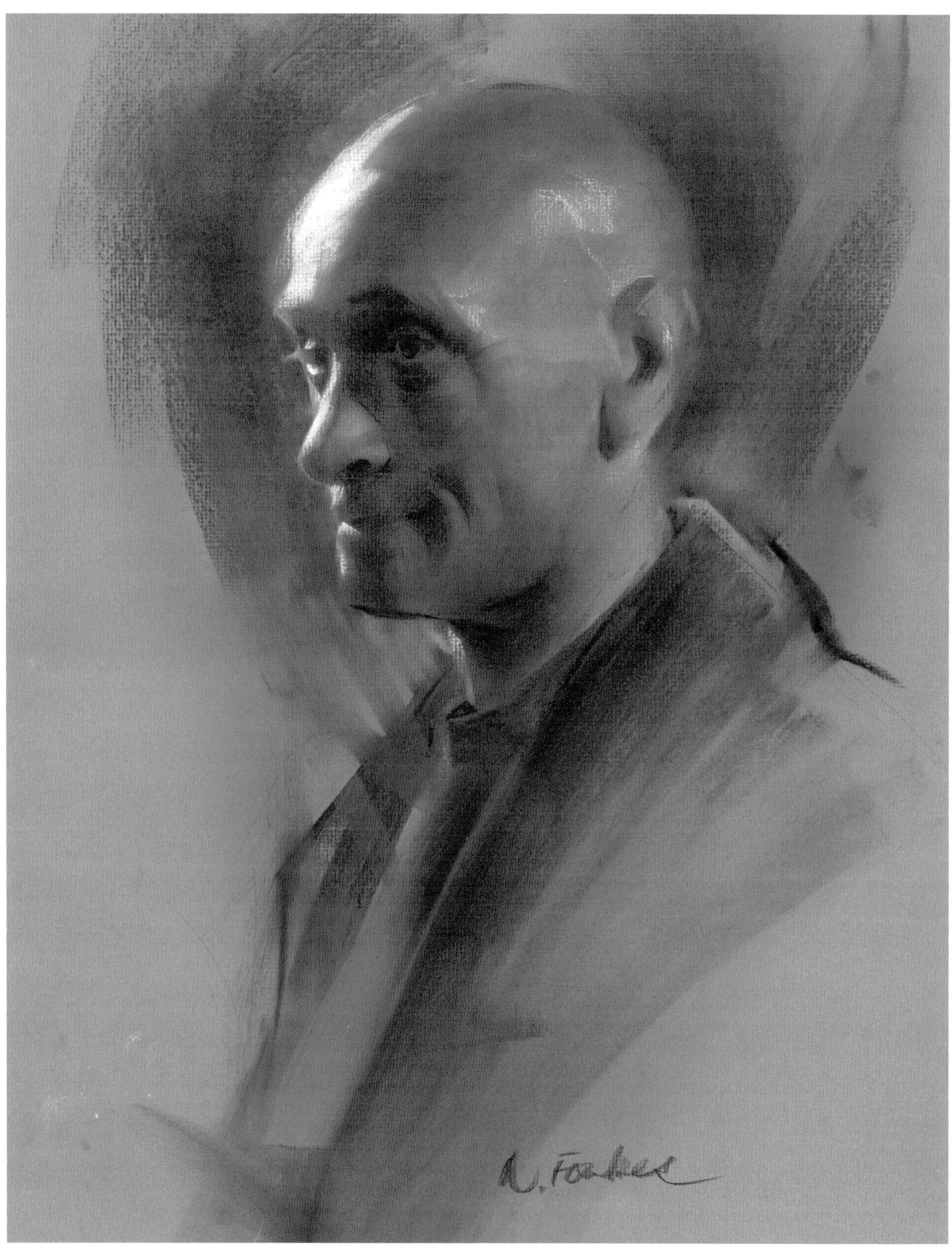

Approach 5: Vine charcoal on Strathmore charcoal paper

I haven't mentioned vine charcoal yet because I rarely work with it. The reason is that I like to be fairly rough with my drawings and aggressively push the charcoal around, but vine charcoal is so delicate that if you so much as sneeze, it blows right off of your page. Nevertheless, many artists including masters like John Singer Sargent, successfully used vine charcoal so I felt I should include it here as well.

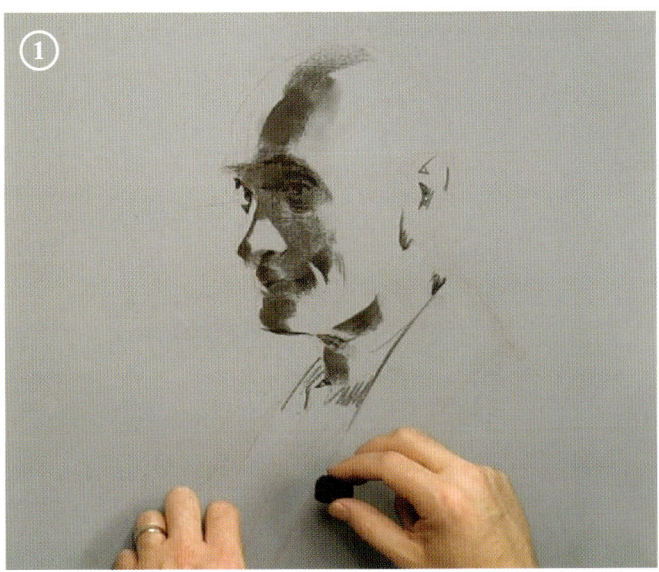

I'm using a toned paper again for the same reasons as in the last demonstration. This time I'm using Strathmore charcoal paper: it has a heavy tooth and really grabs and holds the charcoal, which is a requirement for vine charcoal. I prefer only to use the softest and largest sticks of vine charcoal to get the dark shadows and broad strokes that I need.

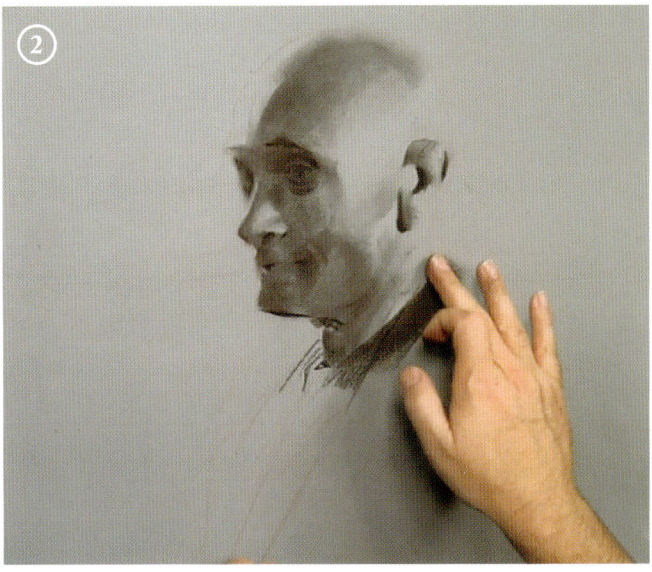

Vine charcoal is exceedingly blendable so I'm taking advantage of that quality to model the forms of the head, once again using my fingers. The surface is still so delicate that if I use a tissue to blend, it will simply wipe all of the tone away.

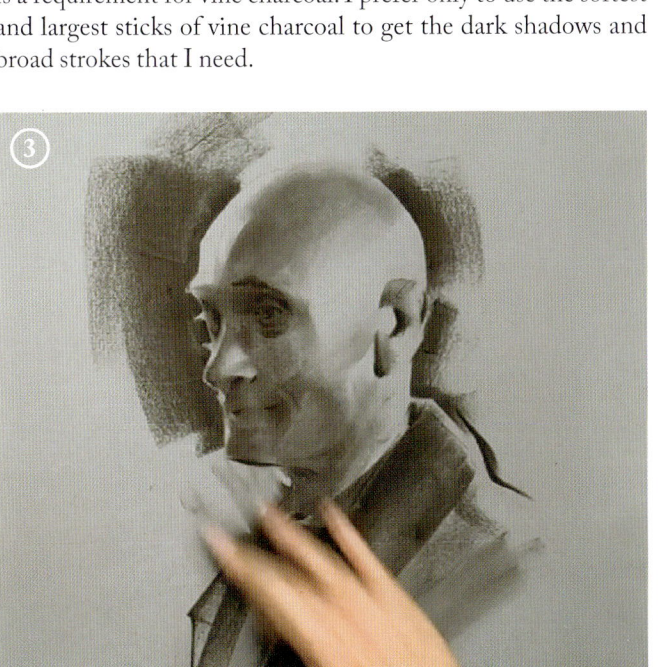

I use broad strokes to fill in the dark jacket and the background, and then once again try and take advantage of the blendability of the medium by pushing the charcoal around in what I hope are interesting strokes.

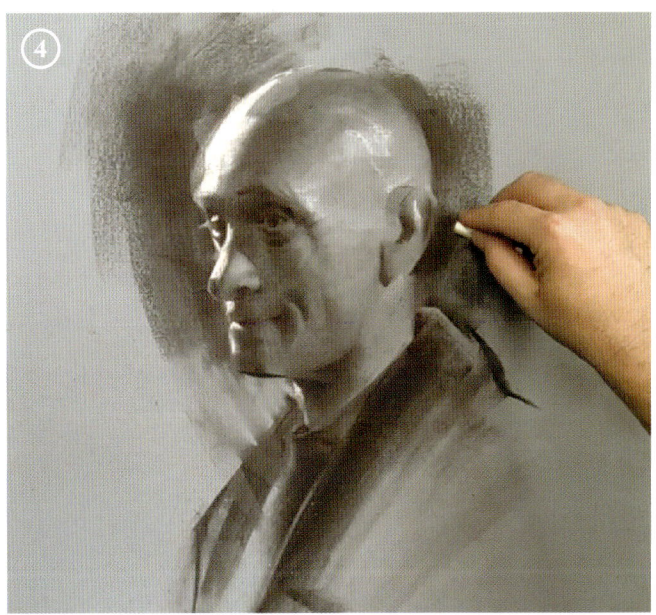

Now it's time to break out pastels to render light! I'm using an ivory Nupastel here to get a hard rim light on the left and a delicate form light on the right. And to wrap up I add the darkest accents in the features and call it a completed study.

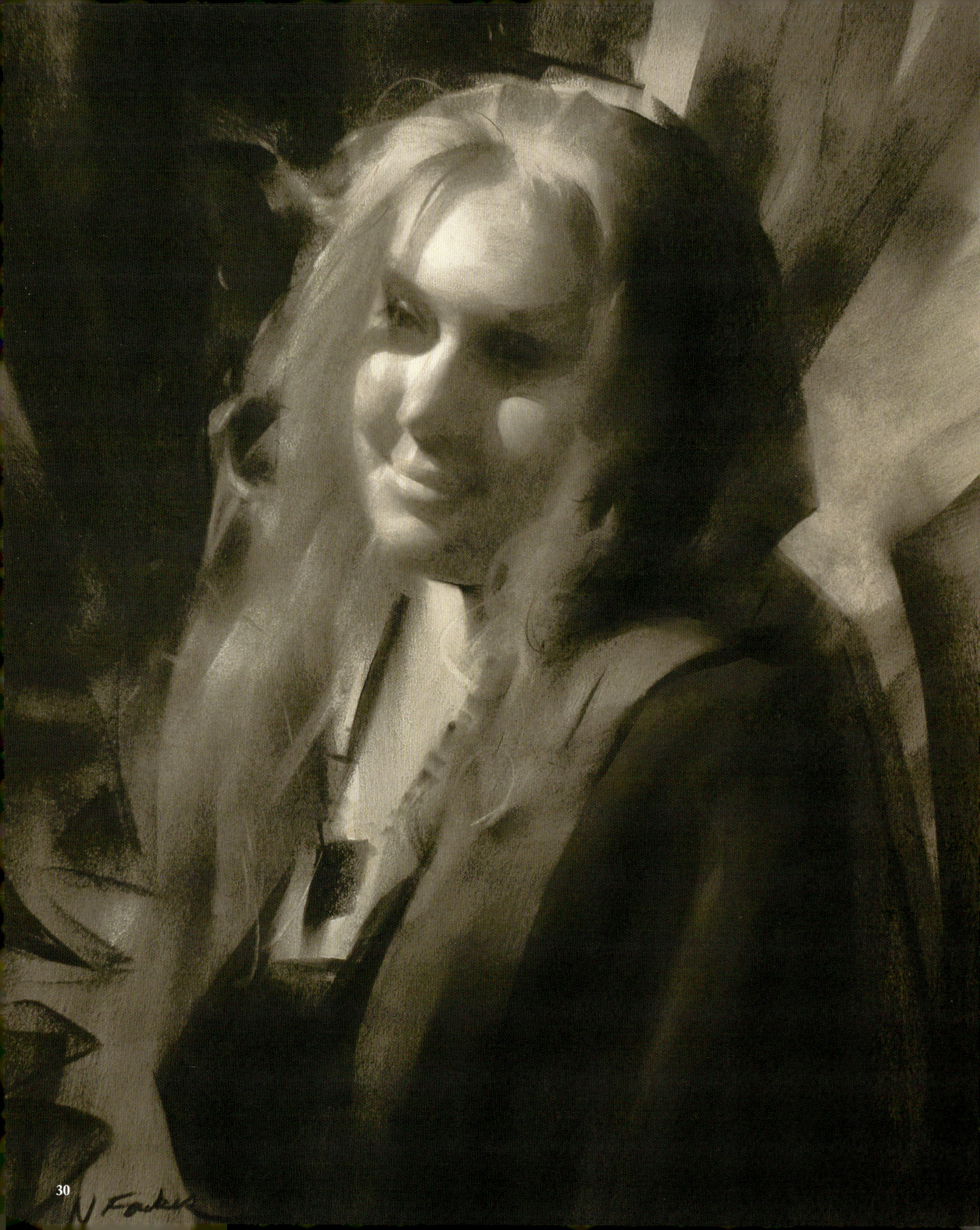

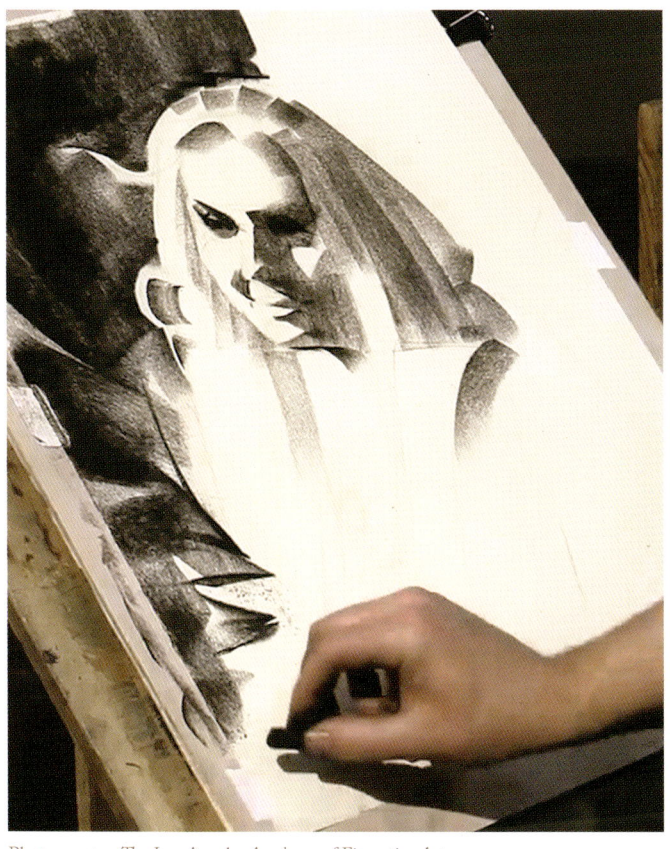

Photo courtesy The Los Angeles Academy of Figurative Art

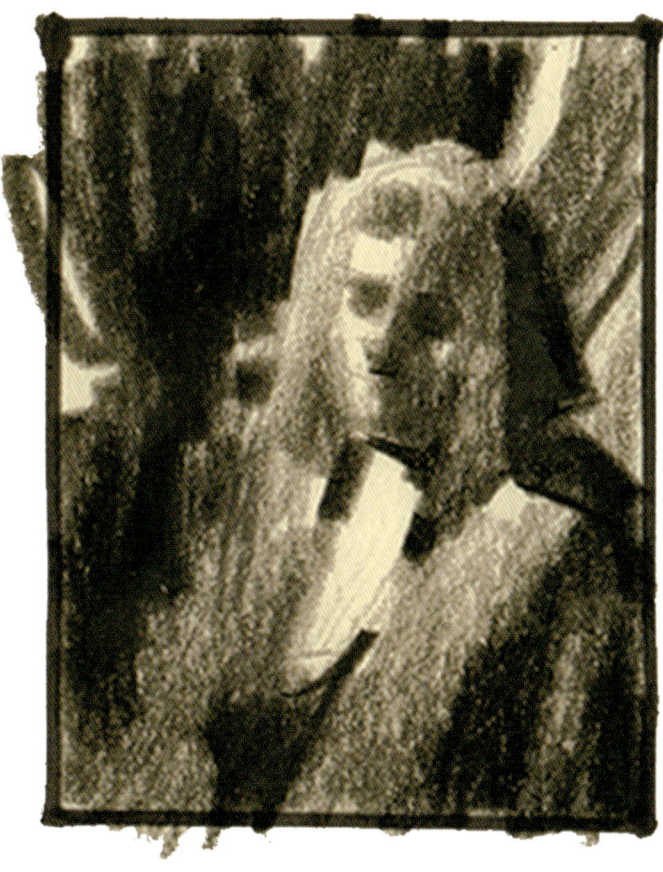

The Four Challenges

As a teacher with more than 15 years of experience in the life-drawing classroom, I believe that the topic we will study here is the most valuable thing that I have to offer. Here's what my teaching experience has shown me: I have watched every single student that I have ever had make some combination of the exact same four mistakes, and I mean without exception. And I've found that students perform much better when we cover these four challenges right up front, so let's do exactly that. Let's identify the four major roadblocks that tend to stop students from achieving the professional level of artistry of which they dream.

The Challenges Are:

① Practice   ② Time Limit

③ Value Limitations   ④ Perception

———

"I have watched every single student I have ever had make some combination of the exact same four mistakes."

———

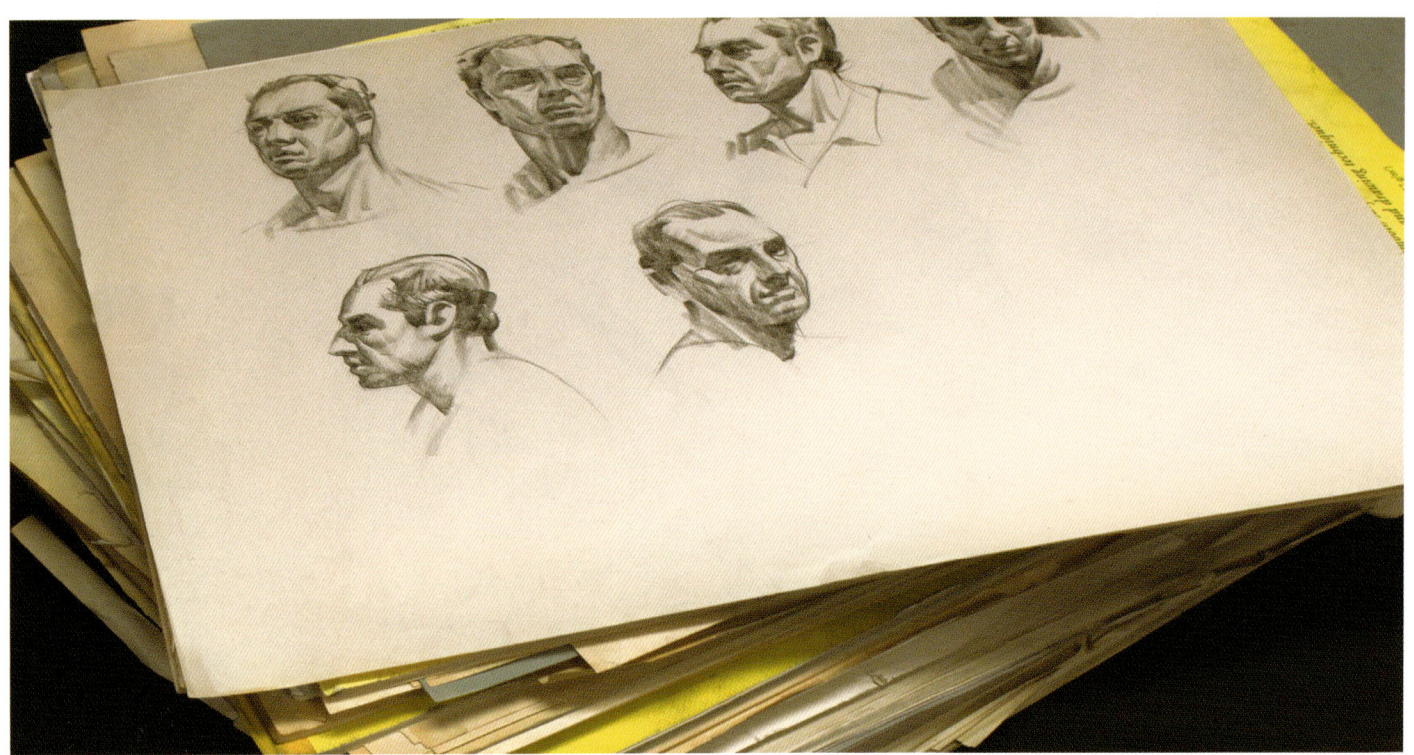

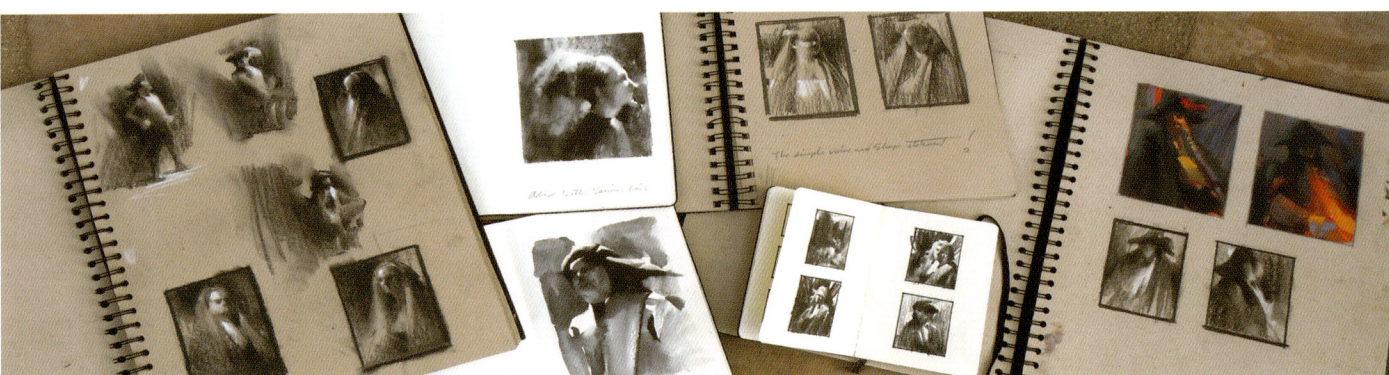

① *Practice, practice, practice...*

I feel very flattered on the occasions when someone says that I have a talent for drawing, but deep down I know it's not true. If I ever manage to stand out in drawing ability it's due to dedicated, unflinching practice. In fact, if I told you the truth about how many feverish hours each week I've put into this for the past 20 years you'd say two things to me: "You should be a lot better by now," and "Get a life!" And I would happily accept both criticisms, but I also think that a part of the good life is having something to show for yourself, something special or unique to bring to the table. And any such worthy endeavor requires dedicated practice.

So our first challenge, practice, is an obvious one; we all know that it's a great challenge to train our eyes, mind, and hands to manage the complexity of drawing a human likeness. We've got to get into the life drawing classroom and practice, practice, practice; there's just no shortcut when it comes to this. And yet the sad fact is that many people, and in my experience, most people who want to learn to draw, ultimately are not willing or not able to put in the amount of time necessary to achieve this highly difficult skill. But not to worry; you'll see as we move forward that it doesn't always have to be as hard as we make it. I've taken the long way to get here, and so the purpose of this book is to take the lessons I've learned and shorten the learning curve for you.

② *Time Limit*

When working from life, there's usually a tight time limit. Outdoor light changes quickly or the indoor drawing session comes to an end. The model gets up and walks away, and we're left only with what we were able to get down on paper. The clock is always ticking, and we are required to render a very complicated subject in a short period of time. Since beginners have no experience in what to emphasize and edit in their subjects, they are initially crippled by this. But there's good news here: in the chapters that follow we will discuss how to find a clear, simple statement within the complexity of our subject. We'll learn how to turn this limitation into an advantage! We'll work toward an understanding of drawing that will ultimately give greater clarity and artistry to our drawings in a shorter period of time.

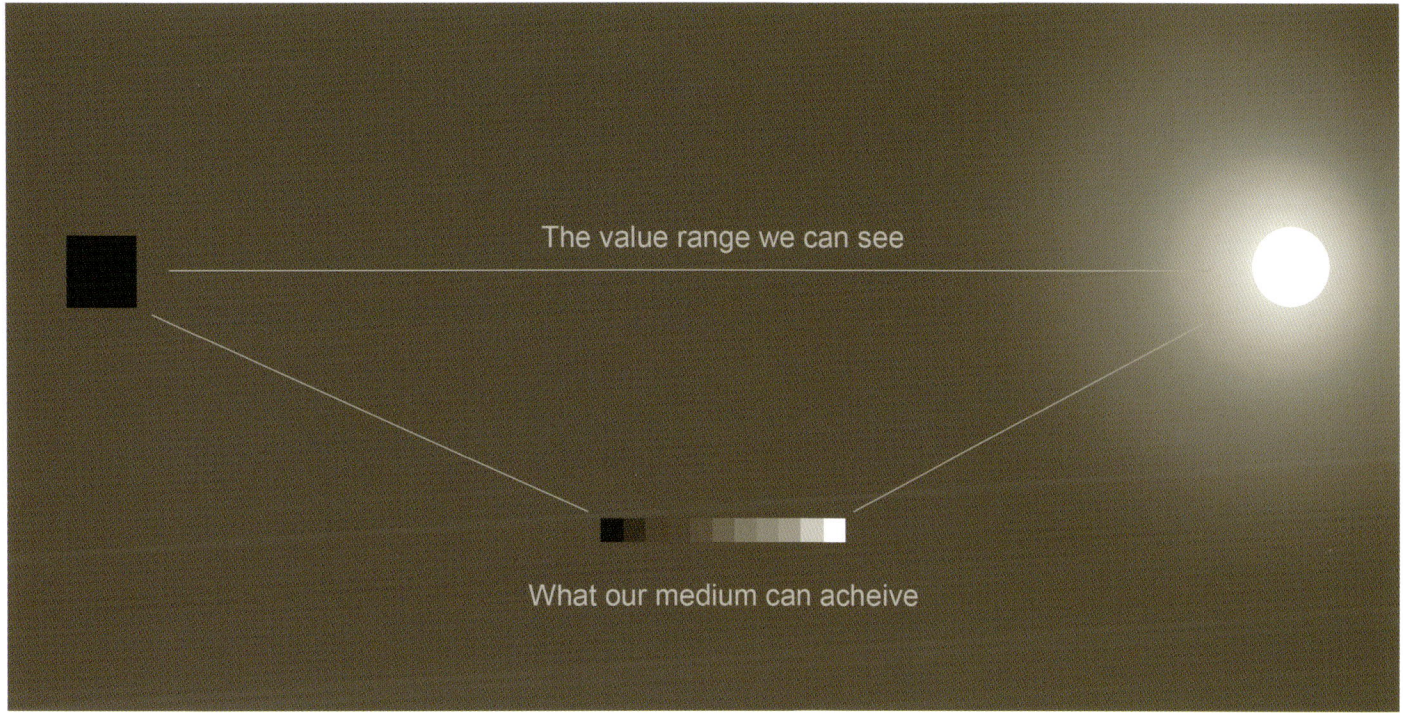

The value range we can see

What our medium can acheive

③ *Value Limitations*

Have you ever heard an artist or teacher suggest that you limit your drawing to just four values of light and shadow? (Value is an artist's term which refers to the scale from light to dark.) Why would we do such a thing? Why would we limit ourselves when the visual world is filled with such intricate complexity? The answer is because sometimes we have to. Our medium, a stick of charcoal and a sheet of paper, is not able to reproduce all of the subtleties we can see, not even close.

Take a look at the chart above; the top line represents what we can see, ranging from the brightest light to the black of a complete lack of light. The lower, much smaller value scale suggests what our medium is able to achieve. Even the whitest paper reflects a limited amount of light, and the blackest pigment still reflects some light back to our eyes. So do you see the huge problem emerging here? We're trying to represent what we see with a medium that is not capable of reproducing it! You literally cannot draw all that you can see, and since beginners do not yet understand this, the results are predictably disastrous.

"One of the first things we must learn is that our drawings will always be an interpretation of what we see, not a one-to-one reproduction."

Let me try and carefully explain what I mean by "perception" because this challenge is the big one. It's the challenge that some students never seem to get past, the one that destroys their ability to work from life. I'll go so far as to say that in my experience this is the battlefield on which most life drawing students die. So let's do our best to understand and tackle it:

The job of our eyes is to glean as much information from the visible world as possible, and information comes in the form of contrast. We understand what we see as one object contrasts with another. And so we are hardwired to most strongly notice that which varies. It's a survival trait; it's something that keeps us alive in the natural world. But ironically it's the very thing that kills us in the life drawing classroom.

Take a look at the images below. The first is a photo of a favorite model in my life drawing classes; he has a lot of character and is a fun challenge to draw. But here's what always seems to happen; students study his features and anatomy carefully in an effort to draw as accurately as possible. But when the model takes a break and the students step back to see how their drawing is coming along, they are often horrified to see that their drawing looks more like a sack of walnuts than a human head. "But I was drawing it exactly the way I saw it," they say.

"How did this happen?" But they weren't drawing it the way they saw it; they were noticing the contrasts and rendering those individually without giving attention to how those parts relate to each other. That's where drawings three and four apply; they show that rather than emphasizing individual contrasts, we can find how the parts relate, and then we're much more likely to properly interpret what we see.

So let me say it again: we all have a strong tendency to make the perceptual error of overemphasizing individual contrasts. Darks get darker or lights get lighter; bumps get bumpier and the sad result is that enthusiastic students get results that are disheartening. And worse, the harder they try to reproduce what they see, the more they falsely exaggerate. Eventually they throw their hands in the air and proclaim that they have no natural talent and walk away. And it didn't have to happen. We simply need to learn to reverse our natural way of observing and emphasize relationships rather than contrasts. It's easier said than done, which is why we need so much practice; we have to overcome our own innate nature when we endeavor to draw representationally.

"But I was drawing it exactly the way I saw it," they say. "How did this happen?" But they weren't drawing it the way they saw it; they were noticing the contrasts and rendering those individually without giving attention to how those parts relate to each other."

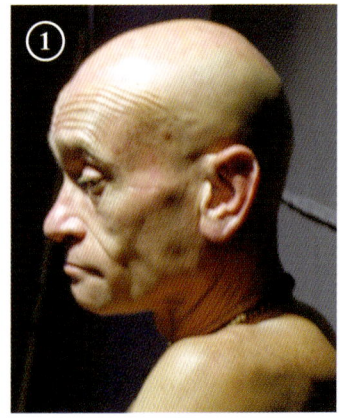 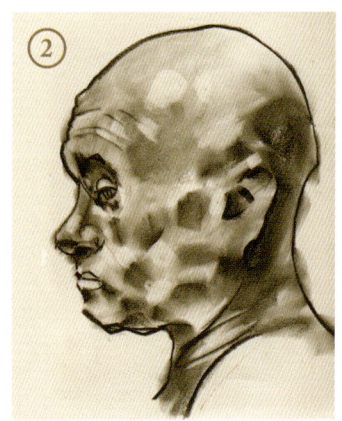 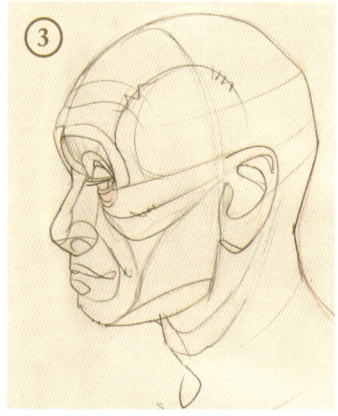 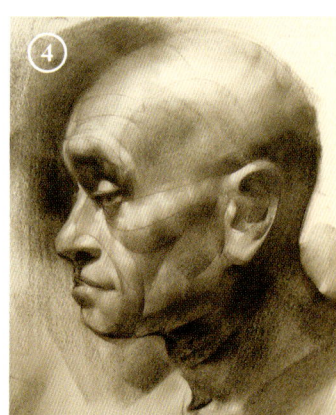

This step-by-step example illustrates solutions to challenges of perception that we will be discussing fully in the chapters to come. Take note that in each stage I'm looking for ways to simplify and organize my subject into manageable steps.

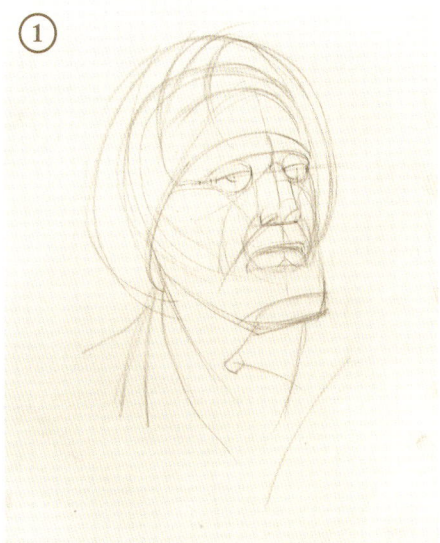

Find simple relationships that emphasize the three-dimensional nature of the head.

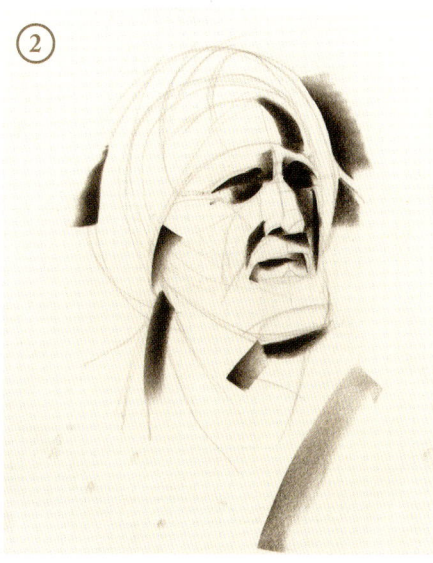

Find simple landmarks.

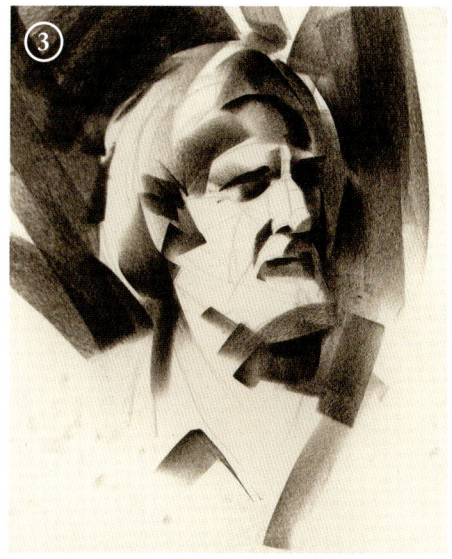

Group the entire head into simple masses of light and shadow.

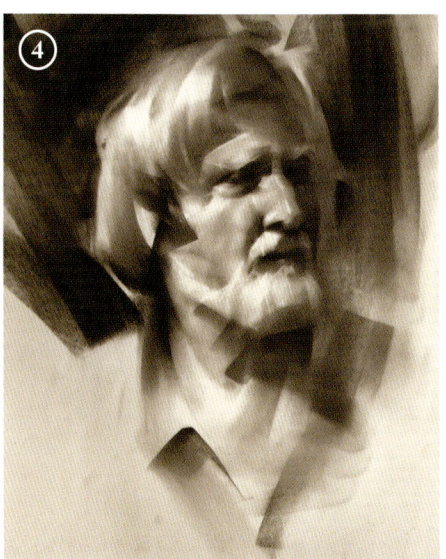

Now we are prepared to tackle the greater complexities of the portrait! At this stage the light areas are organized into simple turning forms and the direction of the strokes follow the contour of the forms.

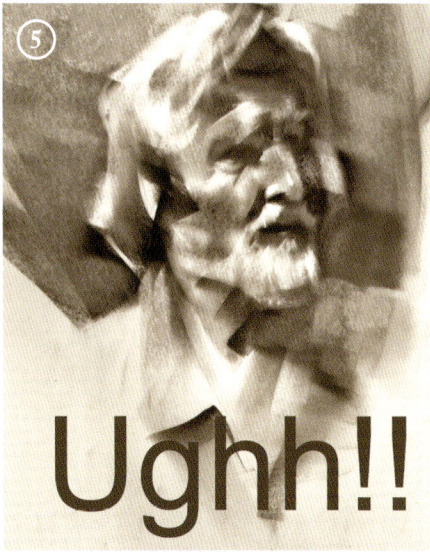

Here's what not to do. "Ughh!!" is right, and yet I have never once had a student in my 15 years of teaching whose drawings didn't tend to drift in this direction. Once again, it's an example of most strongly noticing "that which varies" (details, contrasts, anatomical bumps, highlights, wisps of hair, etc.). And so we unconsciously give these variations undue emphasis, which leads to bumpy, out-of-control drawings like the one above.

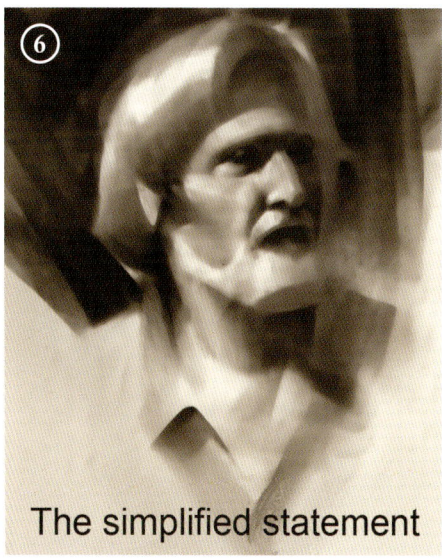

Avoid the bad drawing problem by seeking a "simplified statement" as shown in the above image. For this one I fussed with the original drawing digitally to show how the parts simply relate to the whole. You can put all the fancy, splashy technique you want into a representational drawing if it sits on the foundation of a clear, simple statement.

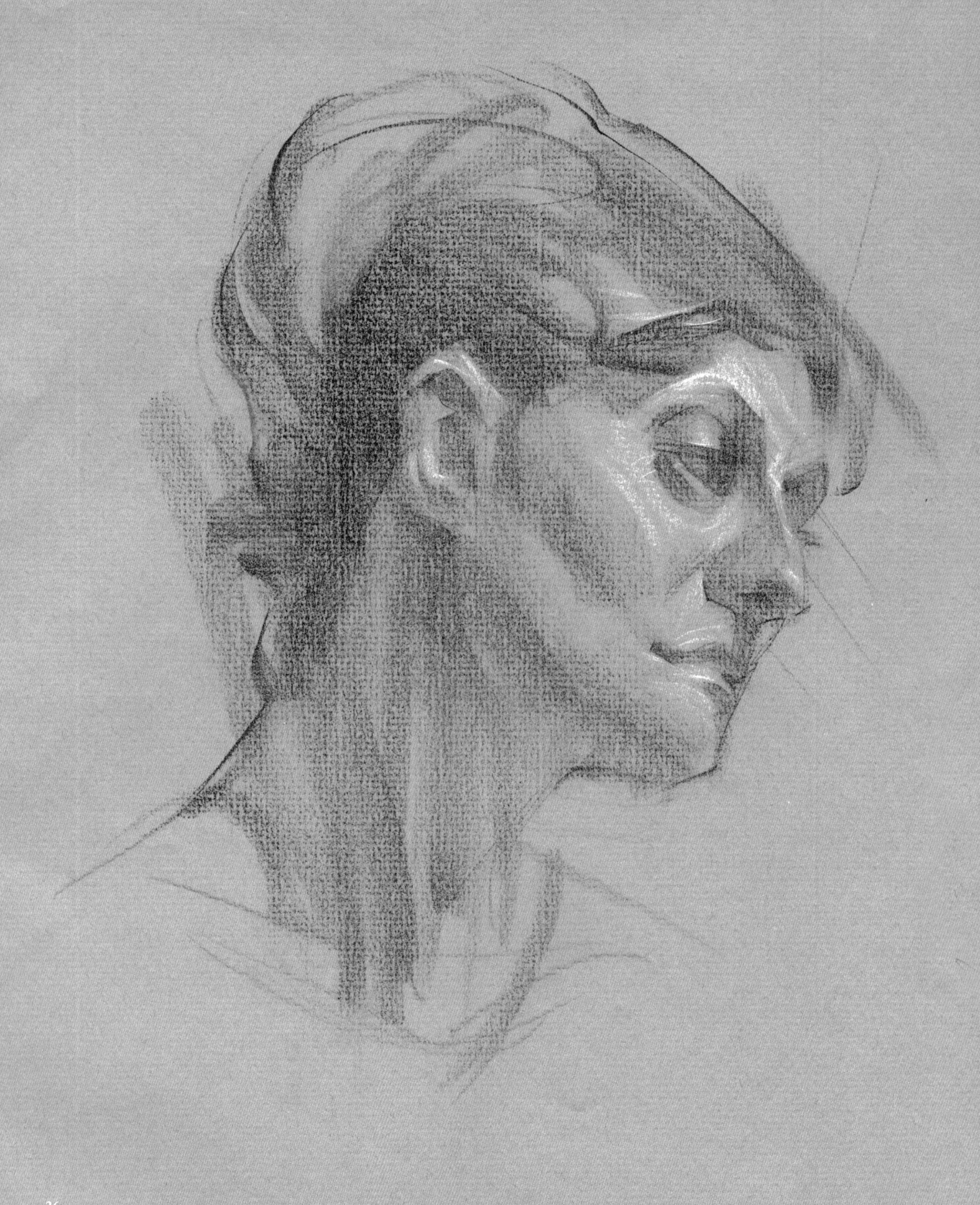

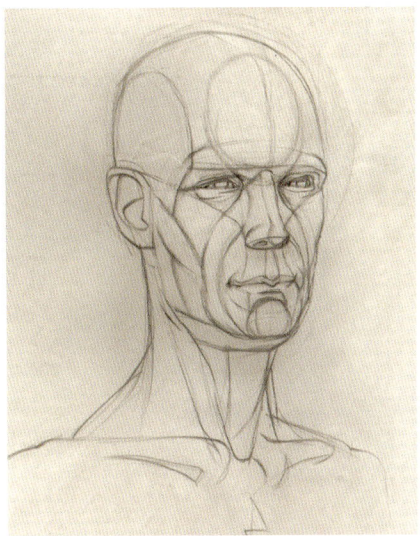
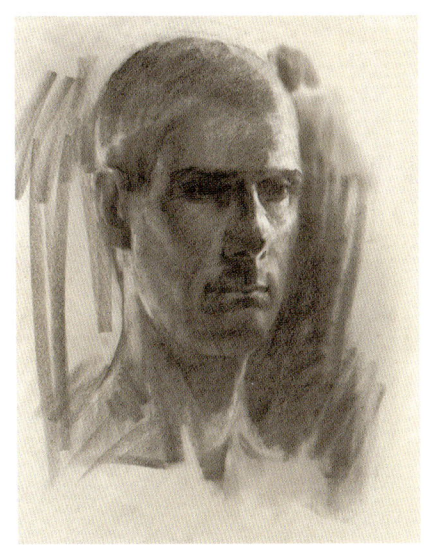

Structure

In the introduction to this book, I described leaving my job in animation for a drawing sabbatical that was critically important in my development as an artist. As we begin our discussion here on the topic of structure, I'd like to share with you a little bit more about that experience.

In the 1990s and 2000s in Los Angeles, there was an atelier called Associates in Art. It had very good instruction for drawing and painting and was under the direction of Mark Westermoe, a talented figurative artist and illustrator. I approached Mark with an offer to teach at the school in exchange for taking classes myself. I shared with him my resume of animated films, and Mark was enthusiastic about having a DreamWorks artist on staff. He put the school's classes and uninstructed drawing sessions at my disposal for the next six months. Mark's drawing approach was quite extraordinary, and I quickly learned that it was inspired by the "Reilly method."

"The purpose of Frank J. Reilly's approach was to help his students understand and organize the anatomy of the human form without getting lost in its complexities."

Frank J. Reilly had been a respected art instructor at the Art Students League of New York and had been actively teaching from the 1930s through the 1960s. His influences date back to the French Academy of the 19th century, having studied with George Bridgman, who studied with Jean-Léon Gérôme, one of the most prominent artists of the French Academy.

During Reilly's tenure as a teacher, he developed approaches to drawing designed to help his students understand and organize the complexities of the human form. On the following pages, you'll see my own interpretation of his approach as handed down through generations of teachers. The Reilly Method was brought to Los Angeles by Fred Fixler. Fred had been trained by Frank Reilly at the Art Students League of New York and then came out West to work as a professional illustrator. Fred also became a popular drawing teacher in Los Angeles and trained several highly successful artists, illustrators, and teachers, such as Glen Orbik, Morgan Weistling, and Mark Westermoe. The traditions carried by this group of influential artists and teachers helped create a resurgence of representational art at a time when the burgeoning Los Angeles entertainment industry was demanding a new generation of artists with exactly those skills.

And so my personal and professional work has greatly benefited from the concepts passed on to me, which I will lay out for you as best I can in the following pages.

The Reilly Head Abstraction

Now that I've shared with you the tradition of excellent artists who have inspired me, I want to advise great caution. With much respect to all the artists mentioned, we are not here to become disciples of any individual artist, dogmatically adhering to one person's idea about how to draw. Rather, we use good ideas wherever we can find them; we apply them where they are useful and ignore them where they are not.

Below you can see my line drawings of the "Reilly head" with a demonstration of how I use it to help me organize the complex forms of light and shadow. Please, please, please use this head diagram as an idea and not as some kind of exact formula. The Reilly abstraction is useful only inasmuch as it gives ideas on how to simplify and organize the complexity of the human head.

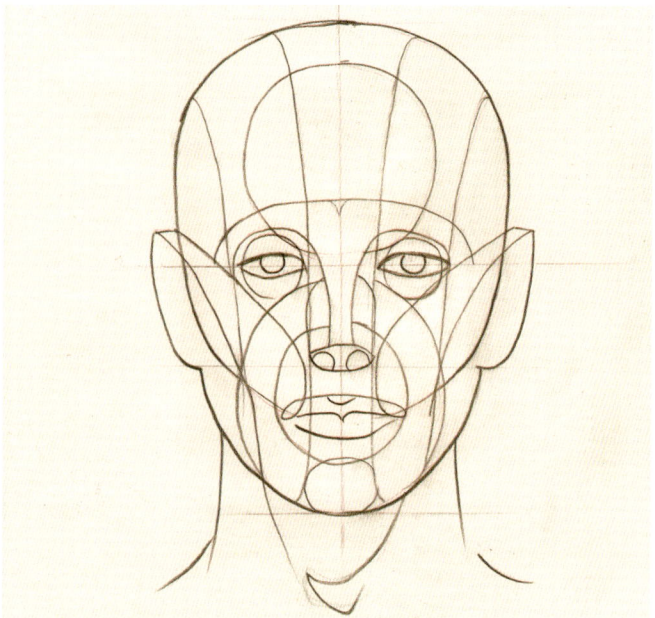

Reilly head abstraction.

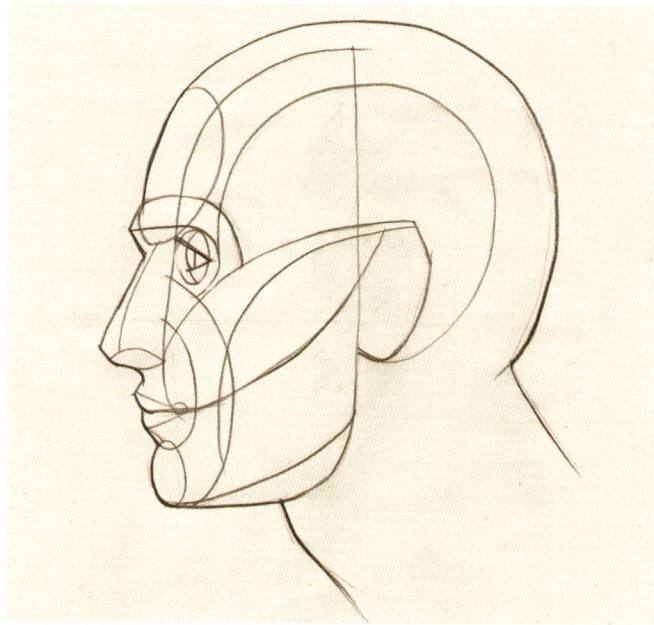

Reilly head abstraction, side view.

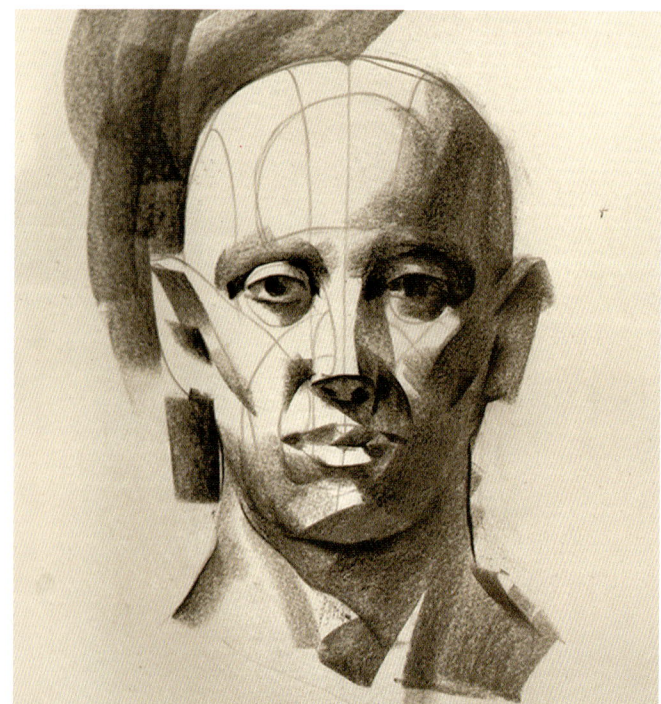

The Reilly abstraction informs the placement of light and shadow.

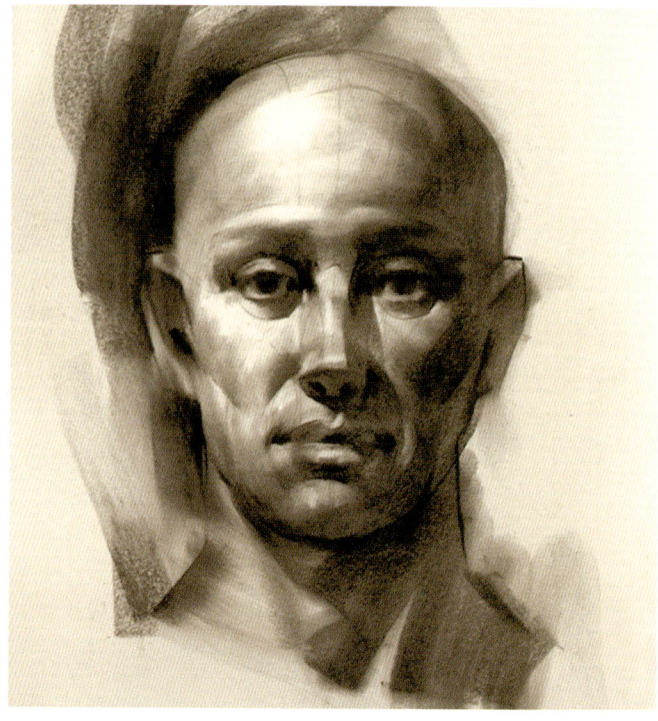

The Reilly abstraction informs the modeling of the forms of the head.

My experiences as a teacher have shown me that nearly all students more readily succeed when they organize their subject into a simple, manageable structure. It's true that I find this particular approach to be highly useful, but in the end I only care that every line you draw and every tone you put down is designed to convey the underlying form.

Let me share an example. One of my former students was struggling with the Reilly abstraction, making the mistake of treating it as an exact formula. A fellow instructor with whom he was also taking classes told him: "You've got to quit doing this Reilly thing; it's ruining your drawings." I was in complete agreement. The student was observing the subject and would then reproduce a generic version of the Reilly head at whatever angle the model was posing. He wasn't using the idea to help draw the character of the person; he was using the person to draw a generic Reilly head. In this case the approach was completely backwards and in no way helpful. Another student who was a bit more experienced, and, in fact, an animation modeler, said, "Oh, I get it; it's like a computer wireframe rendering. It helps you visualize the whole head in 3D!"

He was exactly right and excelled in the class. I hope my further explanations help you avoid formulaic thinking while benefiting from the approach. In fact, you'll be glad to hear that the first student's work greatly improved when he learned how to use our approach more naturally.

Now turn your attention to the sphere and line drawing demonstration below; the most basic idea here is to use your line drawing to recreate the three-dimensional nature of the head on the two-dimensional surface of your paper. This is of primary importance because the act of drawing is a translation of the three-dimensional world onto the two-dimensional page. Since a drawing has no actual depth we have to fight and even exaggerate to create the illusion of depth. Again, think of your structural line drawings like a computer wire frame, a digital rendering where lines wrap around form to create the illusion of space.

You can see how these ideas are put into practice in the demonstration here, and on the following page I'll describe for you step by step how I like to use this approach.

---

*"Every single line you draw and every tone you put down
must be designed to convey the underlying form."*

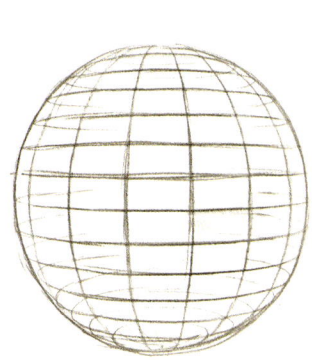
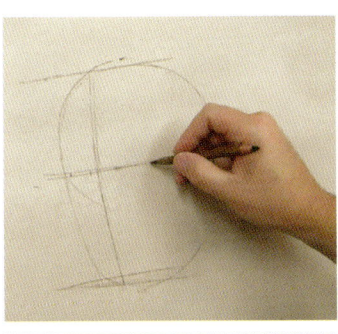
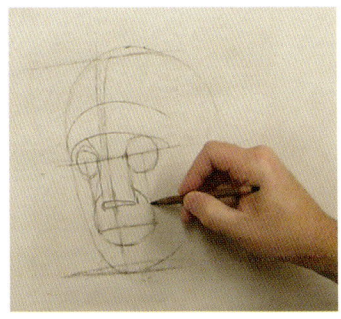
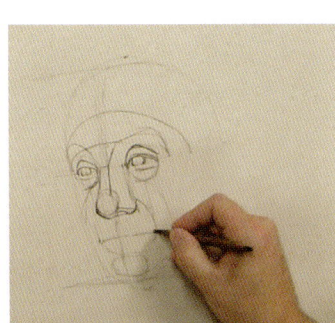
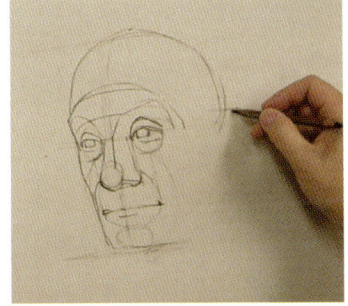
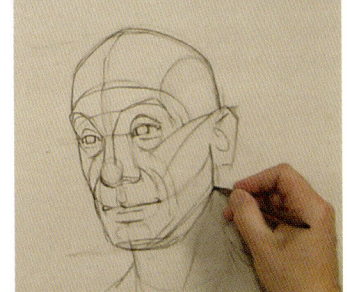
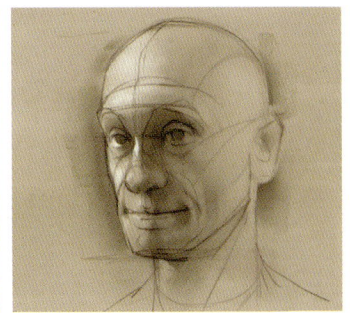

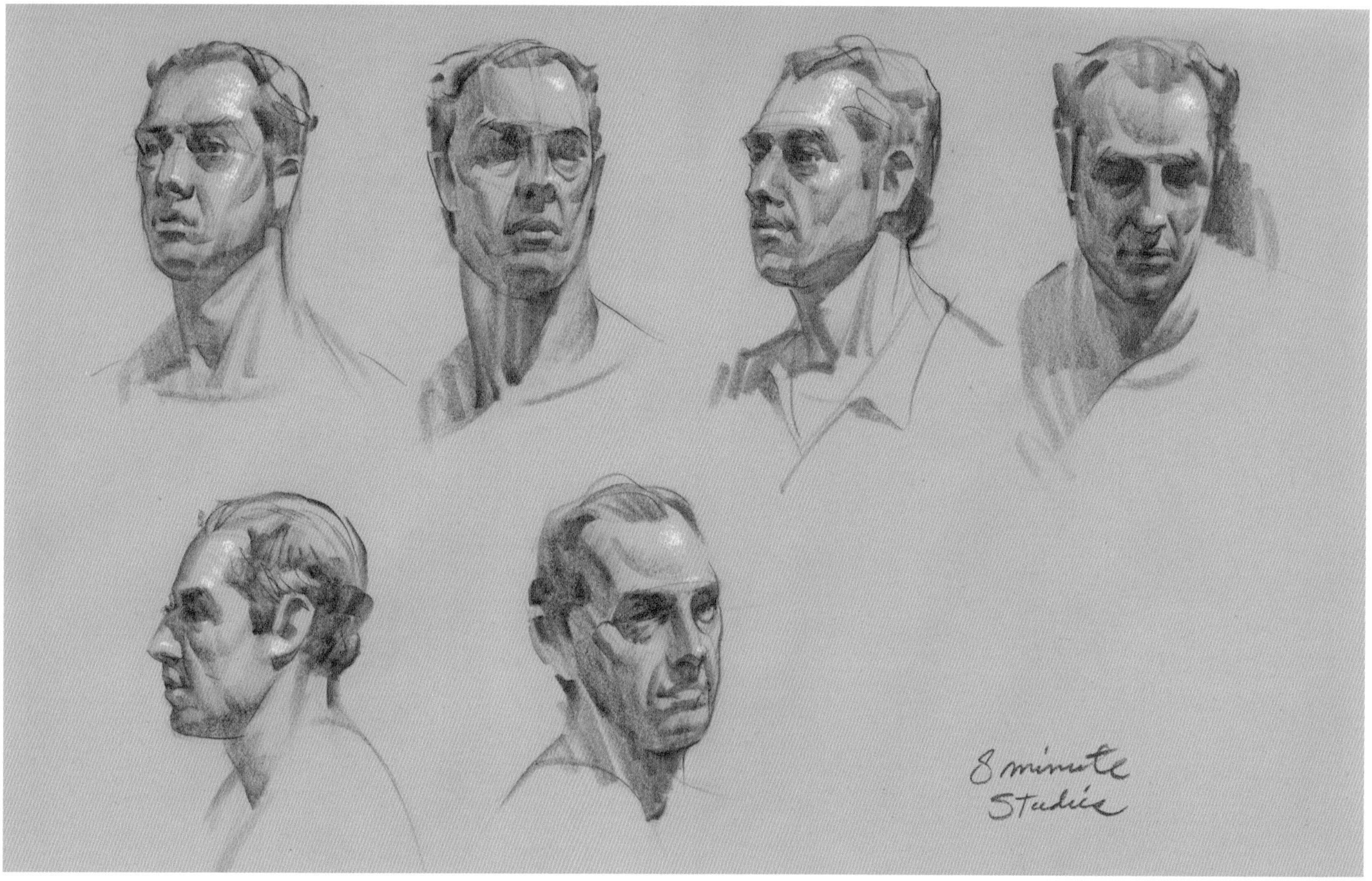

8 minute
Studies

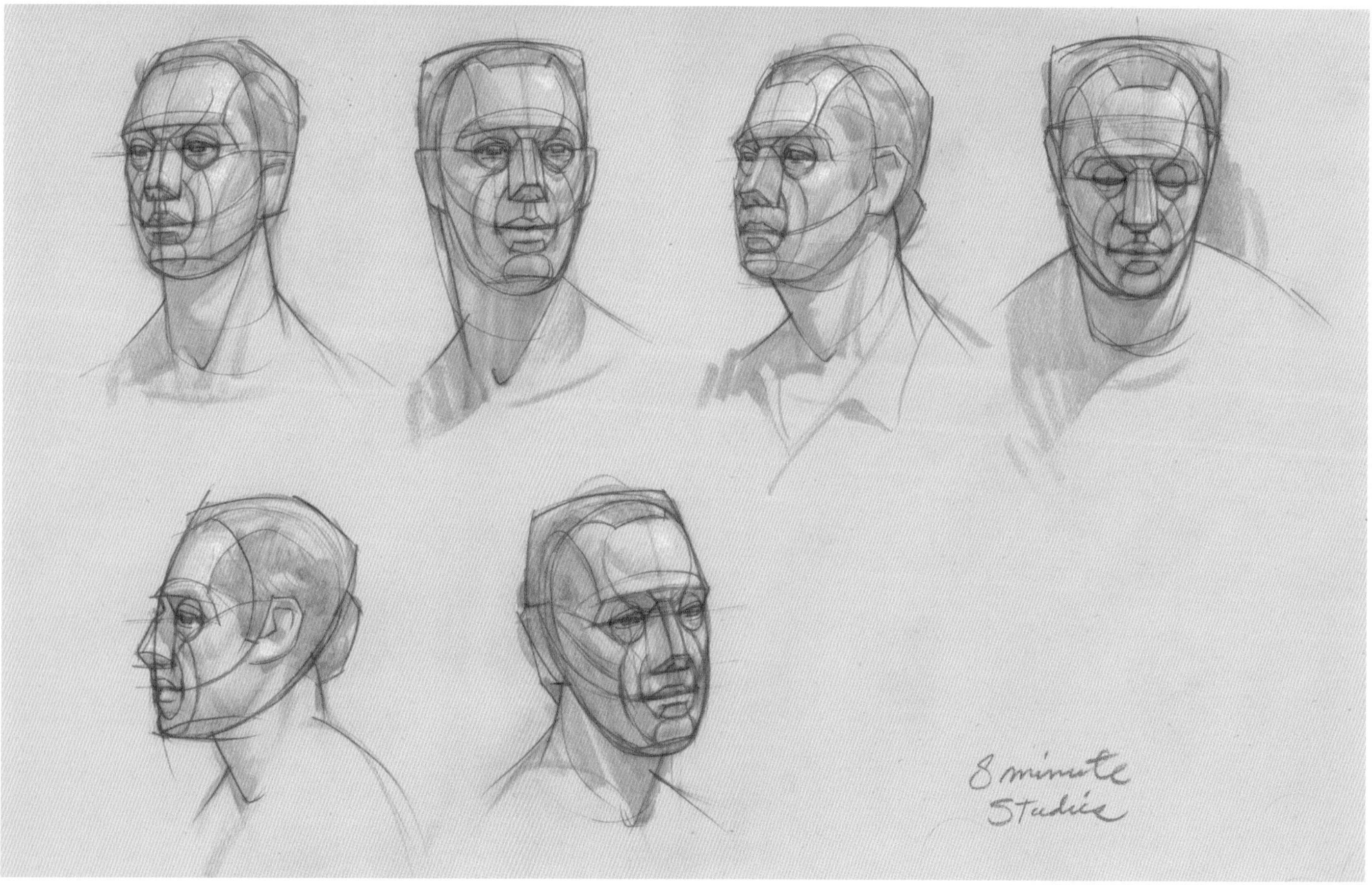

8 minute
Studies

Let's put our organizational principles into practice by quickly sketching the head from multiple angles. The head studies you see at the far top left attempt to render my sitter in full light and shadow in just eight minutes each. Such "quick-sketch" drawings are an excellent exercise; they force us to find a clear simple statement in our drawings. In the lower left overlay, I show how the Reilly style approach helps me organize the complexities of the head. So let's break down the process here into three simple steps:

Head-Study Demonstration 1: Reilly Method

Step One: Put down the simplest ideas first.

I start with the simple egg shape of the head with a vertical dividing line down the center, and then the eye line which is at the halfway point of the head. I eyeball the placement of the nose and mouth by observation of my sitter, and then I add a quick suggestion of the neck and shoulders.

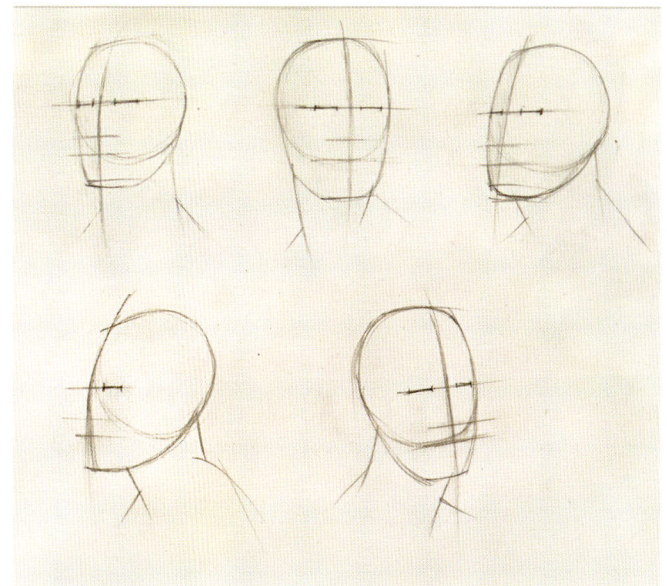

Step Two: Identify simple alignments.

The simple alignments of the features are quite helpful in keeping the face symmetrical. The inside corners of the eyes tend to line up with the outside corners of the nose, and the center of the eyes tends to align with the outside corners of the mouth. Representing the eyeballs as simple circles can help manage the complexity of the eyes. Instead of a mass of complicated details, they can be treated as simple spheres that slightly protrude from the head.

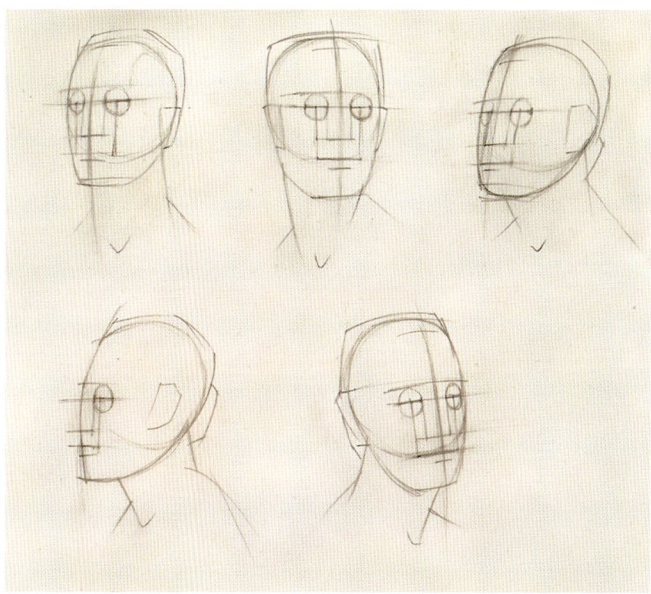

Step Three: Focus on features and large forms of the head.

The brow ridge above the eyes is one simple shape wrapping around the head, and the mass of each cheek is one simple shape along the side of the head. The area around the mouth can seem quite complex but can be simplified into the muscles that wrap around it from below the eye to the chin, and then the muzzle of the mouth is treated as one large sphere that slightly protrudes from the head. Additionally, features, such as the nose, can be broken down into simple planes, such as front plane, side plane, and under plane. Don't forget that the hair has form and can be broken down into simple planes as well.

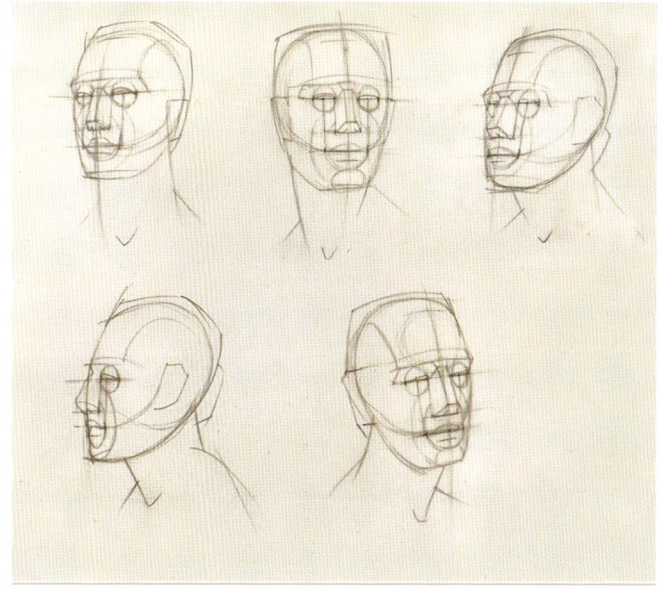

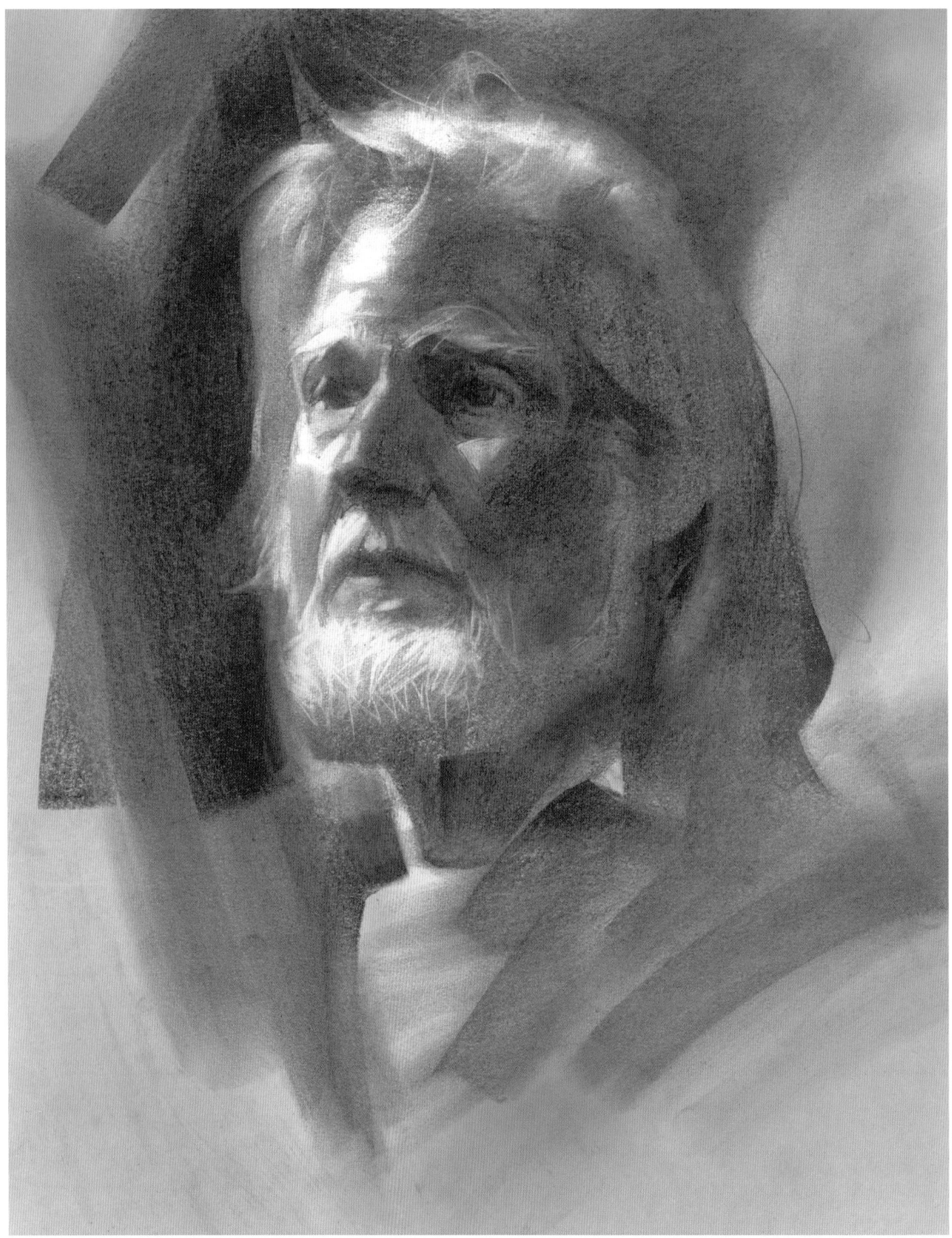

Head-Study Demonstration 2: Reilly Method

Now let's use our simple approach to take on an even more complex subject. Take a look at the finished drawing at the left; see how active the hair is? But I'd also like you to notice how simple the larger silhouetted shape of the hair is; I'm much more able to render complexity when I look for the simplest shapes first.

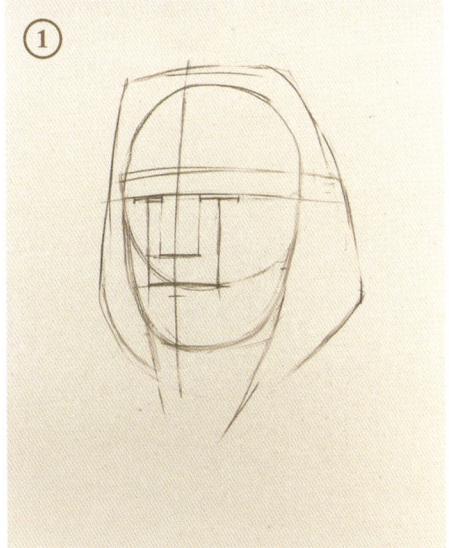

I'm sticking to simple shapes and alignments, especially the overall silhouette of the hair.

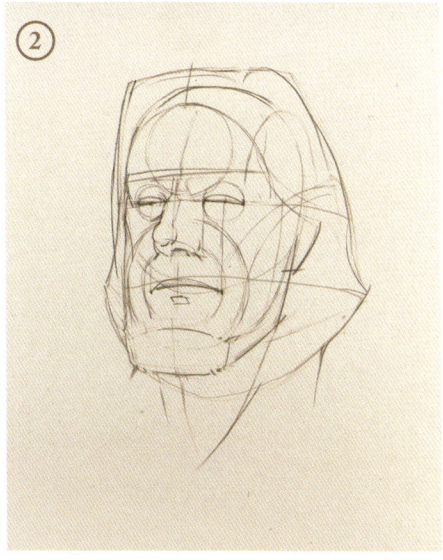

As I work out the three dimensional forms, note that the beard is also treated as having 3D structure.

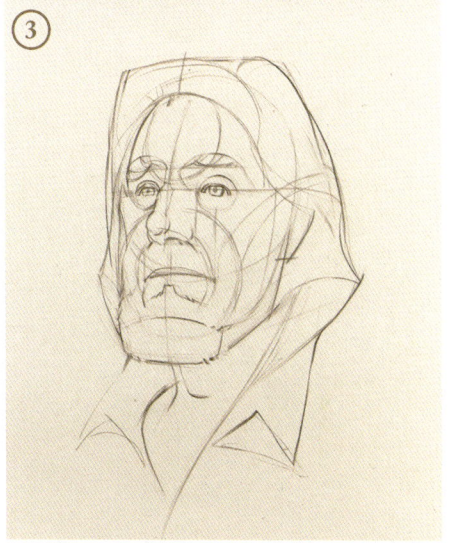

I continue to refine the construction, making sure the hair is given three dimensional structure as well.

For me, this process is an absolute necessity to create the illusion of real, three-dimensional life on a two-dimensional piece of paper. We'll be discussing the intricacies of light and shadow in an upcoming chapter so for now I'd simply like to point out how beneficial a strong construction drawing is for organizing light and shadow.

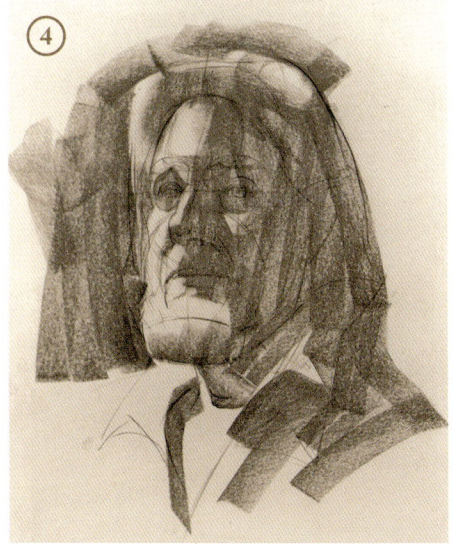

Here I make the simplest statement possible by blocking in a dark tone for everything that's in shadow and leave the light.

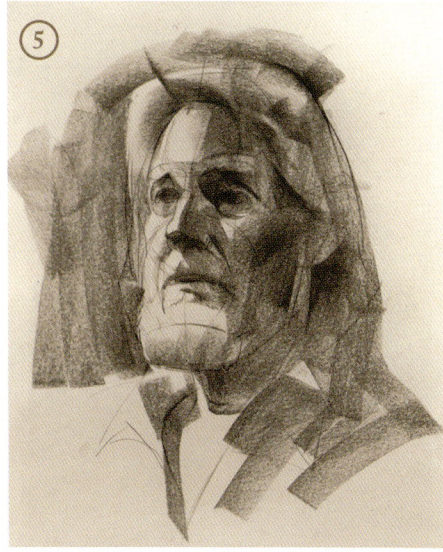

Then, I simply add the darker accents as they conform to the established structural drawing.

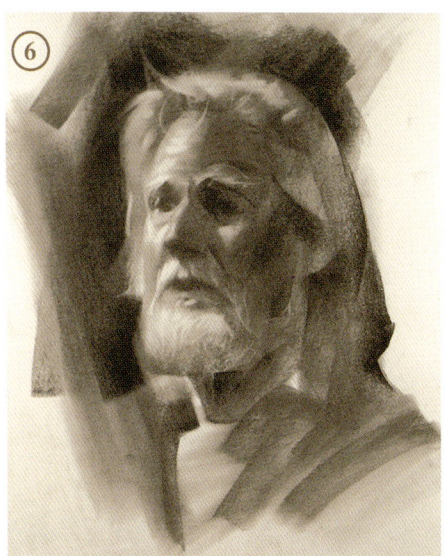

I blend softly turning forms and finish up with the detail work done in pencil and a sharpened eraser. And with these six steps, the completed drawing you see to the left emerges!

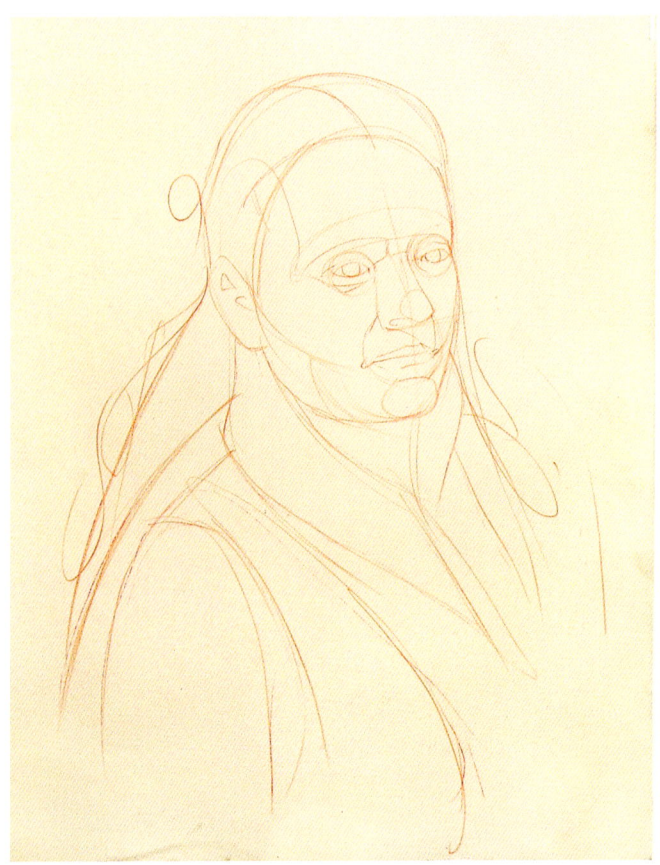

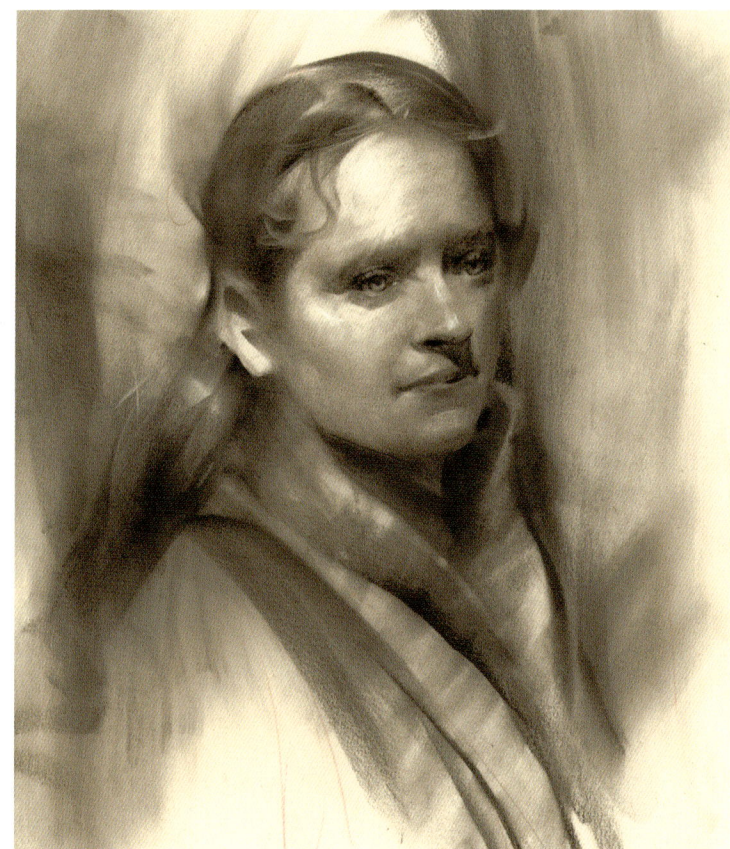

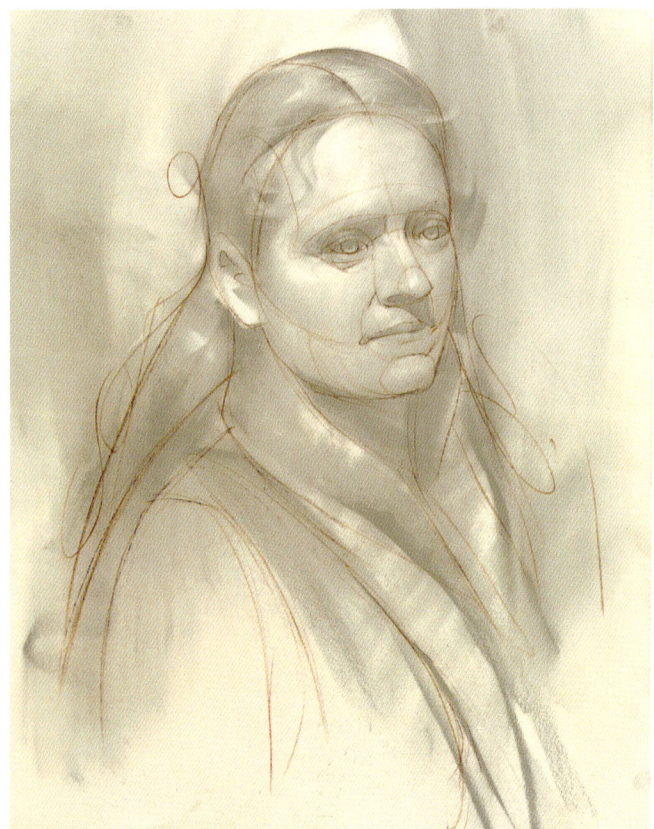

Let's take on a different subject with this female model with long hair wearing a scarf. Here I use an orange Prismacolor pencil on Rives lightweight paper to lay down my construction drawing. The subject was difficult for me to draw, but I'd like you to take notice of how helpful the initial line drawing was. Take a look at the cheek and how it's treated as one big shape that wraps around the head from ear to nose and mouth. Look also at the mouth and surrounding anatomy. It's complicated, but it reads more clearly with the help of the circular shape that wraps from the lower side of the nose to the top of the chin. The hair is also complicated but begins with a very clearly silhouetted shape. For the scarf and clothing, I choose to simply represent the forms that wrap around the neck and fall down the shoulder. There was much more there that could've been rendered, but it was important to edit and keep only what would be useful for the drawing.

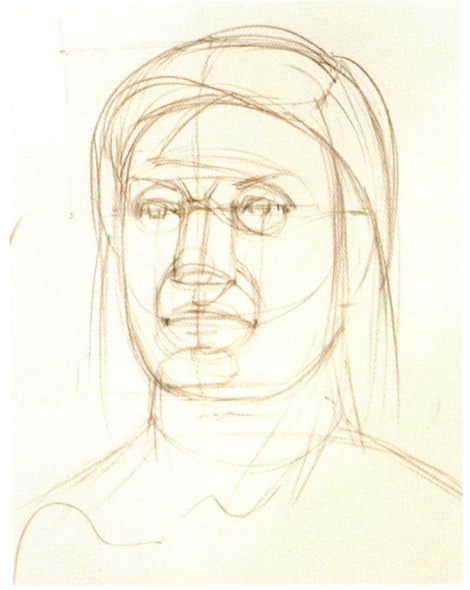

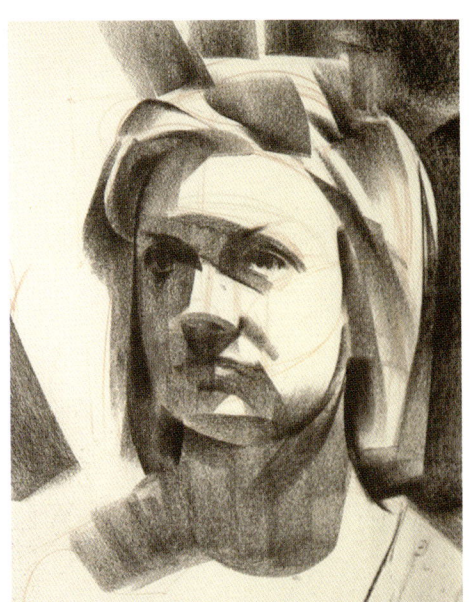

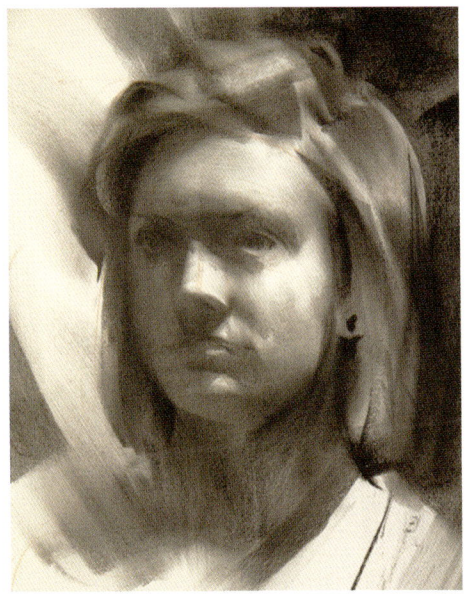

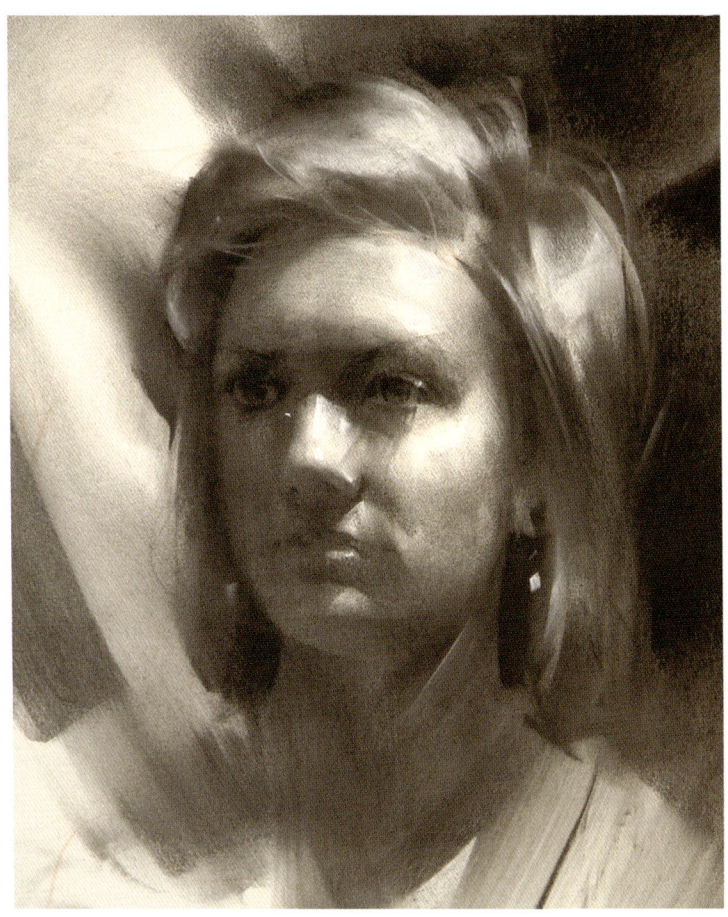

How I really draw

Many of the examples that we've looked at thus far were specifically done not as personal drawings but as demonstrations for students. In such cases the initial line drawings are done meticulously to clearly demonstrate concepts. But for myself, I sketch my initial drawing much more quickly and loosely, adhering to the ideas suggested by the Reilly method but not bothering with any kind of exactness. The step-by-step demonstration here is a quick one-hour drawing that requires economy. I'm using the minimum amount of lines, strokes, and shapes to best represent my subject within a limited period of time. I use the "spirit" of the approach we've been studying rather than adhering to it "by the letter."

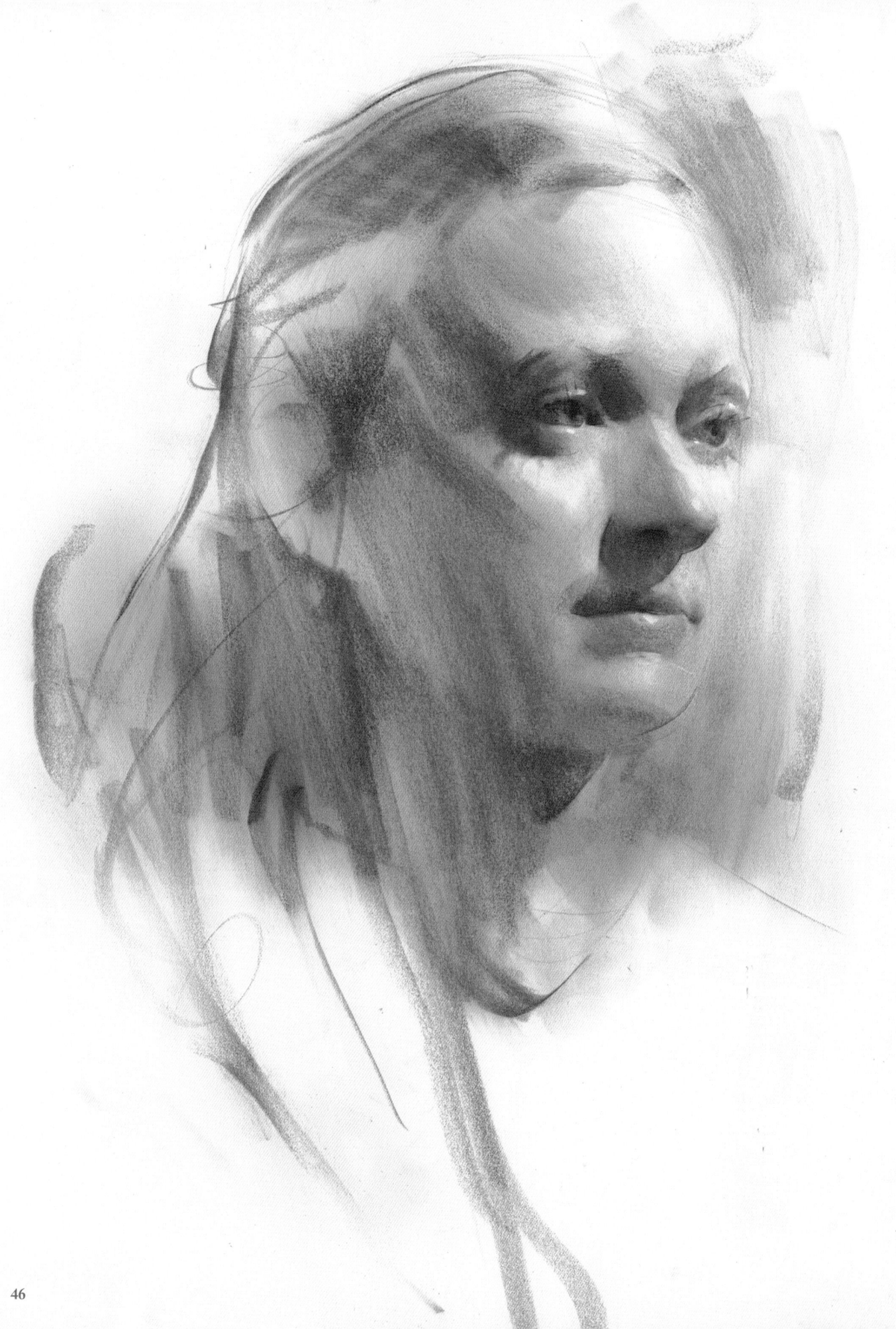

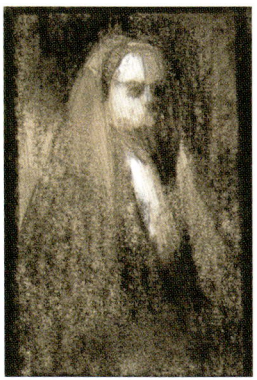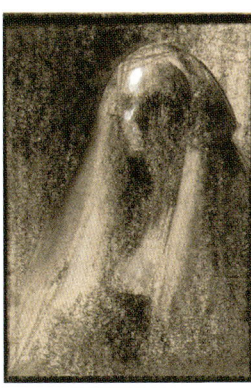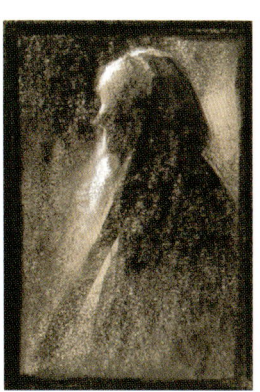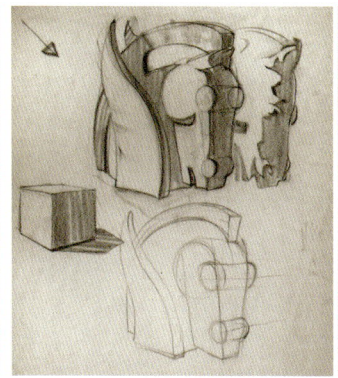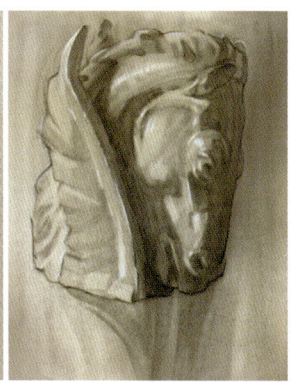

Chapter 5

High-school class demonstration from 1993

Clarity with Artistry

Back in the early 1990s while I was in art school, I got an interesting phone call asking if I was interested in teaching an art class at one of the local Los Angeles high schools. But there was a catch; the catch was that this particular class was for "at risk" students. These were students who had two strikes against them, one more and they'd be kicked out. They were serious behavioral cases and so someone who knew me had the idea to bring in an outside artist in hopes of engaging them in the subject of art.

I hesitated, I was in the middle of art school myself and wasn't sure I had all the answers; but at the same time it was an opportunity and a challenge and so I decided to take it on. I showed up for the class and one of the first things I did was grab a carved Pegasus bust off their shelf. I put it on the table under lights and started to draw. What I tried to do was to show the students a simple process. I showed them that if they were to do nothing more than the line drawing you see above, then add shapes of shadow and a few of the natural curves, they could have the beginnings of a beautiful drawing.

I pointed out that every single student in that class, at that moment, was capable of doing all of these things. When I had first walked into the class, the stance that I got from them was arms folded, slumped in their chairs conveying an attitude that there was nothing I could do or say that would interest them. And so I cannot tell you how much fun it was to watch them start to crack, clearly getting interested while trying not to show it.

Each of us loves the idea of being able to draw, of learning to look at something that's special and fascinating and make it last forever, and these high school students were no different. It wasn't a perfect situation and I was far from a perfect teacher but we were actually able to find some real success in the class. Today that classroom feels like a lifetime away but the challenge for us is exactly the same. Every single one of you in view of these words, no matter who you are, or where you are in life, can take the simple steps that build up to a finished drawing worth being proud of.

"No matter who you are, or where you are in life, every single person in view of these words can take simple steps that build on each other to create a drawing worth being proud of."

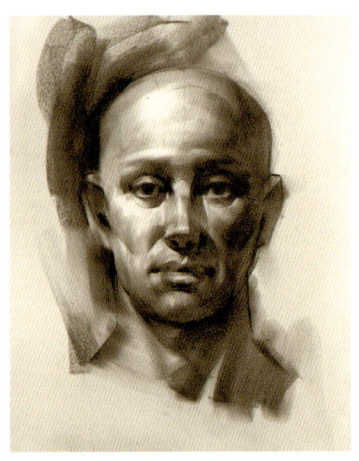
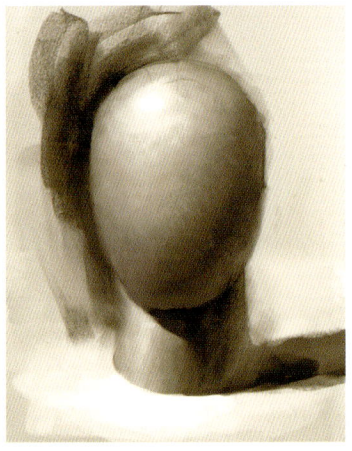

So far in this book we've discussed people's tendency to get lost in details instead of emphasizing how the parts of the head relate to the whole. One of the simplest and most useful ways we can avoid this pitfall is to remember that the entire head can be simplified to a simple shape. Imagine yourself as a sculptor, you wouldn't dream of sculpting individual details then try to piece them together, rather you would sculpt something like the big egg shape shown here and then work the individual features into it. Drawing is no different.

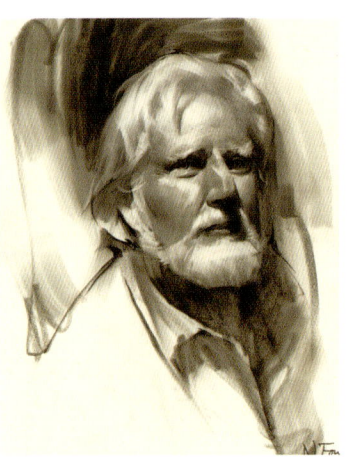
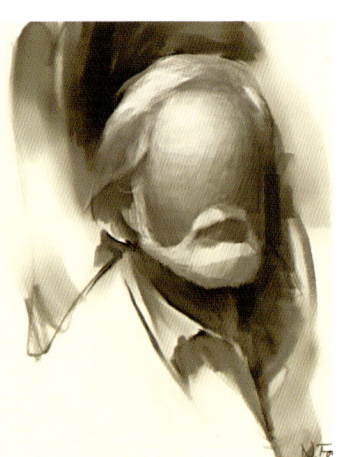

Think in terms of the simple overall form of your subject.

I always have to remind myself to seek the simplified statement. For instance take this portrait of an older gentleman with a beard. The highlights on the far cheek and lower lip might feel very bright when viewed directly, but they must be kept in context with the overall lighting. In the simplified version we see that these areas would receive far less light than the crest of the forehead and hair. It serves as a reminder to properly conform the parts to the whole.

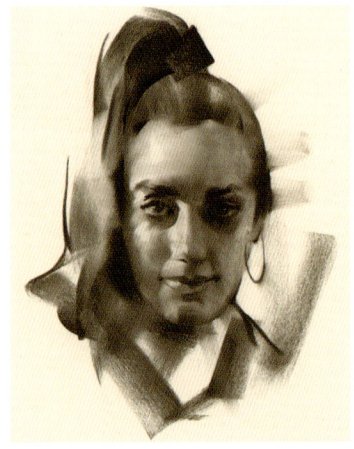
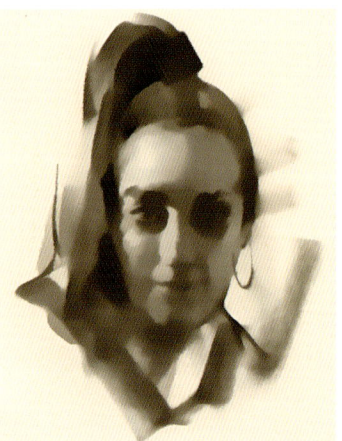

Learn to see big masses of light and shadow first, rather than individual features.

When observing our subject, we have an overwhelming tendency to see all of the features as separate elements; a nose, a cheek, an eyebrow, etc. But as artists we must learn to see differently. In this example notice how the shadows have a simple organization that extends beyond individual features. The light falls across the left side of the head then curves into a simple shadow plane on the front of the face. The side plane of the nose and mouth are illuminated then the front planes fall once again into shadow. And finally the far right side of the head groups in an illumination of ambient light. We tend to believe that if we can just get the details of the features right we will achieve a likeness but organizing the head into simple planes and groupings of light and shadow is the true key to likeness and clarity of drawing.

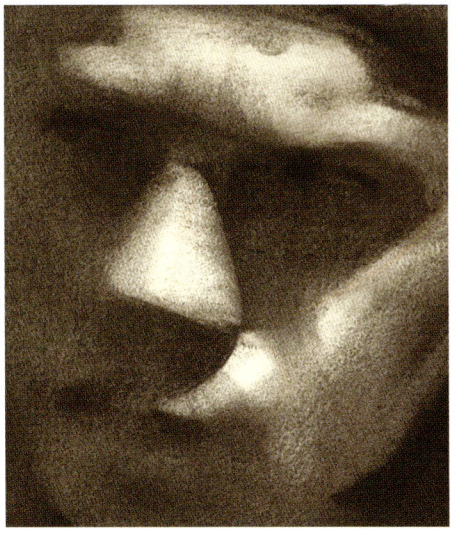

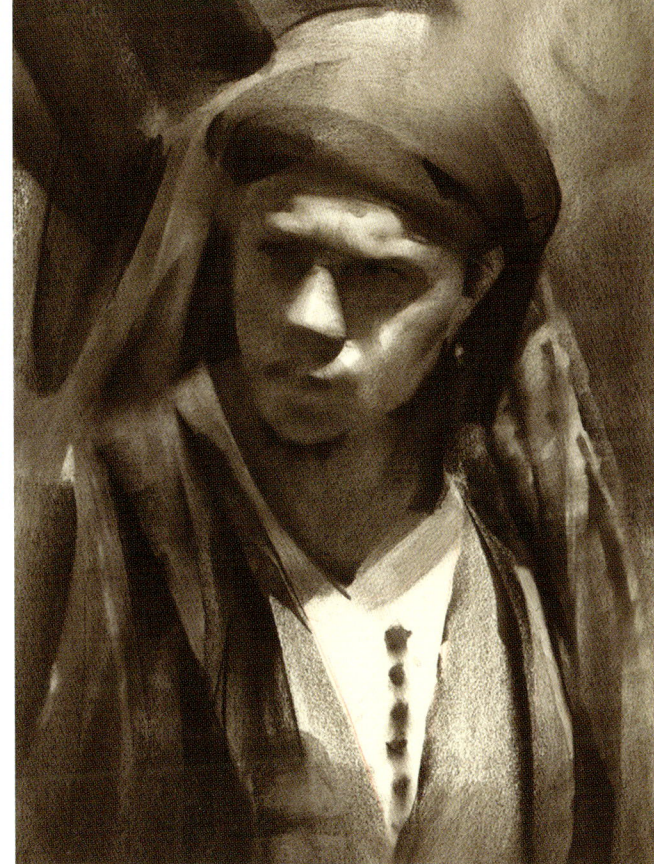

A simplified statement can engage the viewer's imagination.

I did the above right drawing to illustrate our idea of a clear, simple statement. In this light and shadow study, the big masses and simple forms are emphasized and the details are not. This simplified statement can often be more engaging to our viewers than photo realistic renderings, the viewer's imagination is engaged and they fill in the gaps, thus becoming a participant in the drawing process.

Please don't get me wrong, I'm not at all against detail. If your drawing requires detail, put in all that you want, as long as the detail does not break up the clear, simple statement.

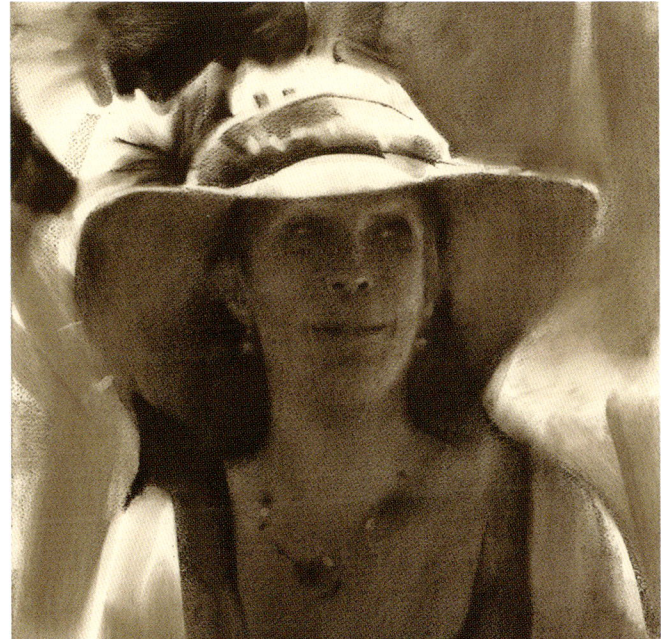

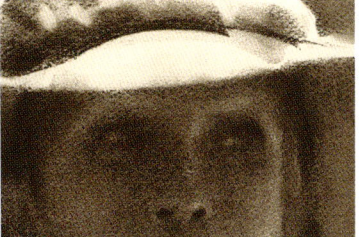

As you can see from this example, I'm an expert at rendering eyes. I say that tongue in cheek since the rendering of the eyes here is negligible, but I hope this illustrates the point of this chapter. Drawing can be far less complicated than we often make it.

Look for simple shapes.

An important way to find the simple statement within our complex subject is to look for simple shapes. In the quick tonal drawings to the right, the challenge was to render my subject with full light and shadow in just five minutes. The face, hair and folds of fabric were filled with complexities but a trained artist will observe that all of these conform to much simpler shapes. The face becomes a simple egg shape, the overall silhouette is just a triangle, and the fabric falls across the shoulders in a simple downward grouping.

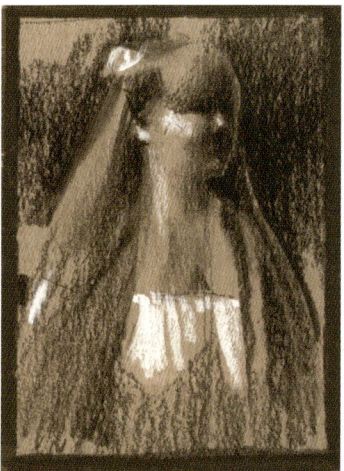
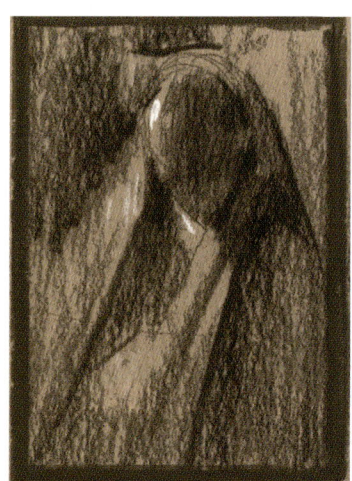

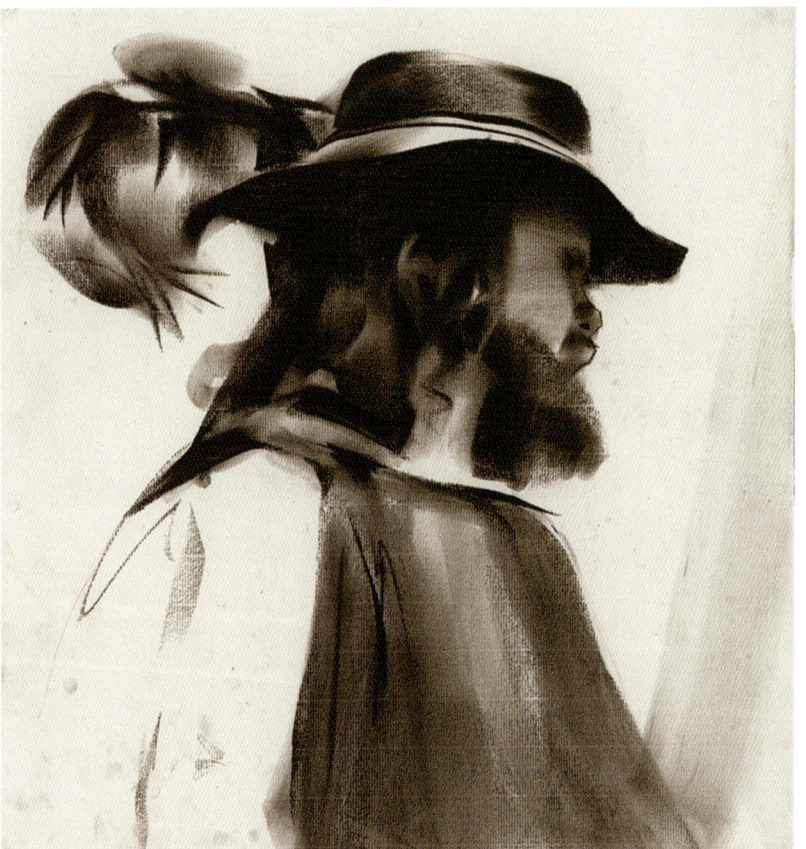

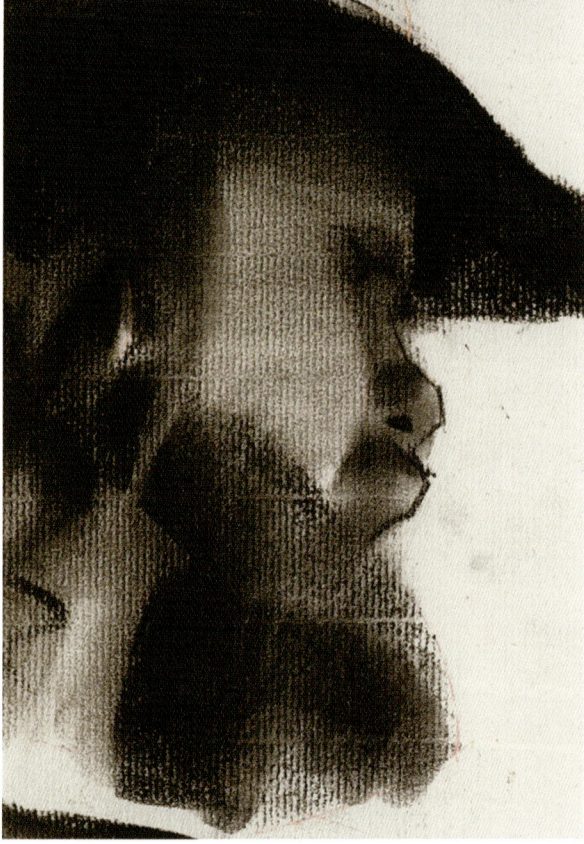

Take as another example this bearded man wearing a feathered hat. Notice how simple the shapes of hat, hair and beard are as seen in the close-up; but note especially the grouping of the features. An amateur will try and carefully observe all the details of the face and render each individually. A professional artist will notice the simple shape of shadow that groups the features together before any details are added.

One of the most helpful things we can do as we observe our subject is to squint!

Next time you're observing your subject, try squinting your eyes all the way down so that you're only looking through your eyelashes. As you do this, extraneous details and complexities of color will fade away and all that's left are simple shapes of light and shadow. By using a digital filter, I've created the equivalent of squinting in the example shown here. Observing and drawing the big simple shapes and relationships first makes us far less likely to get lost in the details and much more likely to achieve the overall likeness of our sitter.

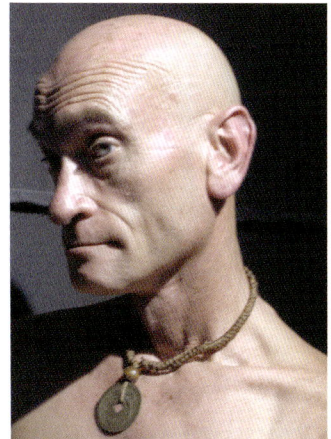 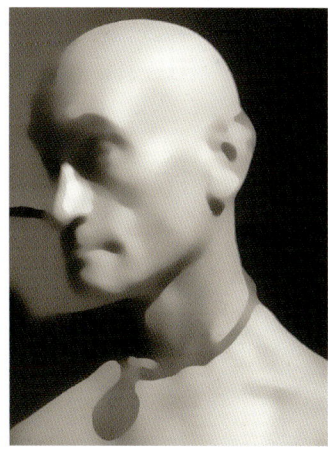

Don't be fooled by individual contrasts!

Remember, the purpose of each of the ideas that we've been discussing is to overcome our natural tendency to be fooled by individual contrasts. Take a look at the versions of forehead shown here. The first one is unaltered from the photograph and the second one illustrates the mistakes we tend to make. As we observe the far edge of the head, it feels very bright in contrast to the dark background and so we draw it that way. Then the tone on the side of the head feels very dark in contrast to the highlights and once again we draw it that way. At this point we cannot understand why our drawing looks so bad, after all we believe that we drew it exactly the way that we saw it. But squinting first would've shown us that the forehead is much more like a simple sphere as shown in version three. Our drawings are nothing more than charcoal on paper but they're brought to life by emphasizing the simpler, clearer three dimensional forms. We can't allow ourselves to forget that our drawings are an illusion of the 3D world on a 2D surface; there's nothing wrong with exaggerating simple form for the sake of clarity.

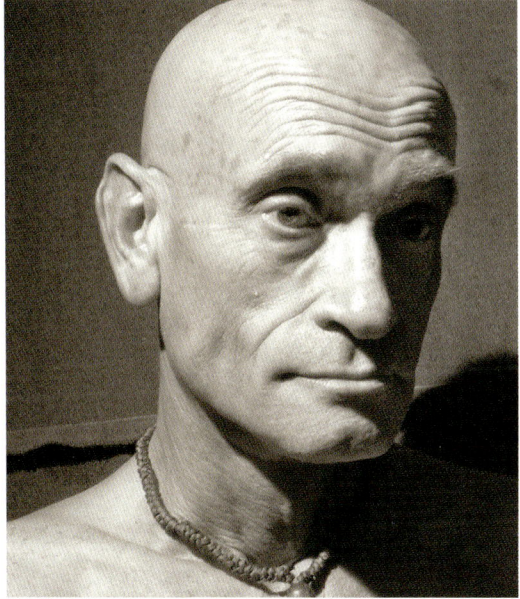

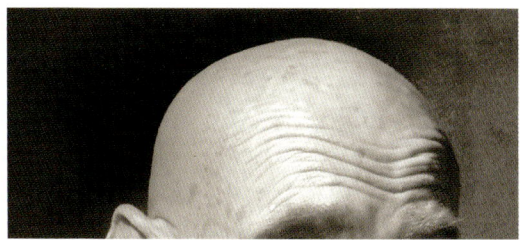

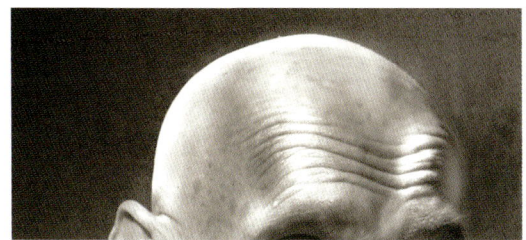

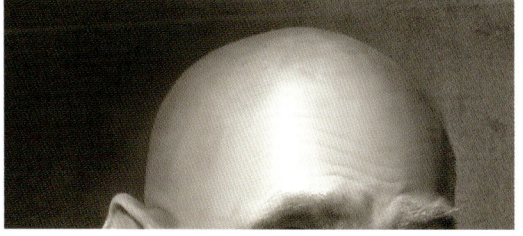

"In drawing it's OK and even necessary to tell little white lies in order to convey a greater truth."

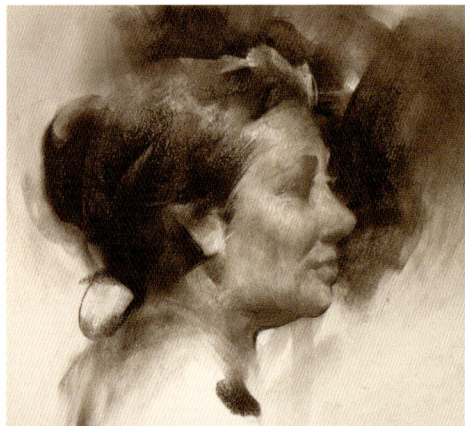
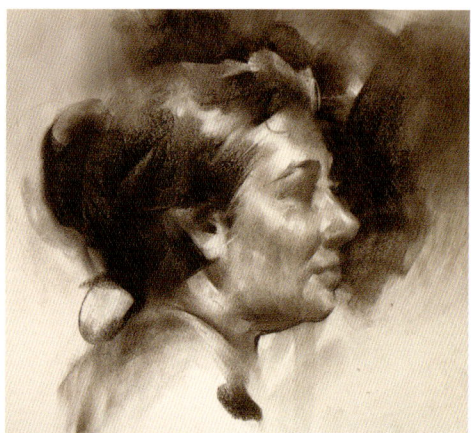

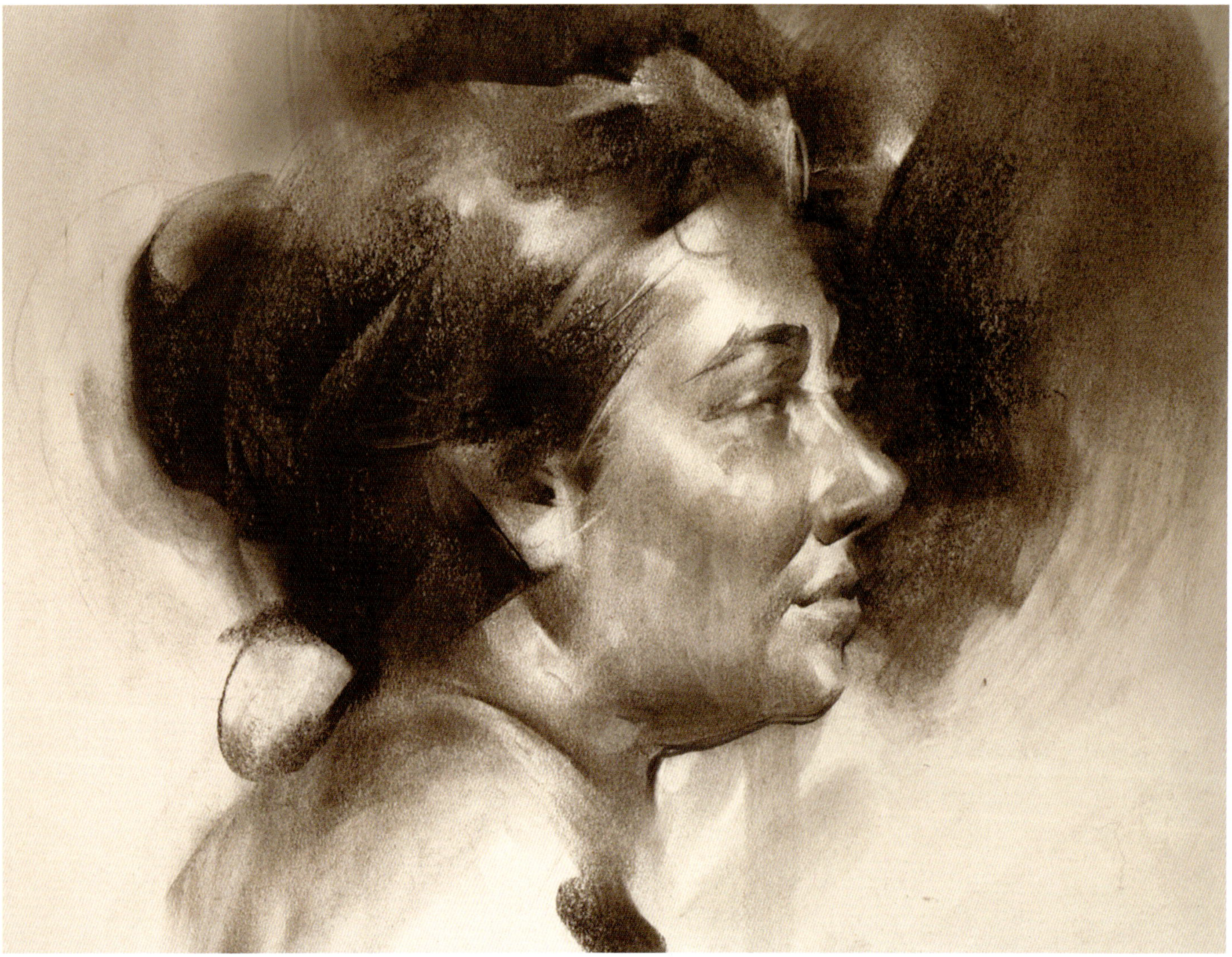

Here's an example that uses the ideas that we've discussed thus far in this chapter. In the first example I'm simplifying my subject into simple shapes and groupings of light and shadow with the help of squinting. In stage two I'm able to add the simple highlights that create the illusion of curving forms. And to bring the study to a finish, I add the details and firm edges that complete the likeness.

Drawing doesn't have to be as hard as we often make it, learning to observe the simple nature of our subject creates clarity of form. And choosing what to edit and what to emphasize creates an artistic statement that will be engaging to our audience.

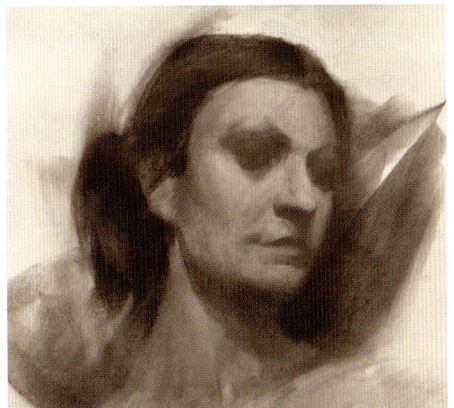 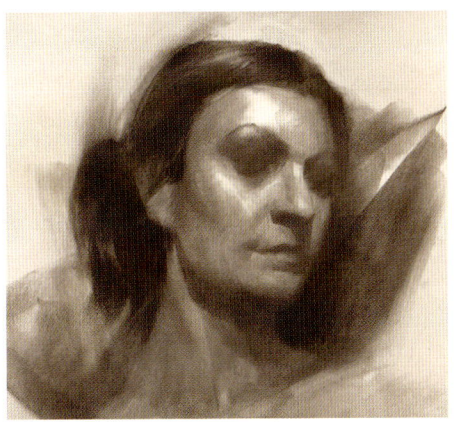

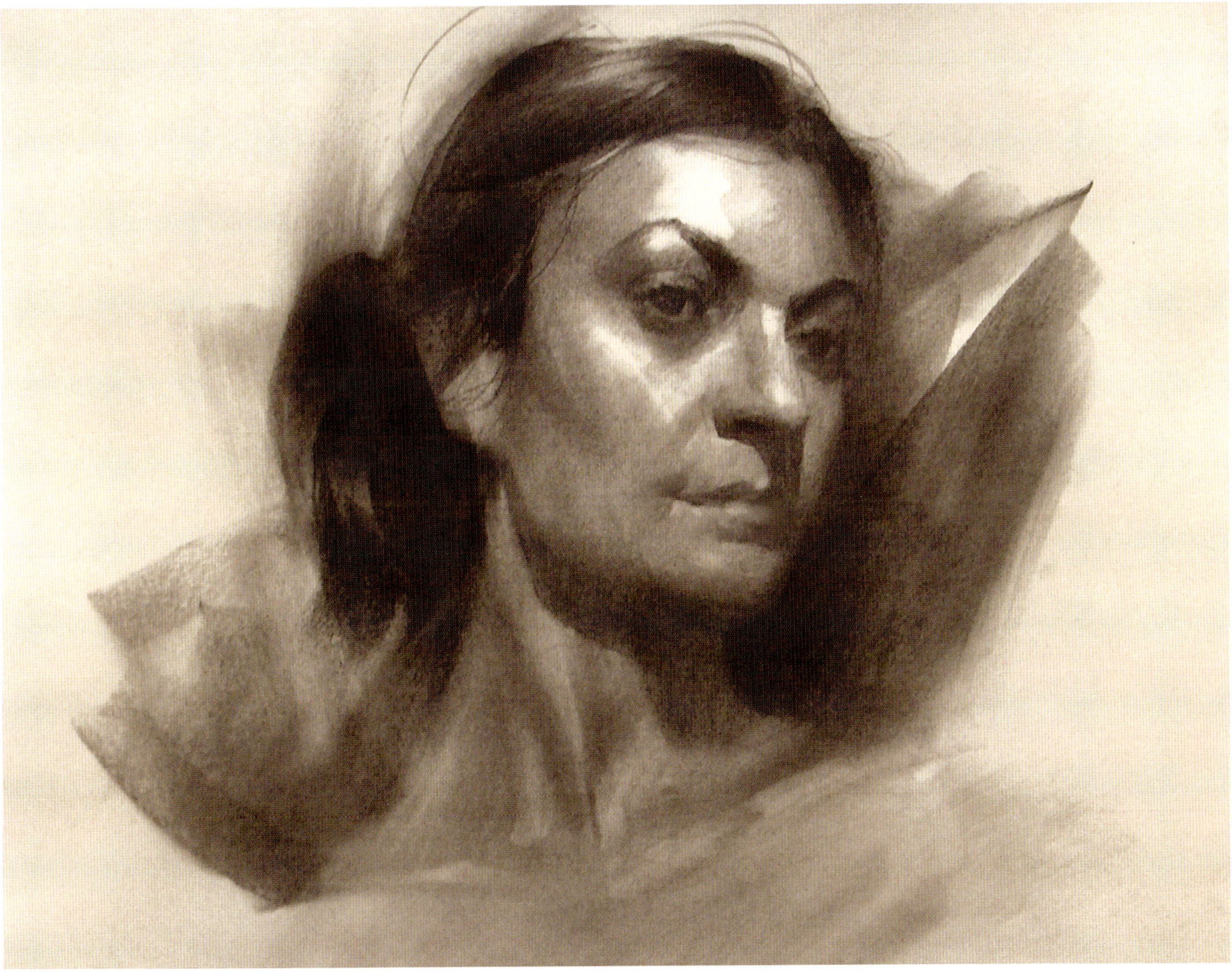

This final step-by-step example shows how simple shape relationships often save my drawings from disaster. I'm just not capable of drawing the subtleties of the head right off, so take a look above at how very simple each shape is in step one. The hair is a simple dark mass, and the eye sockets and features are simple groupings of shadow. The shadow cast from the head onto the neck and background are extremely simple as well.

With this approach I can quickly judge if I'm achieving a likeness and easily make any adjustments needed. Once I'm confident in my initial block-in, I can move to step two and start rendering the curving forms of the head. And once again, for the finished study I simply need to add smaller forms and details to the larger, simpler shapes of the head. For me, this approach turns drawing from being an endless frustration into a great joy.

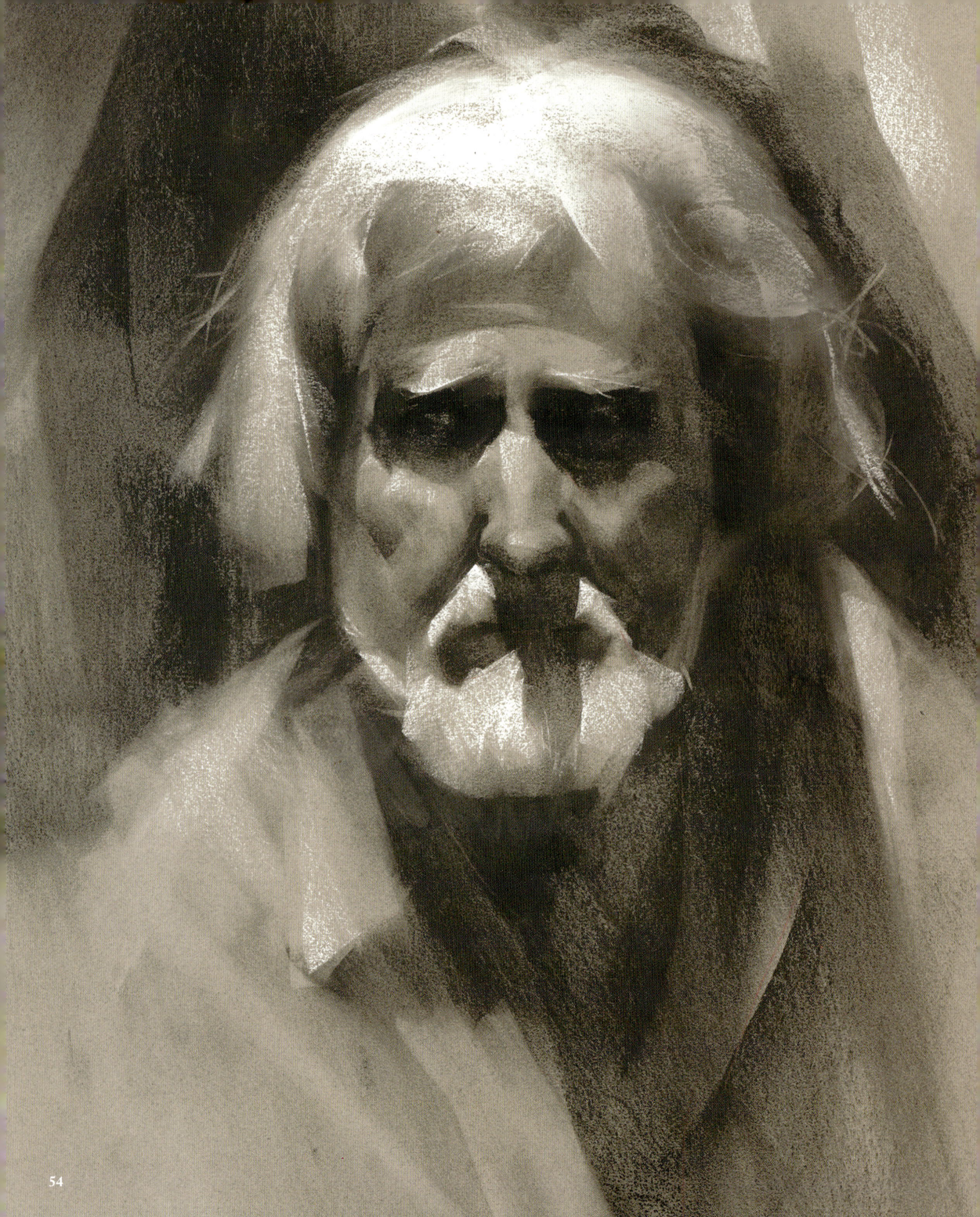

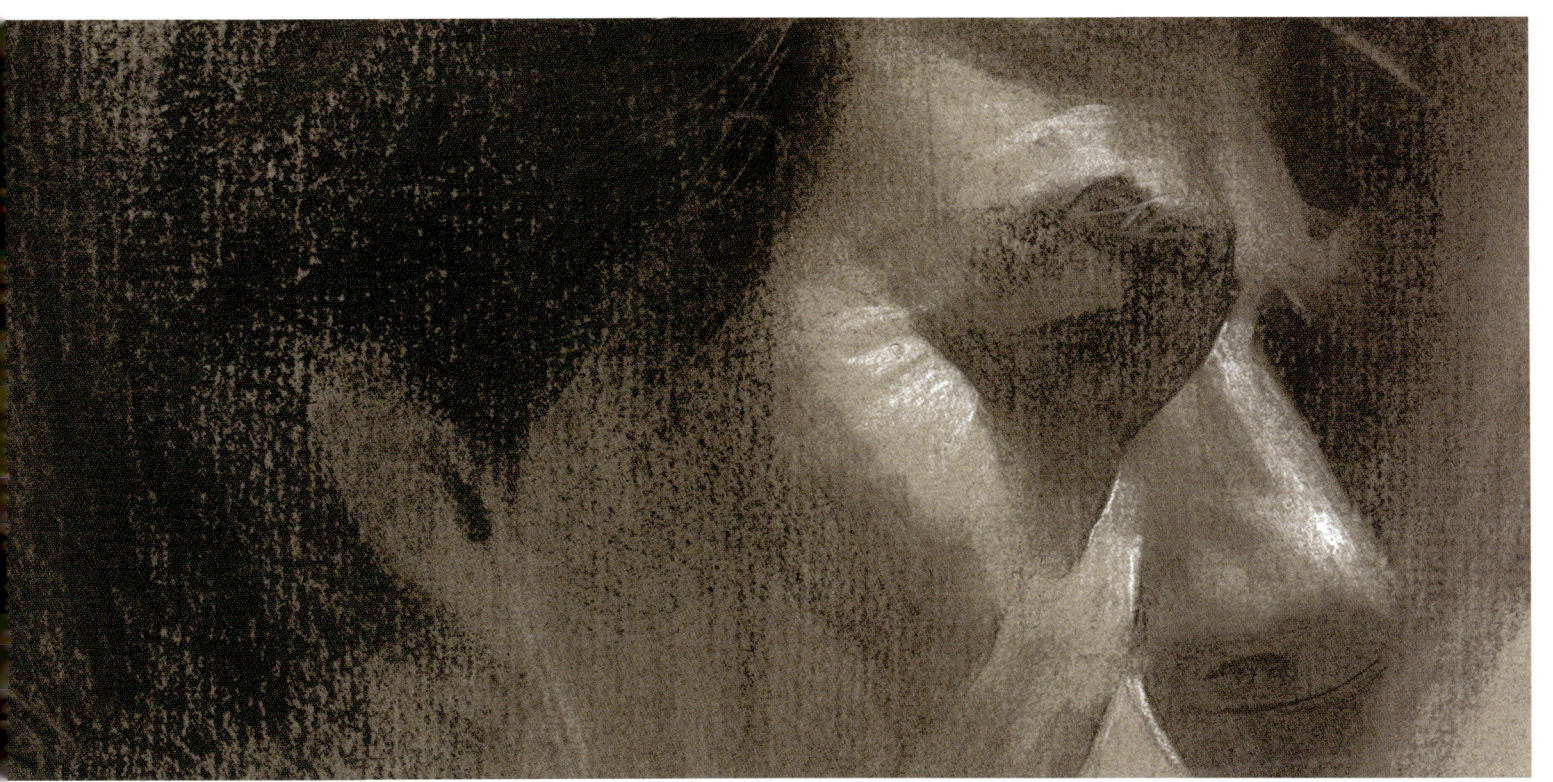

Chapter 6

The Values of Light and Shadow

In my professional work as an animation artist, an understanding of light and shadow has been one of the most important skills in my toolbox. My work has demanded that I have a technical understanding of how light works so that I can give a compelling believability to the scenes that I create. Light has also been a powerful storytelling tool; passages of light and shadow can be designed to give a special emphasis to each moment of a film. And light is a powerful emotional tool. Vibrant contrasts of light can convey an exciting energy, and subtle nuances of light can create subtle nuances of mood. In the end, light is everything: we cannot visually perceive the world without it, and so it behooves us to understand it. Light and shadow can bring the same level of artistry and storytelling to our portrait drawings; long before I began working in film, my understanding of light developed through observational drawing. The study of light on form has been foundational for everything I do as an artist. In this chapter we'll explore how to use light and shadow to convey form and to best present our subject.

"The study of light on form has been foundational for most everything I do as an artist."

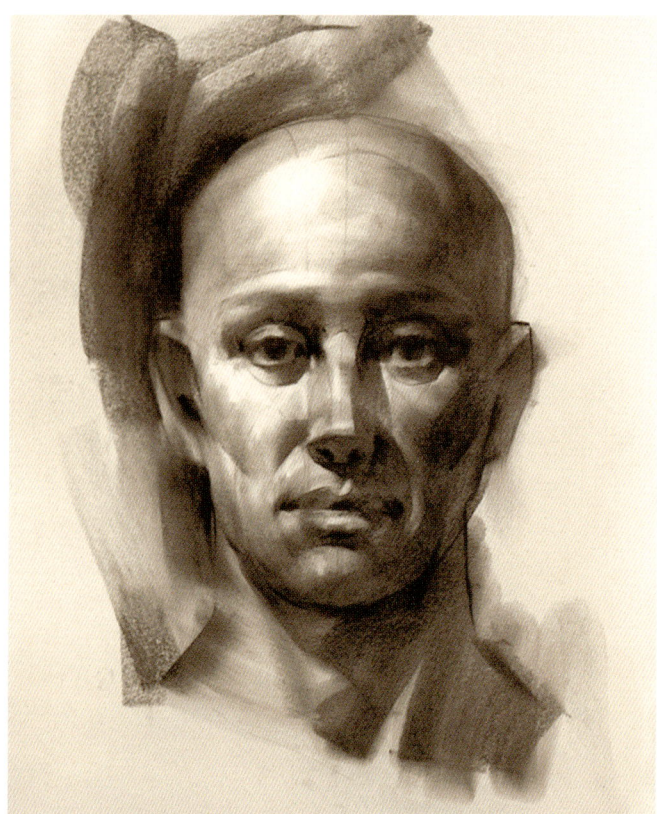

Direct Light Source

Light and Shadow Terminology

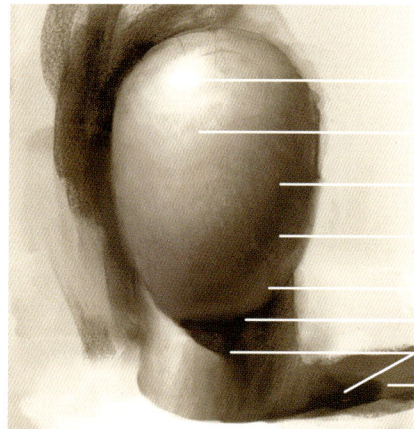

Highlight
Halftone
Terminator
Core Shadow
Reflected Light
Occlusion Shadow
Cast Shadow
Atmospheric or
Ambient Fill Light

First let's review the basics; let's go back to our simple egg shape to establish our terminology for each quality of light and shadow.

After reviewing the diagram above, I'd like you to take a closer look at the generic light-and-shadow head to the left. I'd like you to notice how each major protuberance of the head is like a mini version of our simple egg diagram. For instance, take a look at the nose: it has highlight, halftone, core shadow, reflected light, and cast shadow. Now take a look at the chin, the lower lip, the cheek, and the forehead; each has the same quality of light and shadow. Even the eye, as it protrudes out of its socket, can be treated the way a simple sphere reacts to light. When you learn to observe these simple relationships of light and shadow, rendering form becomes quite easy!

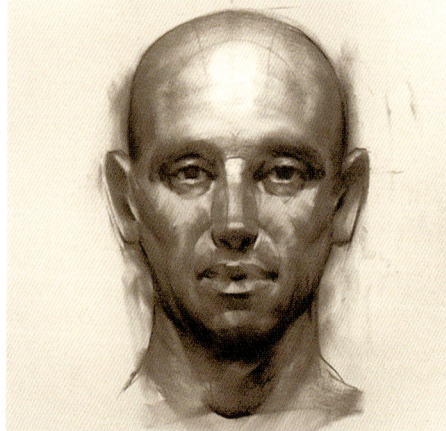

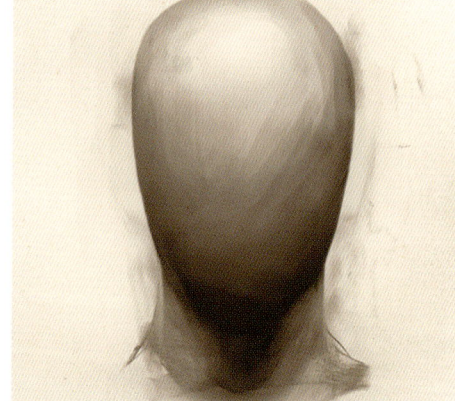

Ambient Light

Now let's take a moment to address indirect or "ambient" light. Common sources of ambient light are things like indirect window light or outdoor lighting on an overcast day. And the good news is this lighting is potentially even simpler than direct light, forms gradually curve away from the light source into shadow, and cast shadows are soft edged and diffuse as shown above. Because electric lighting is relatively recent, there's a long tradition of portraits painted under ambient light sources.

Standard practice was to place the portrait subject in the light of a north-facing window (this is the case in the Northern Hemisphere; the Southern Hemisphere would be a south-facing window), which would maintain a consistent level of illumination for many hours during the day. Still today many portrait artists prefer the soft quality of ambient lighting for a sensitive rendering of their subjects.

> ## "A simple statement of light and shadow is more important than nuance to convey form and likeness."

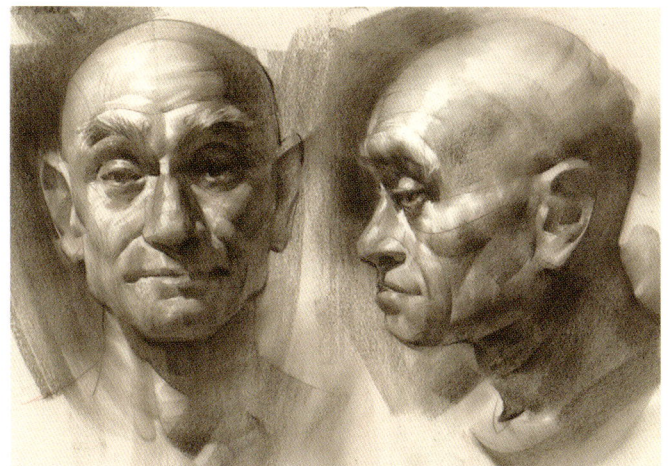

Remember, one of the major goals of this book is to help us find a manageable approach to the complexity of the head so that we have a better shot at doing strong portrait drawings. After mastering our initial construction drawings, the next important simplification is to organize the head into clear, committed masses of light and shadow.

I've mentioned before that in my many years as a drawing teacher I've found that new students nearly always look at individual contrasts of anatomy as they draw, rather than noticing the bigger simpler masses of light and shadow. Their results are just as we discussed in earlier chapters: bumpy overwrought anatomy that starts to look more like a sack of walnuts than like a human head. So before we ever start rendering the nuances of light and shadow, I have students do exercises like the one below. Its purpose is to force students to identify and commit to the simple masses of light and shadow. Additionally we look for and emphasize the quality of the shadow edge; for instance cast shadows tend to have a hard edge, and turning forms tend to have a soft, blended edge. If we emphasize this simple statement of light and shadow in our portraits before we render nuances, we're much more likely to end up with strong forms and an accurate likeness.

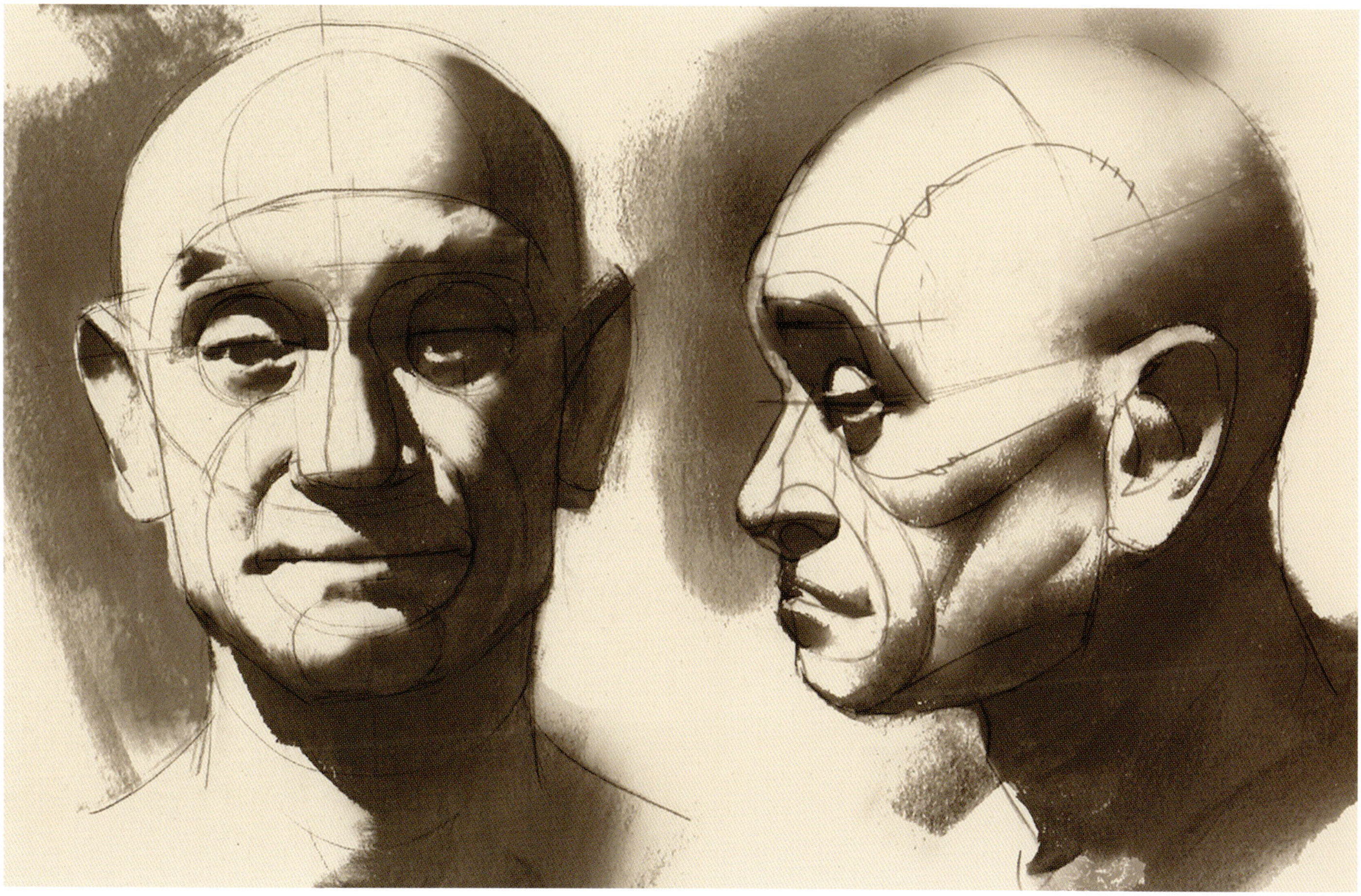

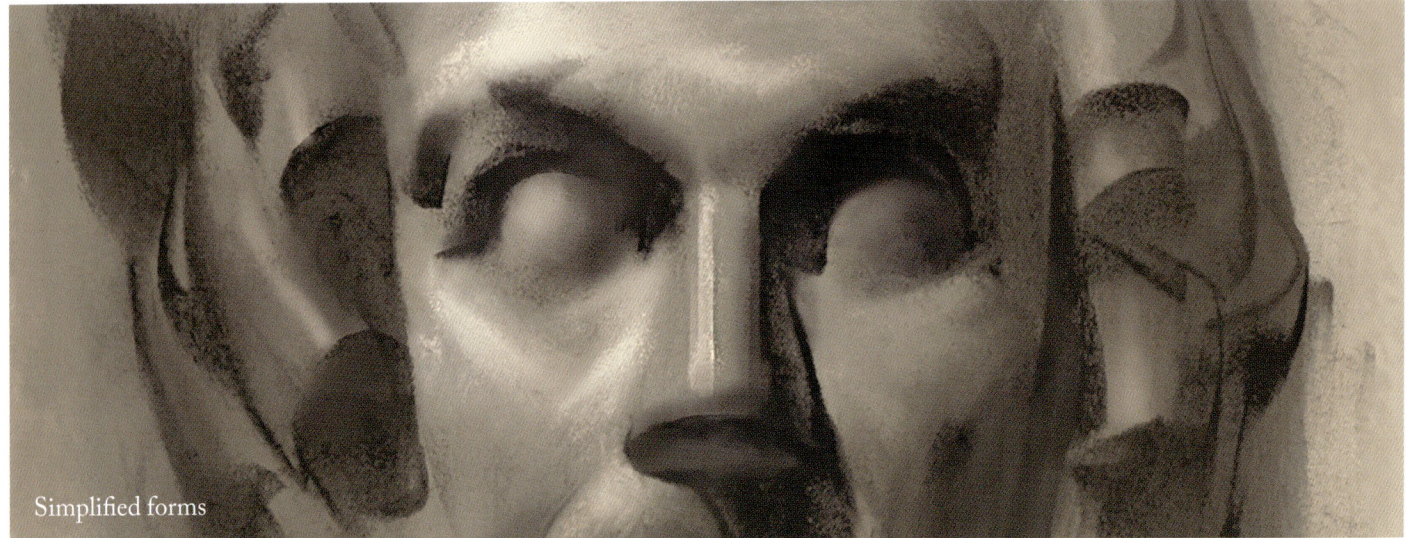

Simplified forms

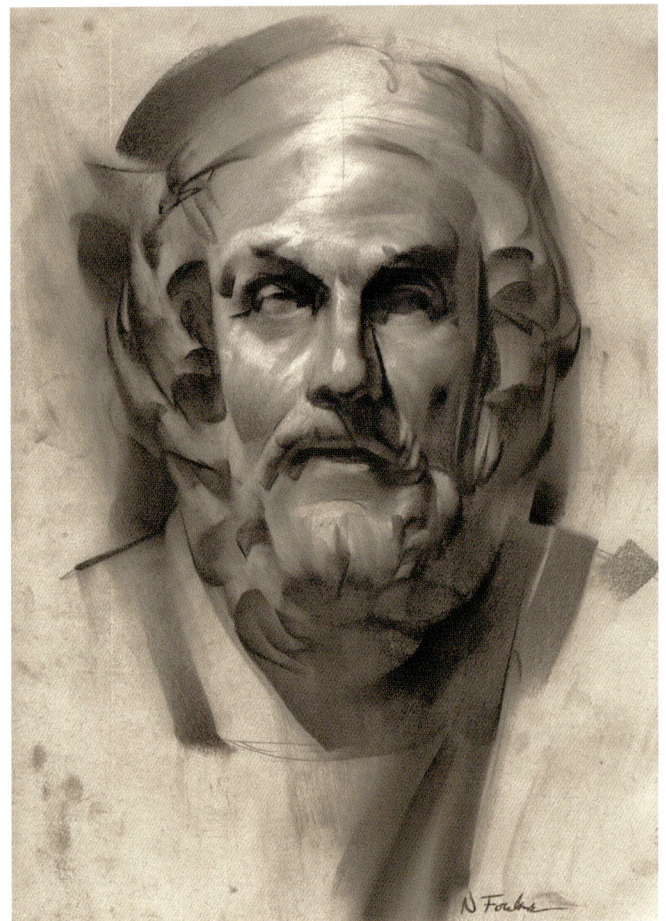

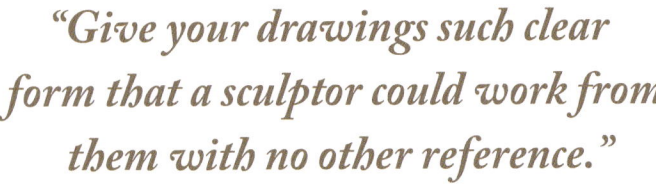

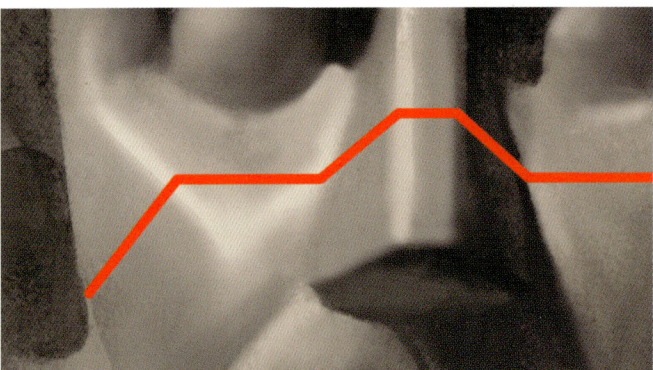

The Importance of Highlights

The drawing of the plaster cast here illustrates one additional observation I'd like you to make when you draw. Take a look at the highlights; see how they tend to fall at the crest of each form facing the light? The placement of highlights is critical to show turning forms. In the upper left I've added a simplified version of the face to show clearly how the highlights describe the curving forms.

A good way to think of this is that highlights tend to fall on the corners between the large planes of the head. Take a look at the red-lined diagram above: there's the side plane and front plane of the cheek with the highlight falling where they meet. It's the same with the nose: the highlight falls right along the edge where the side plane and the front plane meet.

Whenever you're struggling with creating clear form in your drawings, I invite you to fall back on this simple quality of highlights. Even if you end up exaggerating beyond what you see, you're telling the little white lie to convey a greater truth. In fact, several of the instructors I've previously mentioned would encourage their students to give their drawings such clear form that a sculptor could work from them with no other reference.

"Give your drawings such clear form that a sculptor could work from them with no other reference."

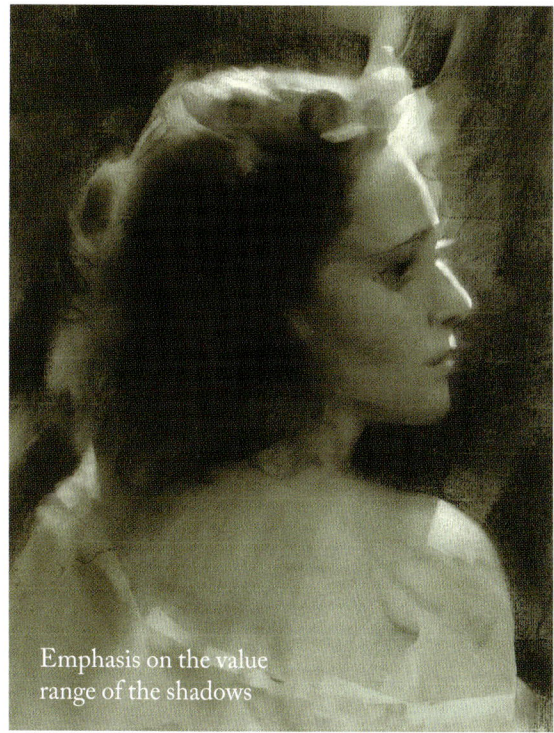

Emphasis on the value range of the shadows

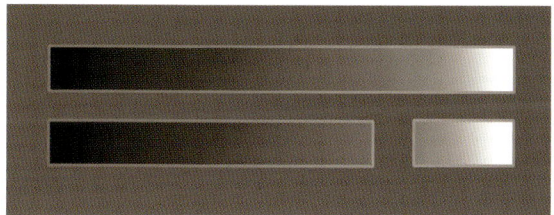

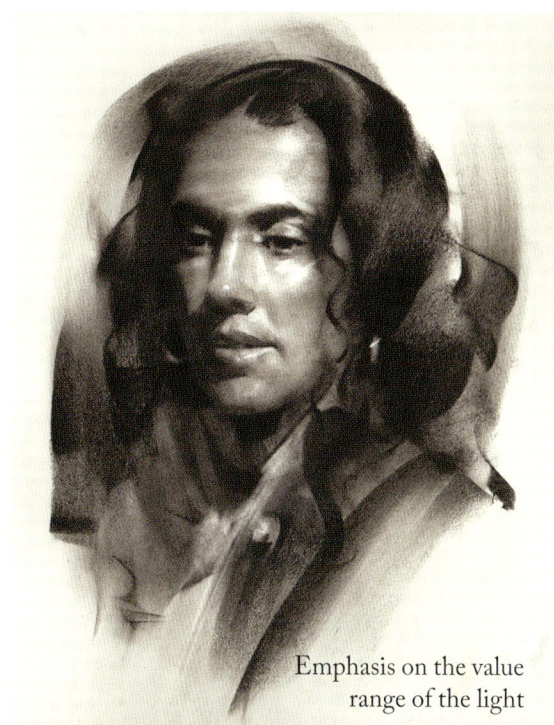

Emphasis on the value range of the light

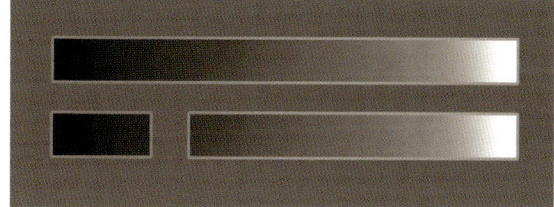

You'll recall that in a previous chapter I described how a stick of charcoal and a sheet of paper are not capable of rendering the range of value that we can see with light. It's now time to take that limitation and turn it into an advantage.

In the two drawings above, the woman on the left is primarily in shadow and the woman on the right is primarily in light. When I was drawing the woman on the left my eyes could perceive a great deal of value range, I could clearly see everything in the light and shadow. But I knew if I tried to render every subtlety, not only would it take all day and all night but the masses of light and shadow would be broken up and confusing. I had to decide what to emphasize about my subject and what to edit. I decided that the rim light on the face should be pushed into a very narrow range of brightness so that I would have the rest of the value range to render subtleties on the shadow side of the face. The value chart below the drawing diagrams the break between light and shadow. The result of making this choice is a clearer more committed drawing.

For the drawing on the upper right, I was most interested in the subtleties of character and form created by the halftone lights. This led me to make the decision to push all the shadows into a very narrow dark range as seen in the lower part of the value graph. That choice opened up a wide range of tone to render strong form and character in the light.

"*Because we cannot draw everything that we see, we must consciously decide what we will emphasize about our subject. In a world of instant digital photography, that choice is what continues to elevate the artist above the camera.*"

Demonstration: Focusing on the Values of Light and Shadow

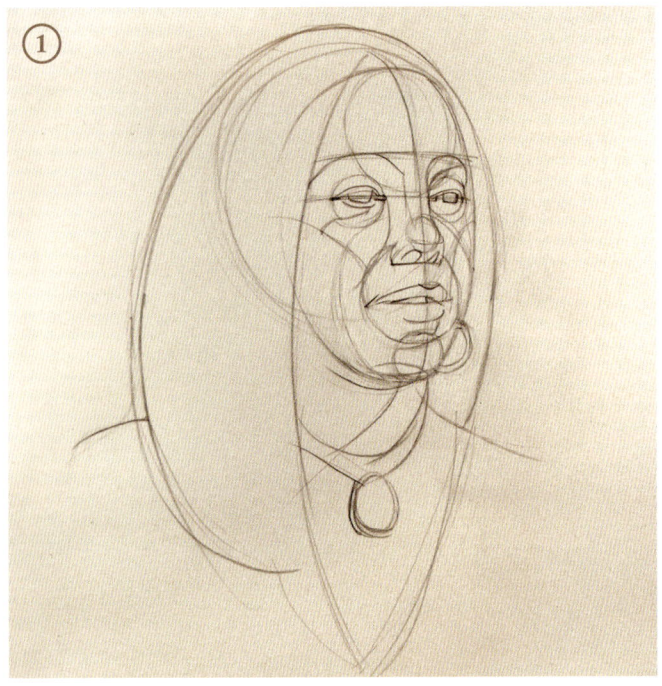

Let's now put into practice our ideas for conveying clear form and character through the values of light and shadow. Here's our standard construction drawing approach; its goal is to establish the simple forms, planes, and three-dimensional nature of the head.

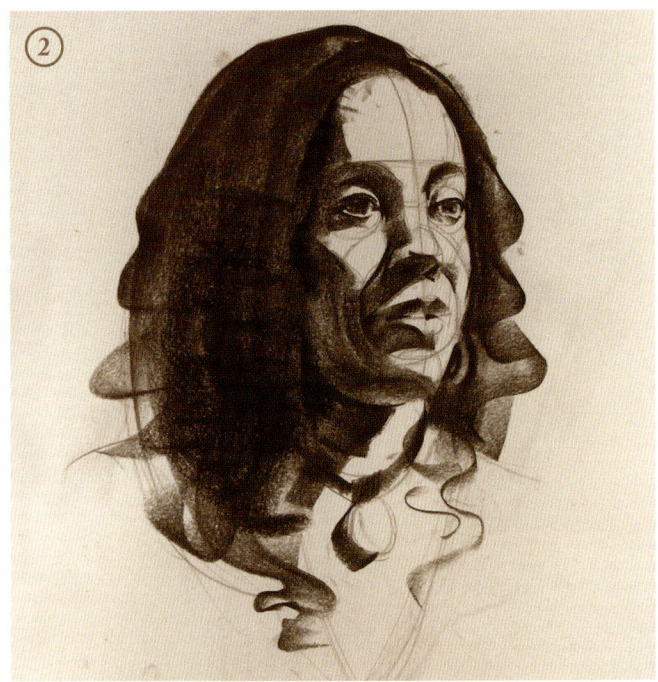

I keep my values as simple as possible by massing them only in the shadow shapes and the darks of the hair. I'm using my construction lines to make sure each stroke properly curves around the form.

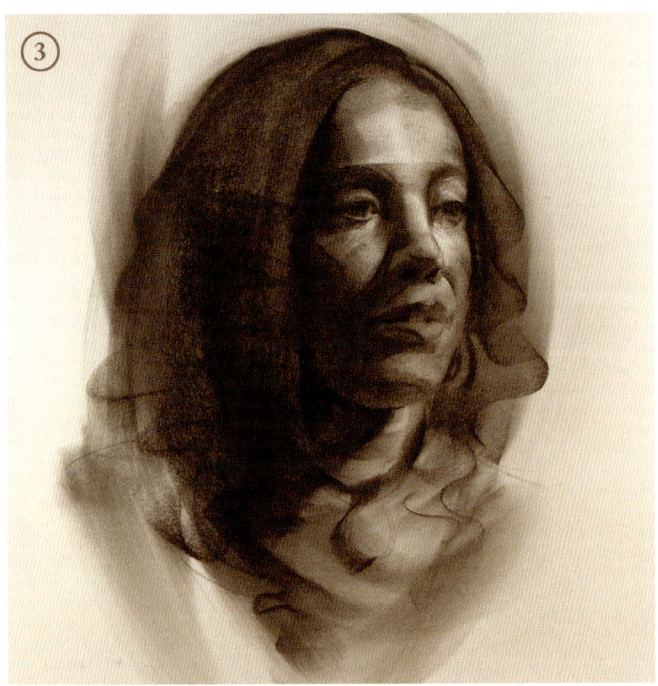

Now I drag tone from the shadows and pull it around the forms of the face to convey the halftones. Notice that my strokes are still carefully following the direction of my construction lines.

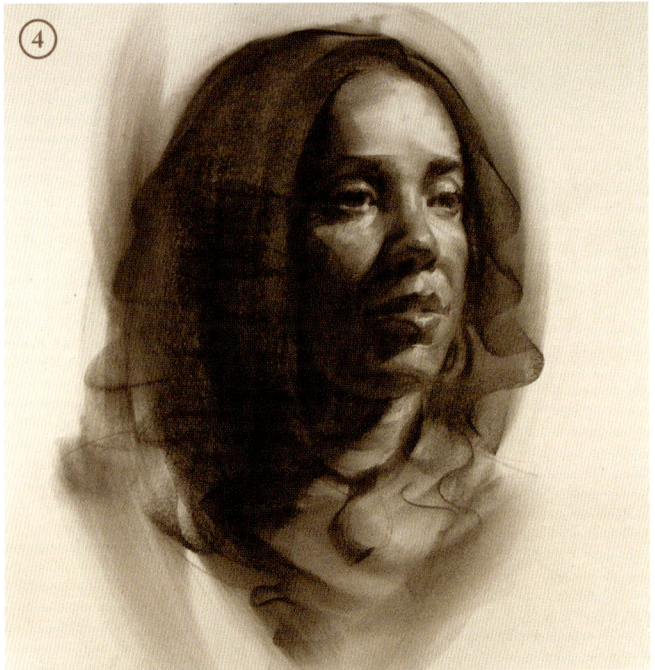

With the big simple statement of light and shadow in place, I'm ready to refine my drawing. I add sharpness to the cast shadows, greater definition to the hair and features, and I use the kneaded eraser to pull out highlights. And we're finished!

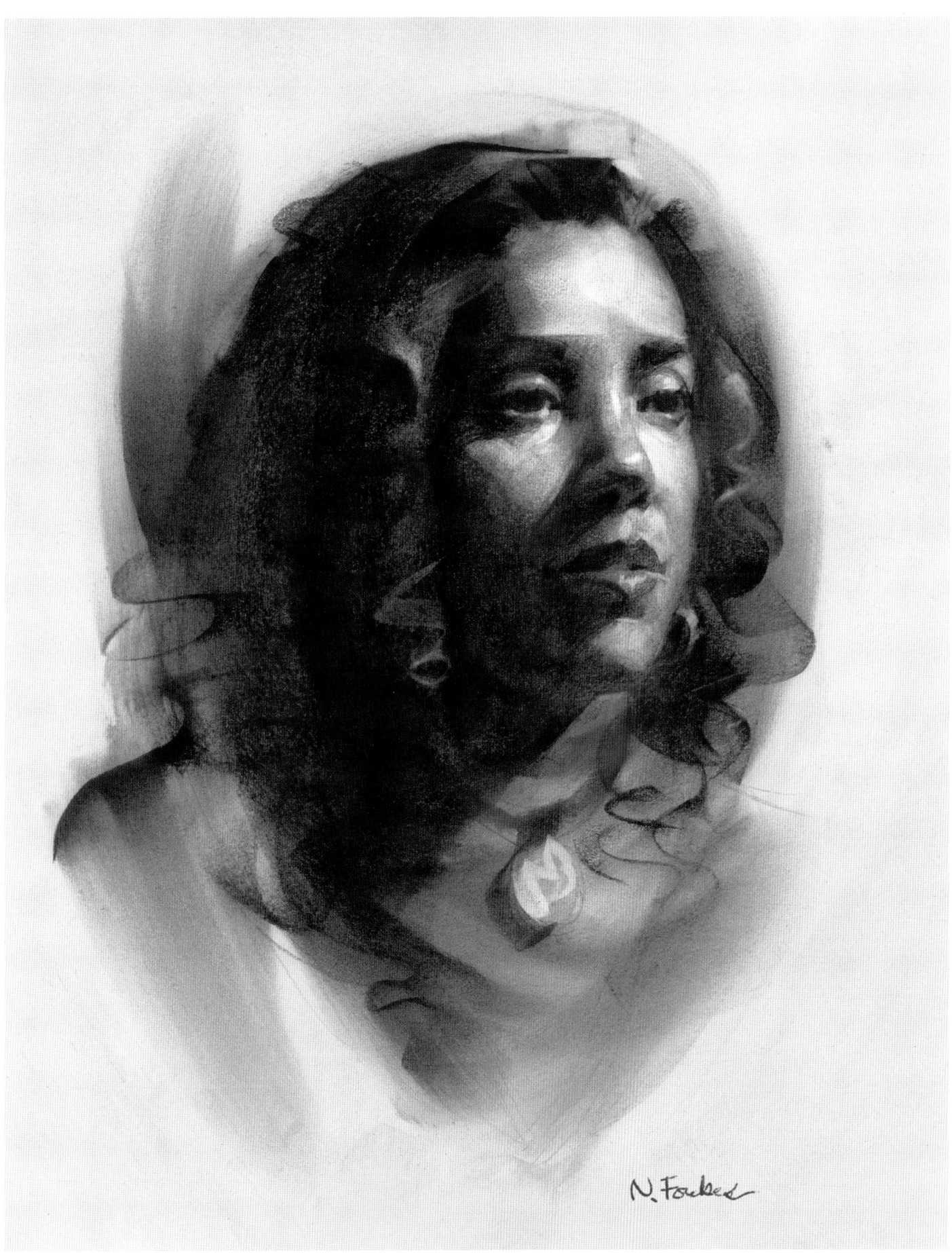

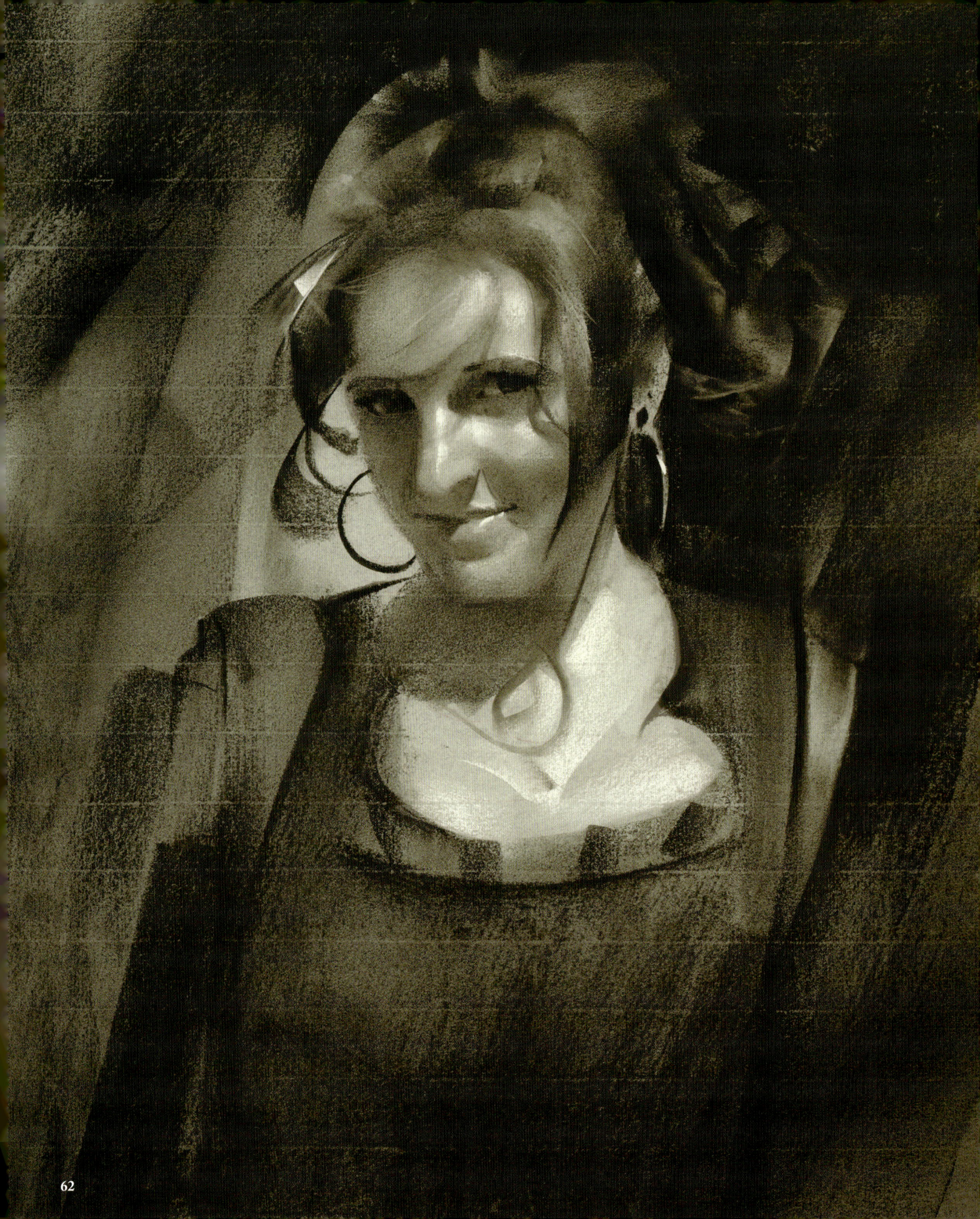

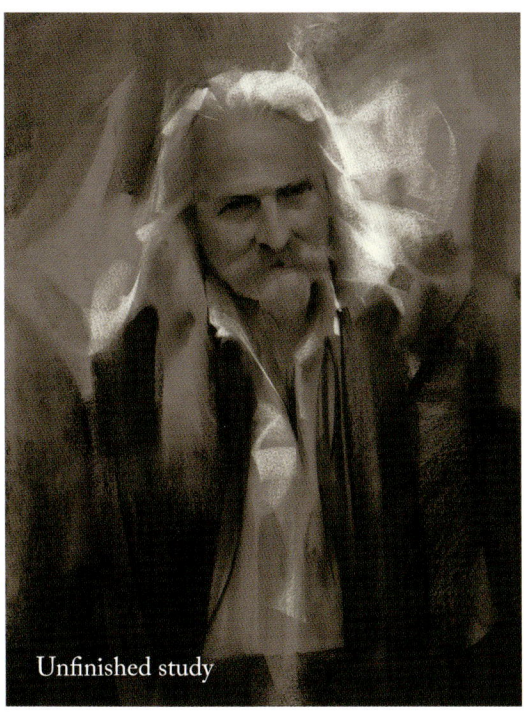

Chapter 7

Unfinished study

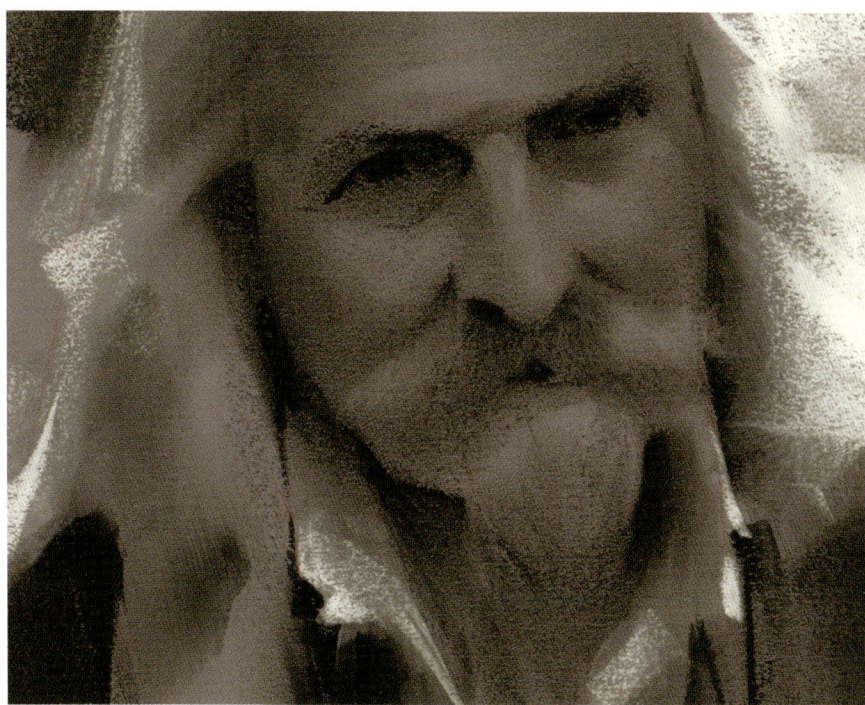

The Design of Edges

A common theme throughout this book is that drawing is not a literal representation of what we see; it's an interpretation of what we see. Our medium is not capable of rendering every nuance of light, and the flat surface of our paper has none of the depth of the world we observe. Additionally our work requires emphasis; we can't look at our subject and say, "What a great face!" and then render folds of the shirt to such complexity that our viewers' attention is pulled away from the face.

A simple and powerful solution to these challenges is the design of edges. In the following pages I'll show you how this can be done, but for now, let me give you a general example. The study of the man with white hair shown above was done many years ago and was a breakthrough for me in my understanding of edges.

I remember looking at the subject and saying to myself, "Uh oh, this is gonna be a tough one." So I decided that the way I would handle the challenge is to do three simple things: **1)** a simple construction drawing, **2)** simple masses of value to describe big forms, and **3)** design hard and soft edges. I figured by doing this the drawing would be about half finished and the remaining 50 percent of my time would be spent rendering the features, the hair, and the clothing. As I did so I was shocked to see that with these three simple steps the drawing was not 50 percent done, it was nearly 90 percent done. I was so pleased with how close to a finish I came in such a short period of time that I set the drawing aside as a reminder that very difficult subjects can be tackled by mere mortals like you and me.

"A simple construction drawing, simple masses of value, and the design of edges makes it possible for very difficult subjects to be tackled by mere mortals like you and me. "

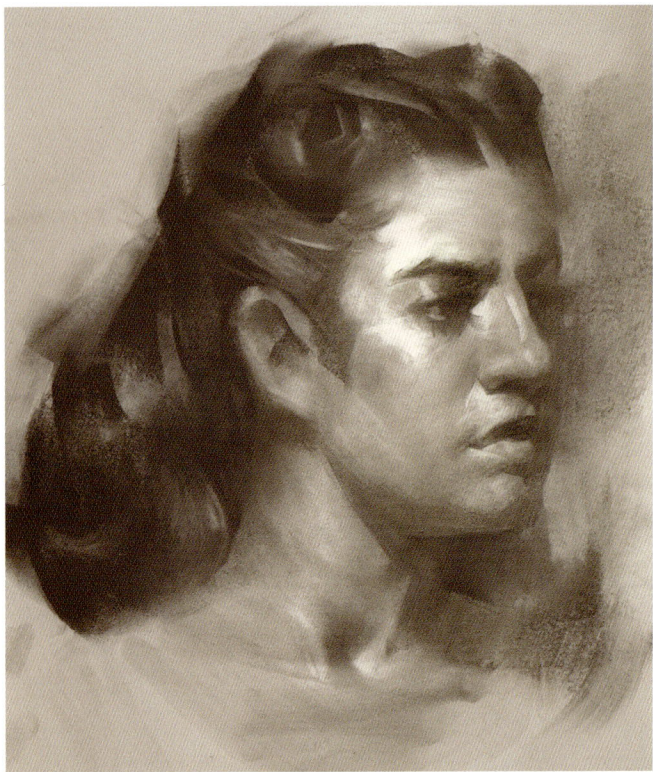

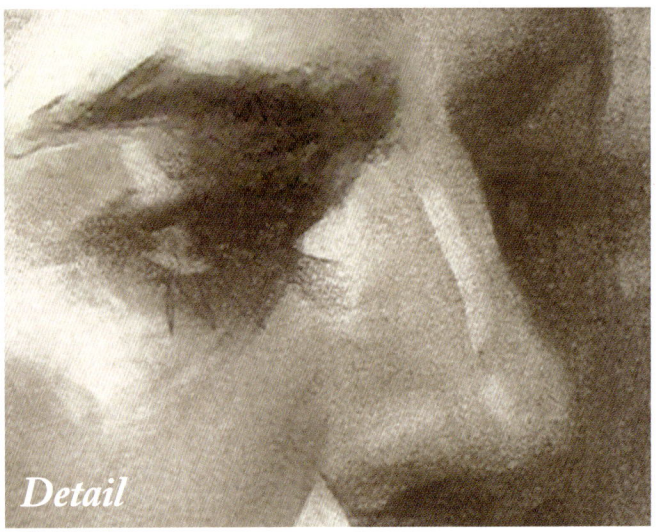

Detail

Designing Edges to Create Depth

Each of the principles that we've studied in this book have addressed the challenge of translating the three-dimensional world onto the two dimensional page. Our construction drawings and value design help achieve this goal, but even those are not enough. It's the design of edges that can help make the 3-D illusion complete. I like to think in terms of three kinds of edges:

Hard edges (I often referred to them as crisp edges.)

Soft edges

Lost edges (Edges that completely disappear into adjacent areas.)

Take a look at the drawing and detail view to the left. One of the things I liked about this drawing session was the front light and the way it curves away from us into shadow. Under these conditions the forms and cast shadows in the features nearest us have crisp edges that tend to feel like they advance forward in space. To complement this effect I've softened the edges on the far right side of the face and have gone even further by creating lost edges where the shadow completely disappears into the background tone. These soft and lost edges are completely artificial on my part. In real life I could see clean, sharp edges on the far side of the head, but had I drawn them that way, the head would feel flat and we'd lose the illusion of the turning form. A sure way of getting forms to feel far away is to connect them with the background.

Let's take a look now at the neck. As a teacher and former student myself, I've seen (and drawn) many, many disastrous necks. I've been guilty of drawing necks as a wretched patchwork of anatomy that makes no sense. And so I've learned my lesson; I've learned to render the neck as its simplest form: a cylinder. You see that happening in this drawing; the tones wrap around the cylindrical shape of the neck and disappear into the lost edges of the shadows. Take a look at the rest of the drawing and notice all the other areas where I'm using hard, soft, and lost edges to create the illusion of depth.

"It's ironic, but sometimes drawing things exactly the way we see them hurts our drawings rather than helps them."

Designing Edges to Give Emphasis

Drawings are often most meaningful when they are clearly about something, and so a valuable principle in art is emphasis. We decide what's most special and interesting about our subject and emphasize that quality to create drawings that have purpose. How do we create emphasis? Primarily through contrast; the eye tends to be most drawn to areas of high contrast. And how to create contrast? We've already discussed the contrasting values of light and shadow; let's add edges to the list. Hard edges inherently have contrast, soft edges have less, and lost edges have none at all. Using edges to create visual emphasis in your drawings is a simple and effective way of creating portraits with real impact.

Take a look at the drawing to the right. In this case I was struck by the sitter's expression and the shapes of light falling across her face; I wanted to strongly emphasize these in my portrait study. I was able to take advantage of the value contrasts and small crisp edges that appear in the features to give a clear emphasis to the face. Then as the head curves away into the hair I used very soft edges to avoid distraction. The hair shows just enough value and edges to give it a little form and a simple silhouette, but most of its edges completely disappear into the background. We often have a tendency to get caught up in rendering all that we can see, but we get our most effective drawings when we carefully choose what to edit out.

"It's not always what we put into our drawings that make them great, but often what we choose to leave out."

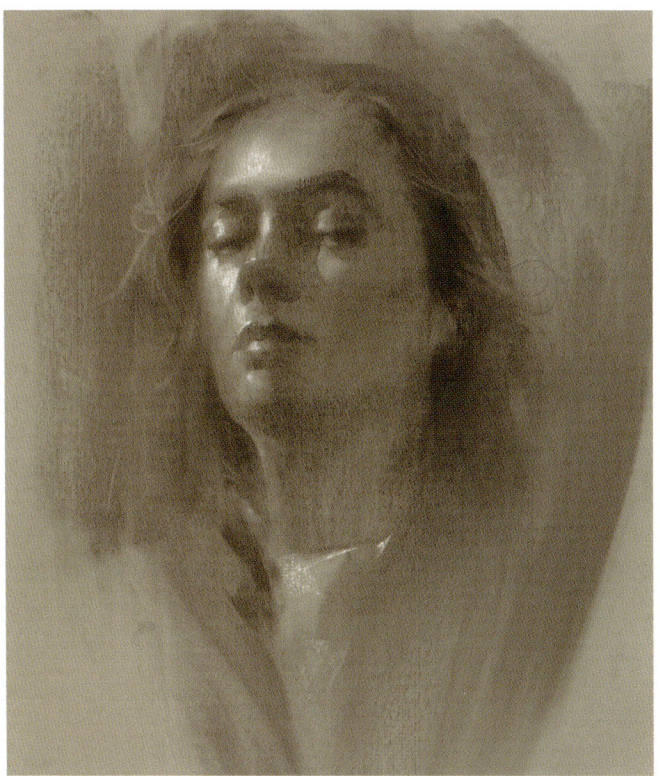

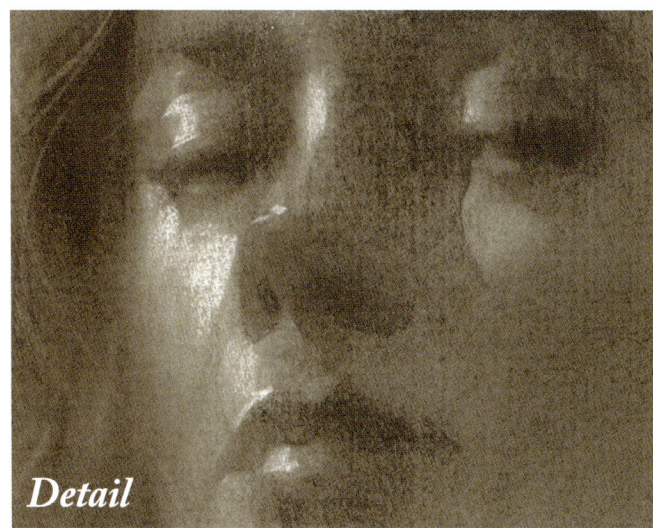

Detail

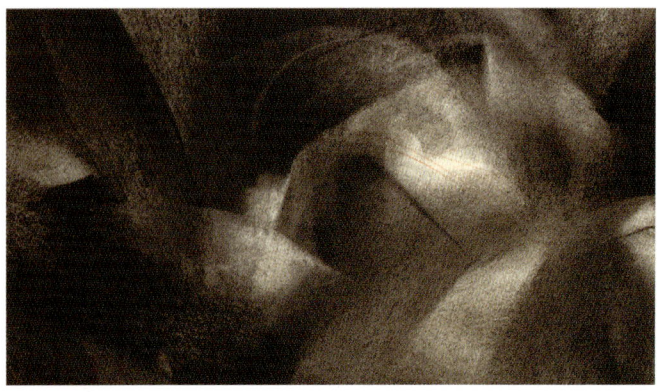

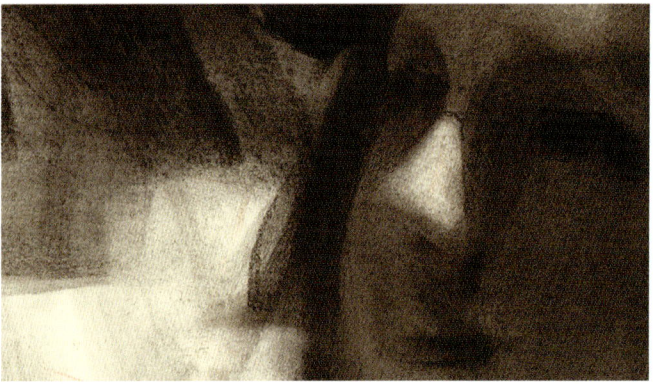

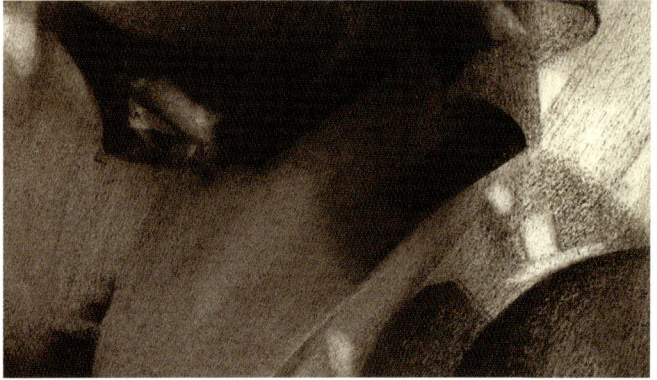

Designing Edges to Create Luminosity

I really enjoyed doing the drawing that you see on this spread, and fellow artists seem to like it, but when I show it to civilian friends and family they tend to say, "Is it, uh, finished?" It's a reasonable response; the expectation is that portrait drawings are about the features and the character of the subject. And I do firmly believe that a part of an artist's job can be to please his or her intended audience. But at the same time, our drawings are an experiment and an exploration of those things that most interest us. And as you know by now, I'm interested in light! And so this study is not meant to be a rendering of the features but an exploration of the luminous and translucent quality of light on the hair, skin, and fabric.

Take a careful look at the drawing and the detail views and notice that wherever the light hits, there tends to be a soft, luminous glow. Hair, cloth, and even skin have some translucency, and light passing through them can create a bit of a glow into adjacent shadows. Additionally, very bright lights can have a "blooming" effect; their luminosity can appear to bloom outside of the lit area. There are plenty of hard edges to be found here, but had I used them too heavily, the soft luminous glow of the subject would be lost.

"Part of an artist's job can be to please his or her intended audience. But at the same time, our drawings are an experiment and an exploration of those things that most interest us."

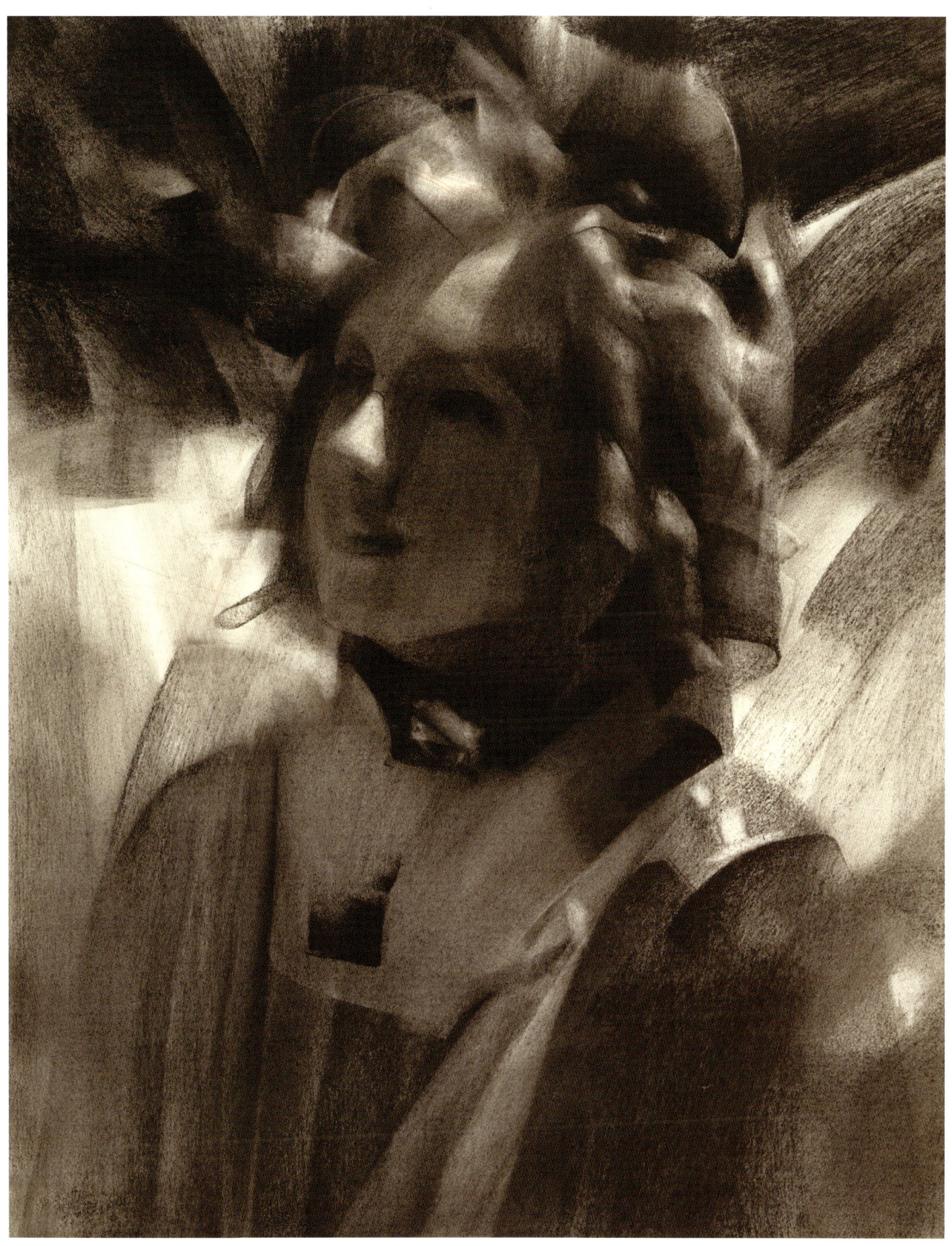

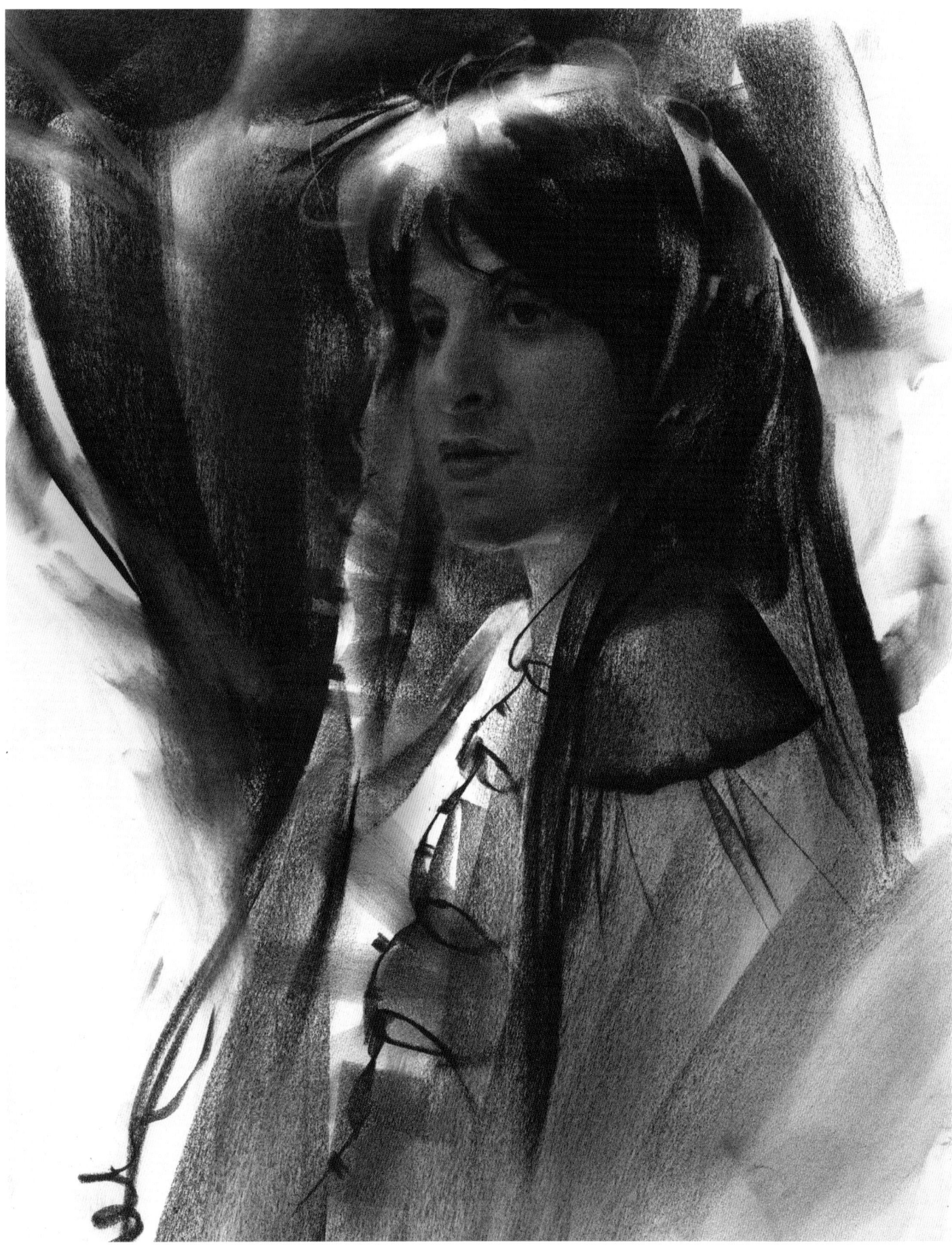

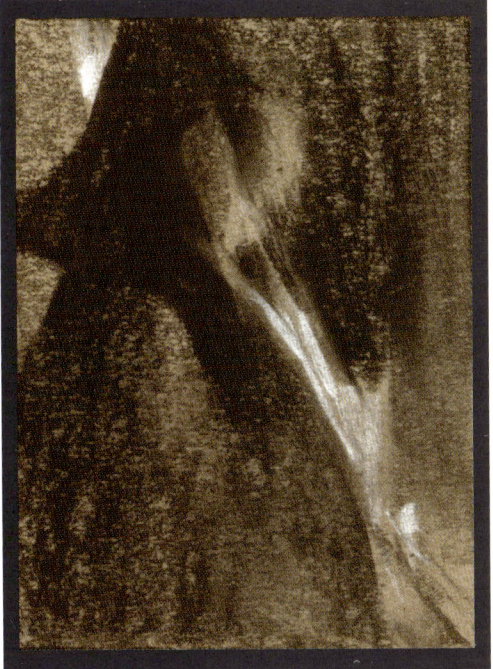
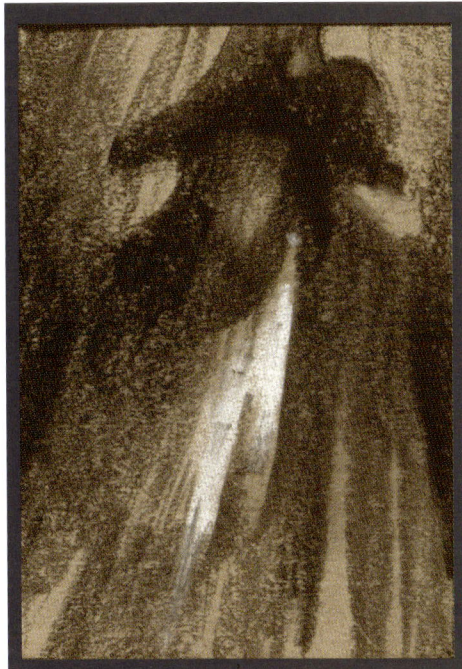
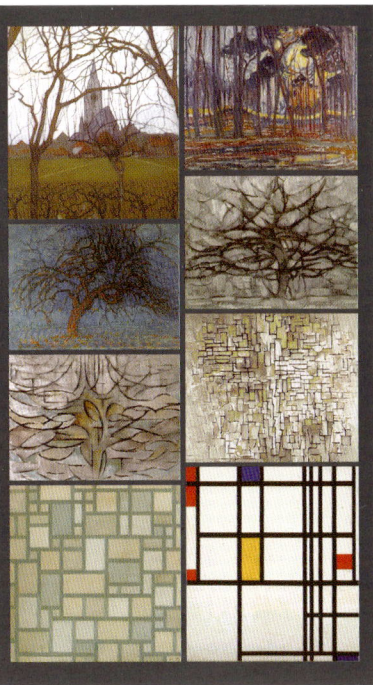

Chapter 8

Piet Mondrian (1872-1944),
style progression over time

Portrait Composition

Are you familiar with the work of the artist Piet Mondrian? He's the guy who spent his last days feverishly painting all of those rectangles you see on the far right in the examples above. Now how would his work relate to portrait drawing? Mondrian's early work was actually very representational; he was quite a good painter and he seemed to have become obsessed with one of the ideas we discussed in a previous chapter: editing the "noise" out of our pictures to focus only on what we believe to be most meaningful. Over time his work appears to more and more seek only the meaningful relationships between the elements that make up his paintings until all that's left are simple rectangles with purposeful alignments to one another. It's certainly not our purpose here to go to such an extreme, but there's a fascinating lesson in work like Mondrian's: to seek and even create meaningful relationships between all of the different elements that make up our drawings.

And if you think about it, that's the very job of our brain as we make our way through the world: we seek that which is most meaningful and useful and learn to edit out the noise. It makes sense then that art with a purposeful design is more likely to resonate with our audience.

Take a look at the drawing of the woman to the left and notice the strong diagonal created by her falling hair and the front of her shirt. It was such a strong alignment that I not only emphasized it, but also I continued it in the background above the head to complete the picture composition. It helps give the portrait an underlying structure and a purposeful quality. You can see the same kind of purposeful organization in the simple composition drawings above. If we are to present our art in the form of pictures, then it behooves us to learn to become master picture makers, and that's what composition is all about.

"Since we present our art in the form of pictures, it behooves us to learn to become master picture makers."

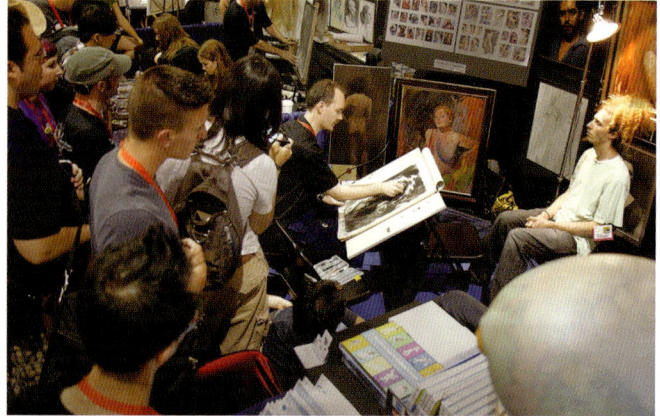

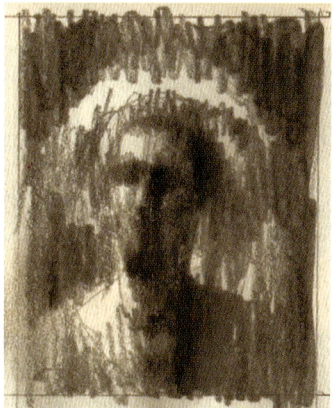
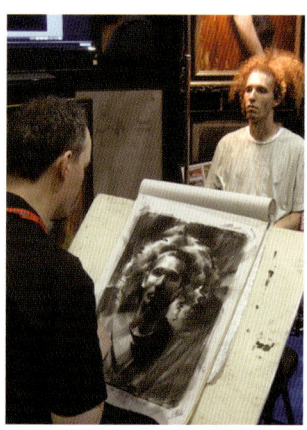

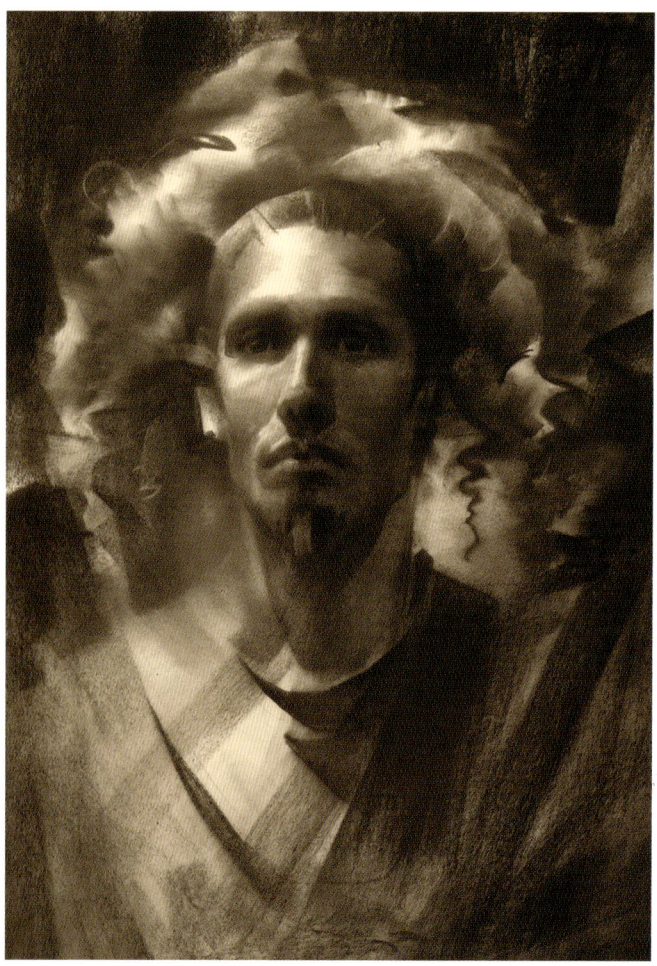

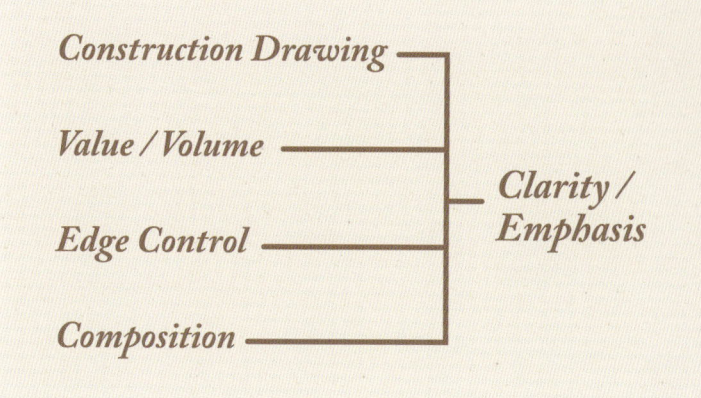

Meaningful Organization

The chart above shows each of the broad principles we've covered thus far in this book. It reiterates the approach we've tried to take with each one of them: to give visual clarity and artistic emphasis to our subject. We've focused on how to achieve this goal in the rendering of our subject, and now it's time to expand it to the entirety of the pictures that we create. It's time for pictorial composition.

Composition helps me avoid great embarrassment; it's true! I often do live demonstrations which are to me a nerve-wracking experience. I rarely do my best work under the time constraints and scrutiny of a demo, so I need a few tricks up my sleeve to make sure I don't humiliate myself in the process. Here's a demo I did at the San Diego Comic-Con booth of the Los Angeles Academy of Figurative Art (LAAFA)—the school where I regularly teach.

Attention spans are understandably short with all the events going on, so I needed to complete a competent drawing in not much more than an hour. I sat down with our model ahead of time and sketched out the simple comp you see to the upper left to be sure I had an uncomplicated idea that could be managed within the time constraints. For the finished drawing, I'd like you to notice how much I relied on a simple light and shadow statement, simple shapes, and a simple design of hard and soft edges. You can also see that a major feature of my sitter was his extraordinary hair, and so I made sure to have a lot of fun with that, but not at the expense of the rest of the drawing. Not only does the hair conform to a simple rounded silhouette, but it also creates an alignment with the rounded folds of his shirt. These ideas helped me manage the potential chaos of the hair into a meaningful relationship with the rest of the picture. And whew! I got the demo done.

Photos above and opposite are courtesy of the Los Angeles Academy of Figurative Art

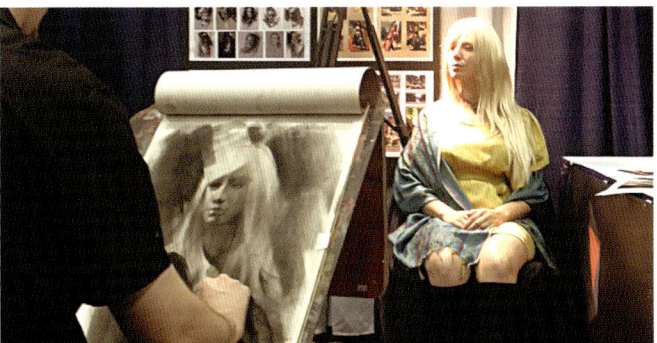

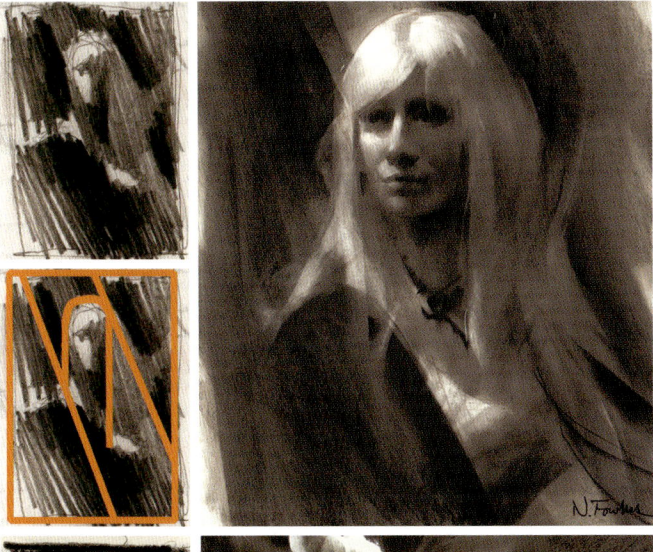

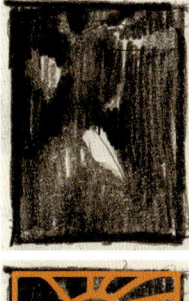

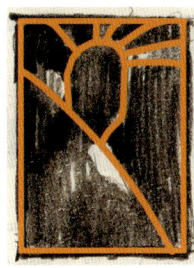

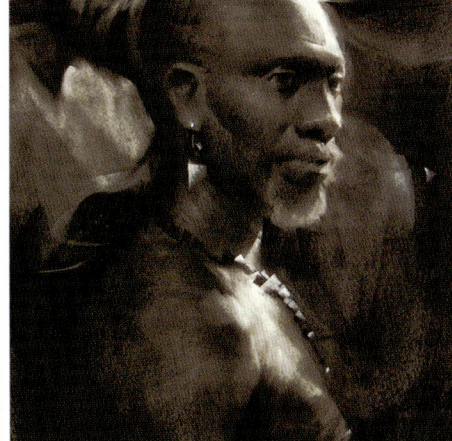

Structure

Here I am again doing another demo, desperately trying to be the man with a plan. And I do have a plan because I am, in fact, desperate. Drawing is not particularly easy, and I've already described the additional challenges of live demonstrations, so once again I prepare. I first sat down with the model before the event to work out ideal lighting; I have to decide what's most striking, and then figure out how to emphasize it within the time limit. In this case I was struck by the shock of blonde hair (a wig that we picked out, in fact) contrasting with her dark eyes. So I set up the light to emphasize the vivid contrast of the hair and let the eyes fall into shadow. This seemed to be a good setup, and so I broke out my sketchbook and did the quick, tiny thumbnail that you see here.

The trick to make light objects that are in shadow still feel light is to put something even darker next to them. So here I put a firm dark in the background until the entire mass of hair reads as a lighter silhouette. I knew that if I drew busy folds of clothing and an overactive background I would weaken my idea of bright hair contrasted by dark eyes, so I felt I needed a simple structure for those elements to play against. The diagonal sweep of her shawl and hair stood out to me as potentially giving a simple line of action to an otherwise passive pose, so I emphasized that idea in the clothing, hair, and background as you see in the diagram. Remember, one of our compositional challenges is to get all of the different elements that make up our drawing to relate to each other in a meaningful way; the repeated diagonal helped me achieve this. Since I wanted the head and hair to contrast from everything else, I also emphasized the simple verticals of the hair framing the head (see diagram). I executed these ideas as best I could in the short time I had, and voila! We have our demo.

For the next demonstration, we have a man in traditional African garb and a headdress. No need to repeat all the steps that I've described in the previous demos; I'll simply say that I took the time to make decisions on how to best present the subject as you see in the comp and diagram. I will admit that in the end I like the design of the comp best, but the students were there to primarily learn about drawing faces, so I spent most of my time on construction drawing and light and shadow without much time left to touch up the structure of the composition. Nevertheless we were happy with the end result, and one of my students ended up purchasing the completed drawing.

"The challenge of composition is to get all of the different elements that make up our drawing to relate to each other in a meaningful way."

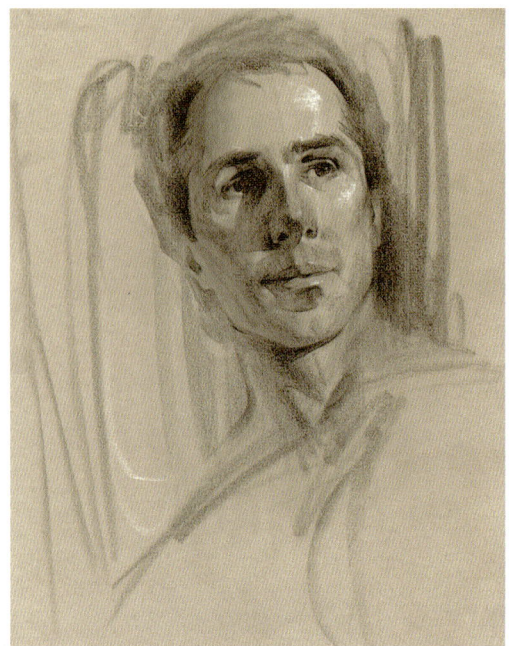

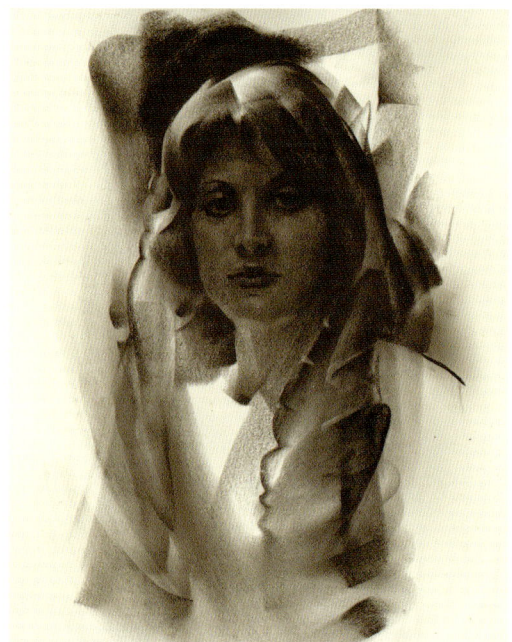

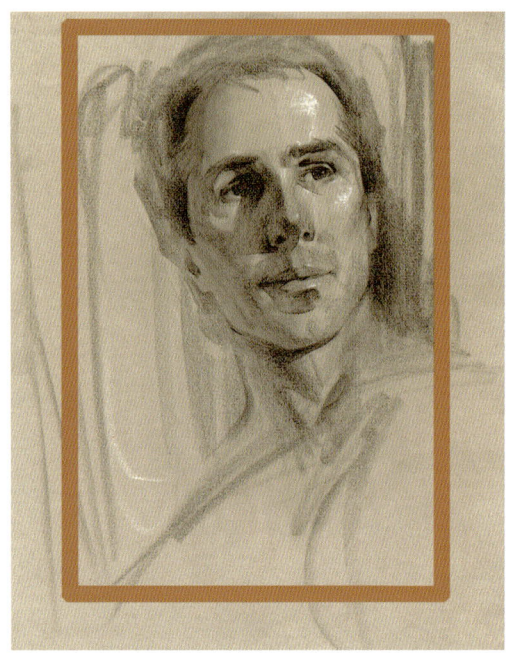

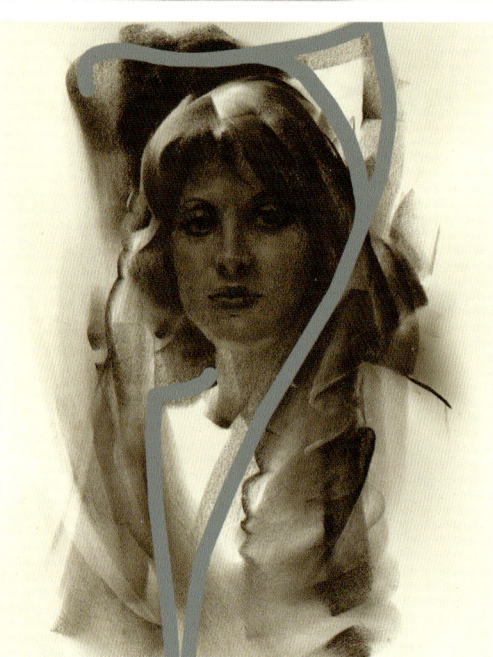

Framing

Let's continue with a series of ideas that will help us bring structure and meaningful design to our portrait drawings; let's take a look at the idea of framing. **Having our subjects pose with their heads at a bit of an angle can create a casual quality that feels quite natural.** The difficulty though, is that we don't see the head in context with the counterbalance of the body; this can sometimes lead to an off-balance appearance. In cases like this I like to conform my background tones to strong verticals for a stabilizing "framing" effect. This subtle support structure helps maintain the casual quality of the pose while compensating for the off-balance feel of the head.

Repetition

A way to get all of the various parts of our drawing to relate to each other is through repetition. I sometimes like to find an interesting shape or idea within the subject and repeat it in other areas of the picture, as shown in the example above. In this particular case I liked the strong triangular shape of light below the neck but felt that it pointed the viewer right out of the picture. A nice solution was to repeat the light triangle shape above the head to hold our attention, and at the same time create a meaningful repetition of shape. I also felt that a repetition of small triangular strokes throughout the image created a faceted quality that added visual interest while conforming to a unifying theme in the drawing.

Active vs. Passive

It's a simple but useful idea that we can give something emphasis by putting its opposite next to it. If we want to emphasize the texture of a stroke, we can simply smooth the tones next to it. If we want an illuminated area to pop, we simply put a dark next to it. And if we want a face, hair, or jewelry to be particularly special, we simply avoid similar contrasts in other areas. It's a simple idea that's easy to forget as we get caught up in rendering all the nuances of our subject. Remember, great drawings are often so because they have a great sense of purpose, and purposeless rendering is a sure way of rendering your drawing meaningless.

To the upper right, you see one of my demonstration drawings with my usual simple rough sketch. This was another situation where a short time limit was actually an advantage because it forced me to emphasize a simple statement about my subject. I felt that the strong areas of light and the glints of jewelry would give a special visual interest to the shadowy silhouette of my subject. I maintained this idea throughout my drawing by using passive vs. active areas; passive areas of dark are placed next to active areas of light, and contrast is reduced anywhere it might compete with the more important areas.

This idea is especially apparent in the profile view of the woman in the middle; she's made to be special because everything else isn't. I've added an overlay to make this point as clear as possible.

Direction

Guiding the eye to the face of your subject can be a useful way to strengthen your portrait composition. In the drawing to the lower right there were two very big potential problems. First, her strong gaze looking downward has the potential to push the viewer right out of the drawing; secondly, her body tipping into the frame is likely to feel very off-balance and uncomfortable to viewers. A simple solution is to place a counter direction running through the drawing, almost as if she has something to lean against, visually speaking. Additionally, notice that the majority of strokes throughout the background are directed to the face; this serves to pull the viewer's eye back to the area of greatest importance.

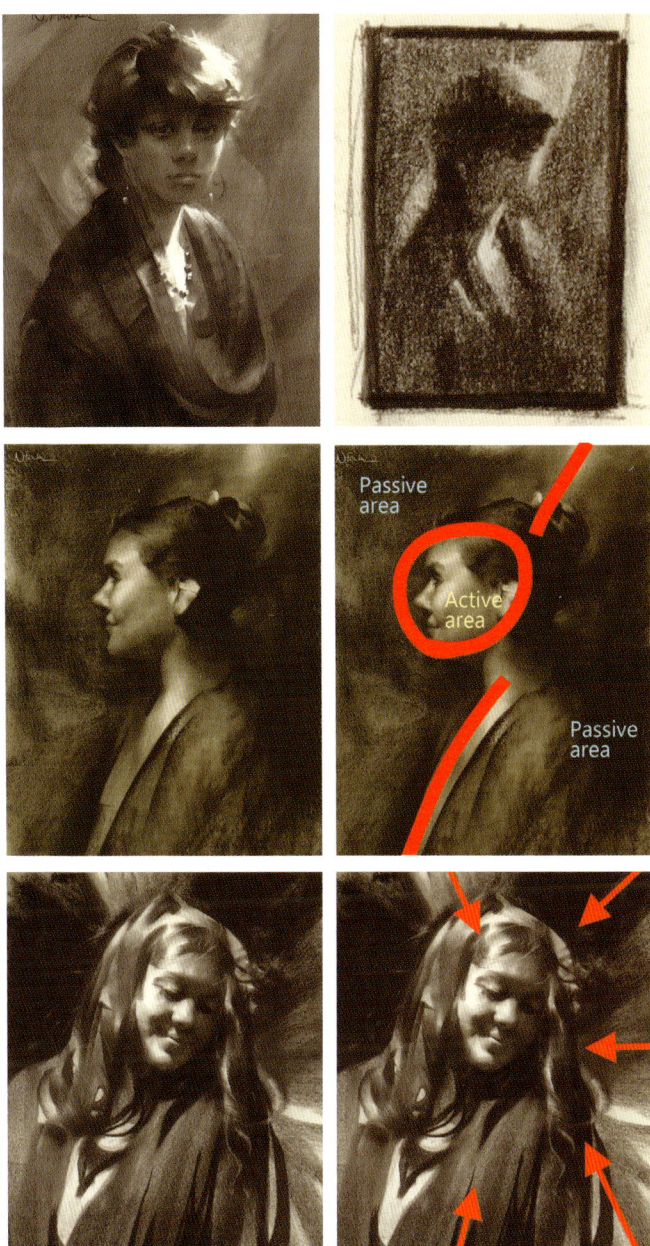

"I like to consider the limitations of drawing an advantage because they force me to use compositional principles for a clear, simple statement about my subject."

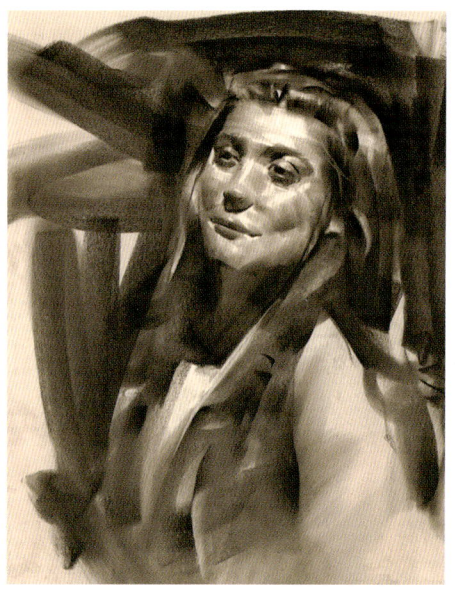

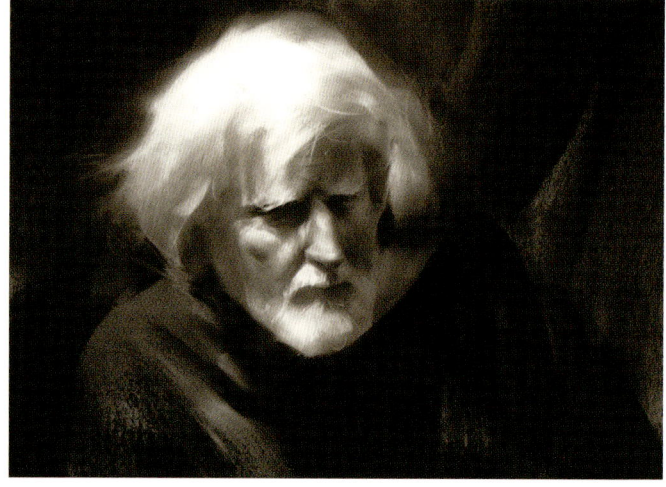

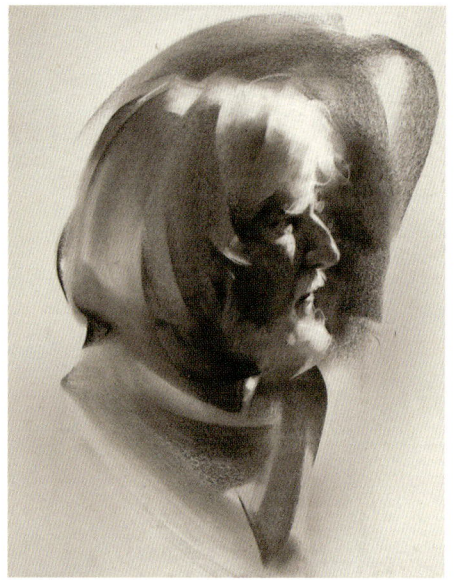

Focal Area

If every part of a drawing is made to be equally important, it also means that every part becomes equally unimportant. This is simple human nature; we tend to think hierarchically. For example, hair tends to feel more important than background, the face more than the hair, and the eyes draw our greatest attention. This is natural to us, and so we respond well to images that reinforce the visual importance of the face and eyes.

This chapter suggests many ways to bring a special emphasis to the face; the primary one is the use of contrast. As discussed in the previous chapter, areas of strong contrast inherently draw our attention, and we can use them to support and strengthen our portrait drawings. Each of the drawings on this page can be found in full-size views elsewhere in this book, but I wanted to assemble them together here as examples of the face and eyes having a special emphasis through contrast. As an exercise, go ahead and take a closer look; how have I used visual contrast to attract the eye to each face as a strong focal area?

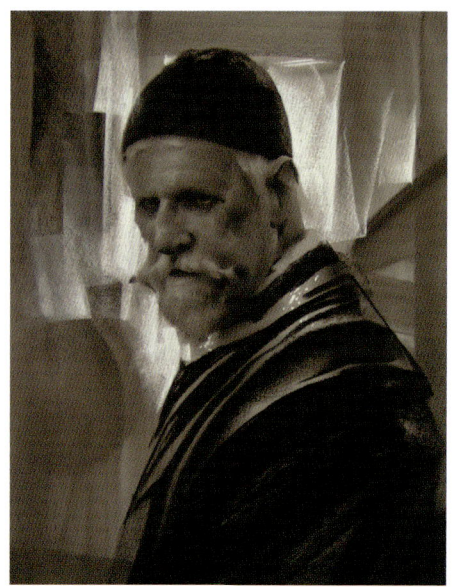

> "*Most portrait drawings are about the face, and so we need a variety of ways to bring a special emphasis to it.*"

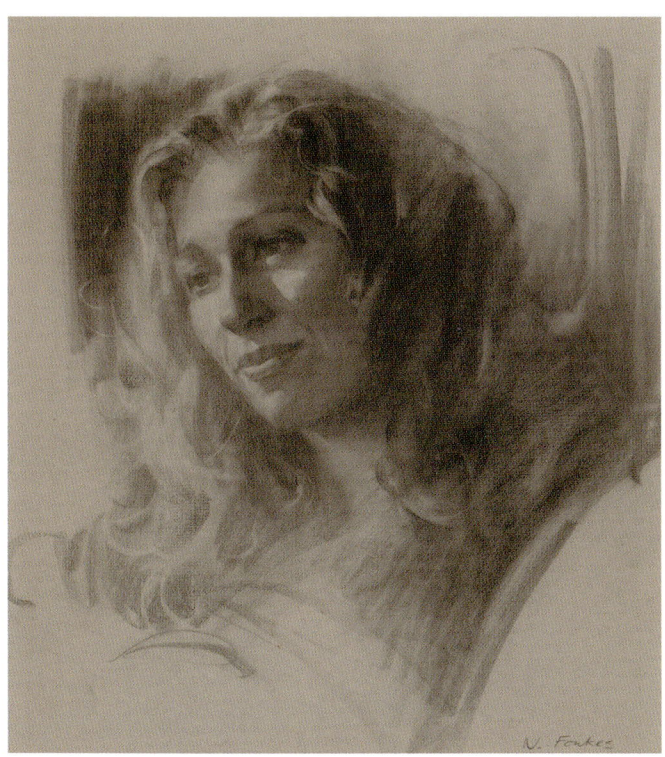

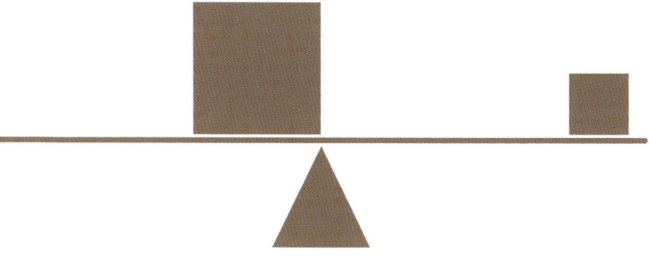

Balance

We've discussed the visual balance of our subject's pose; now let's take a look at giving the picture visual balance as a whole. Balance is a quality that's very important to us unconsciously. If you think about it, every movement of every muscle, every day of our lives is balanced against the force of gravity. It makes a kind of sense that we tend to prefer images that are balanced visually.

In the above portrait of a blonde woman, I wanted the light at the front of her hair to be accented, so I placed a strong dark in the left background. But that contrast combined with the model's left-leaning gaze creates an uncomfortable visual weight. Luckily the solution was quite simple; it was just a matter of putting a few strong vertical strokes and a bit of extra visual interest to the far right side of the picture as a visual counterweight. You can see this concept simply diagrammed in the graphic above.

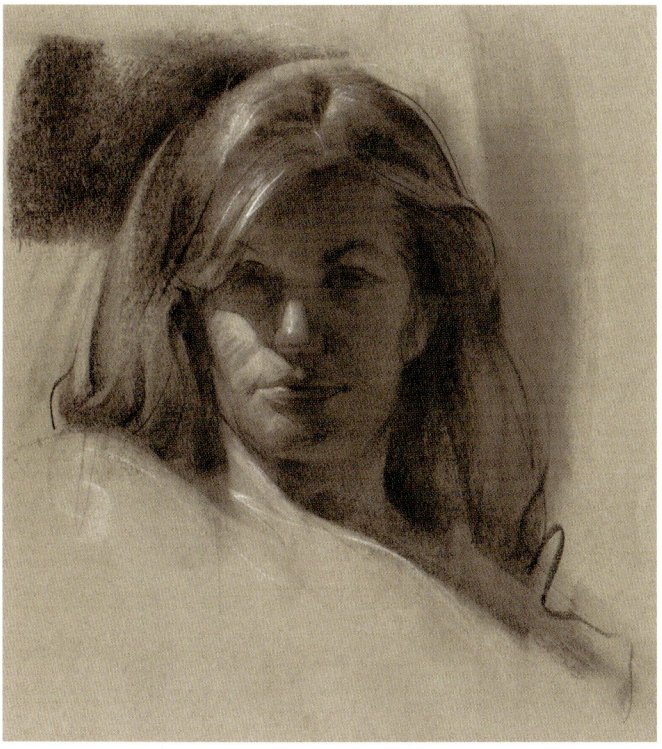

The lower vignette was a quick classroom sketch, and with it I want to make the point that even a quick study deserves a bit of composition. The block of dark at the upper left serves the same purpose as in the previous image and also creates the same problem. The swath of tone coming off the hair at the lower right helps, but mostly it's that little squiggle that adds a touch of visual interest to balance the study. I'm sure it's obvious that I love doing those squiggly shapes with my charcoal, but I'm extremely careful to only put them in places where they add a useful visual interest.

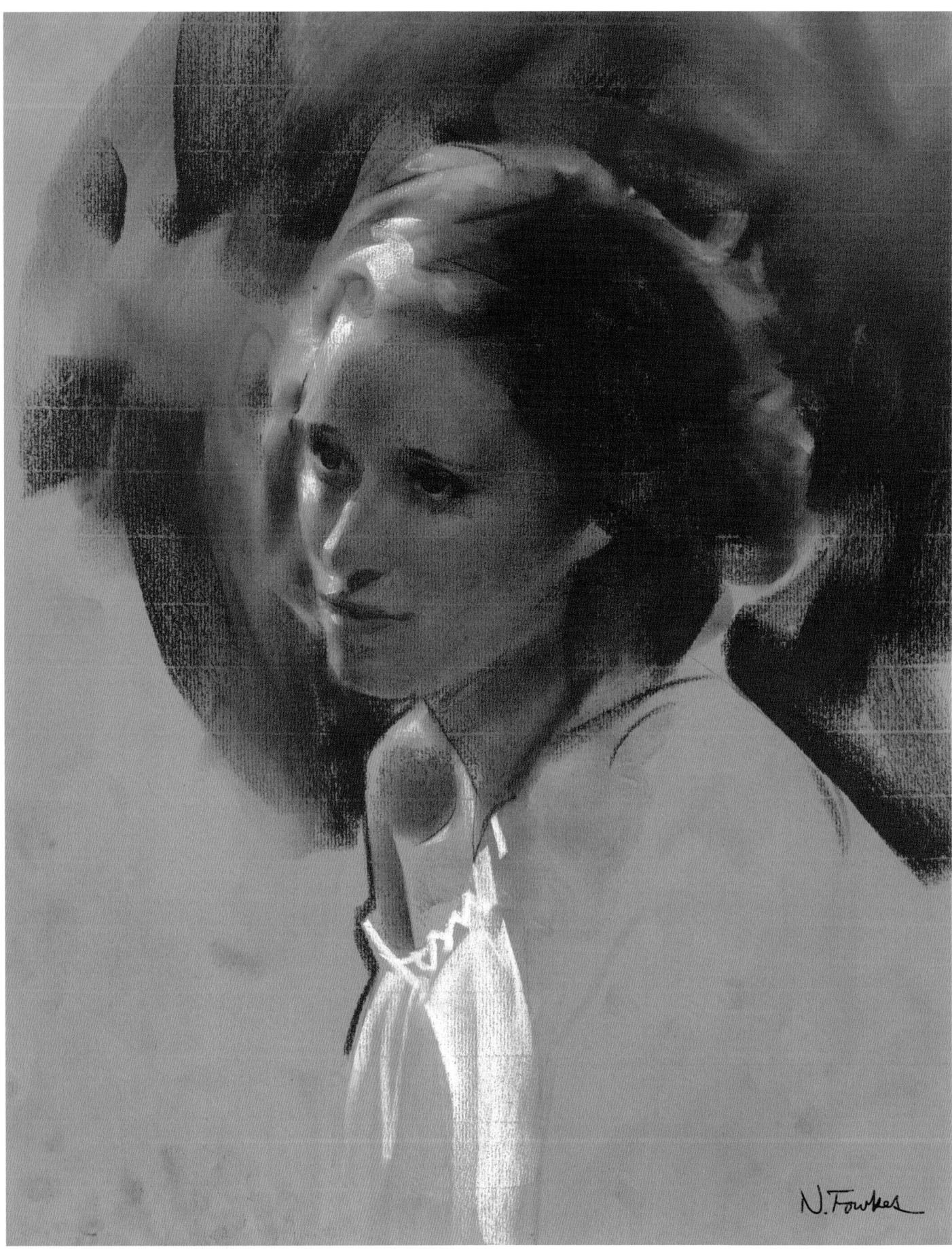

To wrap things up, let's take a look at the compositional considerations and solutions for this drawing of a woman on green paper. This model had dark hair and was wearing a white blouse, and was primarily in shadow. Considering this setup, I thought that I might be able to get an interesting picture by playing the lighter torso against the shadowy mass of the head—kind of a 50/50 split of light and dark in the picture, but with a visual interest being pulled into the face.

I enjoy drawing on colored paper and felt that a green would give a visually interesting pop to this drawing; it also let me take advantage of using white Nupastel to bring out the areas of primary visual interest. I used the pastel for the lights on the blouse and then let the paper do the work by leaving it for the blouse's shadow value. The rim lights gave a nice emphasis to the face as a whole, but the eyes had a kind of smoldering quality that I wanted to be sure to emphasize. They were somewhat lost in shadow, so I wanted to find a way to give them a little extra emphasis. I've had good luck using the natural lines of the pose to strengthen my compositions, so I felt that the direction of the shoulder (orange line) could be used to my advantage. I used it to create an alignment of the body, background, and eyes so that they would all relate to each other and give the extra attention to the eyes that I needed. I also like to create visual interest by the direction of my charcoal strokes and did so around the face and eyes as shown in purple.

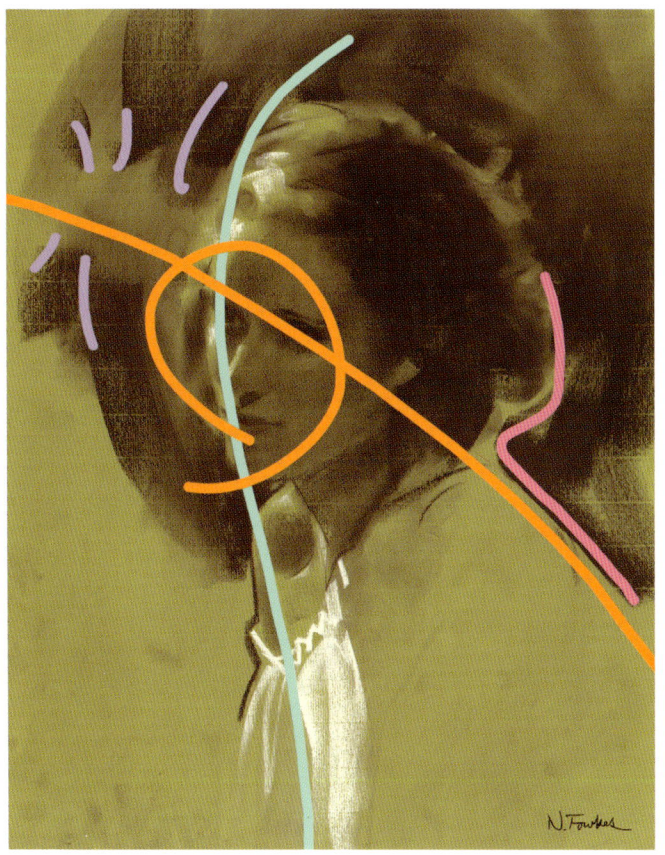

Please keep in mind that my solutions and my style are not necessarily the correct ones; you will surely have different interests than I have, and your compositional designs should reinforce those. Feel free to borrow any of my solutions if they work for you, but it's the big question that matters most: "What am I most interested in about my subject, and how can I design my drawing to support that interest?"

So with this in mind, let me offer a final thought. By now you're aware that I like to strongly emphasize principles but then encourage great caution so the principles don't turn into formulas. The appearance of the subjects we draw are greatly varied, which is why I consider formulaic thinking to be ruinous; a formula means you treat all of your variety of subjects exactly the same way. Your artwork ceases to be about the subject and becomes about the formula. So as always, please don't think of the ideas that we've covered in this chapter as rules that must be followed. **Once again, your first step in drawing is always to consider the "why"—to ask yourself what it is about the subject that inspires you to draw and then use any and every useful idea to achieve that goal.**

"Watch out for formulas, a formula treats all of your variety of subjects exactly the same. Your artwork ceases to be about the subject and becomes about the formula."

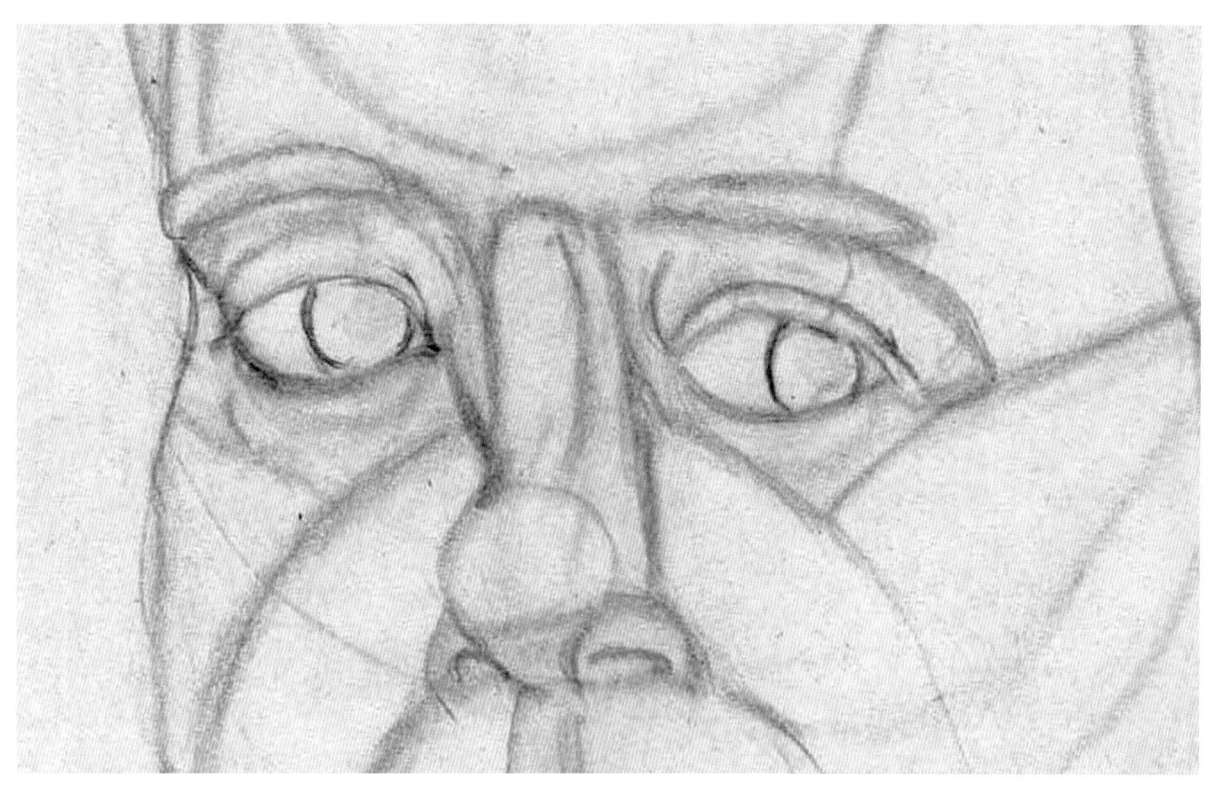

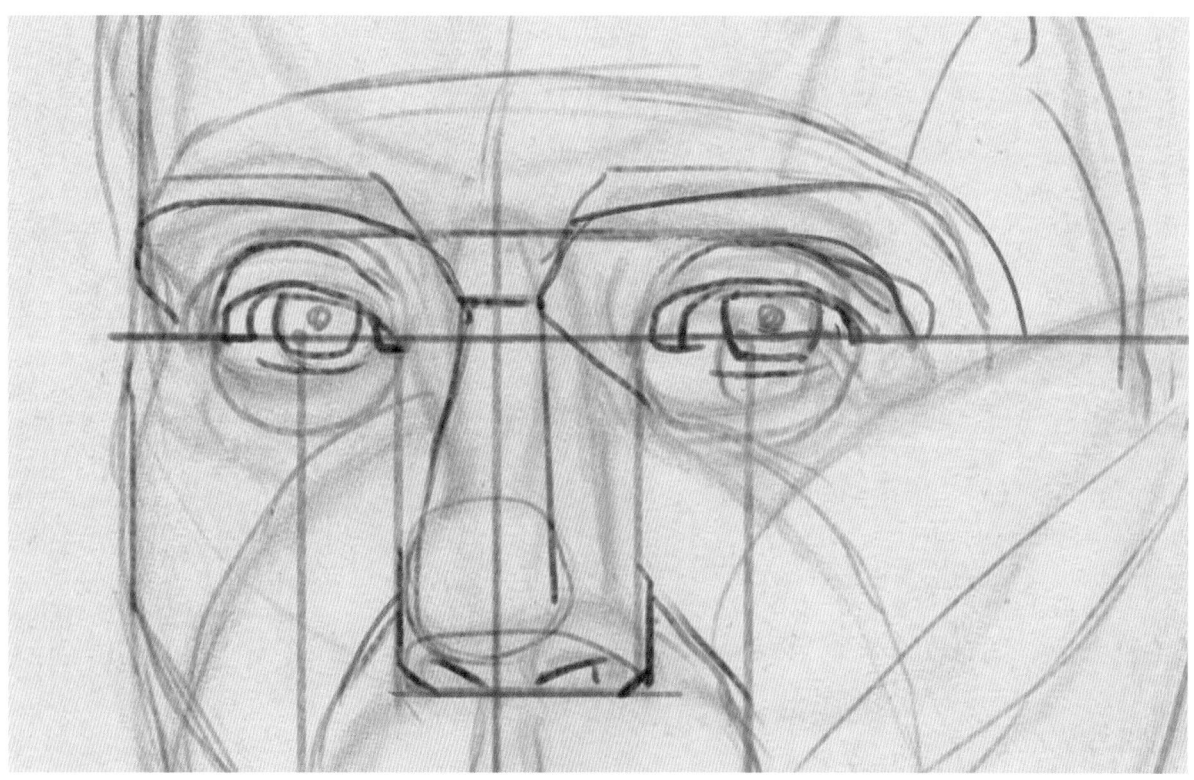

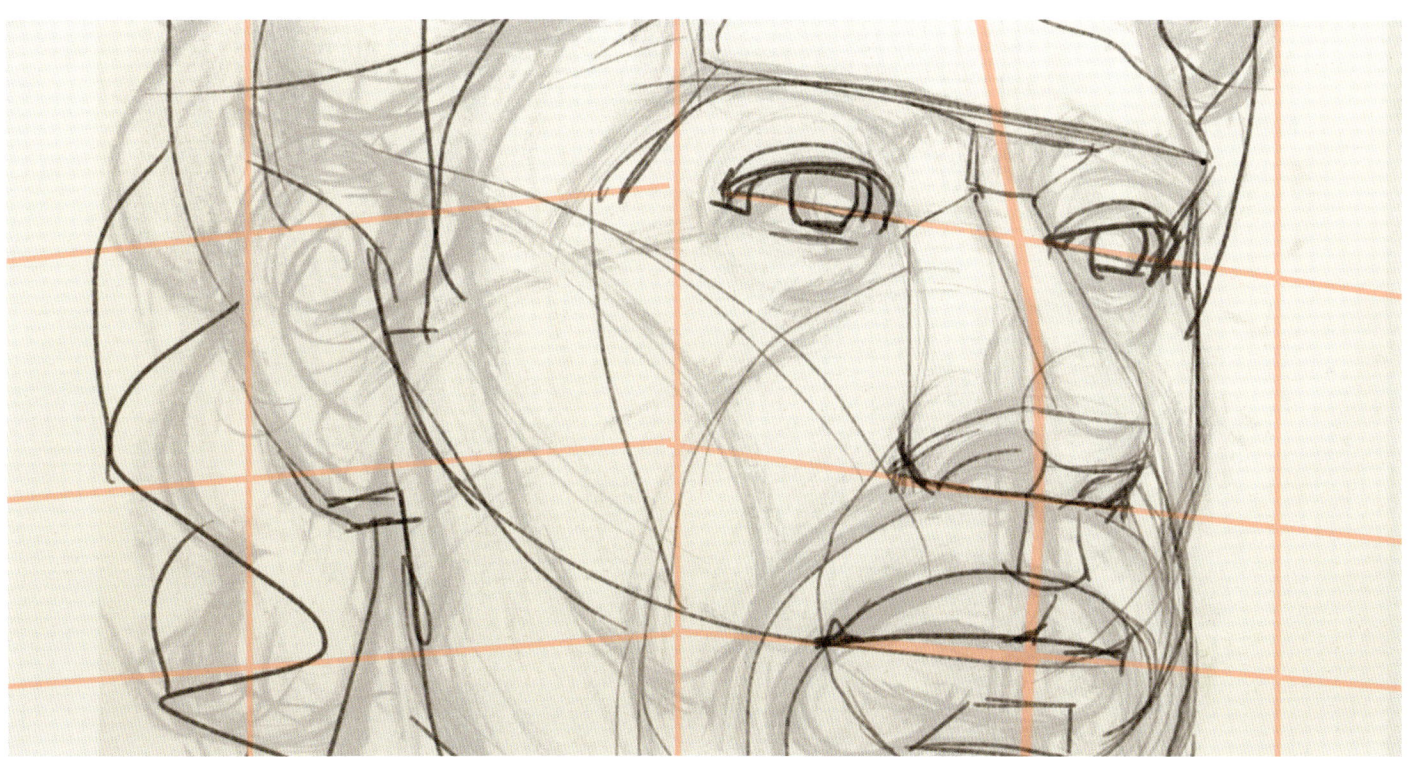

Chapter 9

Common Mistakes

I've been teaching life drawing for fifteen years and I'm convinced that I have the best students. My classes have typically been held on weeknights, which means the type of students who sign up and diligently show up every week are particularly dedicated. They work all day long at their jobs and then fight Los Angeles rush-hour traffic, arriving early to try to get the best spots. They work hard for the next several hours until 10 p.m., and then cruise the lonely city streets to return home. Many take on my challenge to do one portrait study each day outside of class. They're passionate and committed and have been impressive people whom I've considered a great honor to get to know. In the last few years I've ventured into online teaching, which has offered the extraordinary opportunity to work with students from all over the globe; I find them to be equally committed and enthusiastic.

Our class critiques always strive to find solutions to the challenges of portrait drawing, and I'd like to share those solutions with you here in this chapter. The work that follows is from students at various points in the learning curve and includes my draw-overs of their work. Each piece is shown with their permission. So as I show you before and after corrections of student work, it's with great appreciation for them and their willingness to share their learning curve with you. And in fairness to them, you'll find one of my own student drawings tucked in the mix. I'm sure you'll be happy to see how much help I needed as a student as well.

"Repetitive practice leads to a refinement of our abilities and a mastery of our subject."

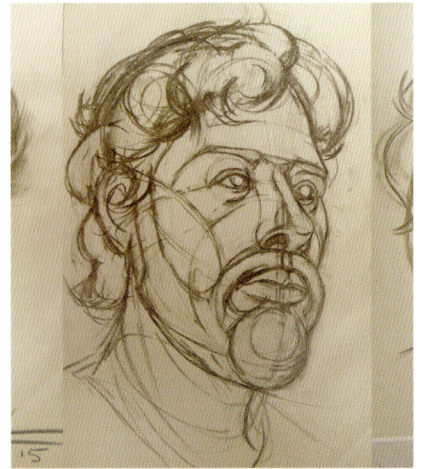
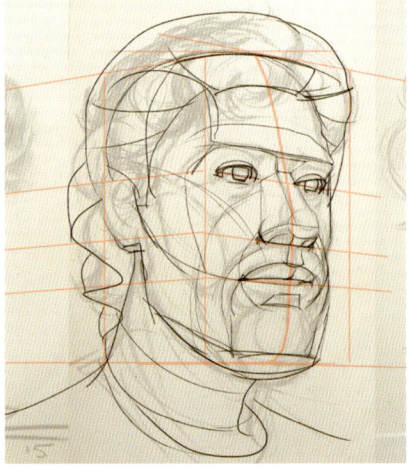

Abstract construction lines that don't convey form.

In this first selection, you can see that some good things are happening in the student drawing, but at times the construction drawing is being treated as a series of abstract lines rather than a method of carefully describing three-dimensional form and character. My draw-over tries to correct this by carefully conforming the construction to three-dimensional planes and proper perspective. The anatomy is grouped into simplified forms, and the hair is treated as a volume that carefully wraps around the head.

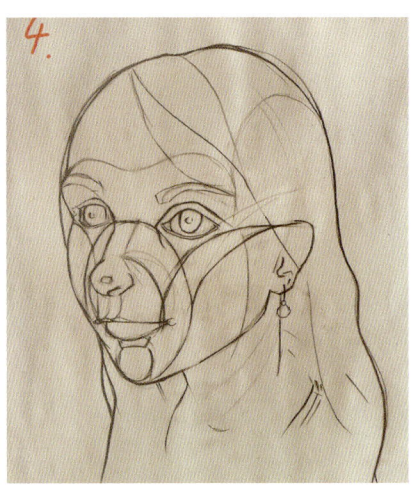
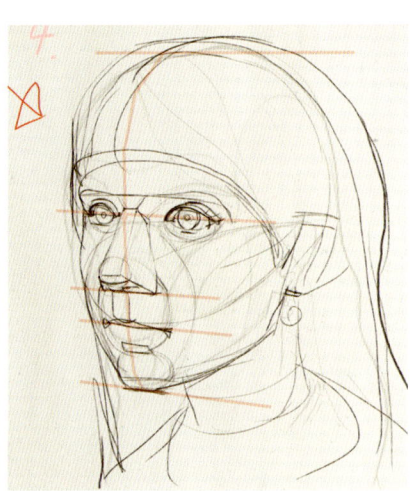

This study struggles with many of the same issues as the previous, and so my draw-over attempts to rework the drawing to emphasize the volume of the forms. For instance, the complexities of the nose have been rendered simply as a front plane, side plane, and under-plane. And take particular note of the eyes; eyes are a spherical protrusion from the head and need careful attention. Here I drew the eyelids such that they appear to wrap around the sphere of the eyes.

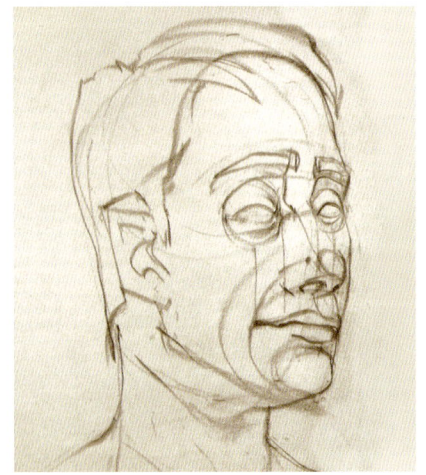
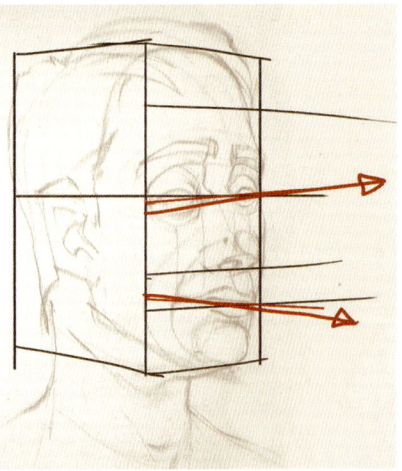

Features don't follow the perspective of the face.

I very much like the expressive quality of this student drawing, and expressive drawings often work better when they have a strong underlying structure. As you saw in the previous draw-overs, perspective is critically important to the accuracy of our drawings. But as we concentrate on so many other concerns, it's very easy to lose track of the way that the features fall along perspective lines. As you're doing simple construction studies, it can be helpful to lightly sketch out a three-dimensional cube with diminishing perspective lines as an aid to accurately place the features of the subject.

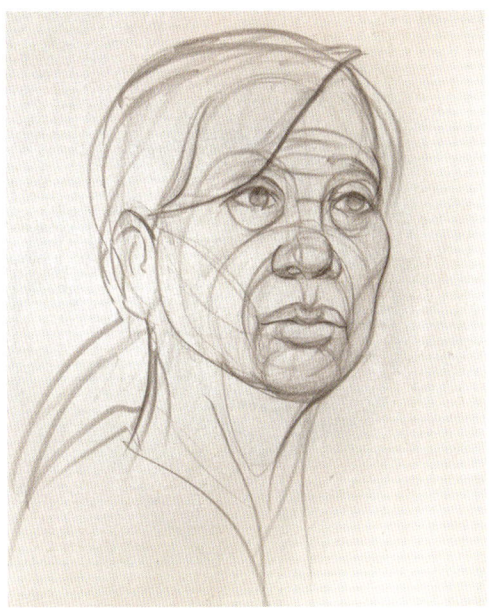

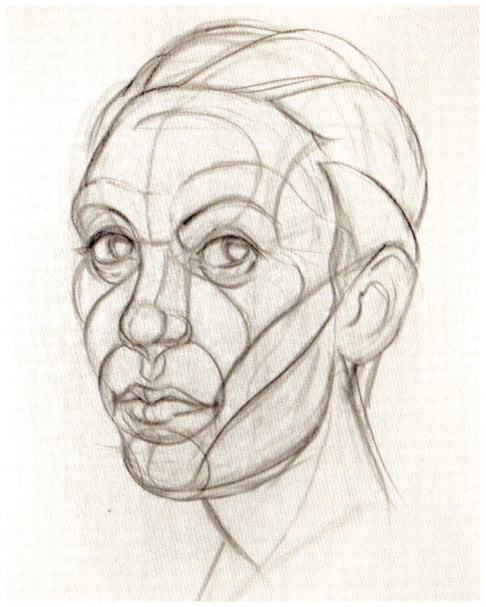

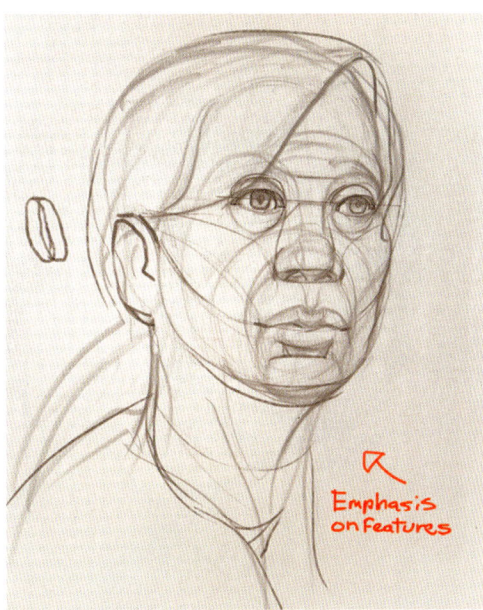

Emphasis
on features

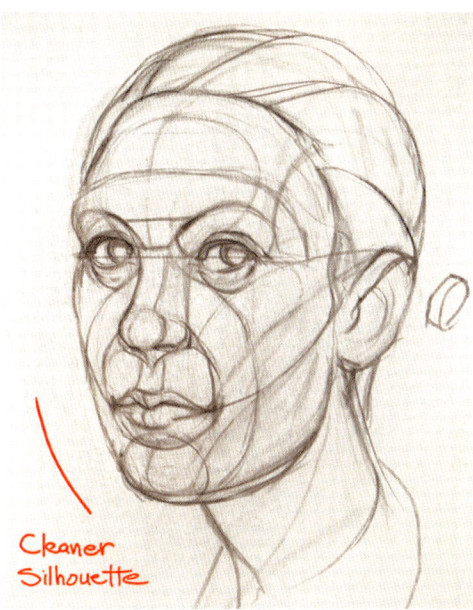

Cleaner
Silhouette

Weak Emphasis on features.

The student construction drawing here is quite good and needs very little help from me, but I did take this as an opportunity to give a little extra umph to the features. As we begin the learning curve to constructing a good portrait, it's good to have constant reminders that the end goal is to represent the form and character of our sitter. So my draw-over adds a little extra firmness to tell which lines are more important than others to give a special emphasis to the features.

Unnatural exaggeration of the silhouette.

Overlapping lines are especially important in construction drawing because as the lines wrap from front to back they suggest the 3-D quality of the turning form. This student's drawing is really getting the hang of overlapping shapes, especially around the outer edges of the head; at the same time it's becoming too much of a good thing. As you can see in my draw-over to the lower right, the outer silhouette of the portrait is quite simple. This is usually the case for front and three-quarter views, so much so that big breaks in the outer forms are usually the realm of exaggerated caricature only.

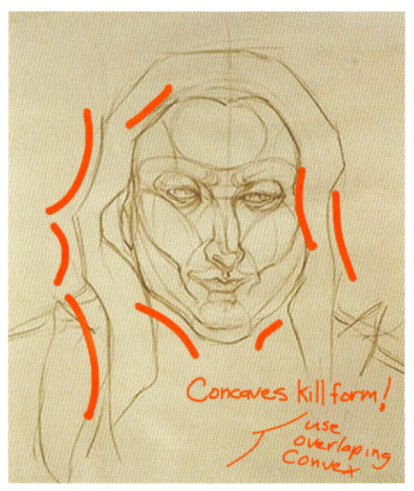

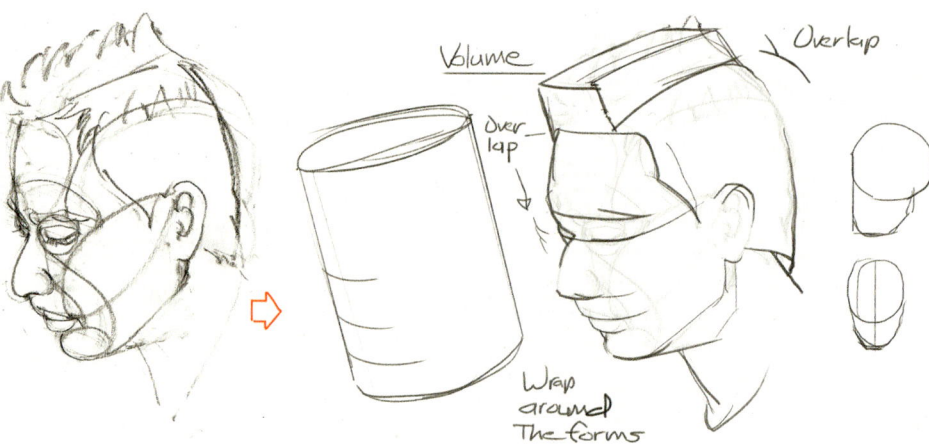

Concave shapes that weaken form.

The drawing here has a lot of great character but also has unfortunate concave shapes that work against the feeling of three-dimensional form. In most cases such concaves can be replaced with two overlapping convex lines which wrap around the forms of the anatomy.

Using Reilly lines at the expense of form.

As helpful as the Reilly construction lines can be, you've heard me encourage caution several times. If you're drawing the head at an angle where the Reilly abstraction seems to work against the form, then rework them to suit the pose or ignore them completely. In this case the lowered view of the head is an important consideration in the construction, and we need lines that reinforce it. We can think of the way construction lines wrap around a cylinder; such lines can give a simple clarity to our construction and create helpful overlapping shapes along the edges of our subject.

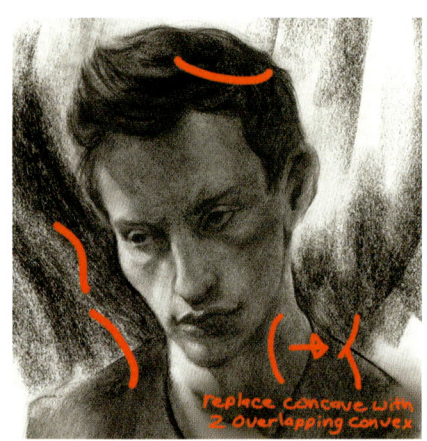
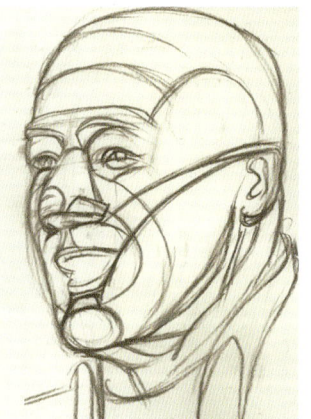
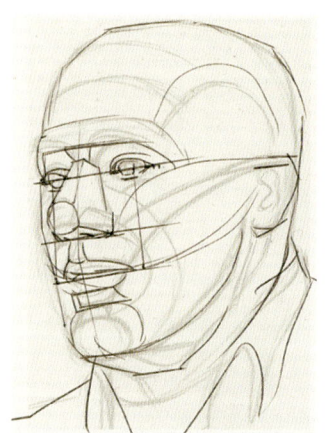
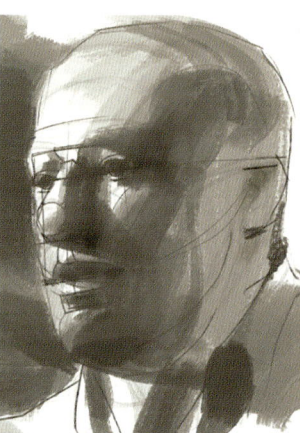

Here's a tonal drawing that is quite well done but also suffers from concave shapes that work against the form. Once again the solution is simple; just replace the concaves with overlapping convex shapes that wrap around the form.

So keep in mind that all of the construction lines represented above are in preparation to create finished tonal studies. Working with a simply constructed drawing like the middle example makes rendering light and shadow a simple matter and a real pleasure. To illustrate this point I spent just one minute brushing in some shapes of light and shadow into the construction, and the volumes of the head and features are already starting to appear!

Tones aren't designed to describe form.

As we move into rendering light and shadow it's important to emphasize, and even exaggerate, the three-dimensional quality that we've worked for in our construction drawings. In the case of this drawing, the subject is positioned such that we're looking up into the under-planes of the forms. Just like the simple cylinder shown, the chin, lips, nose, brow ridge, and hair all should show a strong under-plane.

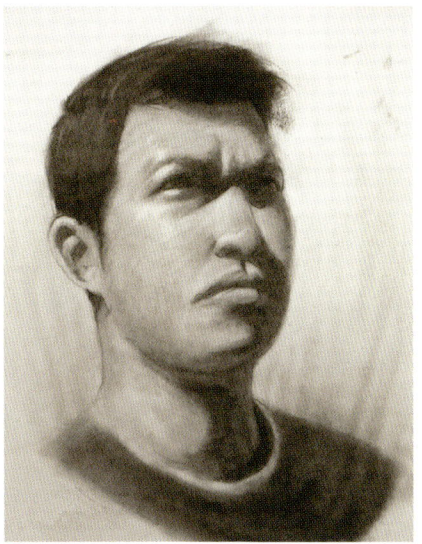
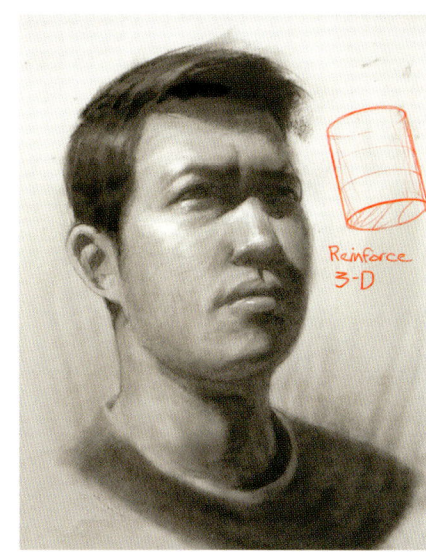

Misinterpretation of light contrasts.

Remember our previous discussions about how easy it is to misperceive individual areas of contrast? This drawing has some nice forms emerging, but it also struggles with the areas of light placed up against dark shadows. For instance, notice the right cheek and the chin. When we observe our sitter, areas like these can feel much brighter than they really are because they're surrounded by dark shadow, and we end up drawing them much too bright. This is why it's so important to view the light and shadow as a whole rather than to observe individual areas of contrast. In my draw-over I'm careful that as the forms curve away from the light into shadow they have the proper half-tone values. Such misperceptions of value are also why squinting at our subject is highly useful; it helps us to see the big, simple value relationships.

You might notice that in this, and the previous example, the shadows are all grouped to be nearly black. This is an exercise we do in my classes that allows the luxury of only having to worry about turning form in the light. We save rendering form in the shadows for a later exercise. With such dark shadows there's a wide value range available to turn forms in the light, and I've tried to take best advantage of that in the draw-over. The misperceptions of value where light meet shadow have been corrected, and the brightest values are concentrated on the left where the forms most strongly face the light.

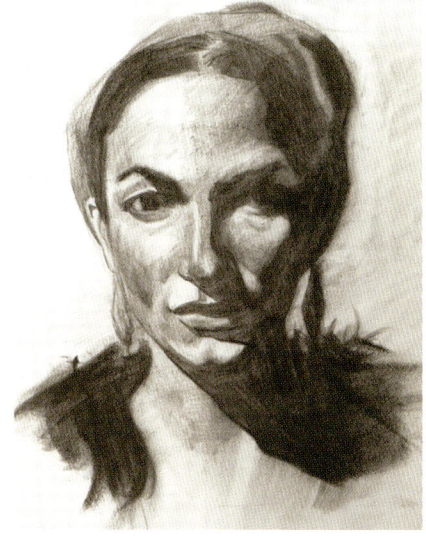
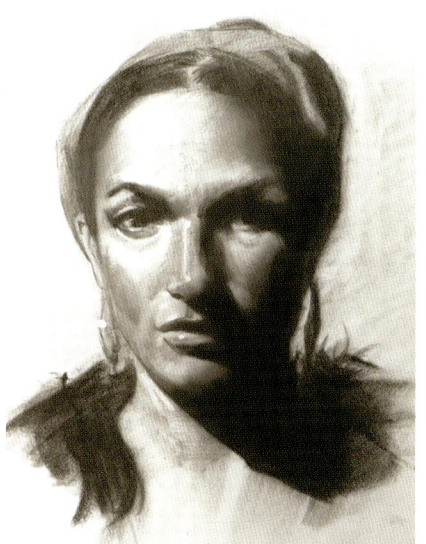
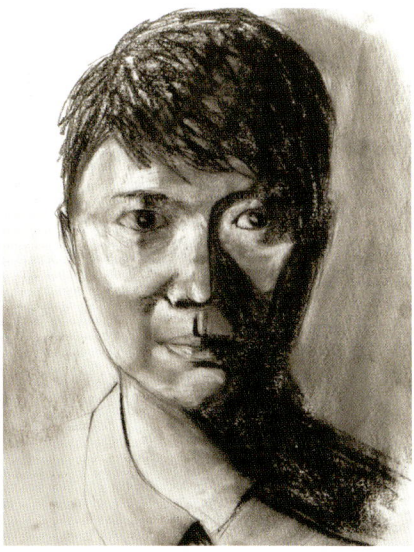
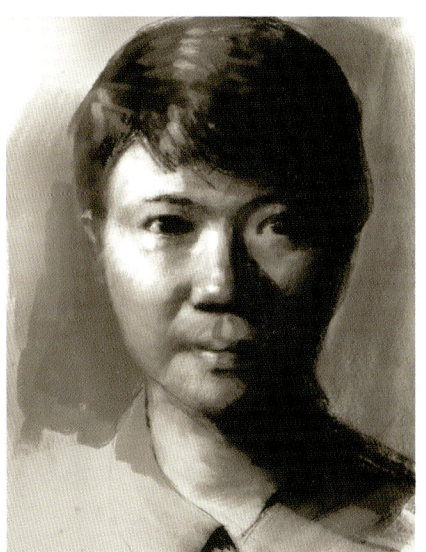

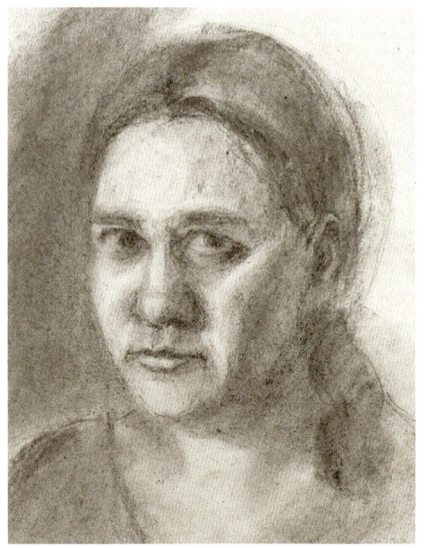
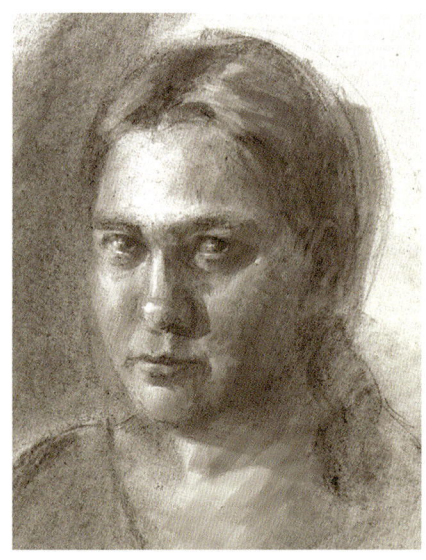

Uncommitted cast shadows.

Another common problem when dealing with a direct light source is cast shadows that have an overly soft, uncommitted quality. I've noticed that students often exaggerate the contrast where light meets shadow (as noted in the previous examples), and then blame hard-edge shadows for the excessive contrast, not realizing that the problem is the value contrast. Their solution is often to artificially soften cast shadows instead of correcting the value contrasts. In fact, in my many years of teaching I've found the struggle of properly rendering hard-edged cast shadows is fairly universal, so I'm here to promise you, your cast shadows will be absolutely beautiful… if you render their values properly.

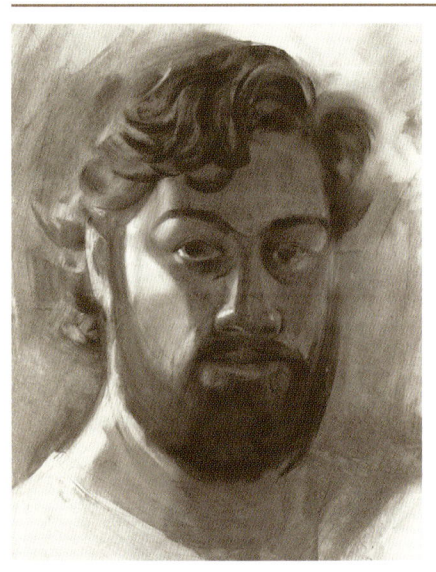
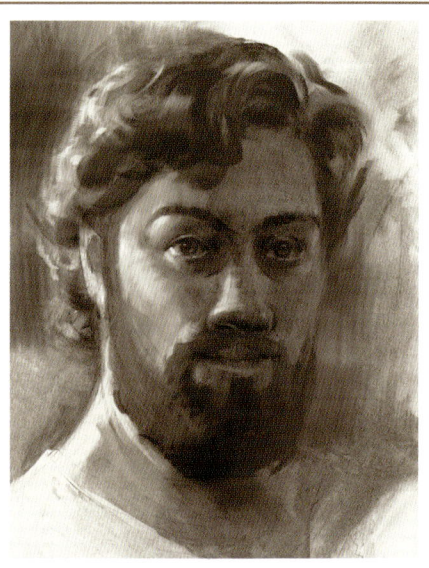

Strokes don't wrap around forms.

We need to do everything that we can to get our two-dimensional drawings to have three-dimensional qualities, so I like to have my strokes of light wrap around the form. In my paint-over for this drawing, notice especially in the left cheek the beneficial quality of the strokes wrapping around the anatomy to help create the illusion of form. I'm also making a point to enhance the quality of light and shadow in the hair, wrapping my strokes around the forms there as well.

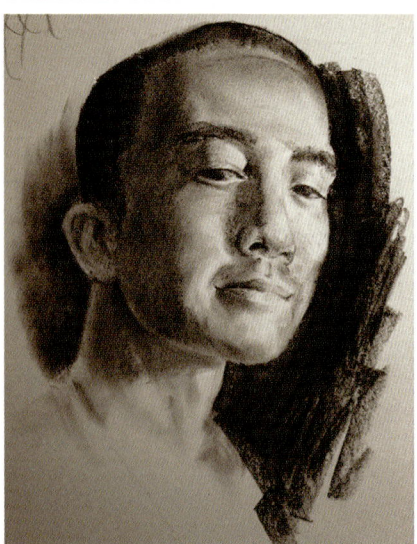
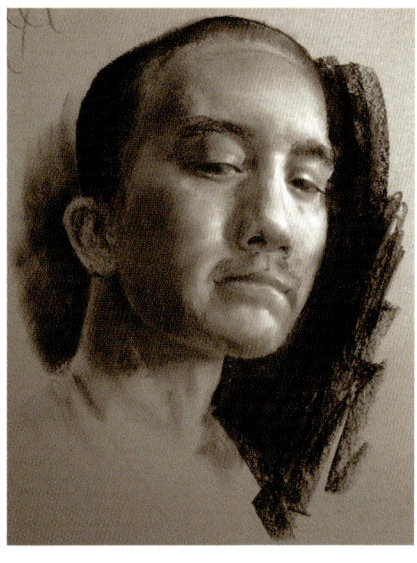

Forms end abruptly at light/shadow border.

Here's a drawing that is coming along quite well and doesn't need much help from me; my draw-over just suggests two subtle but important things. First, skin has a translucent quality. As bright lights transition into shadow there's often an under-glow of light passing directly through the skin into adjacent shadow. Second, forms don't stop wrapping around the head at the border of light and shadow. Take a look at the upper left cheek in the student drawing: there's no continuation of form as the cheek bone wraps around from under the eye all the way back toward the ear. It was important for me to correct this as you see in the draw-over.

False exaggeration of shadow values.

This example and the next are products of a class exercise where we leave the areas of direct light blank so as to focus our efforts entirely on rendering shadows. The student drawing is coming along well and has a nice commitment to form shadows and cast shadows; it just needs a smoother transition from light to shadow. Another area that needs greater consideration is the hair. It's very typical for students in the learning curve to only notice the directional strands of hair and not notice their simpler massing of value. Take a look at the curving masses of hair in the corrected version: the process of squinting as previously described helps us see the simpler value statement as we deal with the complexities of hair.

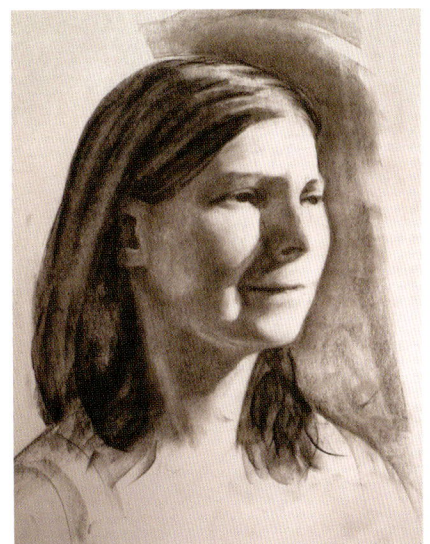 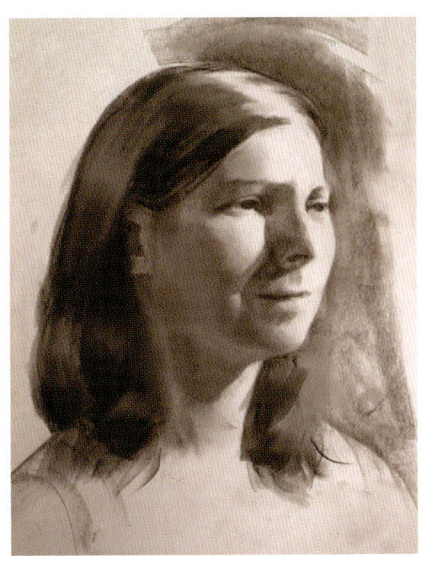

Lack of form in the shadows.

Observing how forms turn in shadow is no less important than observing forms in the light. Most environments are filled with directional ambient lights such as the lighting shown in the corrected version of this drawing. Shadows can feel complicated, but often it's a simple matter to follow the logic of the lighting as softly illuminated side planes curve around into deeper shadow tones.

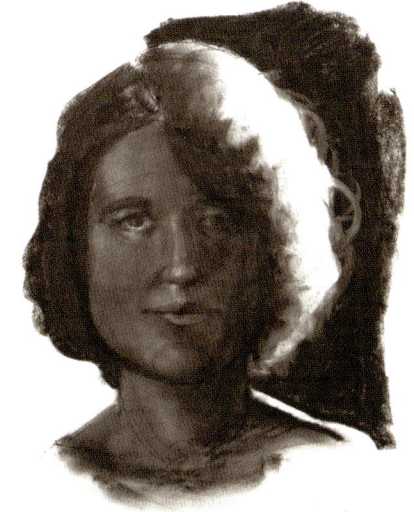 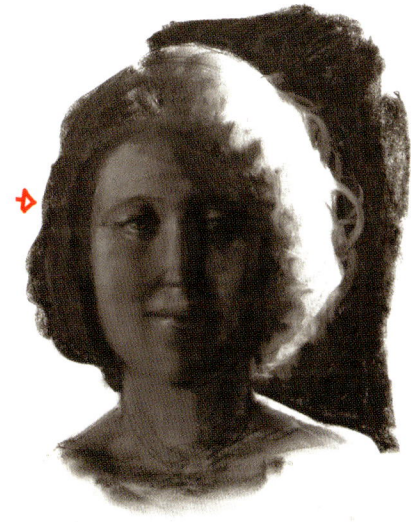

Attempting style without experience.

The student drawing here is trying very hard to be stylish at the expense of clear forms and good values of light and shadow. The student has rendered the features somewhat symbolically without intending to, and there are misinterpretations of contrast throughout the drawing. Plus, the lighting on the hair makes absolutely no sense. I'm allowed to be particularly harsh with this student because it is, in fact, me. You can probably tell by the hairstyle here that this drawing is from the eighties, and I had a whole lot to learn as a student. I invite you to take a close look at how I made many of the mistakes that have been discussed and how the present day me has tried to correct them in a quick draw-over.

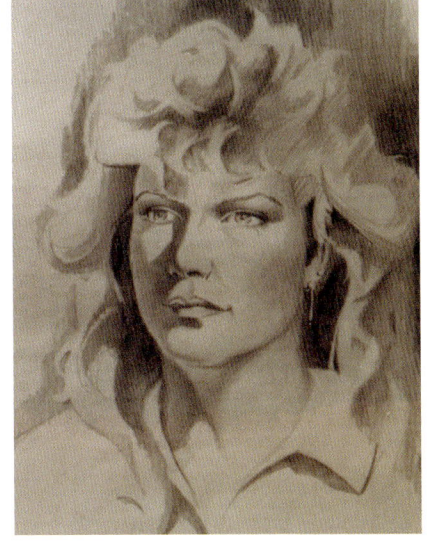 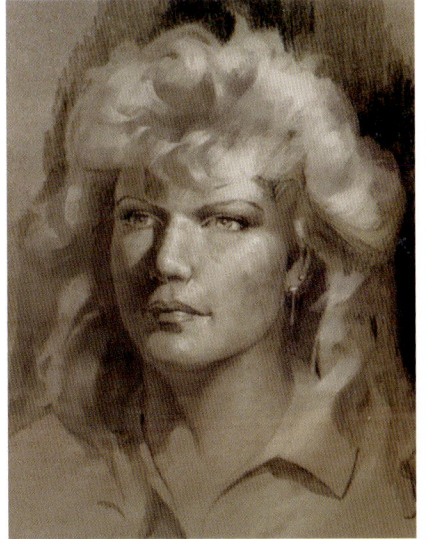

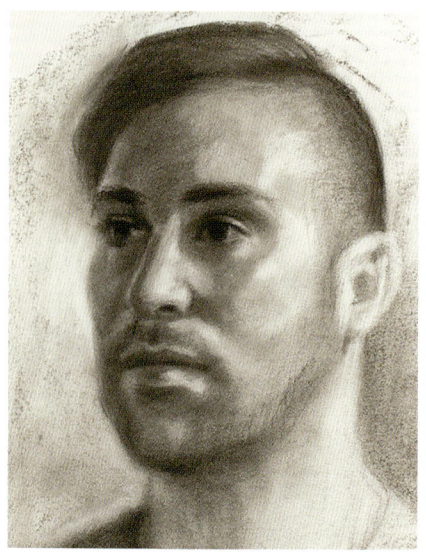
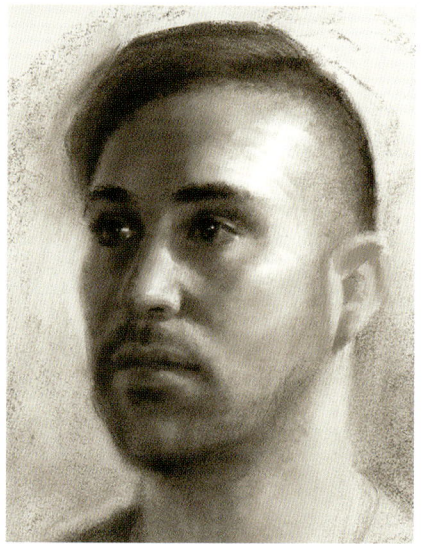

Lack of eye reflections.

Here's a student drawing in full light and shadow that's coming along quite well; it just needs a little cleanup and a special emphasis to the eyes. Notice how the highlights and adjacent halftones are over-rendered and give a bony quality despite an otherwise healthy and youthful appearance. Once again it's the tendency we all have to notice contrasts and accidentally over-render them. Additionally, the eyes feel unfinished because they don't have the natural quality of wetness present. Notice how my draw-over is quite soft and loose, and yet the highlight in the eyes gives the drawing a focused and completed quality.

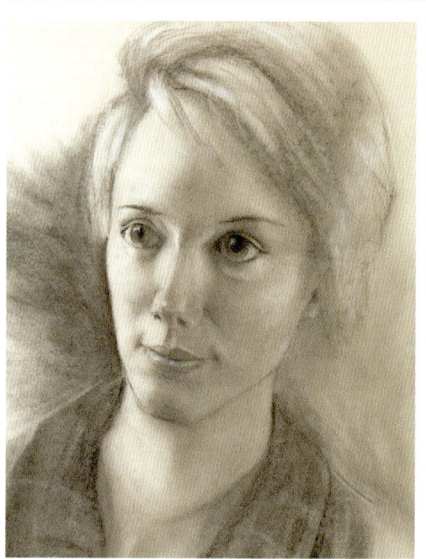
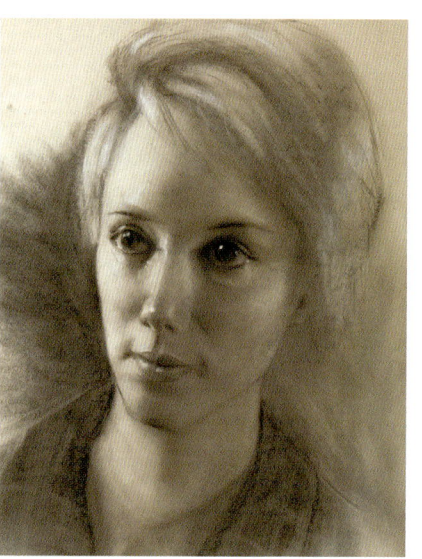

Uncommitted values.

And here we have a very nice drawing that also suffers from an unfinished quality. All it needs is a greater value range for more turning of form and extra attention given to the highlights. Natural oils on the skin give a sheen that picks up highlights, and in this case lip gloss increases the highlights on the lips as well. Finally, glistening highlights on the eyes and eyelids finish off the drawing.

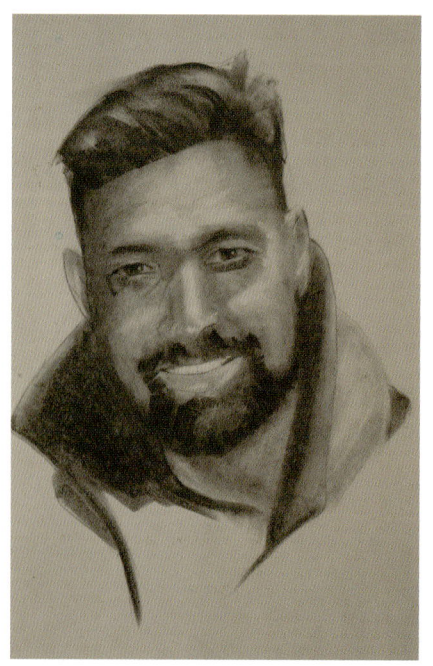
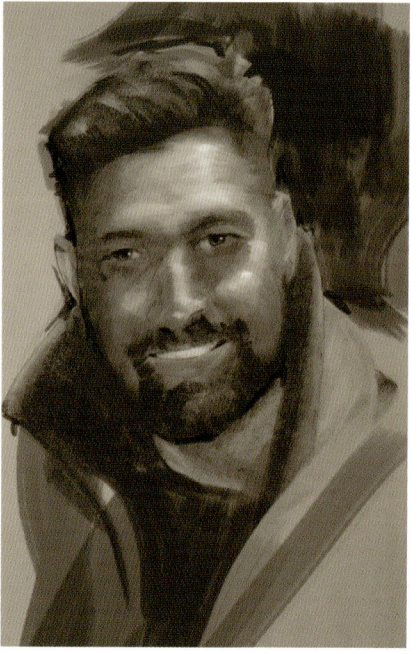

Lack of portrait composition.

Here we have a good start but an unfinished drawing. In my draw-over I'm using the previously discussed ideas of rendering light and shadow to quickly complete the face. Notice also how with a few strokes I'm able to give the study a full-page composition. The dark tones behind the head and of the jacket frame the head as well as create a diagonal movement through the picture.

Symbolic rendering.

Considering my own struggles as well as working with many students over the years, I'm very sensitive to how difficult it is to interpret the complexities of the human head. Our brain sometimes wants to turn the eyes and features into symbols and isolated parts rather than forms of light and shadow that flow into each other. This student, being early in the learning curve, struggled very much with those issues initially, so I took the time in the draw-over to convert the face into a form-driven study of light and shadow.

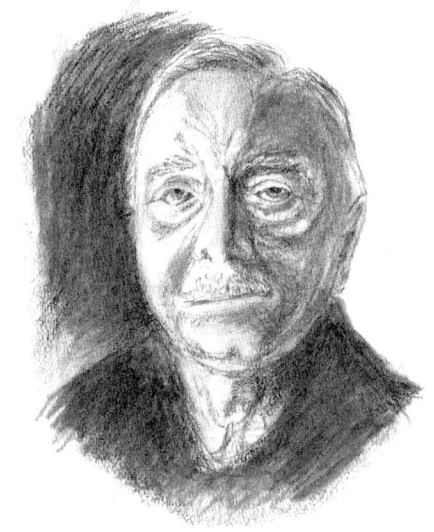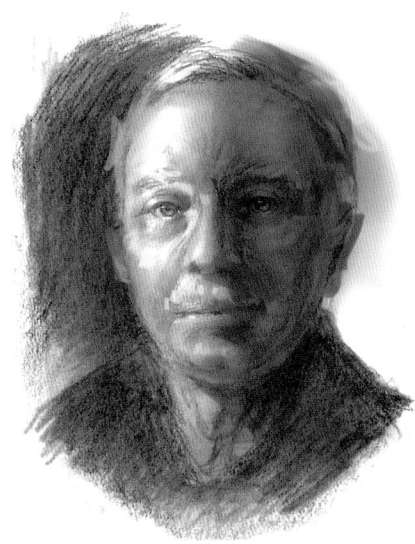

Weak luminosity in bright light.

A sense of luminosity is especially important when our subject is illuminated by the vivid brightness of the direct sun. Under these circumstances, shadows can be quite light since there's so much light bouncing around in the environment. Strong cast shadows are still very important, but there can also be a blooming effect where the radiating glow of brightly lit areas obscures adjacent shadows.

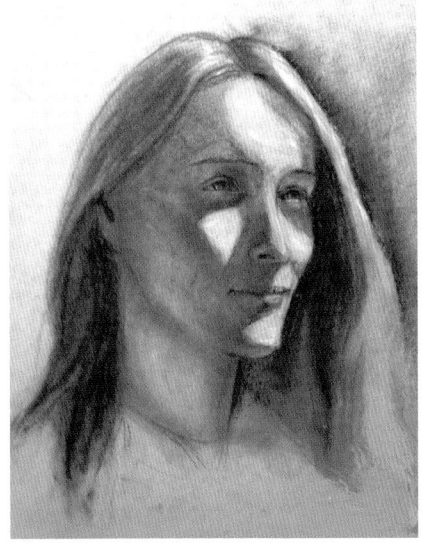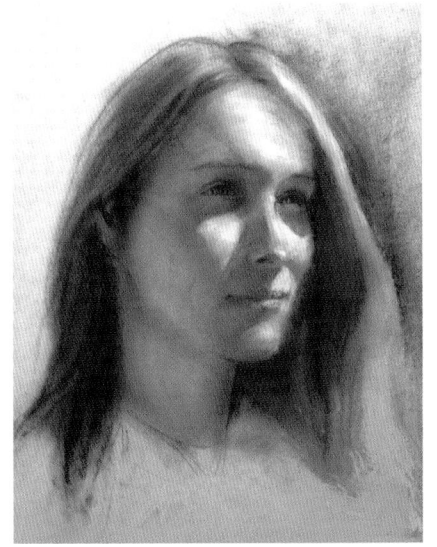

Lack of clarity in the features.

Remember that the goal in most of our portrait drawings is to bring a special emphasis to the features and character of our sitter. The student drawing here is starting to achieve that goal and just needs a little extra emphasis. Notice in my draw-over how the edges on the far right side of the face have been softened or lost against the background to avoid distraction and to create depth. I love the rim light that's coming into the shadows from the right, highlighting the features. Giving that a little extra emphasis does a great job of giving the appropriate importance to the face despite the many possible distractions elsewhere.

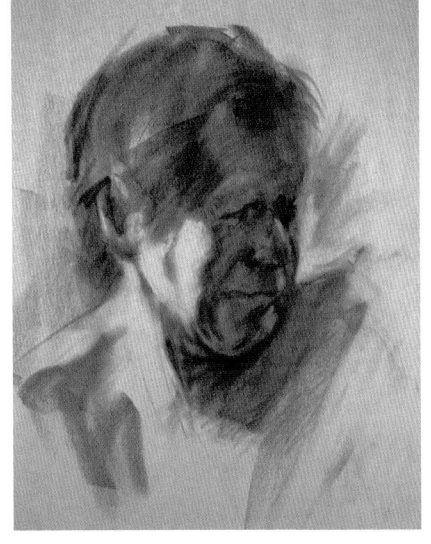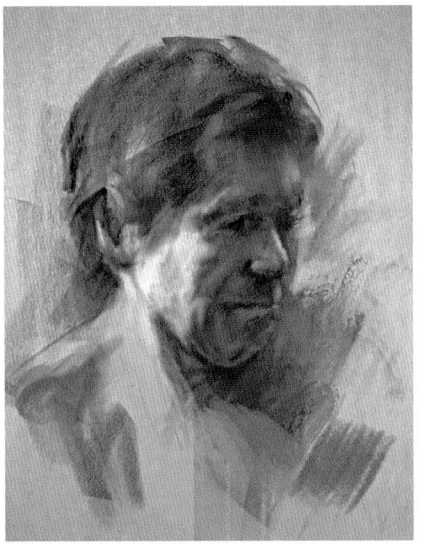

Road to Success

The group of drawings here chronicles one student's excellent improvement made in just nine weeks. As much as I would like to credit my draw-overs, the lion's share of the credit goes to the student's commitment to practice on a daily basis. Repetitive practice leads to a refinement of our abilities and a mastery of our subject. This student launched that process by accepting my challenge to practice on a daily basis. Each week he turned in numerous studies and we carefully reviewed what was working and where improvements were needed. He would dutifully apply what was learned each week and made the consistent improvements that you see here. He finished the class with a toned paper drawing that you see to the lower right, a drawing that far exceeded his abilities just nine weeks earlier. I added a few strokes to intensify the light and add a suggestion of background, but the drawing needed nothing more. On the following pages I'll review with you the exercises that we use in class to make such improvements possible for everyone.

Suggested Exercises

It takes good ideas and focused effort to make real improvement in our drawings, so let's take a moment in the next pages to review the skills required and go through a series of exercises to achieve each skill. And I do strongly suggest that you break your practice down into exercises—the quickest way to make you hate drawing is to try and take on everything at once. It's imperative to break down our learning process into manageable exercises that tackle one skill at a time.

"You can't do sketches enough; sketch everything and keep your curiosity fresh."
– John Singer Sargent

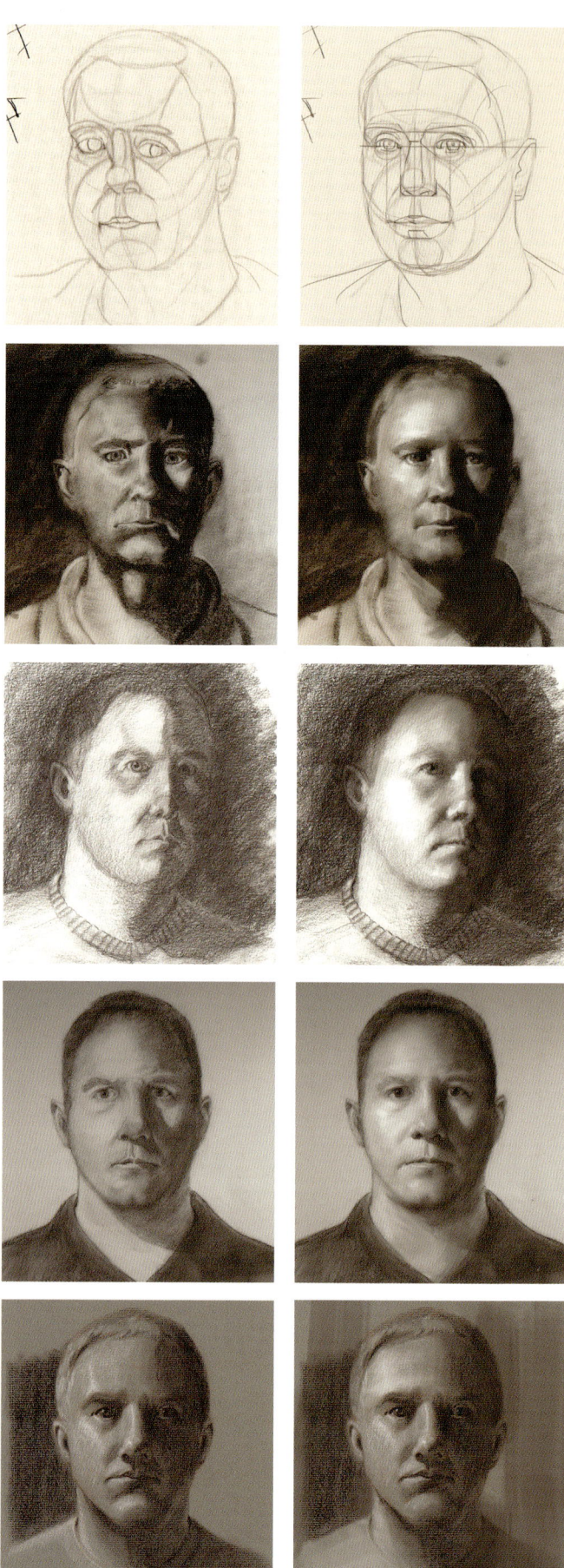

Student Drawing   Instructor Draw-Over

Exercise 1:
Do short pose studies and trace faces.

We keep coming back to the idea of consistent practice to refine our portrait drawing skills, so I recommend quick studies that emphasize construction drawing, the values of light and shadow, and portrait composition. Short pose studies force us to keep things simple and allow lots of valuable repetition. One exercise my students have found quite helpful is to lay tracing paper over photographs of people to practice construction line drawing.

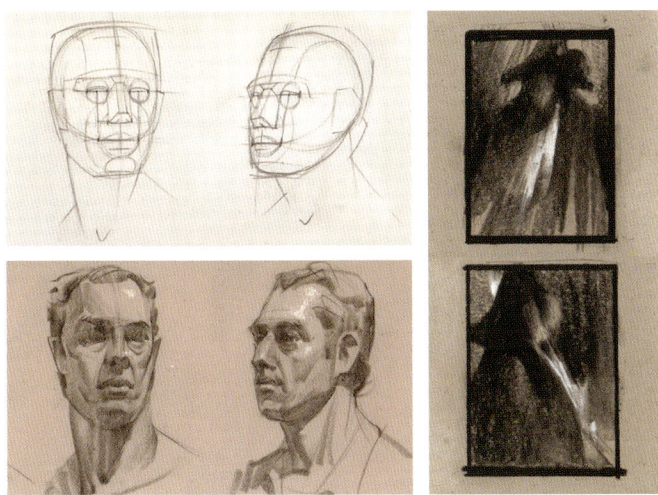

Exercise 2:
Commit to light and shadow shapes.

When working under a direct light source, it's very common for students to lose track of where the light ends and the shadow begins, so I encourage the exercise shown below. Once you've completed your construction drawing, practice making a clear commitment to what's in light and what's in shadow. Pay particular attention to the difference between sharp-edged cast shadows and soft-edged form shadows.

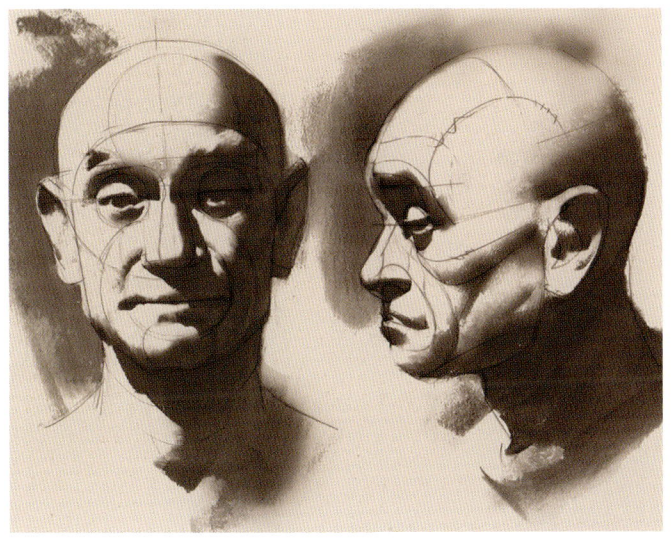

Exercise 3:
Practice with tools and techniques.

Practice and experiment with your tools as much as possible! Explore how the properties of each mark-making tool can best be used to describe form. For instance, here's a page of doodles where I'm exploring using my pencil strokes not only to create turning form but also to find an energy and visual interest in the drawing process.

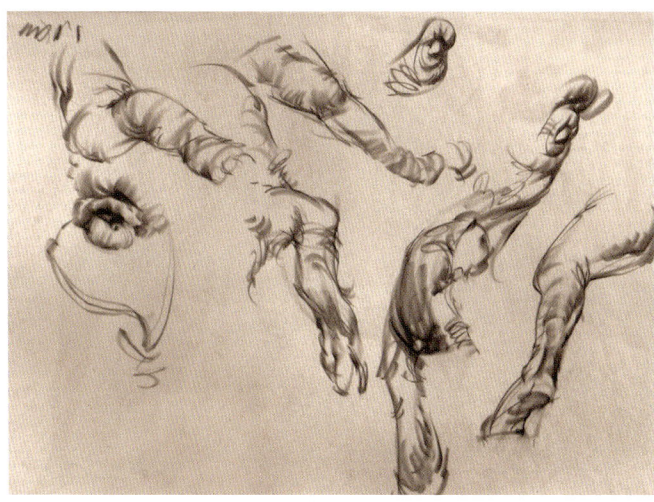

Exercise 4:
Simplify light or shadow for emphasis.

An invaluable exercise for rendering form in light and shadow is to simplify one to give emphasis to the other. Start by creating your shadows as shown in exercise 2; be willing to take them down to pure black with no form or information. This gives you the luxury of only having to worry about rendering form in the lights. Now you can take advantage of a tremendous value range to turn form as shown in the example below of the bald male. To do the opposite exercise of rendering form in shadow, take a look at the female portrait below. The subject is primarily in shadow, leaving the white of the paper for the direct lights. This version allows the luxury of a wide value range to render form in the shadows without having to worry about the lights.

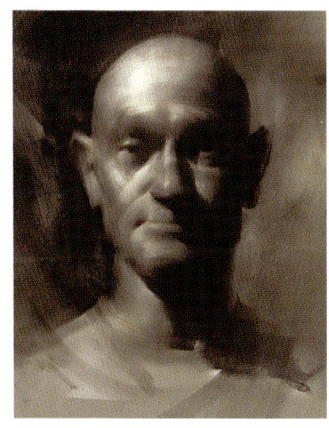
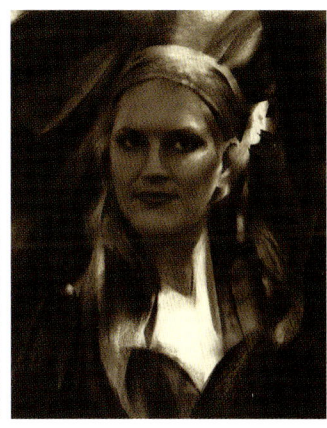

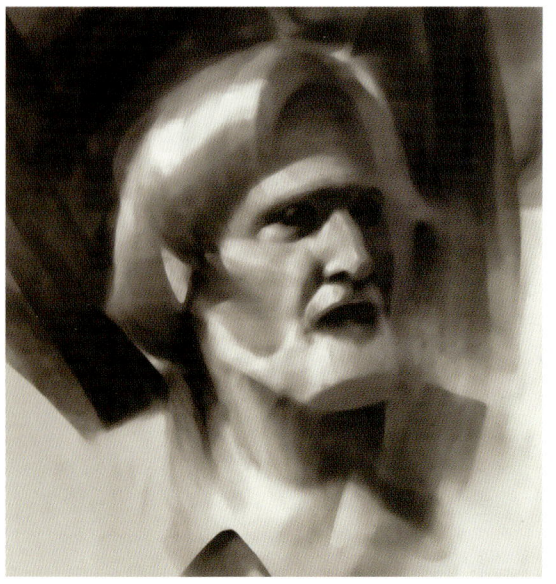

Exercise 5:
Render simplified forms.

Clarity and artistry are our tickets to success; our drawings need to clearly convey form plus a strong level of visual interest for our audience. My overwhelming experience is that our tendency to get caught up in the individual parts of anatomy can spoil the more important qualities of our drawings. So as an exercise, I strongly encourage rendering simplified forms as in the example on the left. Ignore individual details and bumps of anatomy even if they really exist, and instead do whatever it takes to create the illusion of clear turning form on your two-dimensional page.

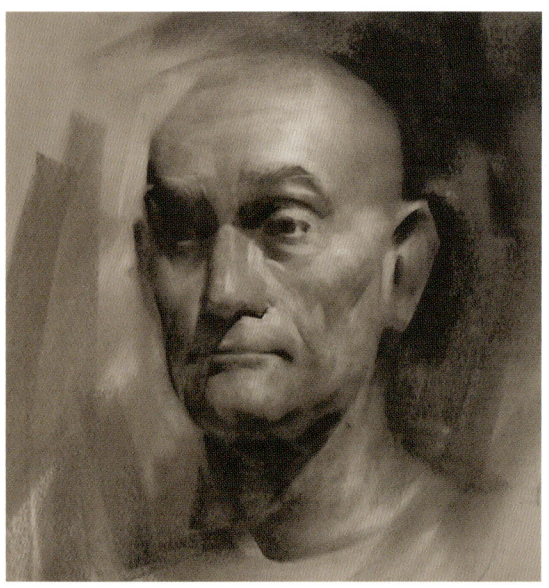

Exercise 6:
Do drawings that emphasize edges.

Be willing to go to an extreme in the design of your edges. Give yourself the exercise of doing drawings that emphasize edges (or the lack thereof) like the one on the left. Notice the firm, contrasting edges that bring a special emphasis to the features. Now notice all the soft edges elsewhere that have been designed to lower contrast and to let further edges drop away into space. Note as well that some edges are completely lost, for instance, the outside edges of the neck where the tones wrap around and disappear into the background.

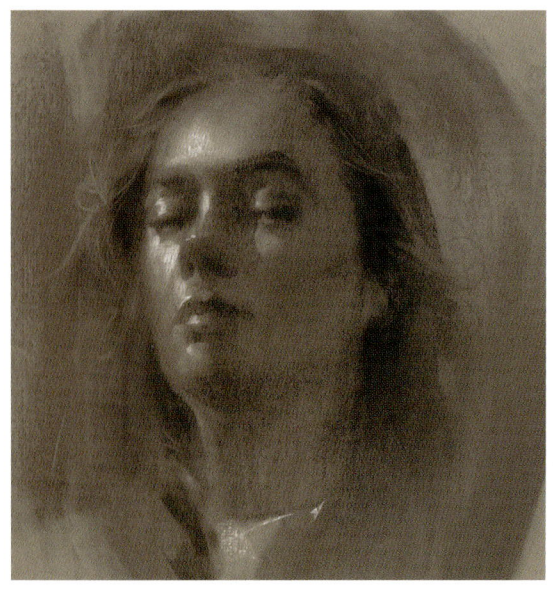

Exercise 7:
Emphasize what inspires you.

As we go through each one of these exercises, we must never lose sight of job number one: that our portraits are about something, that we in some way make something meaningful that didn't exist before we came along. So each time you draw, take a moment to think about why. What was it about your subject or circumstance that inspired you to draw? Once you've made that decision, be sure to emphasize that quality in your drawing every step of the way.

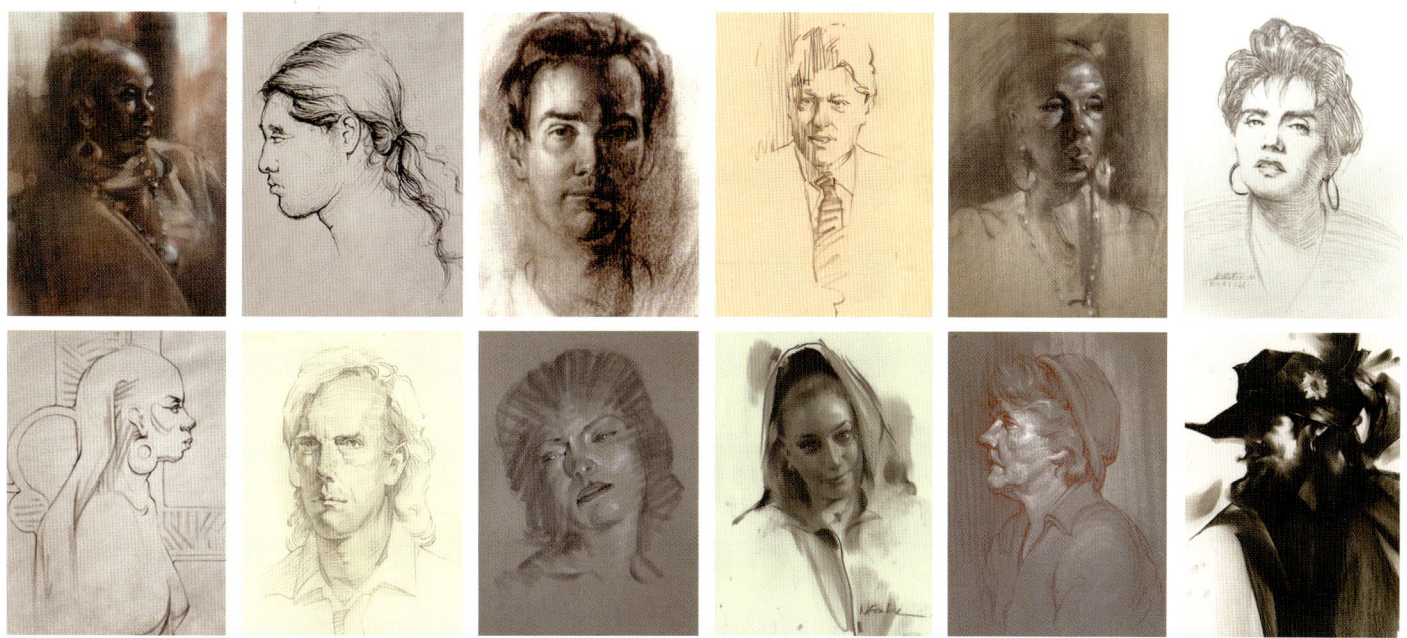

More Tips:

Experiment!

The above batch of drawings span the last 20 years and represent my various attempts to use new tools, new techniques, and new approaches. The drawings themselves aren't necessarily great, but the experience of doing them led to good things. We're all prone to falling into ruts and using techniques that deteriorate into formulas; enthusiastic experimentation helps us avoid these pitfalls as well as creates new and exciting opportunities for us.

Keep a Sketchbook

If we are to constantly practice, then we've got to make that practice fun and convenient; otherwise we won't stick with it consistently. For me, that enjoyable and consistent practice comes in the form of sketchbooks. As you might be able to tell from the photo below, I'm a fanatic on the subject of sketchbooks. And so I have stacks and stacks of sketchbooks, and I keep them in convenient spots at home, in my car, and on my work desk. Anywhere I spend any significant amount of time I make sure there's a sketchbook handy. I encourage the use of hardbound sketchbooks; not only do they hold up well, they also lend an importance to themselves that a paper-cover sketchbook might not. Happy drawing!

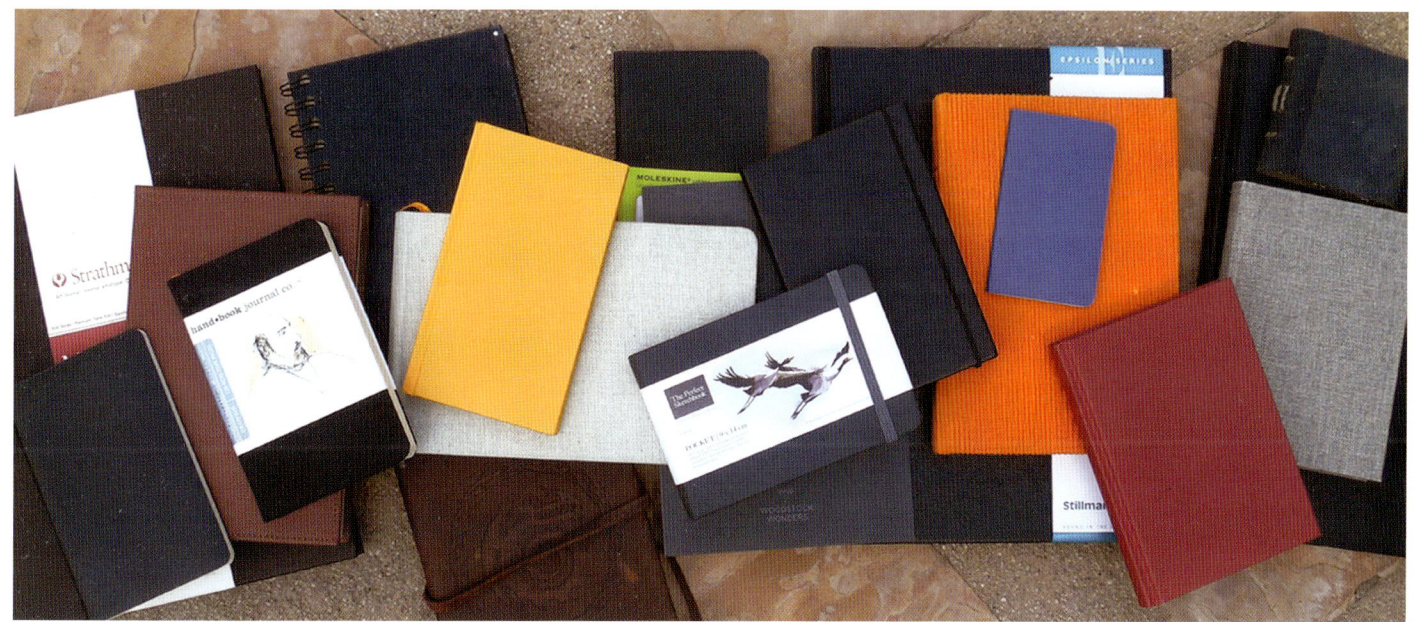

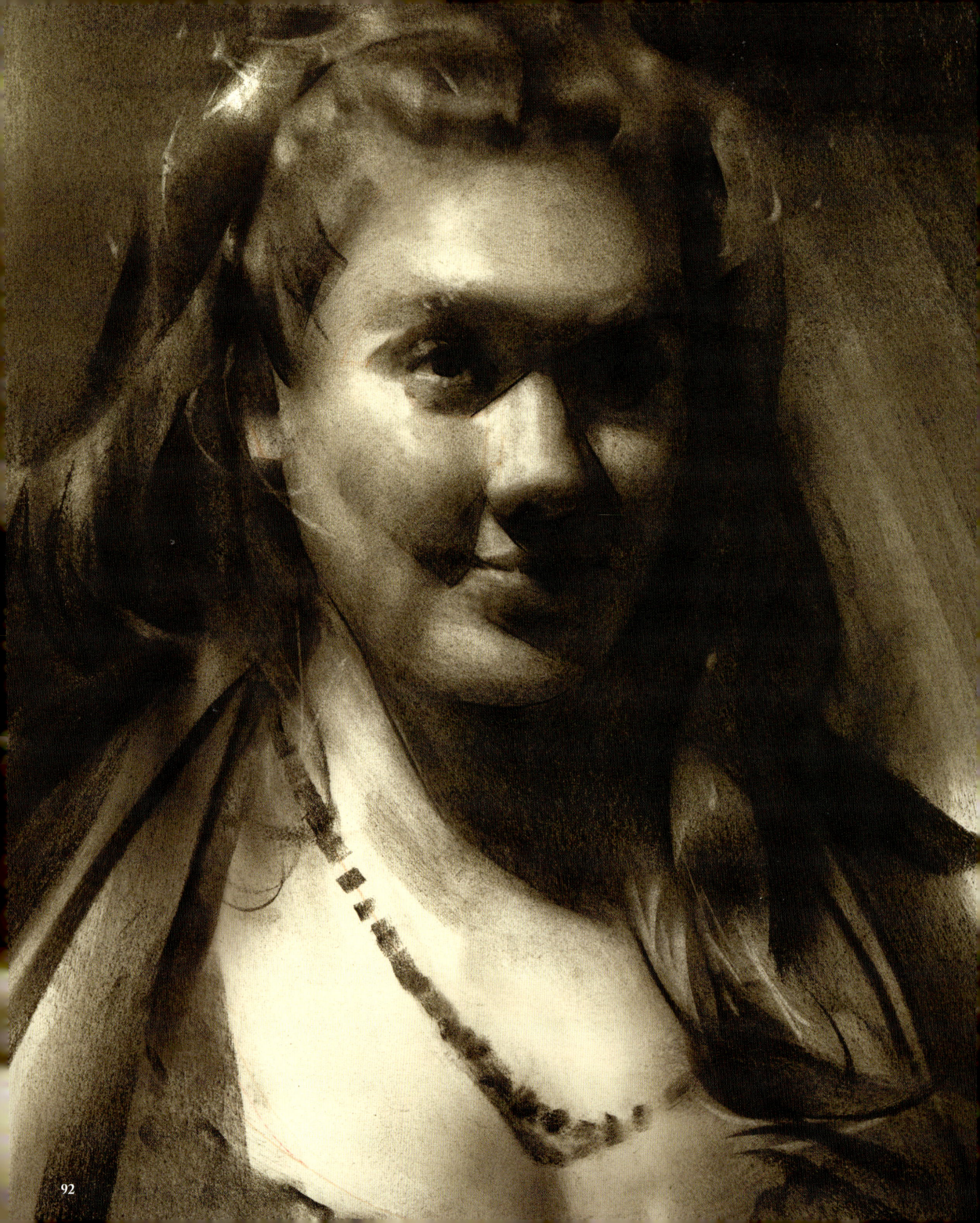

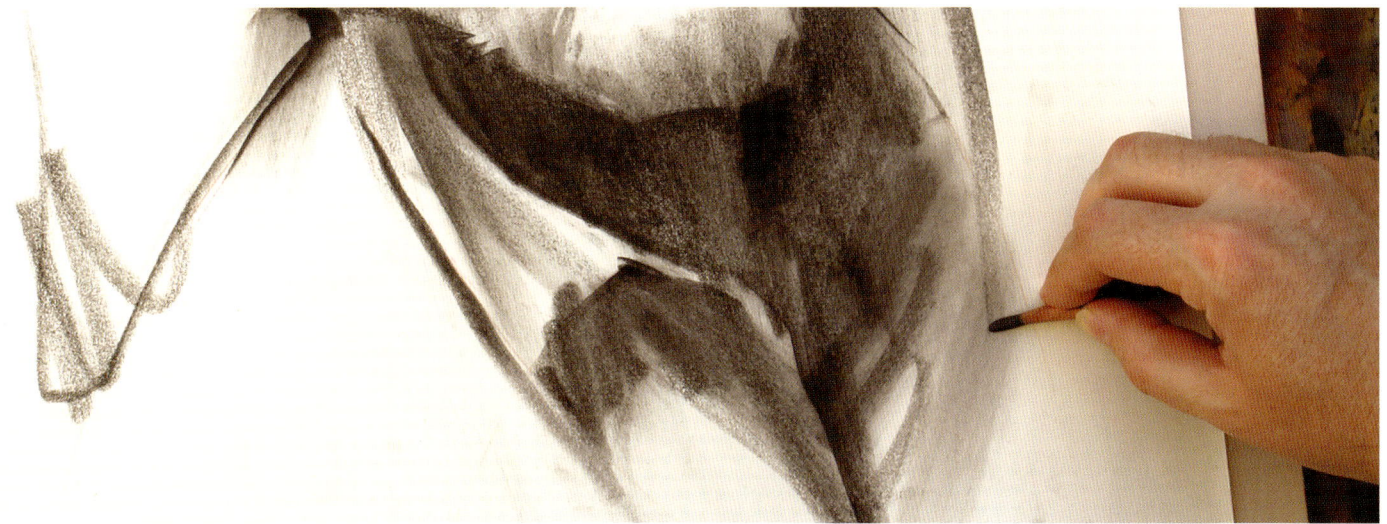

Chapter 10

Putting It All Together

When I was 15 years old, I had a summer job in Parks and Recreation. Most of the time I was very busy conducting arts and crafts projects for kids, but there were also the dead moments when I had the luxury of empty time to fill. You might be assuming that this story is ramping up to be another self-congratulatory speech about how I used that time to practice drawing, but I didn't. I used it to practice juggling.

There was a box of juggling balls handy at the park activity center, and I had always wanted to learn, so I gave it a shot. The balls spent more time on the ground than up in the air, but I stuck with it just enough to get comfortable juggling three balls. The real frustration came when I tried to introduce a fourth ball. One moment I could impress kids with my three ball juggling prowess but adding a fourth left me incapable of keeping a single one of them in the air. And that was it for my juggling career; it was just too much of a bother.

Well, learning to draw felt very much like learning to juggle. When I was coming up, I dutifully practiced some basic drawing skills and got pretty good at them, but whenever I tried to introduce a new skill, my drawings would completely fall apart—when just a moment before they had been working pretty well. I suddenly couldn't keep a single ball in the air, so to speak. I remember being shocked and discouraged at these low points in the learning curve, but I cared about drawing more than I cared about juggling, so I stuck with it.

Each chapter in this book includes the challenge of learning a new drawing skill, and so I want to assure everyone out there who is struggling that these low points are completely normal. Our work tends to get much worse as we add new skills but it's temporary; you'll come back as a much better artist if you're willing to fight through the pain. In this chapter I'll share examples and demonstrations that I hope will make your learning curve a little smoother.

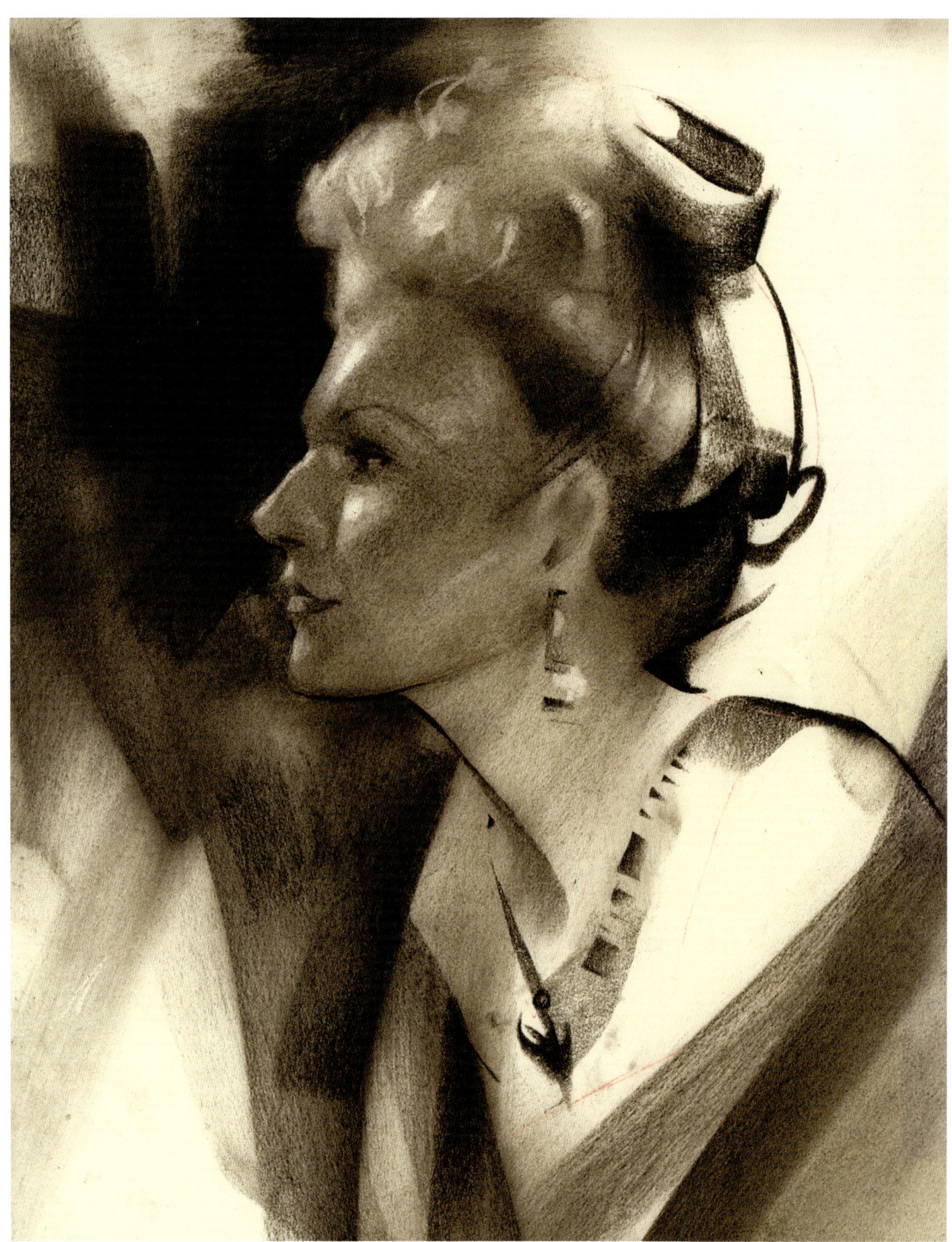

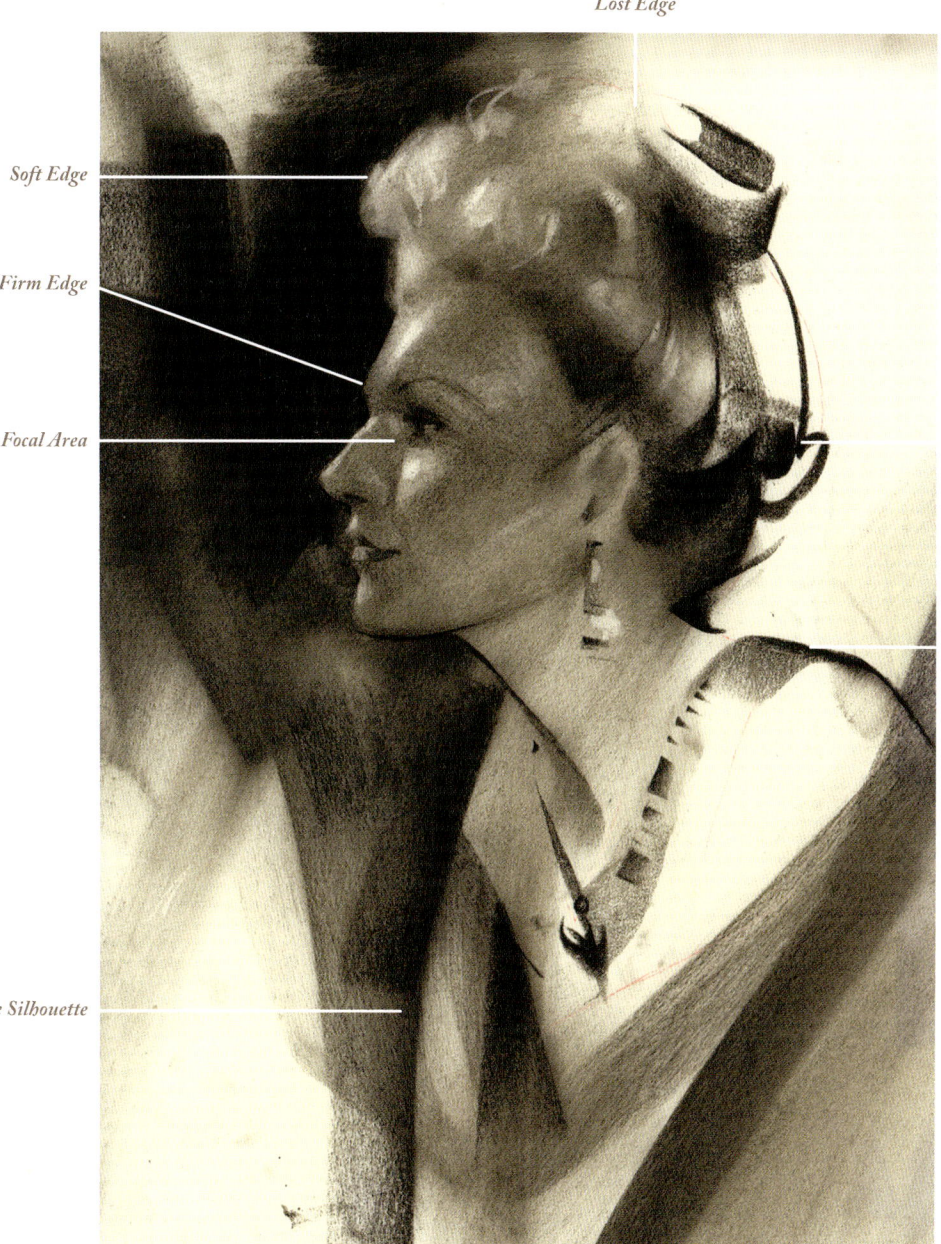

Lost Edge

Soft Edge

Firm Edge

Focal Area

Simple Silhouette

Silhouetting and Balancing Elements

Simple Silhouette

Let's use this drawing as an example for putting together our principles of drawing. I've charted out for you where each principle has been applied, and I'd like to add an additional note. I've been deeply flattered when people have liked the way that I push charcoal around and have attempted something similar in their own drawings. Sometimes though, students early in the learning curve will do so as a matter of style without regard to the specific needs of the drawing. For example, take a look at my squiggly doodad that represents the back of the hair. I love doing expressive strokes like these; they've become a noticeable part of my style. But I'd also like to point out that the same doodad serves two very important purposes beyond mere style.

First, it carefully completes the silhouette of the head, giving the portrait a cohesive presence. Second, it creates visual balance; the left side of the drawing is heavily weighted with visual interest and a counterweight is very much needed for balance on the opposite side.

On the following pages I've put together several demonstrations for you. I'll add a few notes where needed, but at this point my hope is that our principles are firmly in place and the steps will speak for themselves.

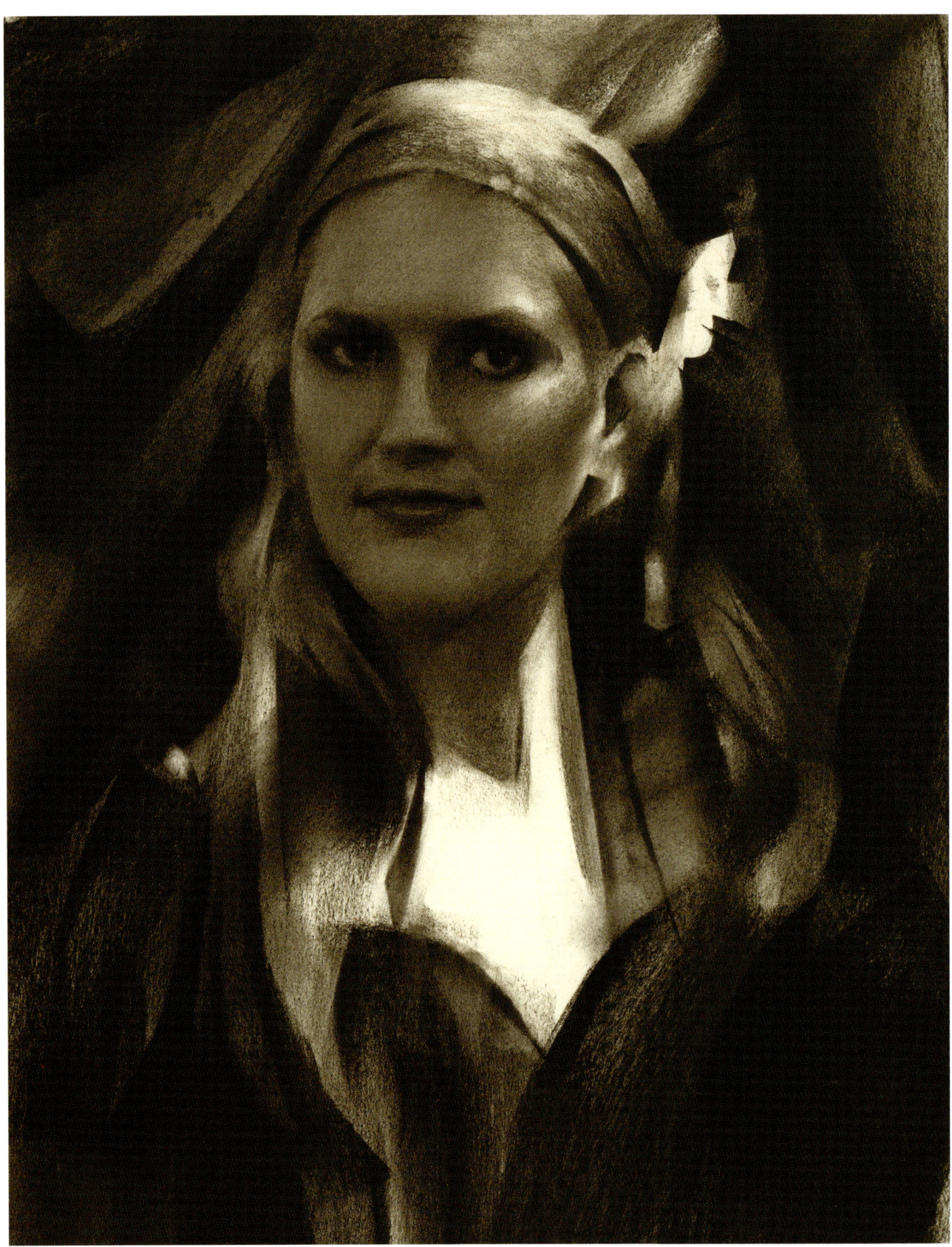

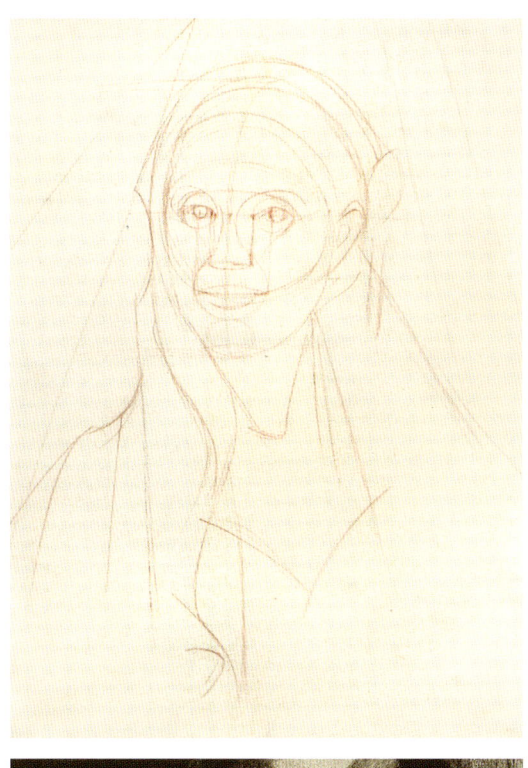
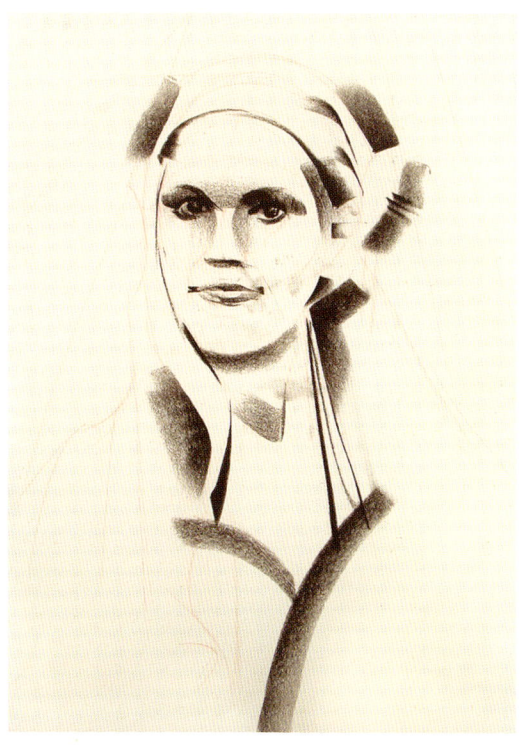
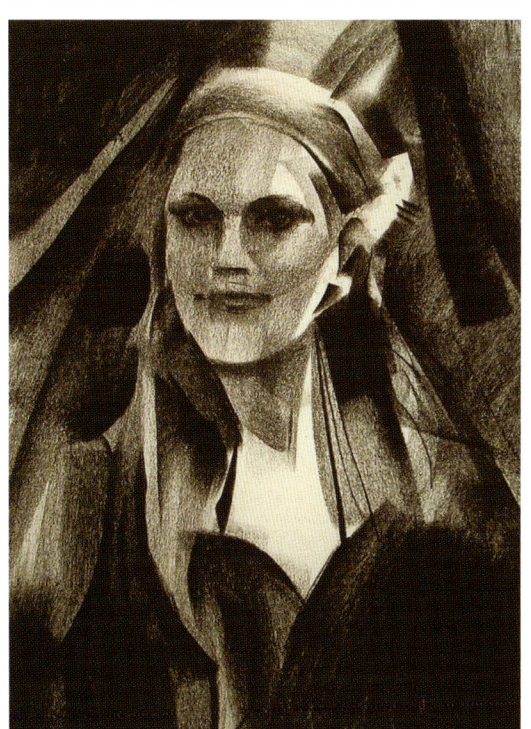
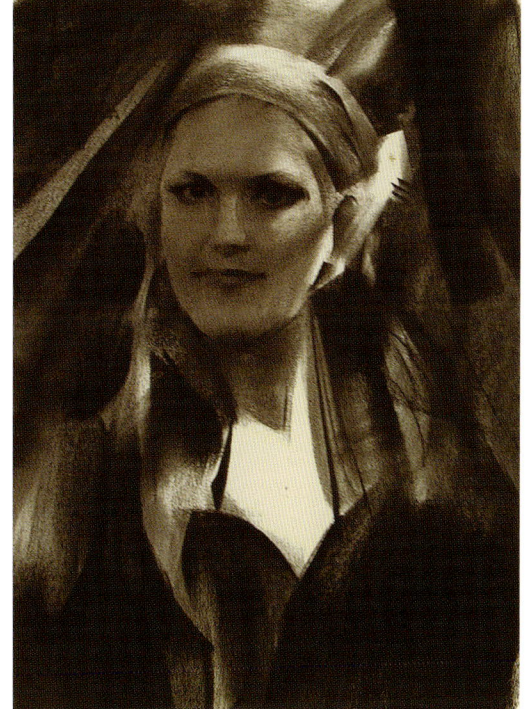
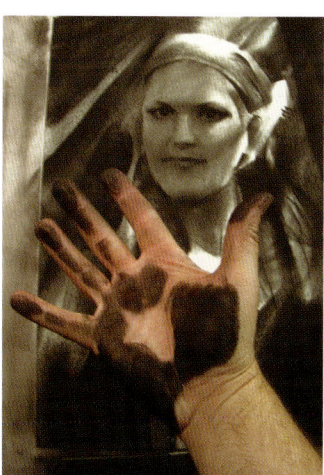

This demonstration gives you a firsthand look at the toll my technique takes on my personal cleanliness. Some students come to my classes interested in learning my specific technique, but then when they see what's required they're sometimes not so enthusiastic. I consider this to be a good thing; I don't care how exactly they get to their end result as long as they carefully design for clarity and artistry in their portraits. Personal style and technique will slowly emerge over time as they strive for those goals.

For this drawing, the sitter had an intense gaze and was primarily in shadow. I tried to take advantage of this by letting the light shapes add a strong visual interest surrounding the face and by pushing the background and shirt into a simple, dark mass. Note that in the first step, I've artificially darkened the lines here so that you can see them clearly. I actually drew them very lightly as you can see in the second step.

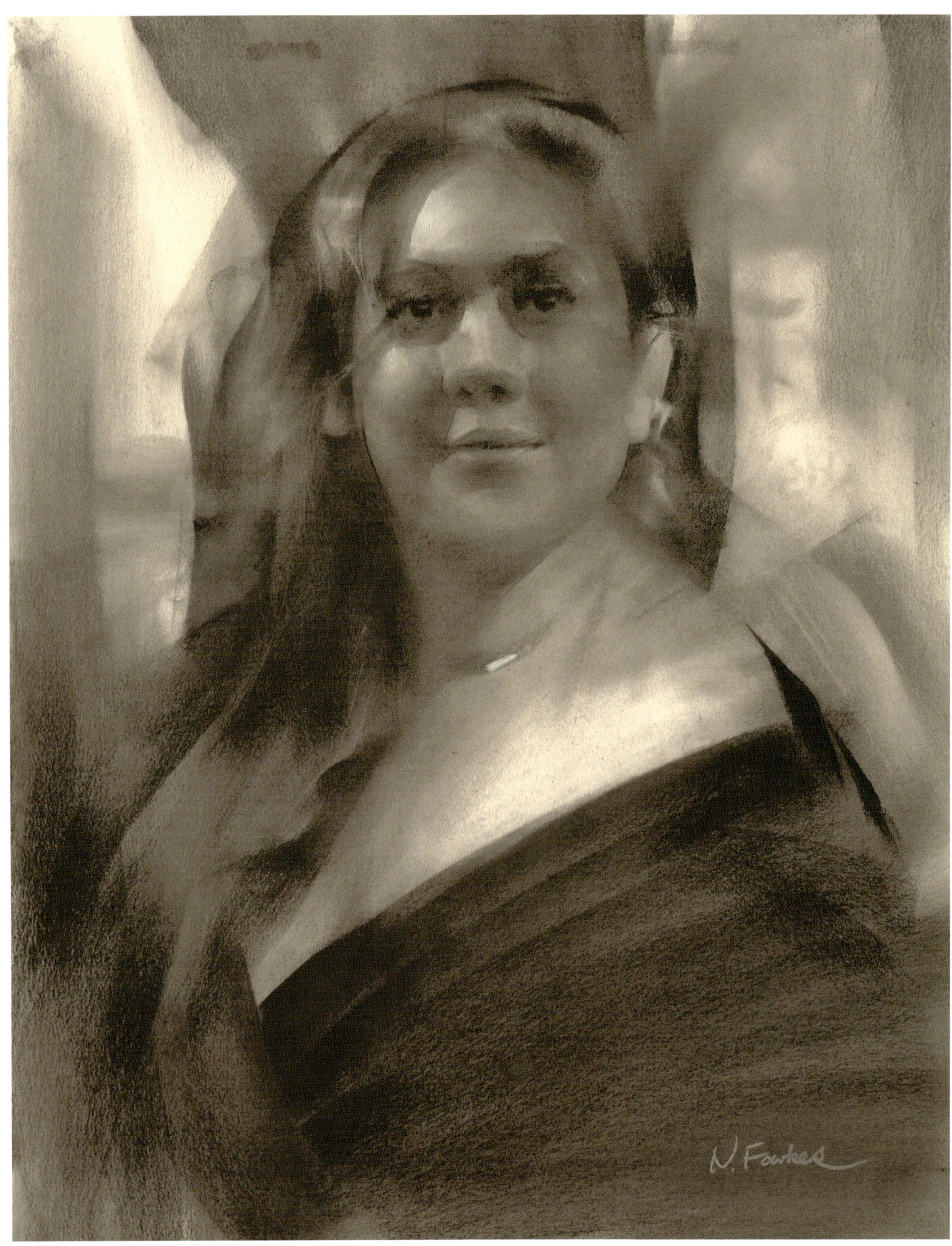

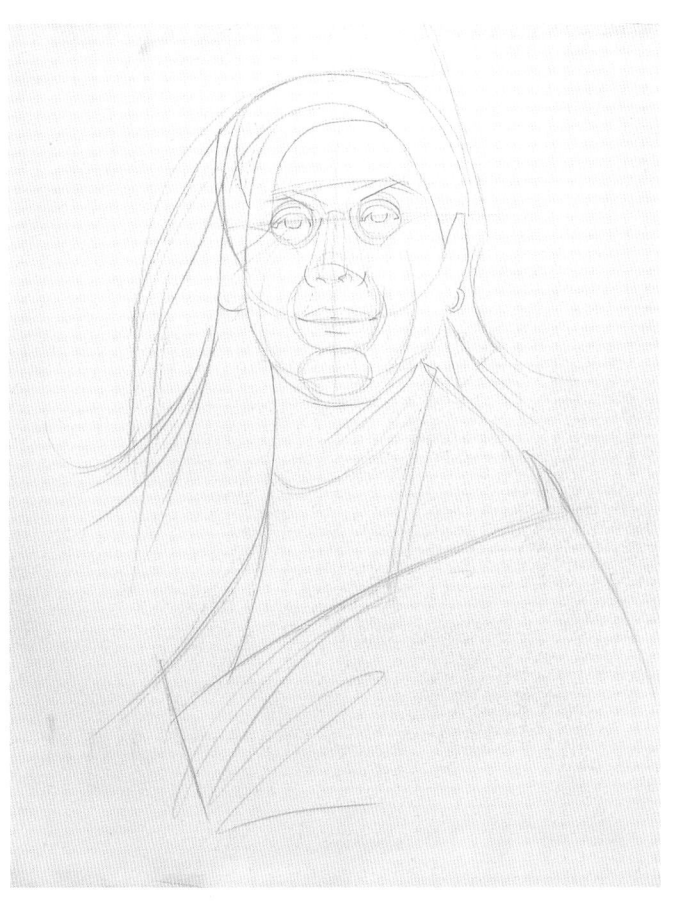
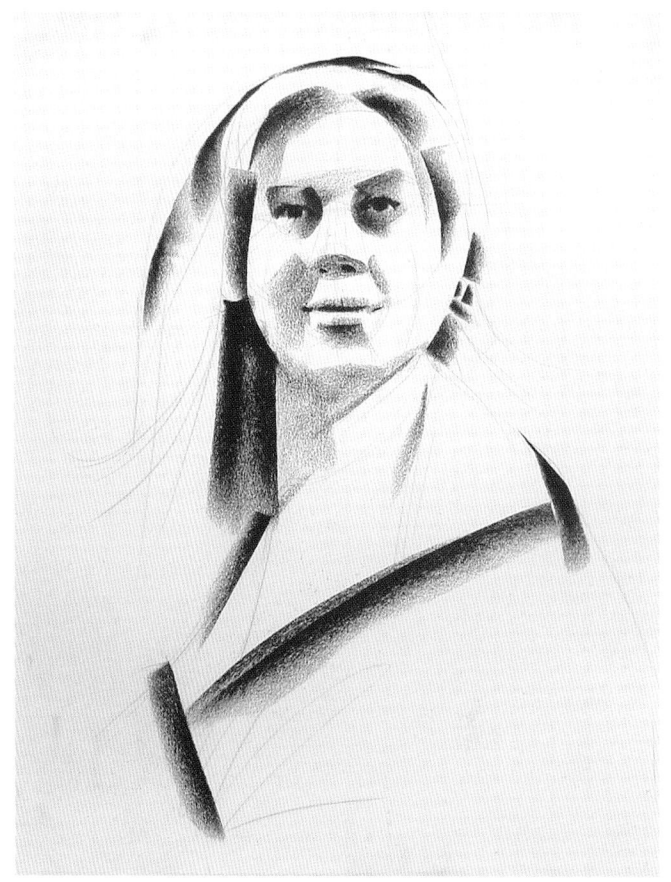
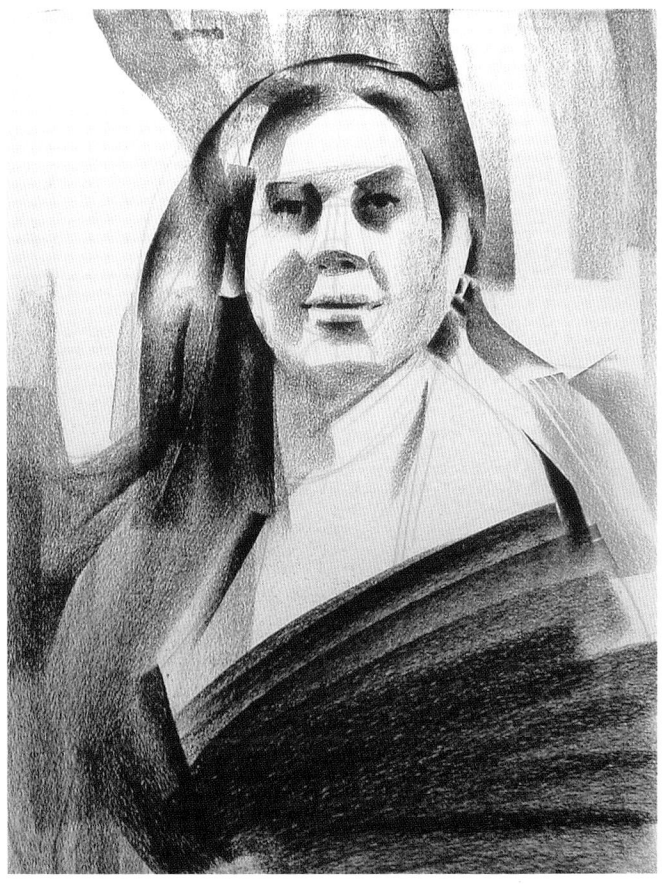
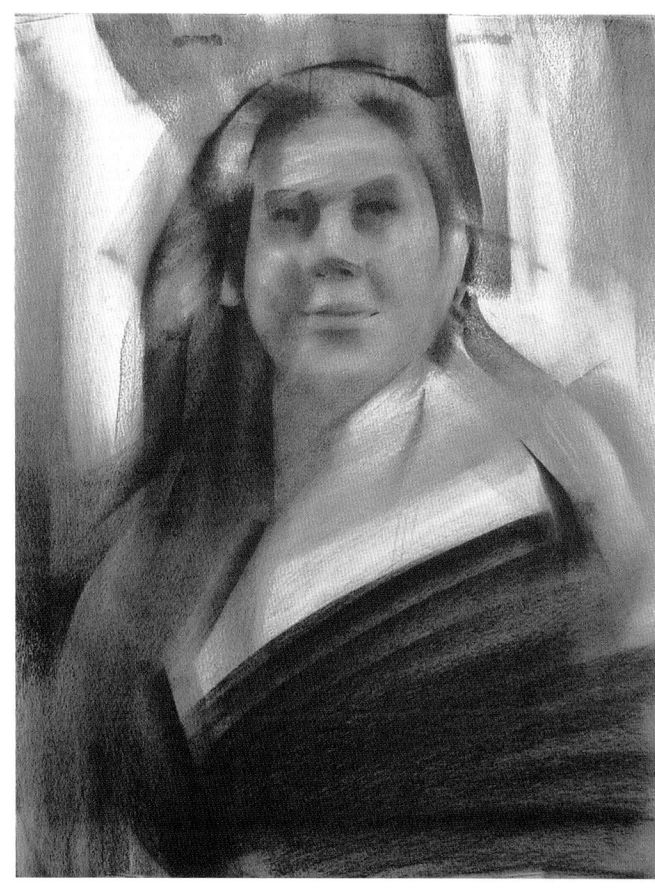

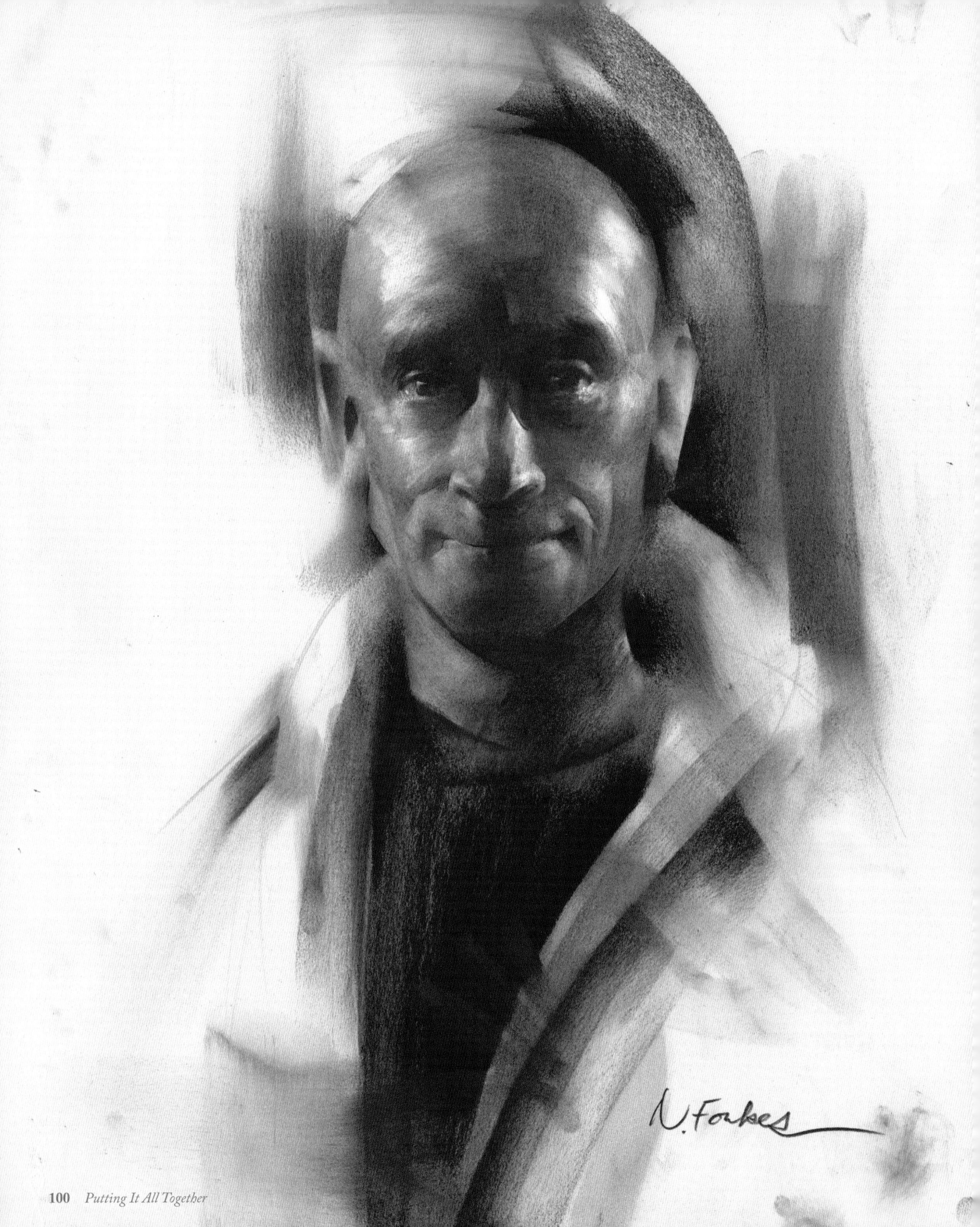

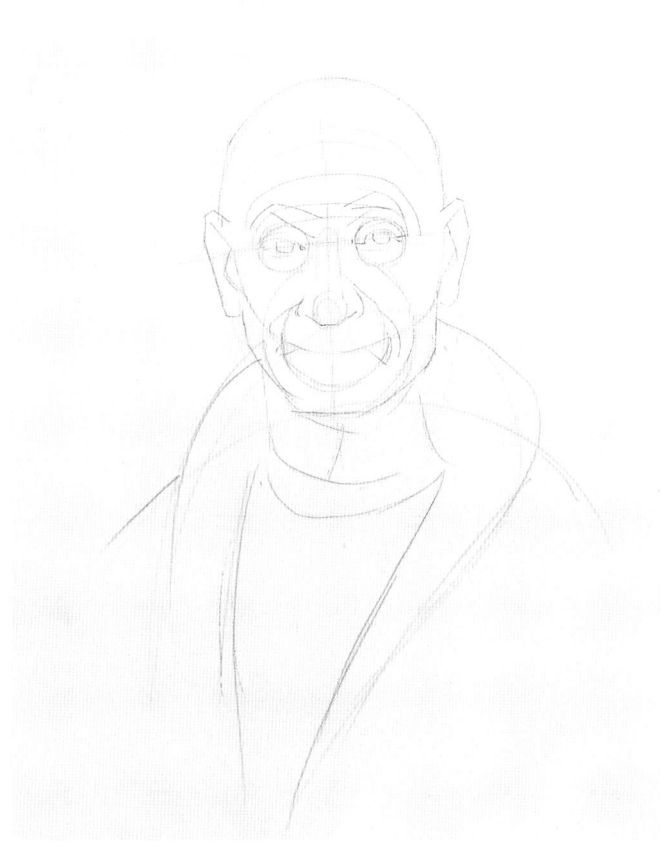

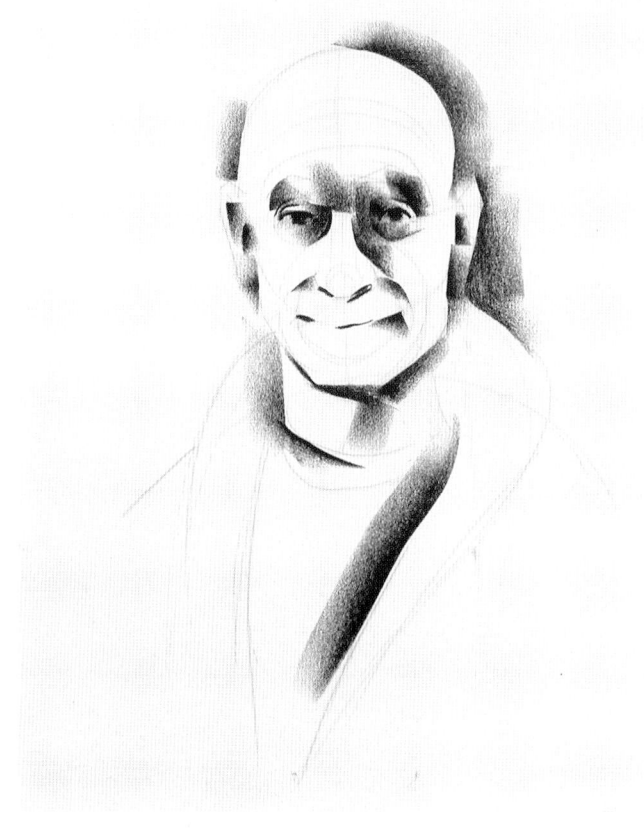

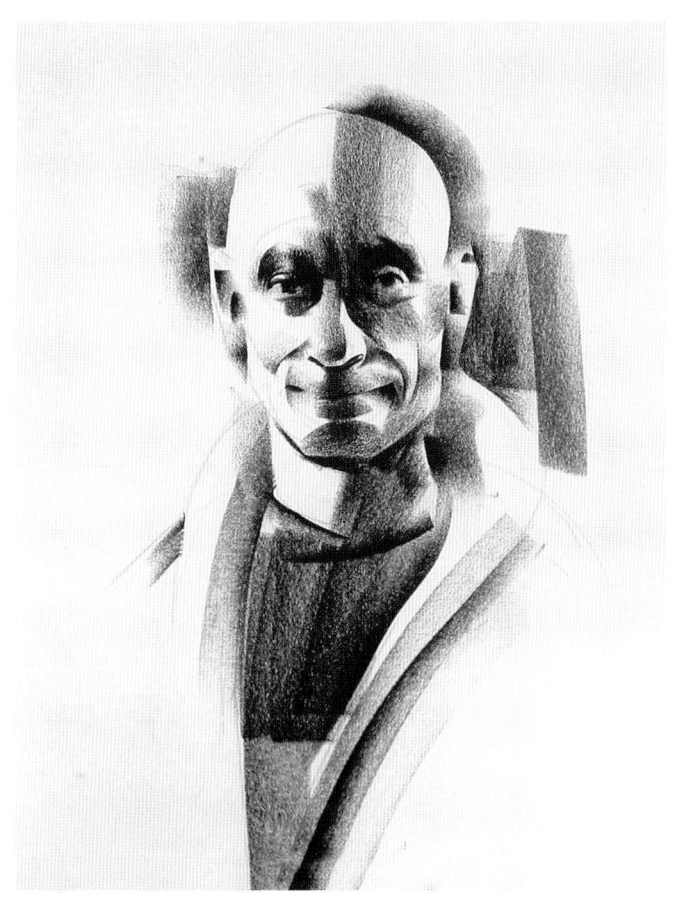

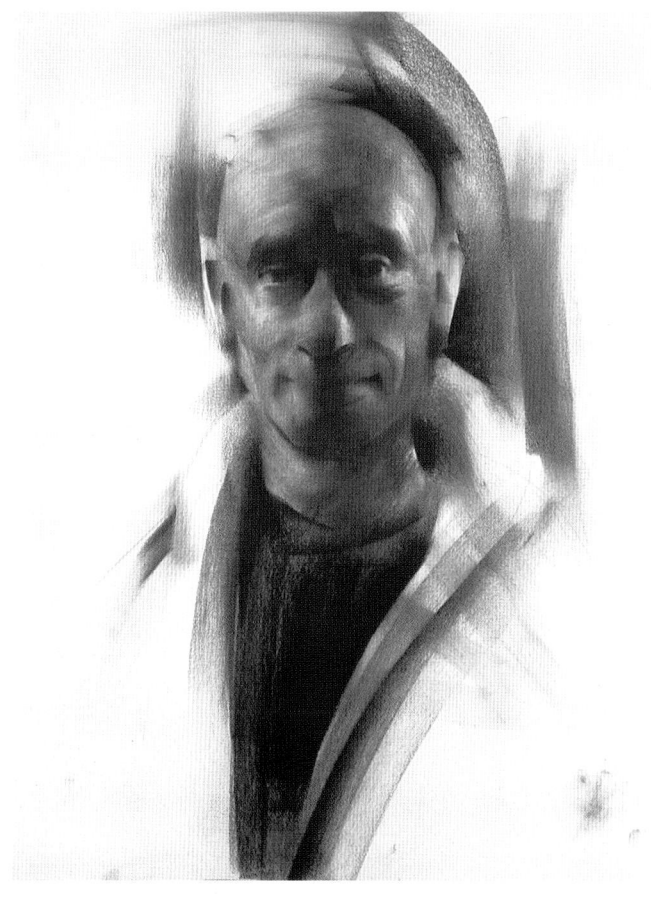

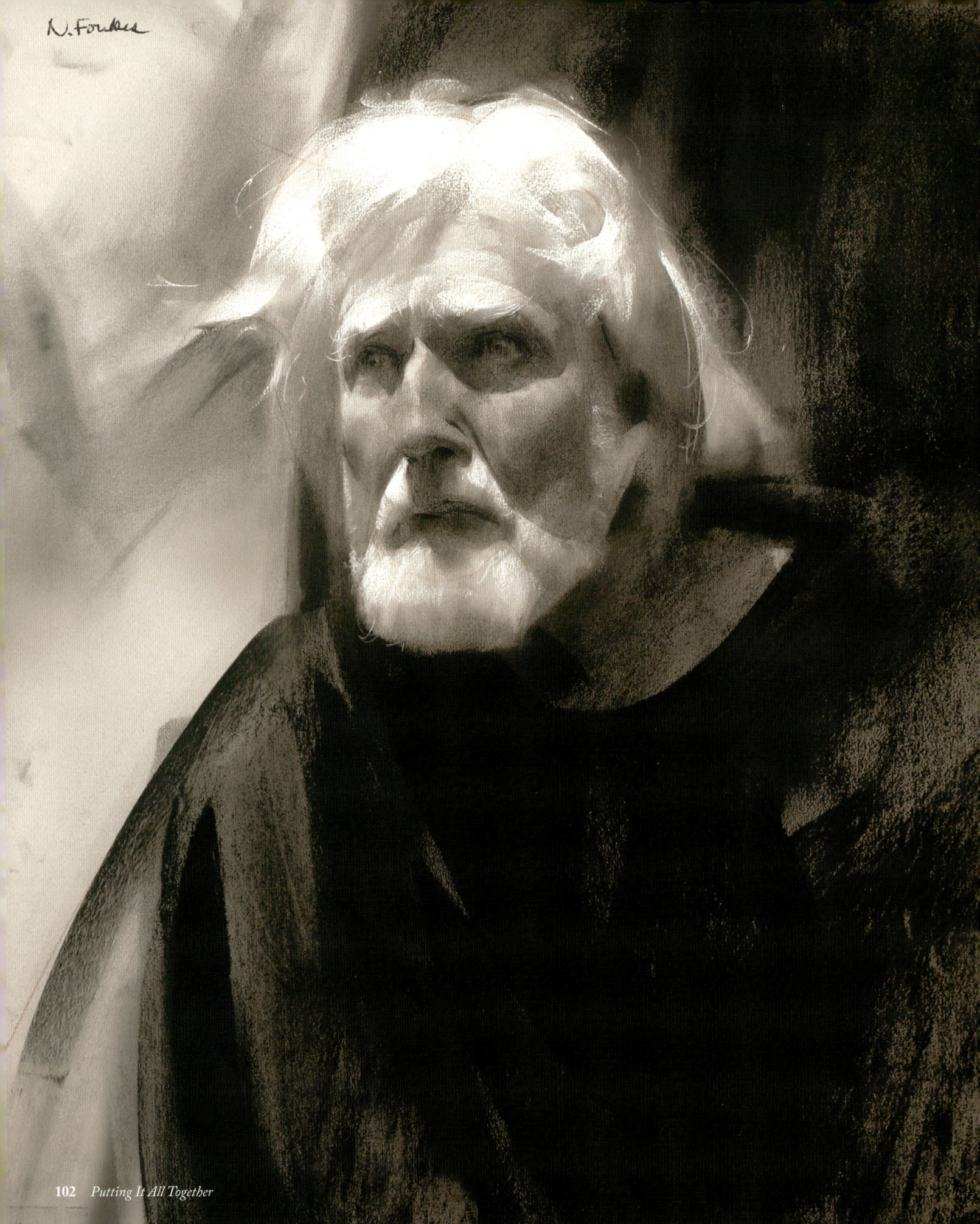

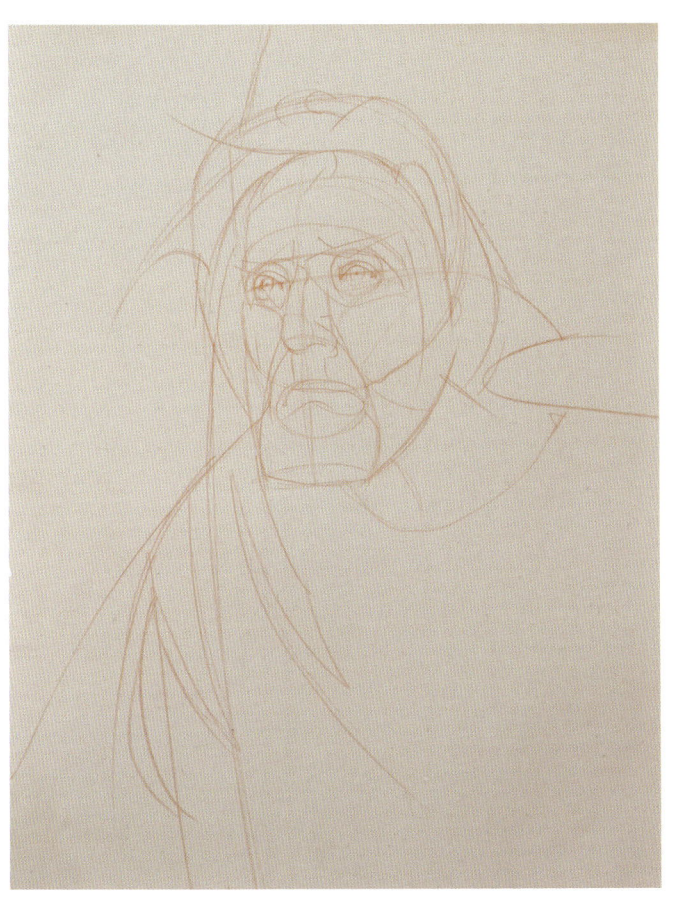
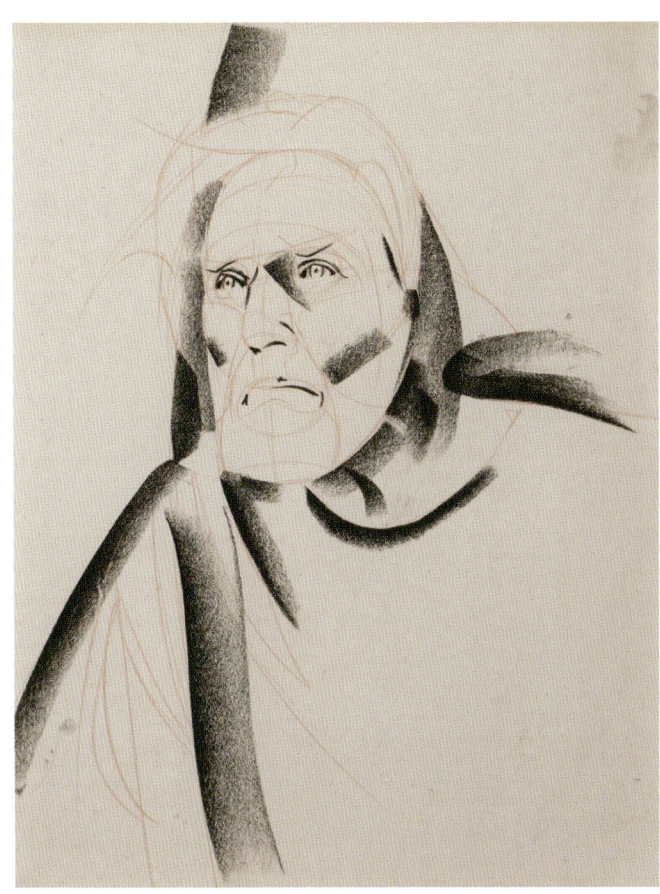
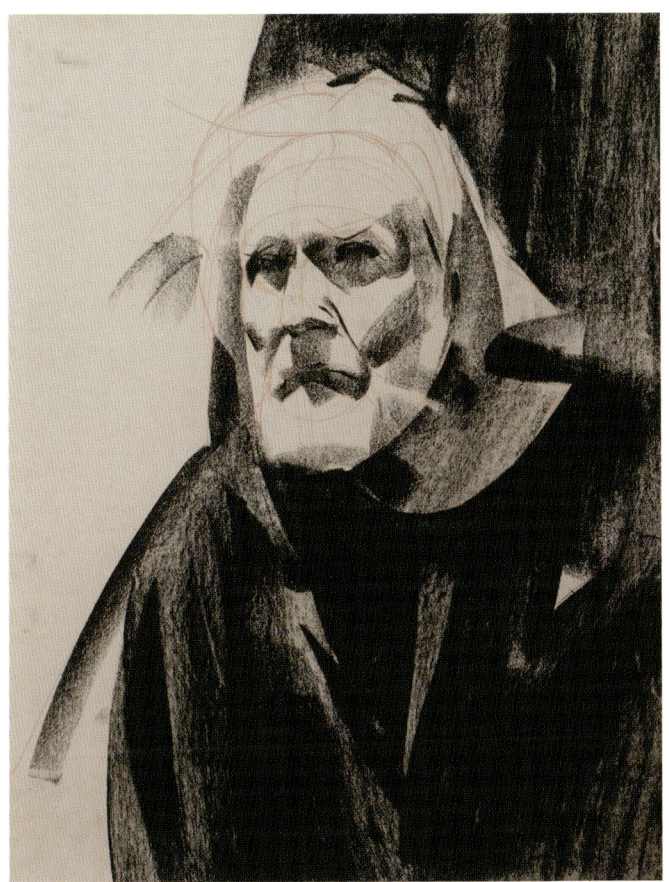
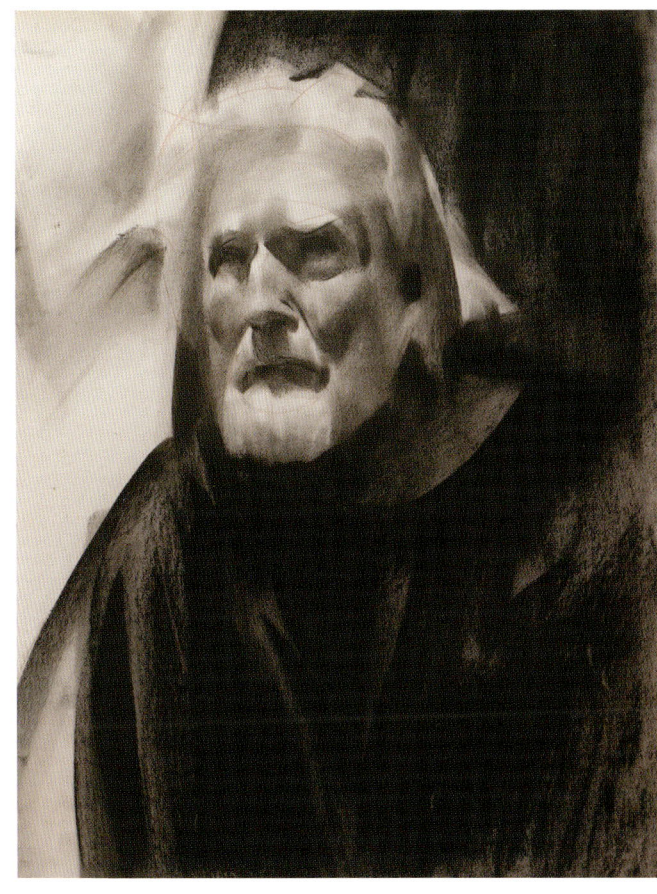

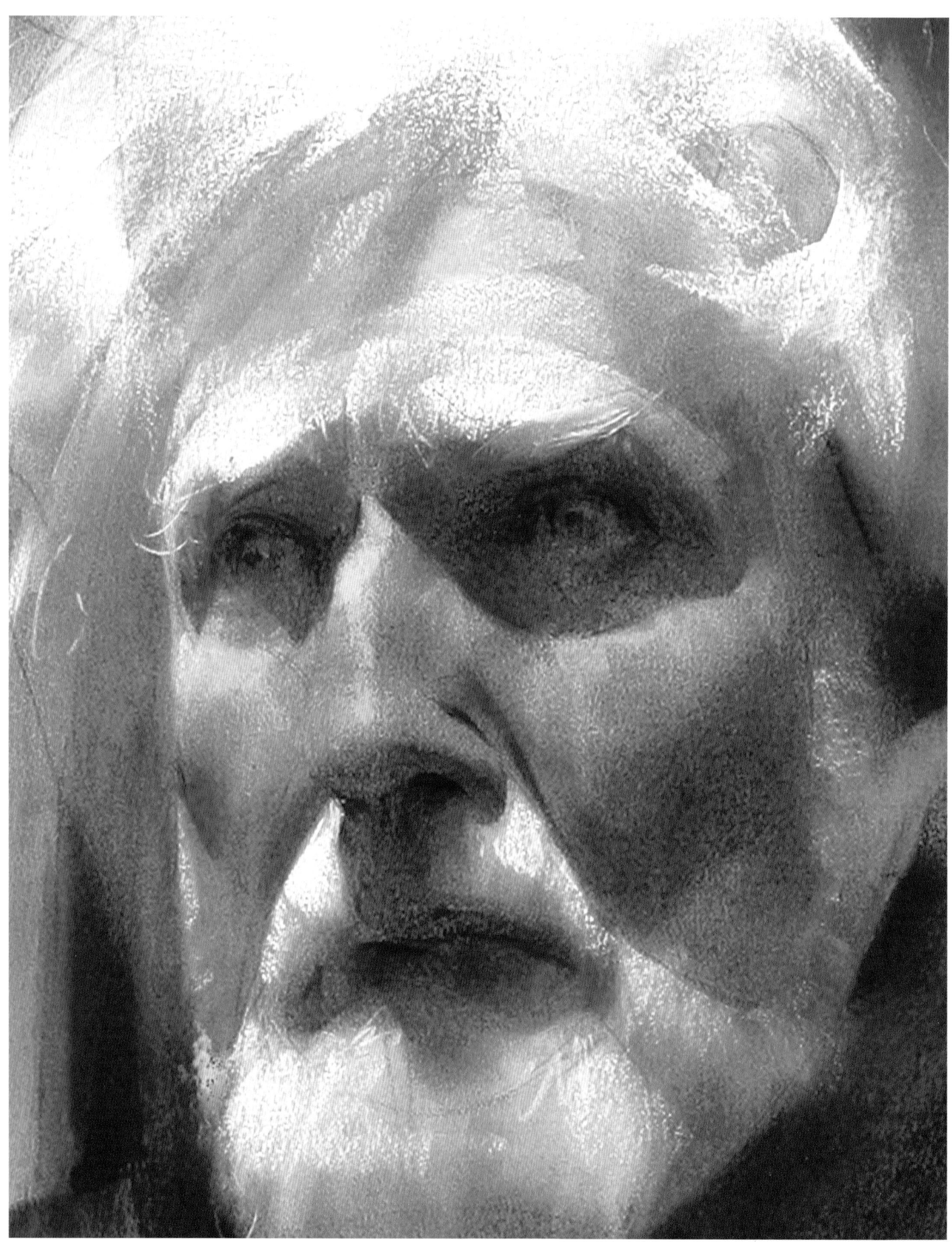

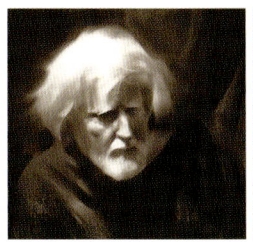 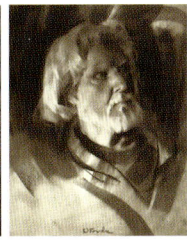 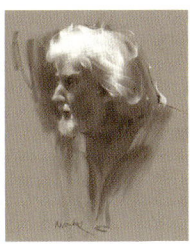 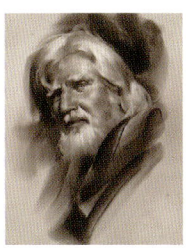 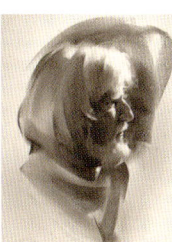 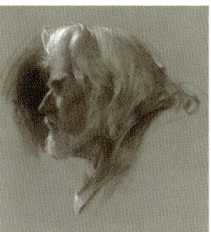 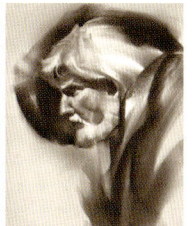

Story of the Person

With all of our discussion on rendering form let's not lose sight of the end goal; our portraits are a study of the character of our sitter. A good likeness comes from good observation, which has been a theme throughout this book; let me add an additional tip.

It can be helpful to slightly caricature your subject so look for the characteristics that are especially unique about your sitter. Is the shape of the head more round or more square? Is it long or short? Does the person have a prominent nose? Deep-set eyes? Start off your drawing session by making a careful observation of character, and then be careful to emphasize it throughout the drawing process.

To emphasize this point, let me share with you the story of the man shown here. This is Clark Allen, a favorite model of Los Angeles art students until his passing a few years back. Clark had a great face, framed by his extraordinary mane of white hair and beard, but his personality and backstory went much deeper than outward appearance. Clark was one of those people you very much hope you have the opportunity to meet and work with as an artist because he was a colorful character from the very beginning.

I first met Clark when I was studying at the Art Center College of Design in Pasadena, California. Clark was a regular at the school as a costume and portrait model, and years later, when I started teaching, he became a regular in my classes as well. During long drawing sessions he would tell stories of his past escapades, and frankly, those experiences were so outrageous that you just had to believe he was weaving tall tales. They may have been based on a kernel of truth but then became bigger and bigger as the years went by.

Well, one night I was over at Clark's house going through his extensive costume collection for an upcoming drawing session; he had an entire room of his house dedicated to his amazing costume collection. He also let me thumb through his volumes of photo albums before I left. Clark had told stories about being on the set of the film One-Eyed Jacks with Marlon Brando, and about Marlon Brando making a pass at Clark's wife right in front of him. He told stories about touring the country with Bette Davis as a performer and that she, in fact, made a pass at him during the tour. He told stories about appearing as a character on the Twilight Zone television series and eventually becoming the owner and operator of the El Cid, an iconic Hollywood flamenco club. As I thumbed through the photo album, there was Clark on a movie set with his arm around Marlon Brando, and on the next page there he was, touring the country at a variety of venues with Bette Davis, along with dozens of other colorful events, venues, and costumes. The "tall" tales that he told were all true!

From that point forward I always asked Clark for more stories and learned much more, eventually hearing about the tragic turn his life took. Late one night after hours at the El Cid, Clark was robbed, and during the encounter he was shot and left for dead. It was a very long recovery for Clark; he left his old life behind and eventually began working full-time as an artist's model. That was Clark's backstory at the time that I met him.

The portrait detail shown to the left was the very last portrait that I did of Clark a few months before he passed away. He knew his health was failing and carried a forlorn expression and the thousand-yard stare of a man at the twilight of his life. Those were the circumstances of this particular portrait and its expression. I did dozens of portraits of Clark over the years, a handful of which are shown here and can be found full-size elsewhere in this book. I hope very much that as a group they represent the man and his delightfully expressive character.

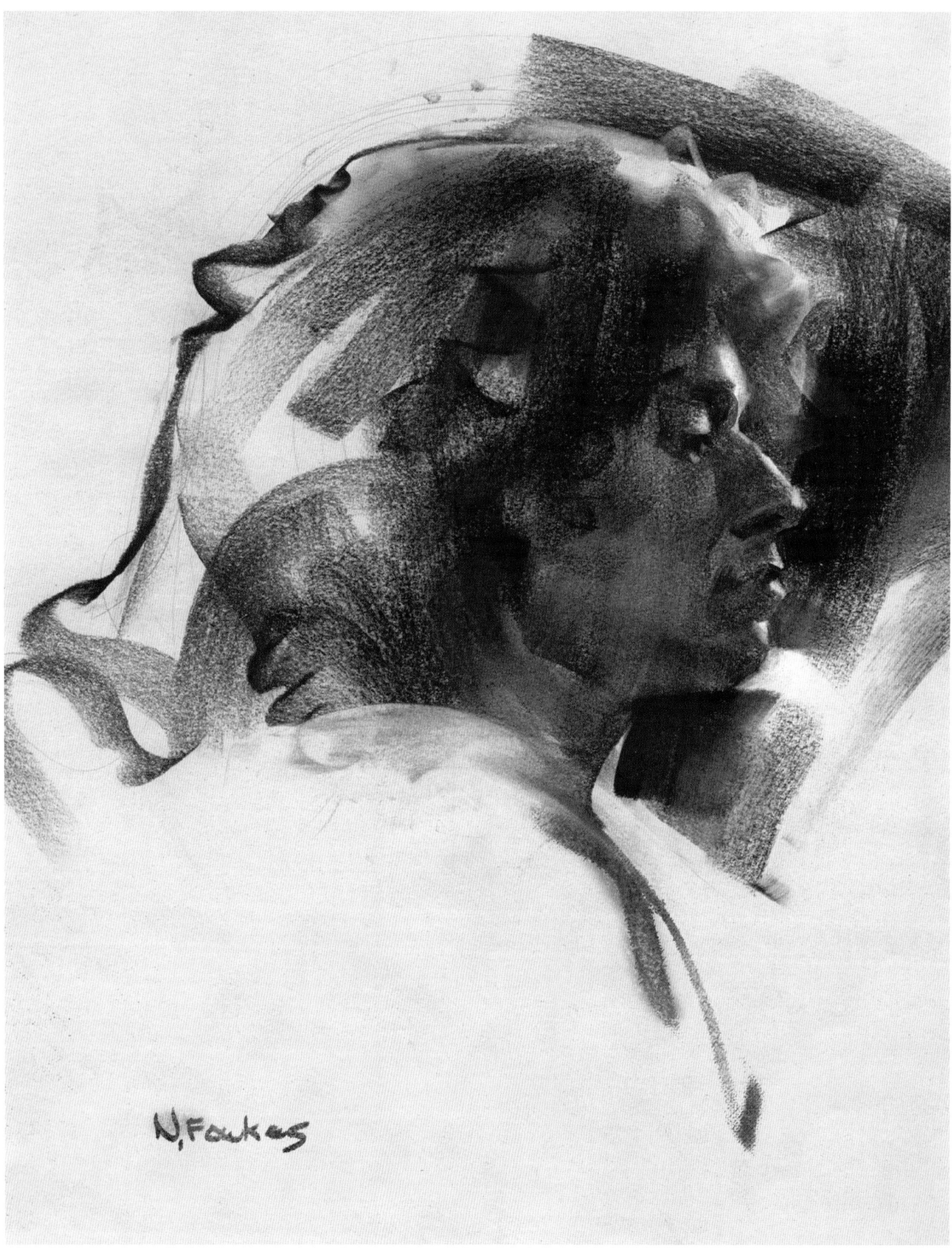

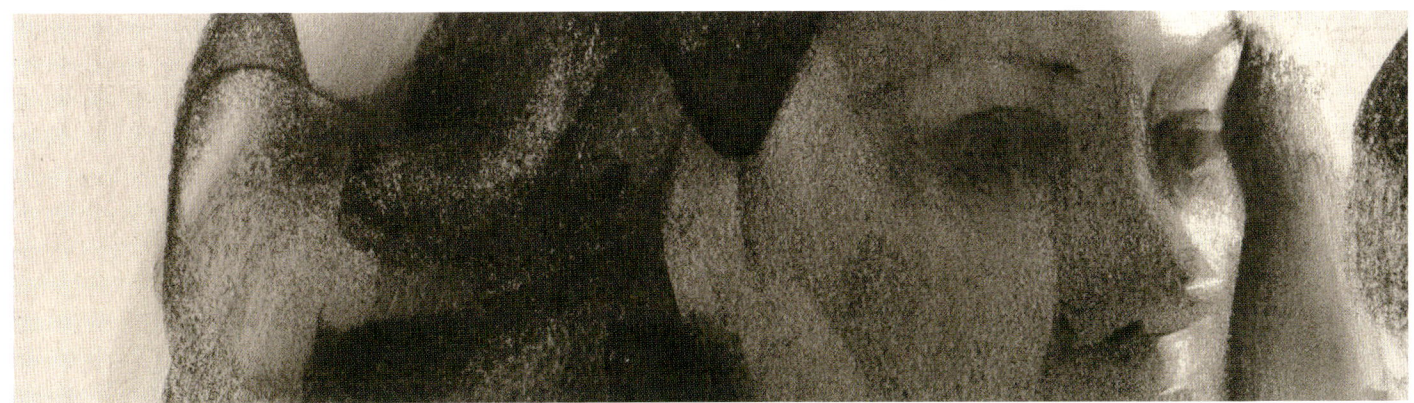

Chapter 11

Quick-Sketch Drawings

Spending a long time doing carefully detailed studies of the human form certainly has great value for hopeful artists. Equally important, though, are shorter studies with a built-in time limit. Such exercises force us to look for a clear, simple statement in our drawings and avoid getting lost in the details. In previous chapters we've looked at quick-sketch exercises spanning just five to ten minutes, but now I'd like to show examples that are completed in less than an hour. The drawings in the following gallery are finished portrait studies done in that period of time. I typically draw them ranging from near life-size to one-half life-size. As a bonus you'll find a demonstration at the end of this chapter that tackles a very complex costumed subject with a time limit of 50 minutes.

"Quick-sketch exercises force us to look for a clear, simple statement in our drawings and avoid getting lost in the details."

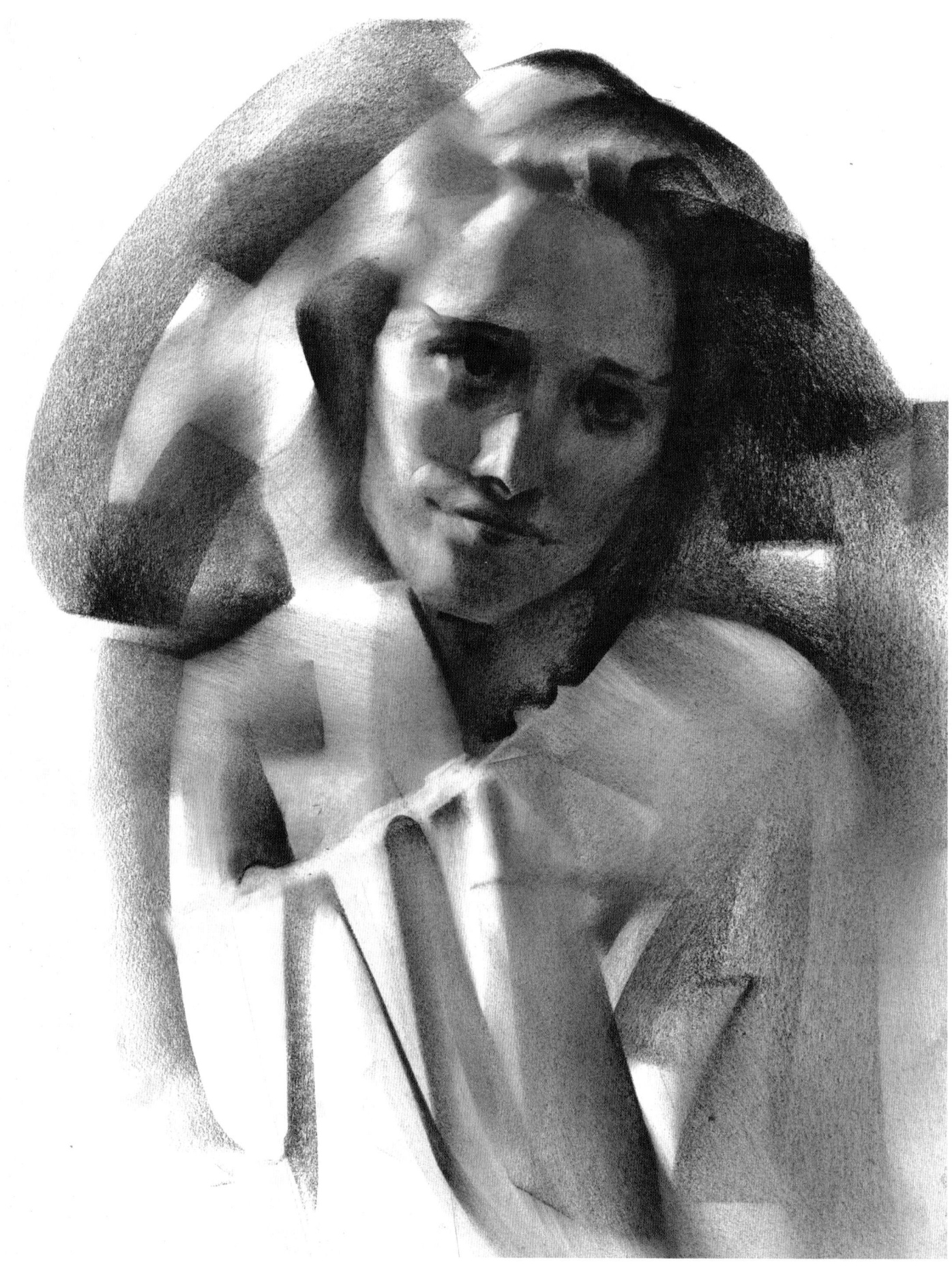

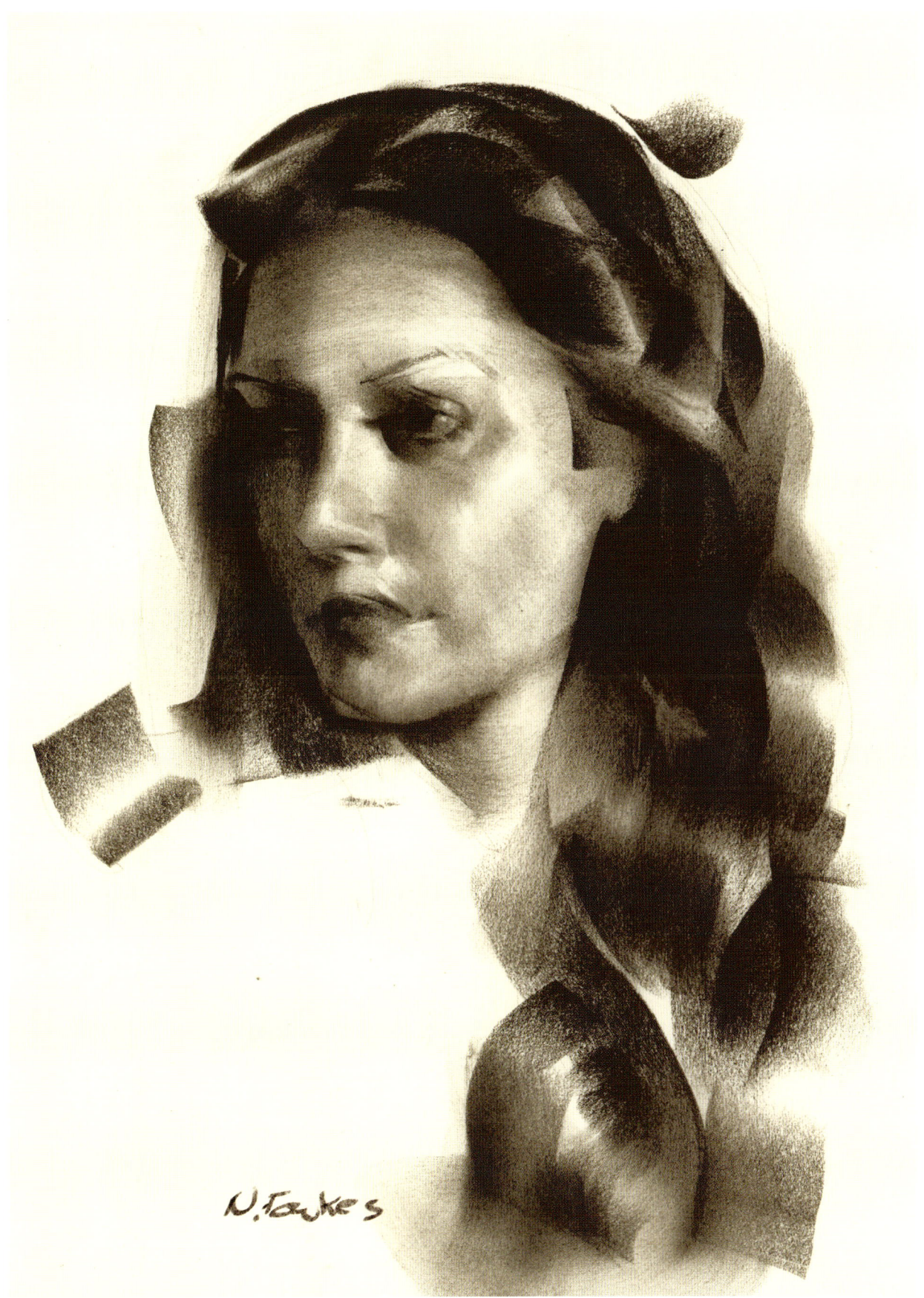

Above: Compressed charcoal on Rives lightweight cream paper.

Opposite: Compressed charcoal on Rives lightweight cream paper.

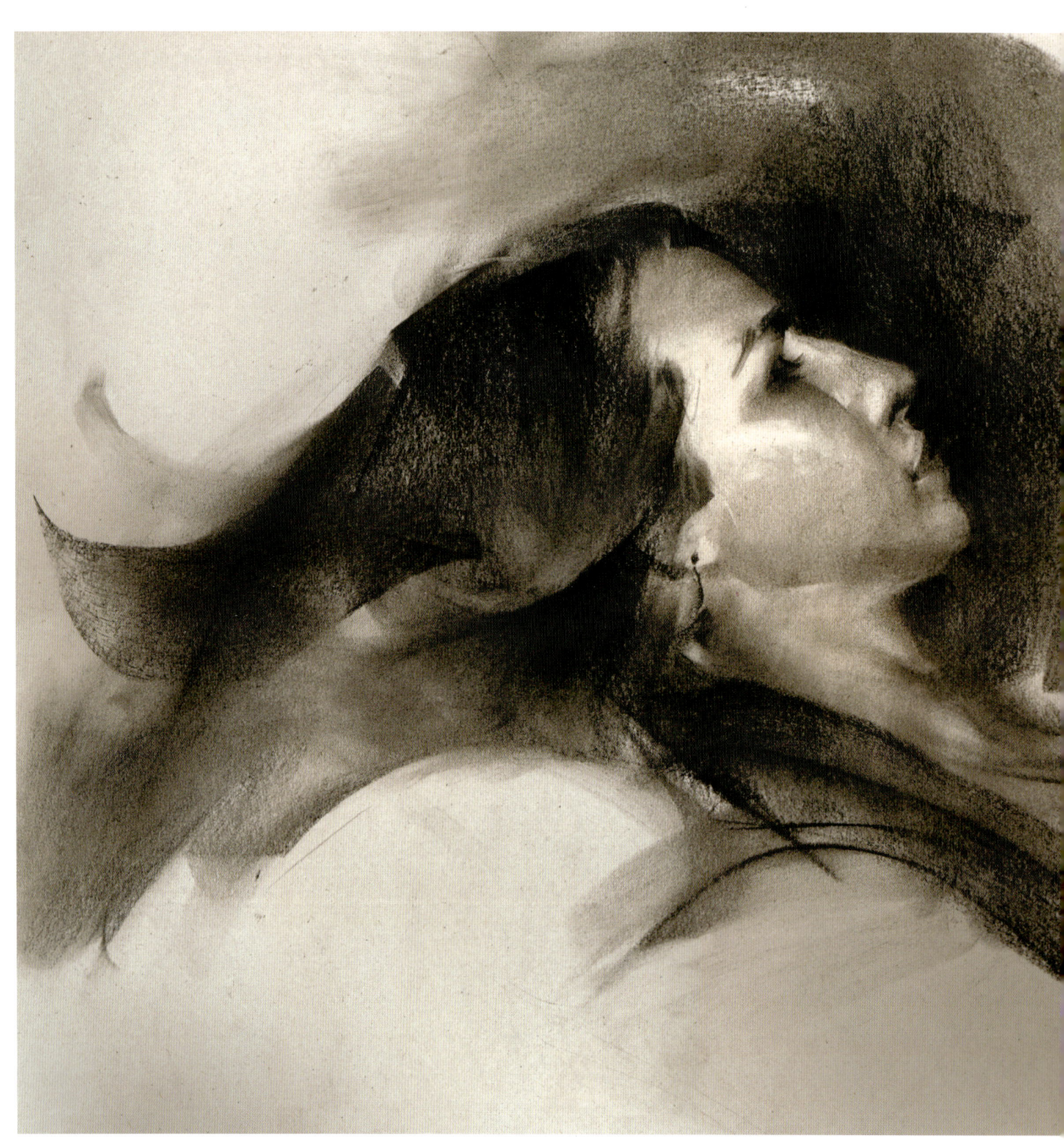

Compressed charcoal on rough newsprint.

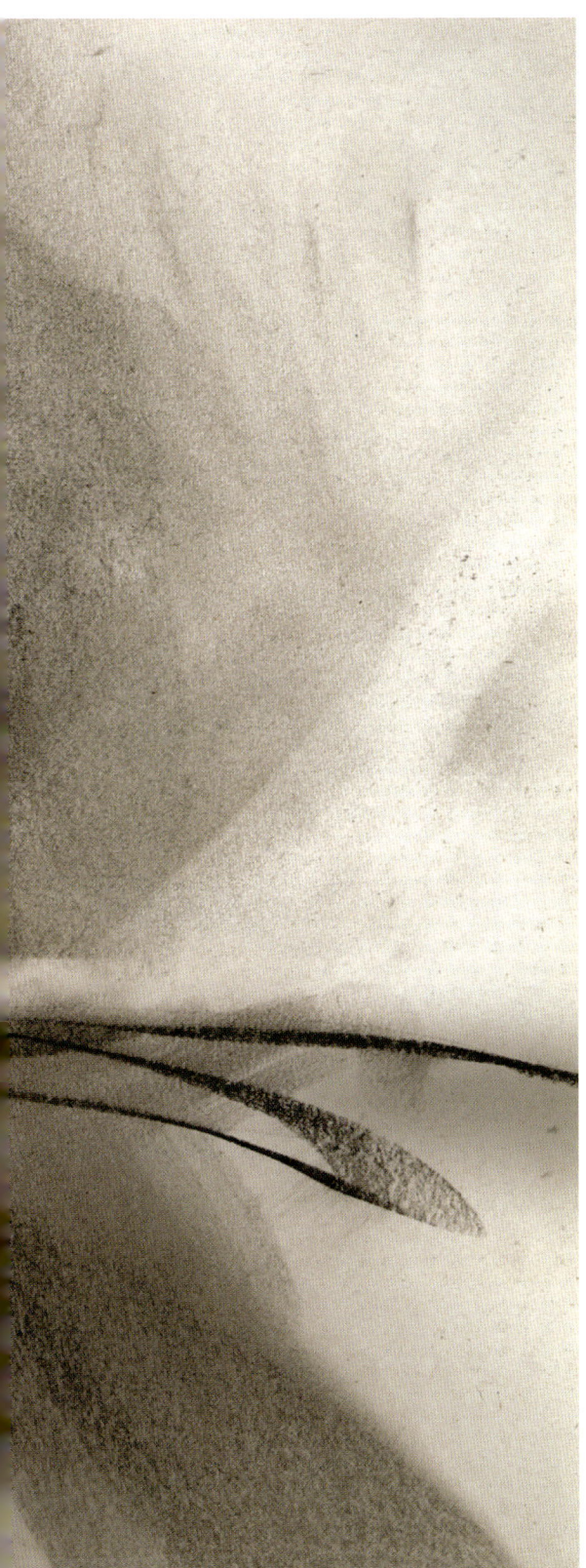

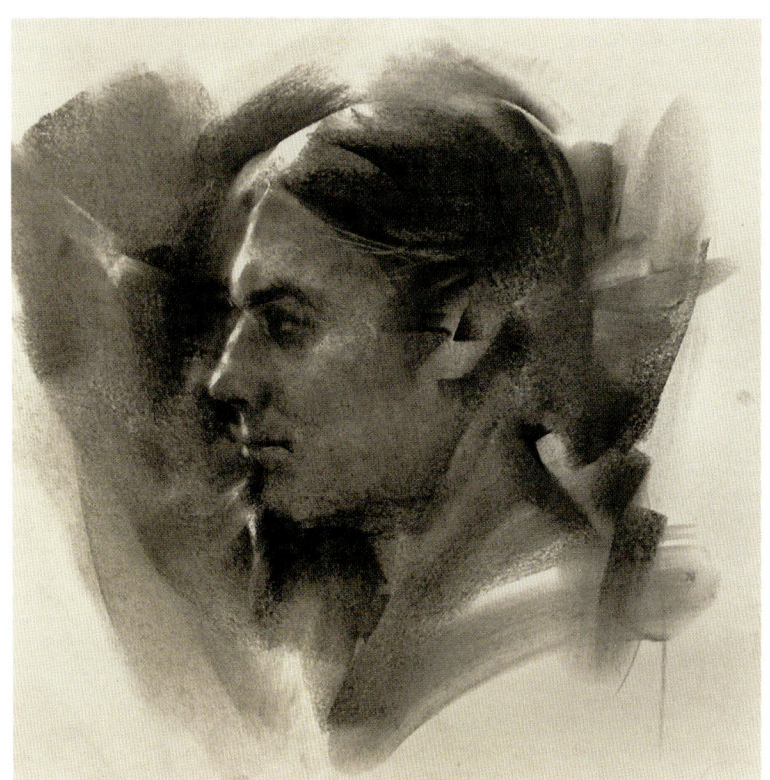

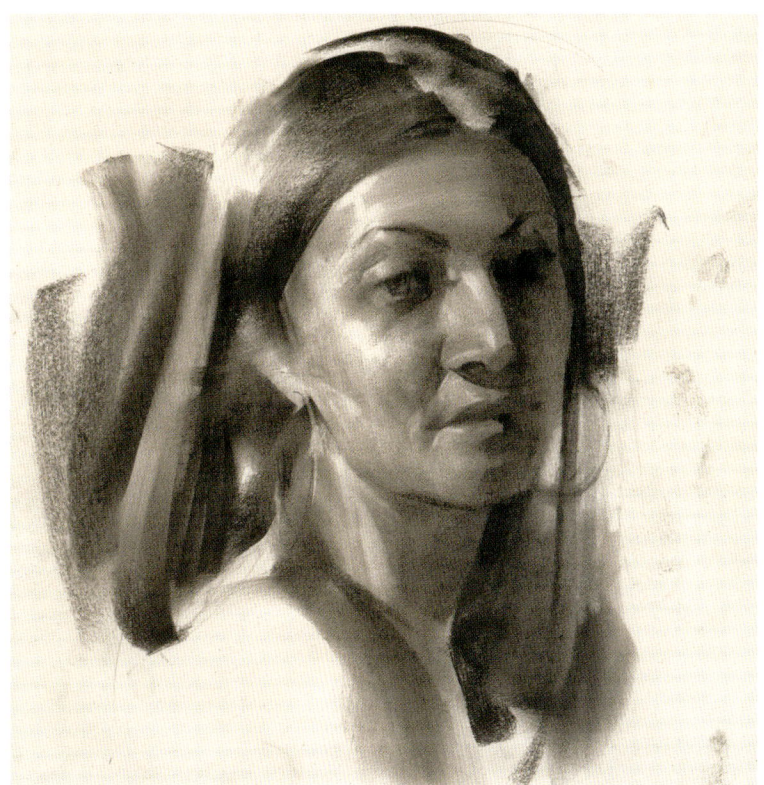

Top: Compressed charcoal on rough newsprint.
Bottom: Compressed charcoal on rough newsprint.

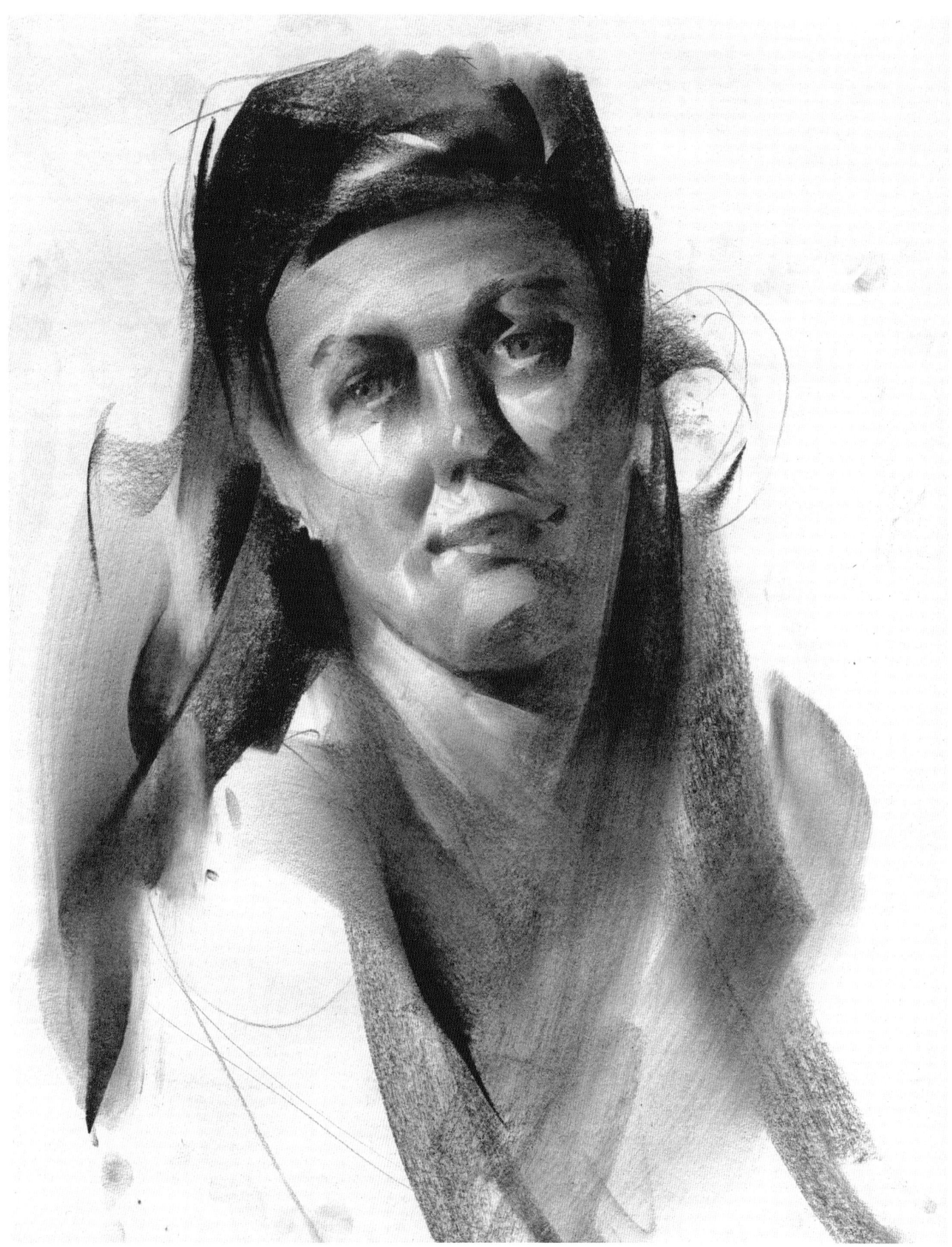

Opposite: Compressed charcoal on rough newsprint.

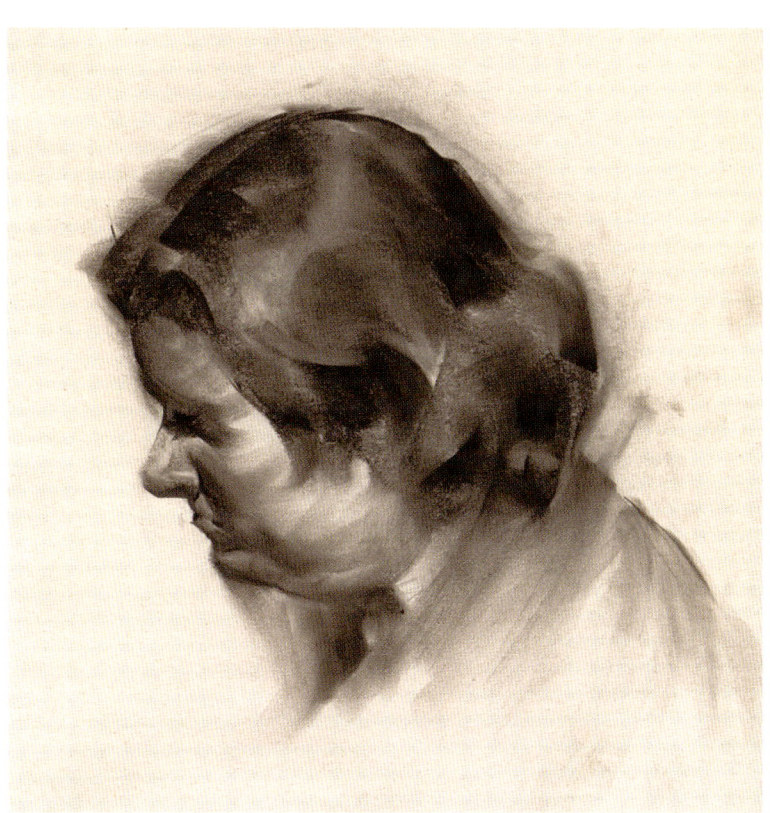

Compressed charcoal
on rough newsprint.

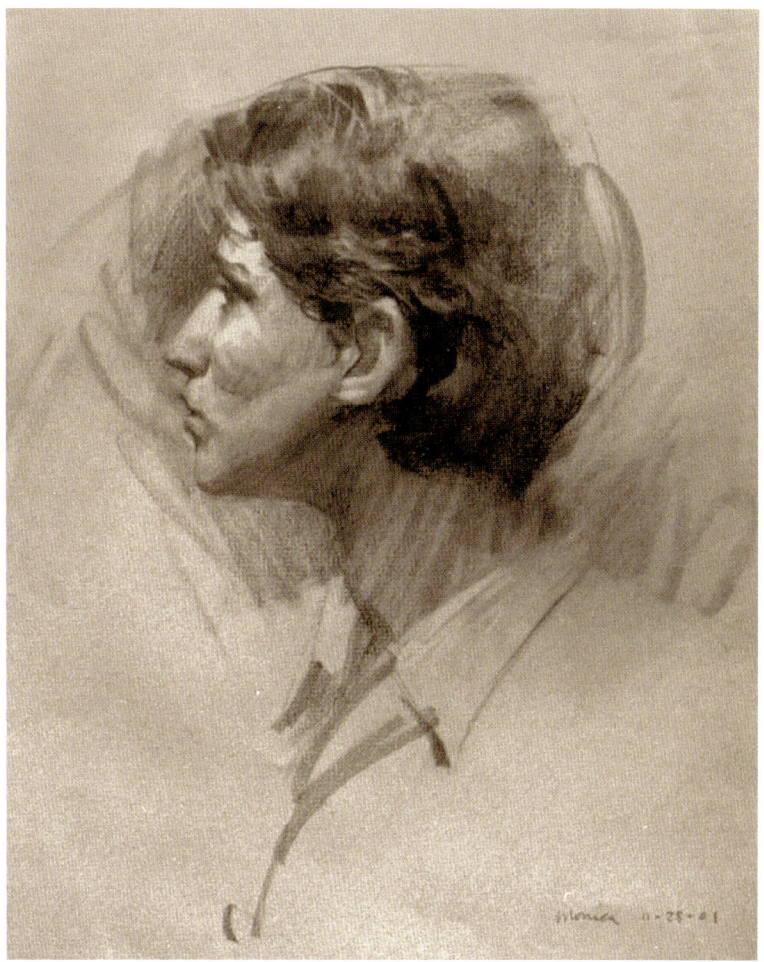

Ritmo charcoal pencil on
Strathmore charcoal paper.

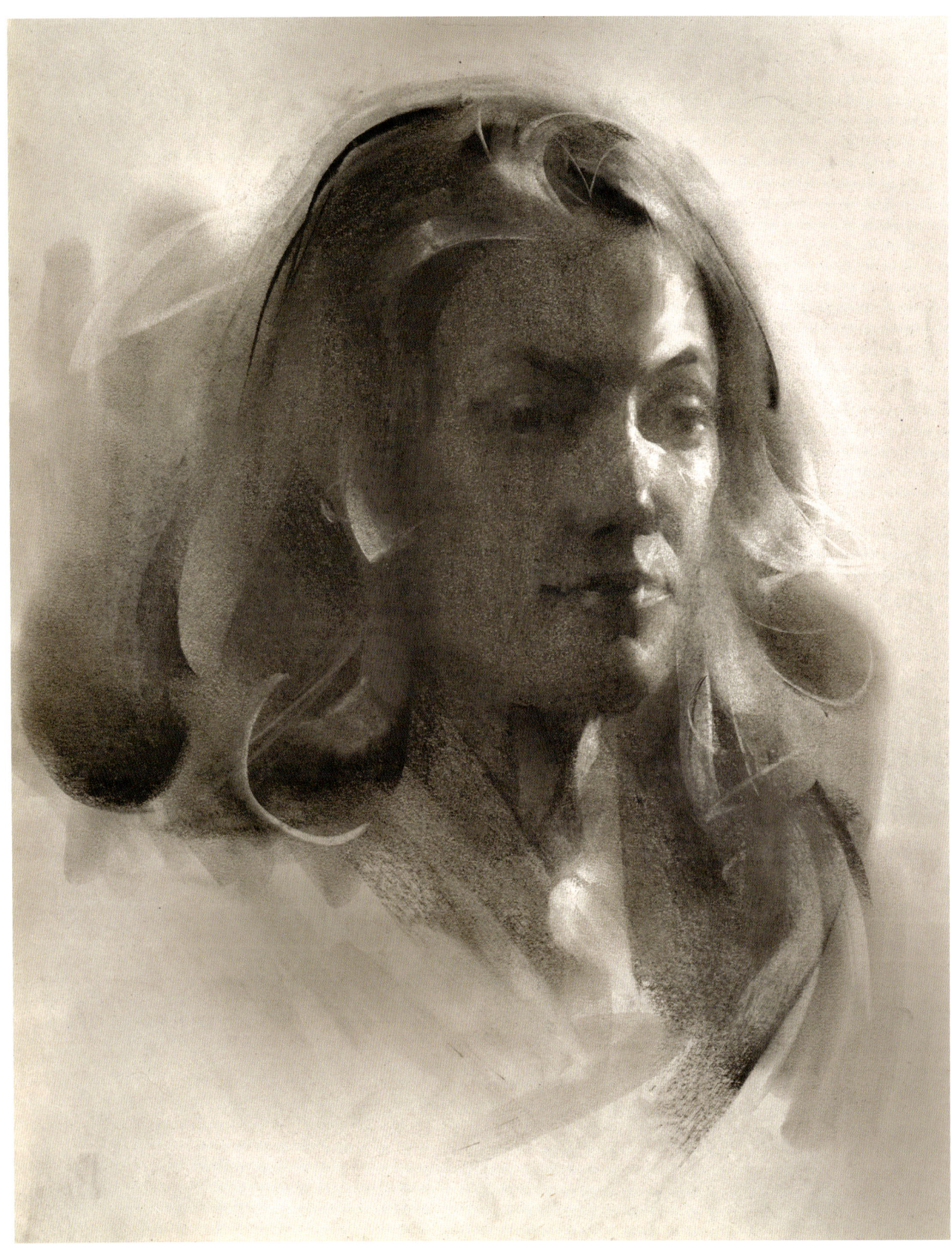

Opposite: Compressed charcoal on toned Bristol paper.

Ritmo charcoal pencil and white Nupastel on Strathmore charcoal paper.

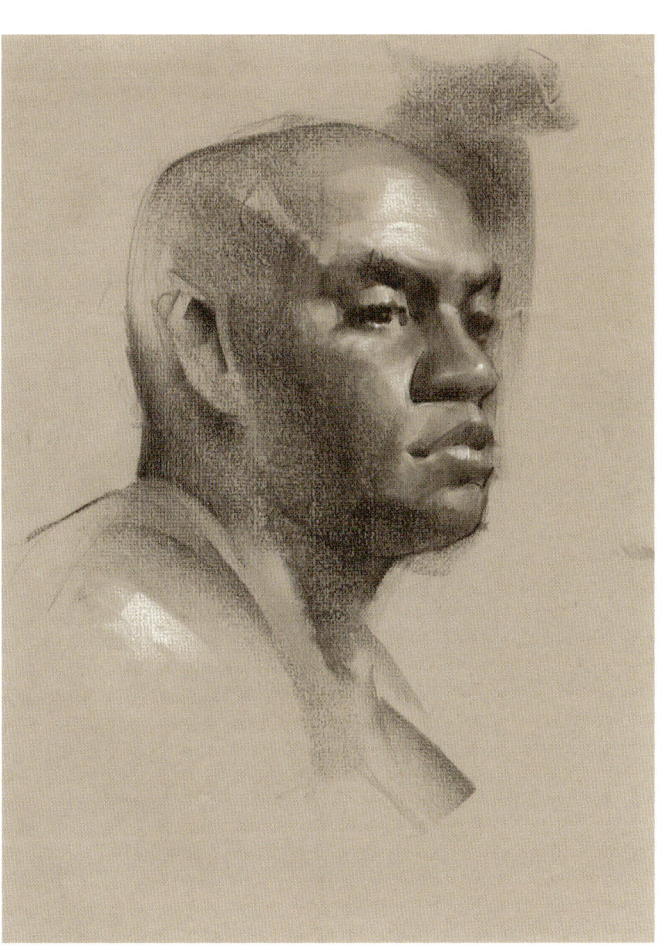

Compressed charcoal and Pitt charcoal pencil on Strathmore charcoal paper.

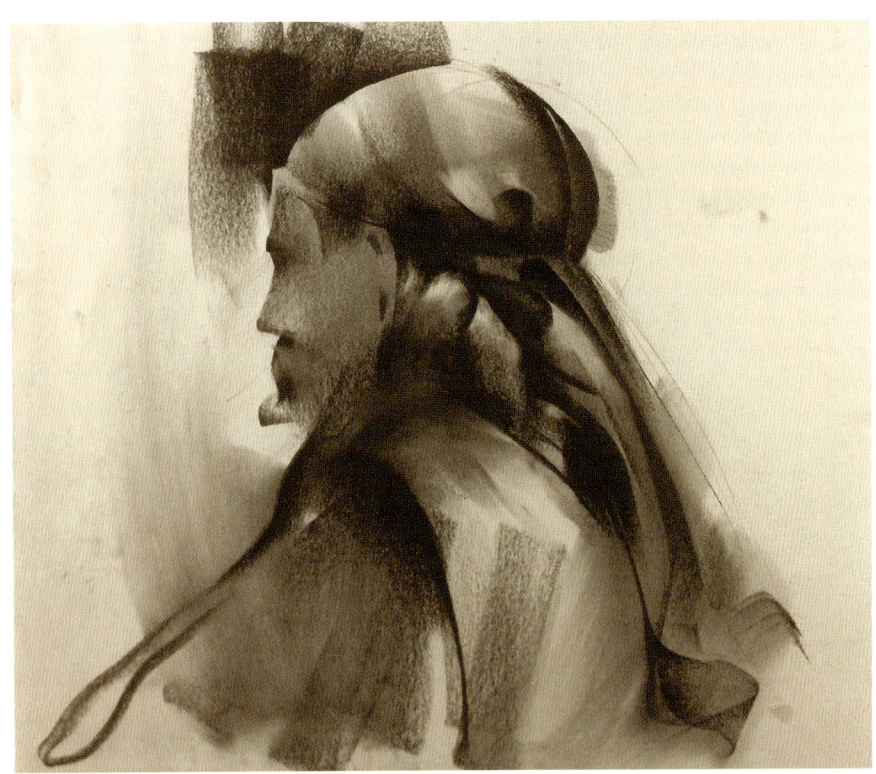

Compressed charcoal on
rough newsprint.

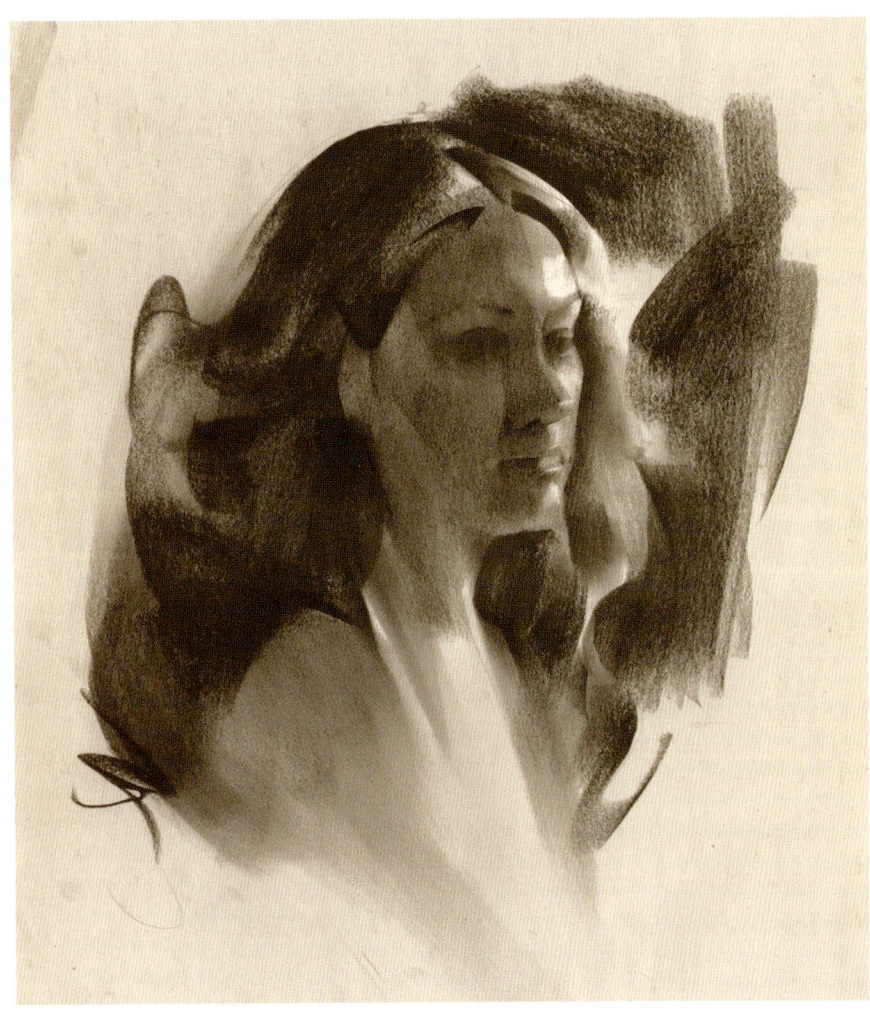

Compressed charcoal on
rough newsprint.

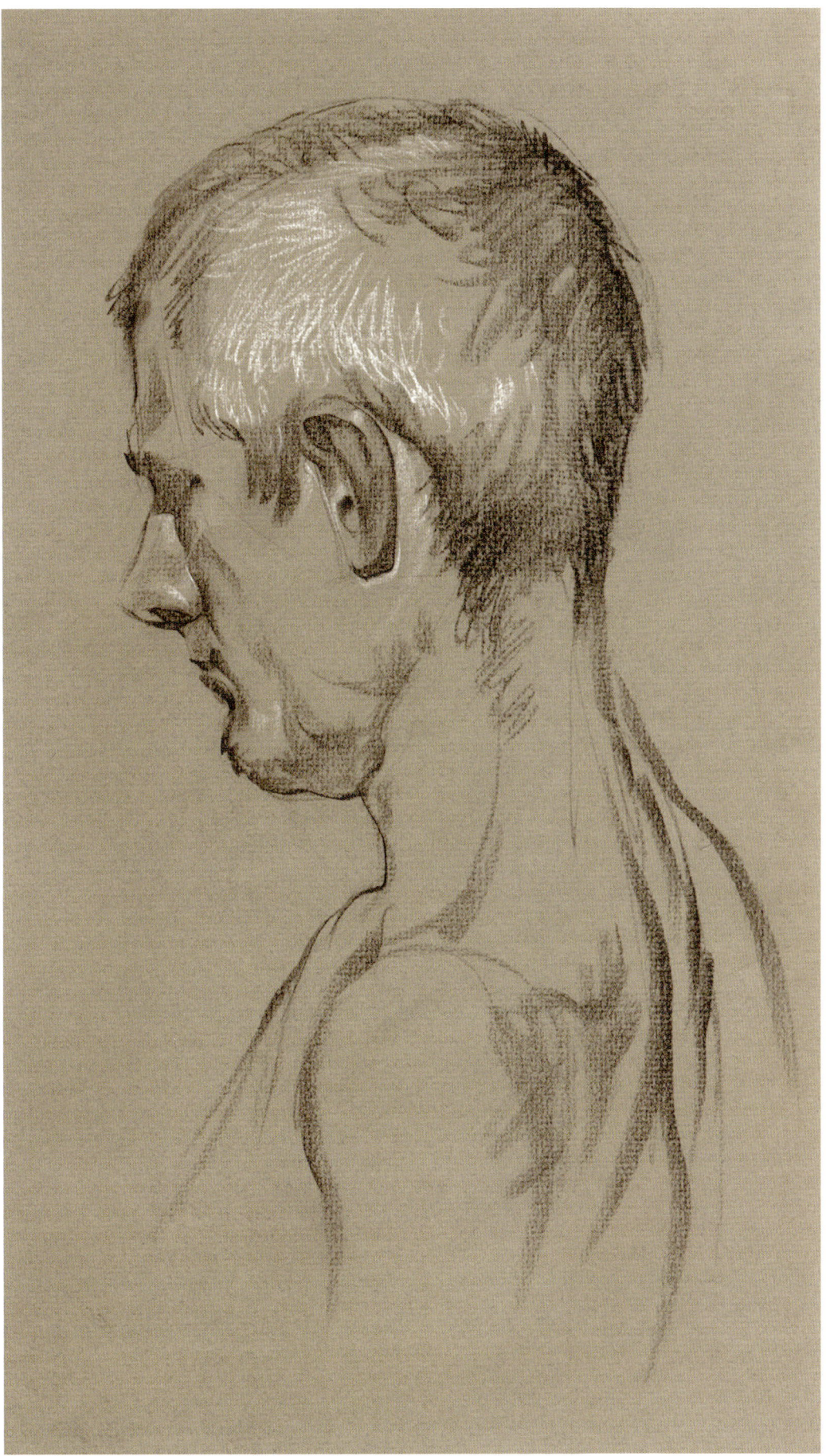

Ritmo charcoal pencil on
Strathmore charcoal paper.

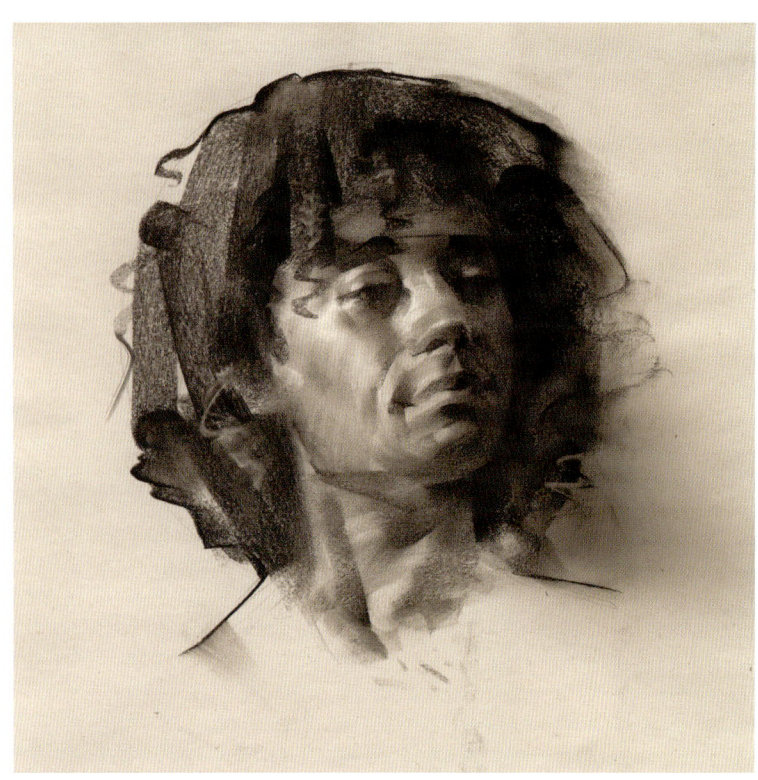

Compressed charcoal on
rough newsprint.

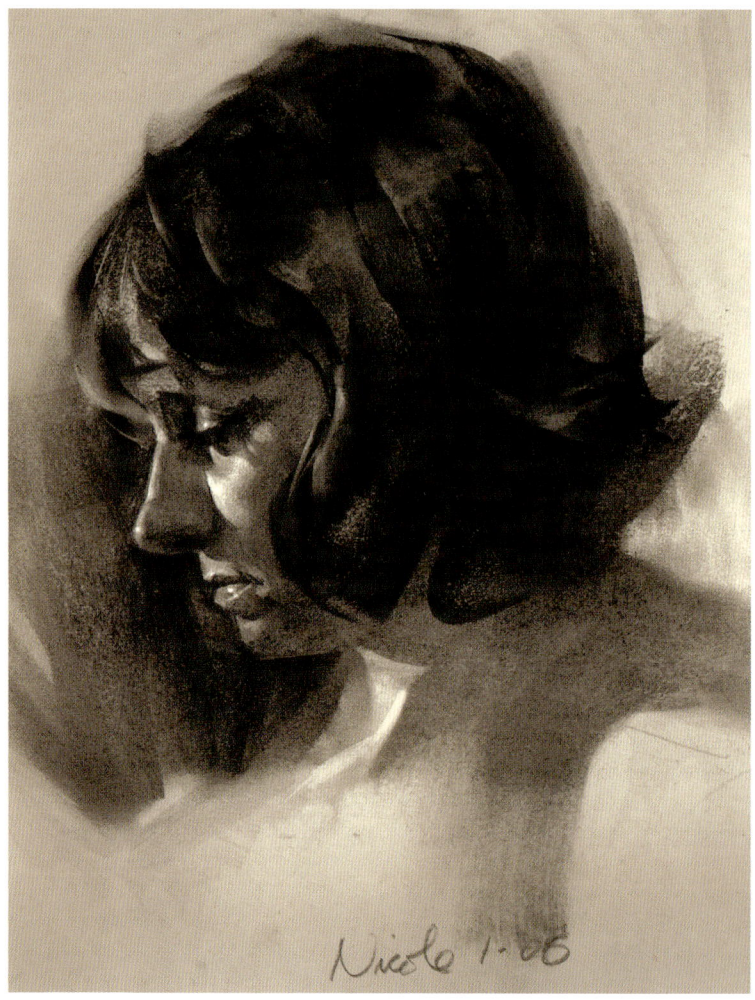

Compressed charcoal and white
Nupastel on rough newsprint.

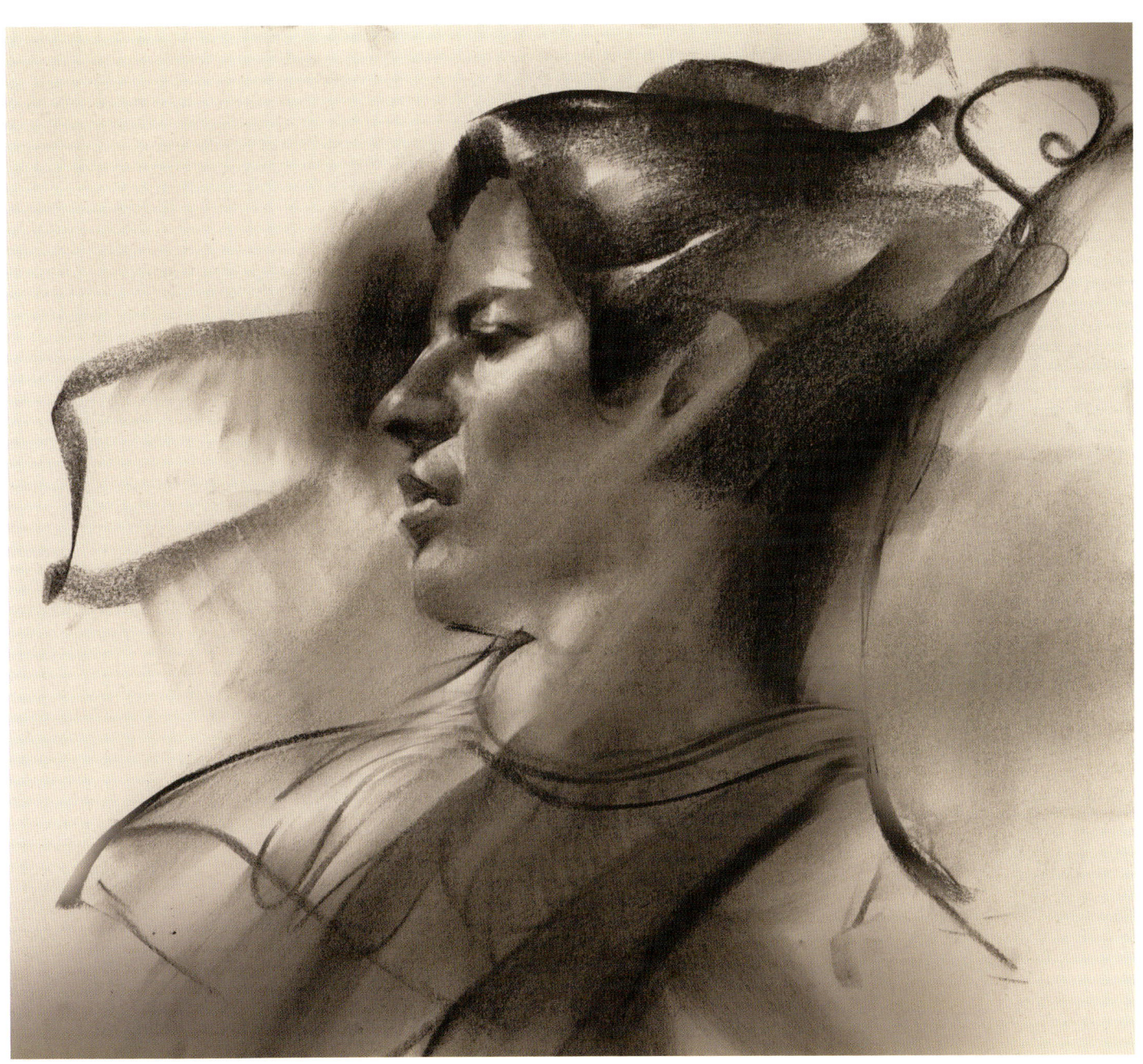

Compressed charcoal on rough newsprint.

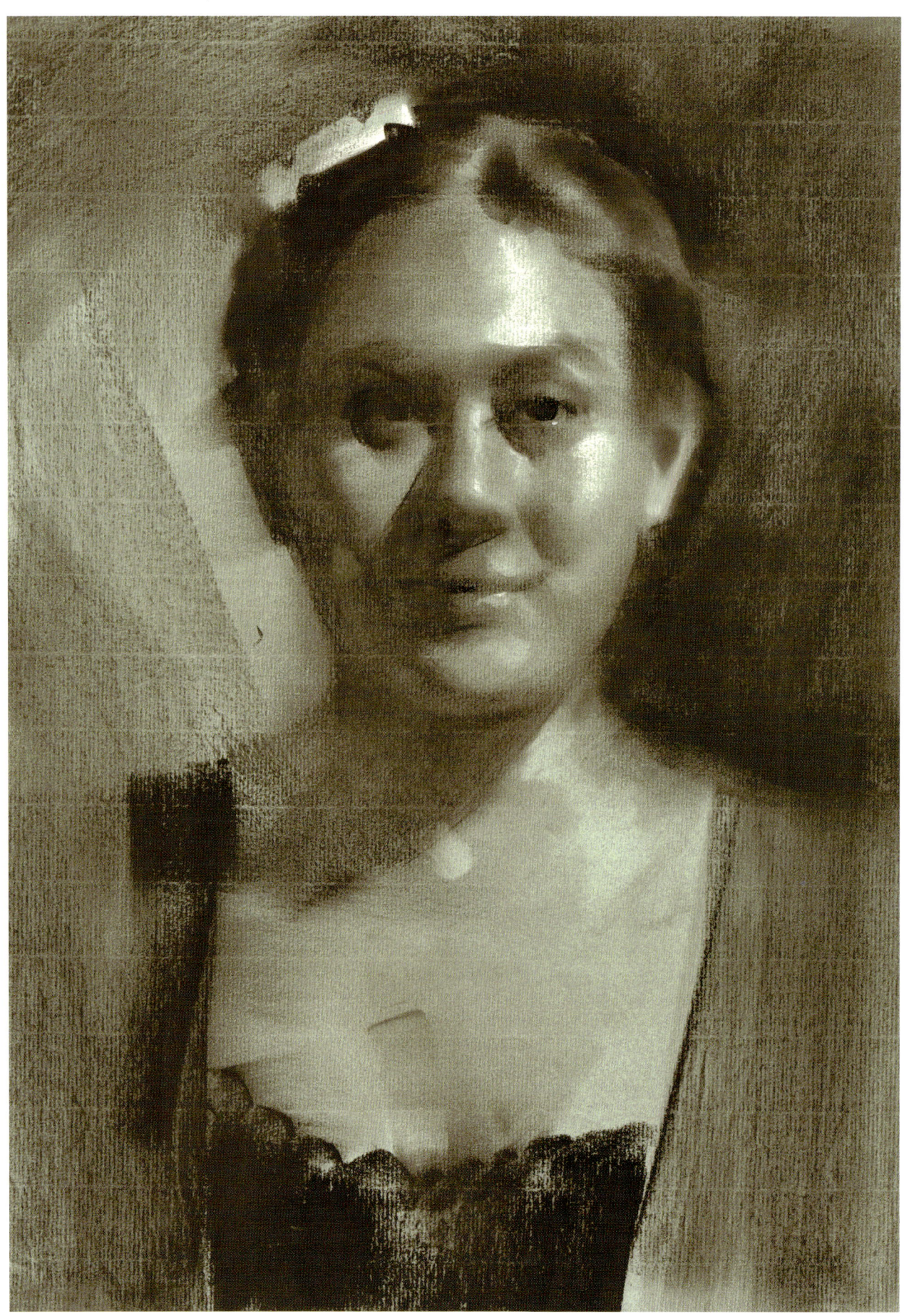

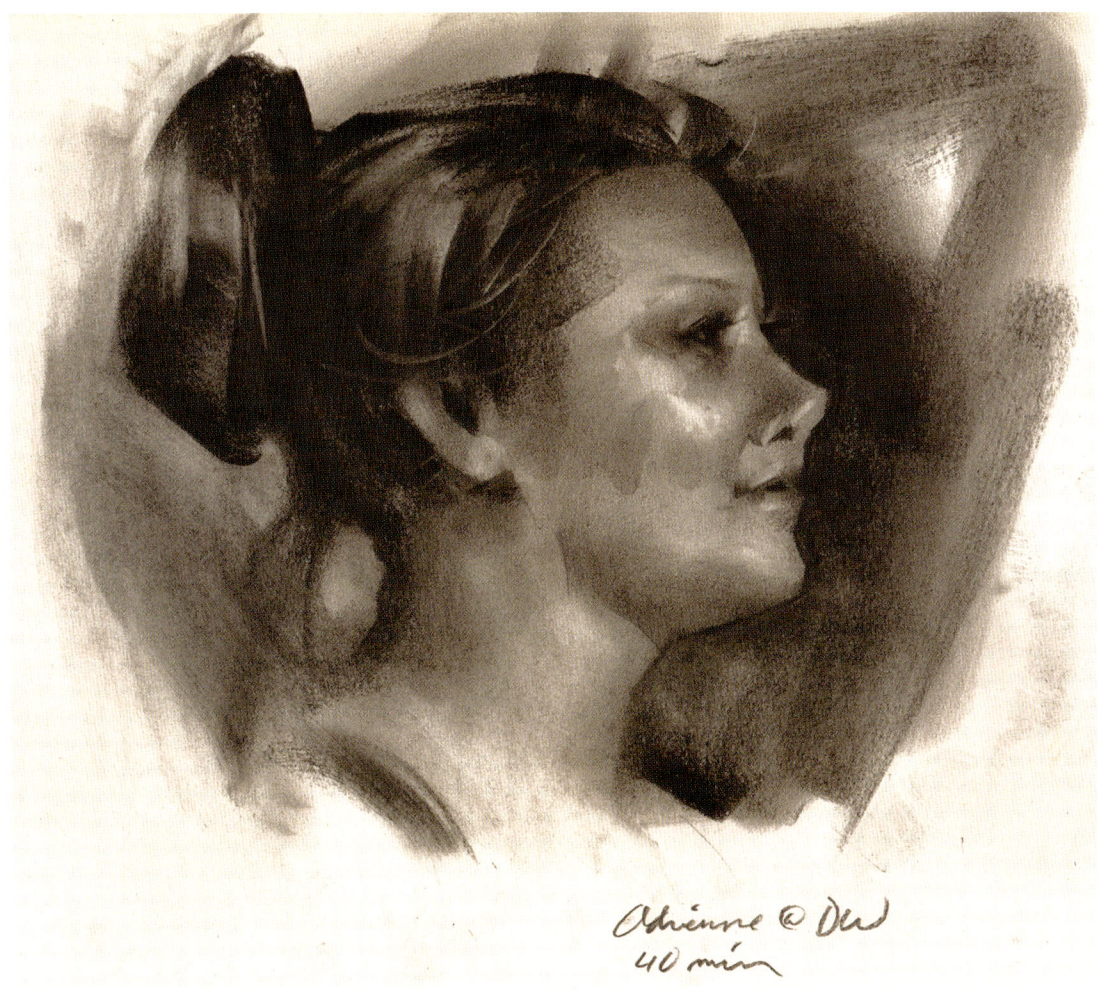

Adrienne @ Otis
40 min

Top: Compressed charcoal on rough newsprint.

Bottom left: Compressed charcoal on rough newsprint.

Bottom right: Compressed charcoal on rough newsprint.

Opposite: Compressed charcoal and ivory Nupastel on Strathmore charcoal paper.

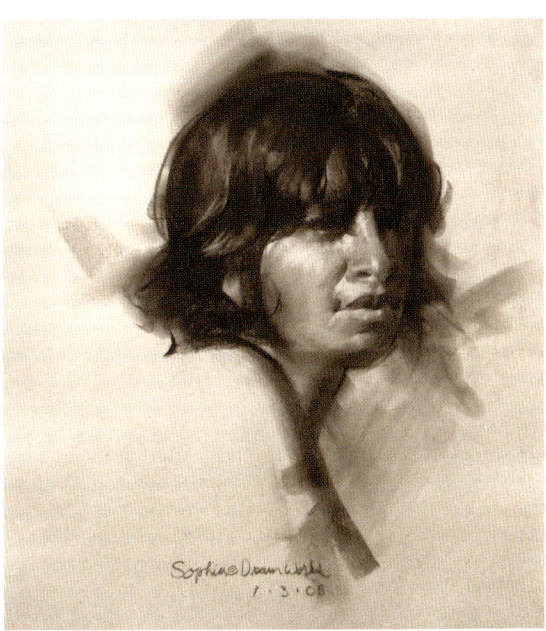

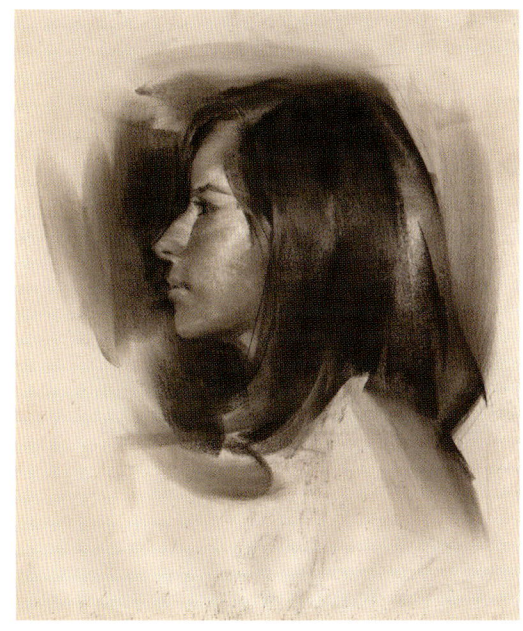

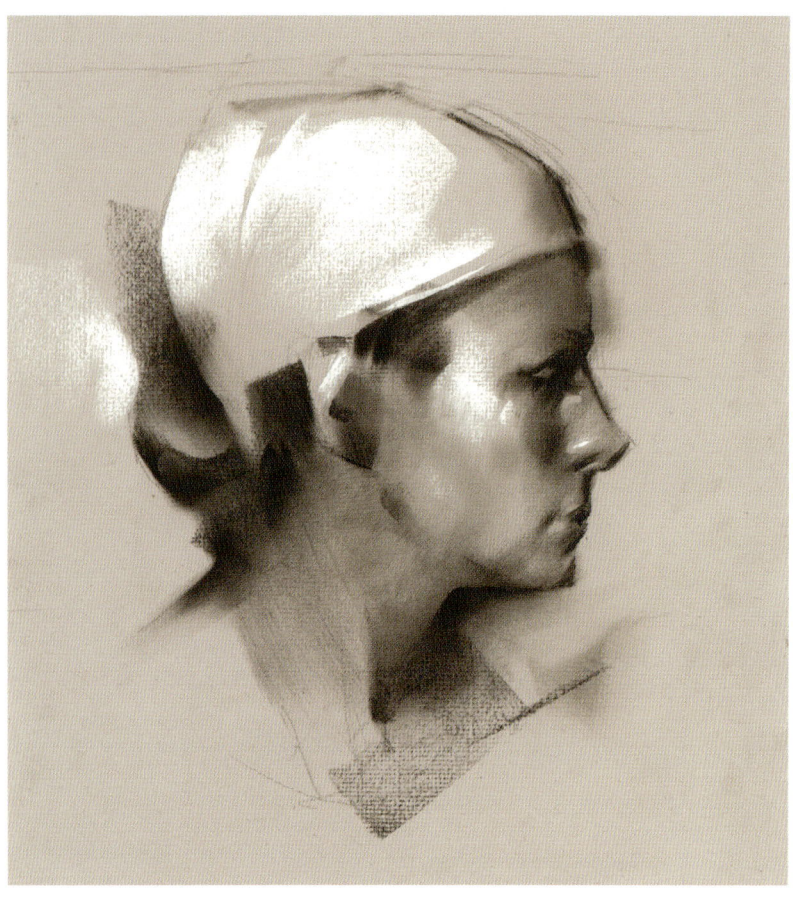

Compressed charcoal and white Nupastel
on Canson Ingres Vidalon drawing paper.

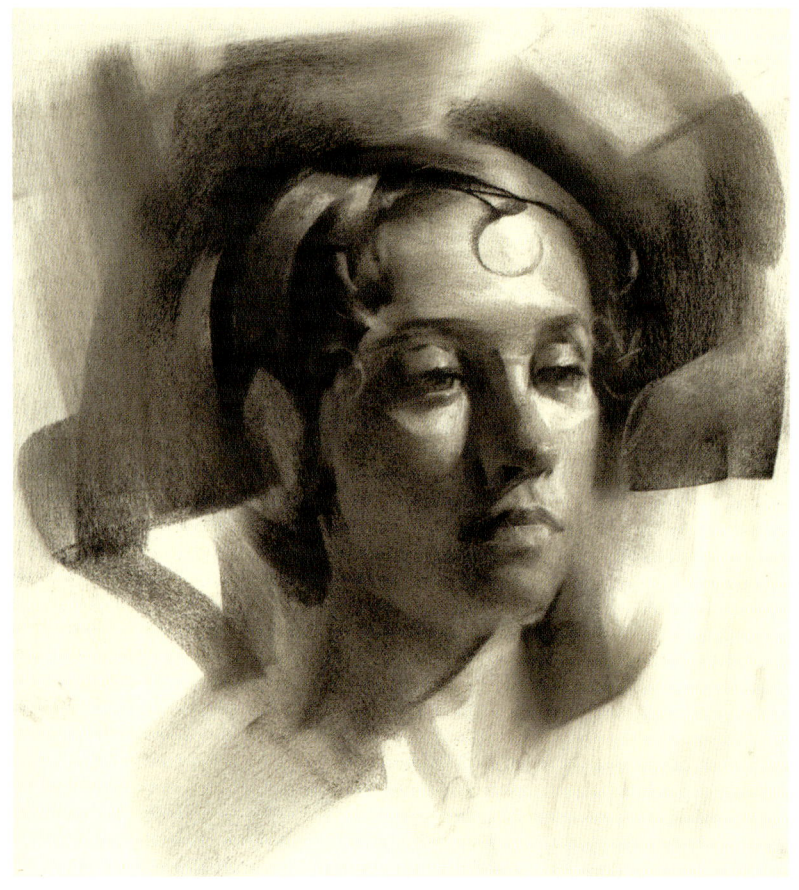

Compressed charcoal on Rives
lightweight cream paper.

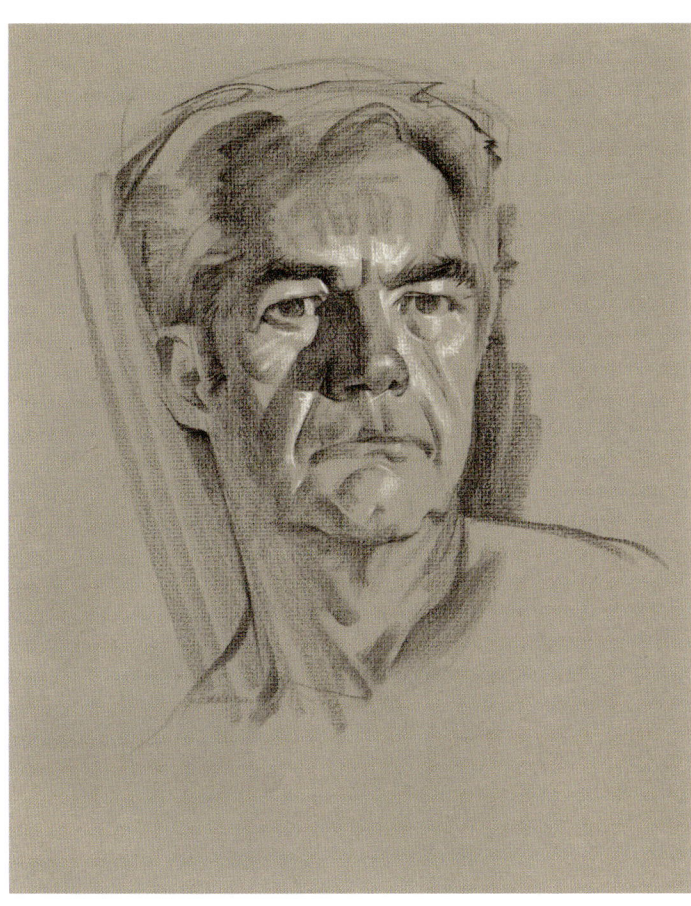

Ritmo charcoal pencil and white CarbOthello
pencil on Strathmore charcoal paper.

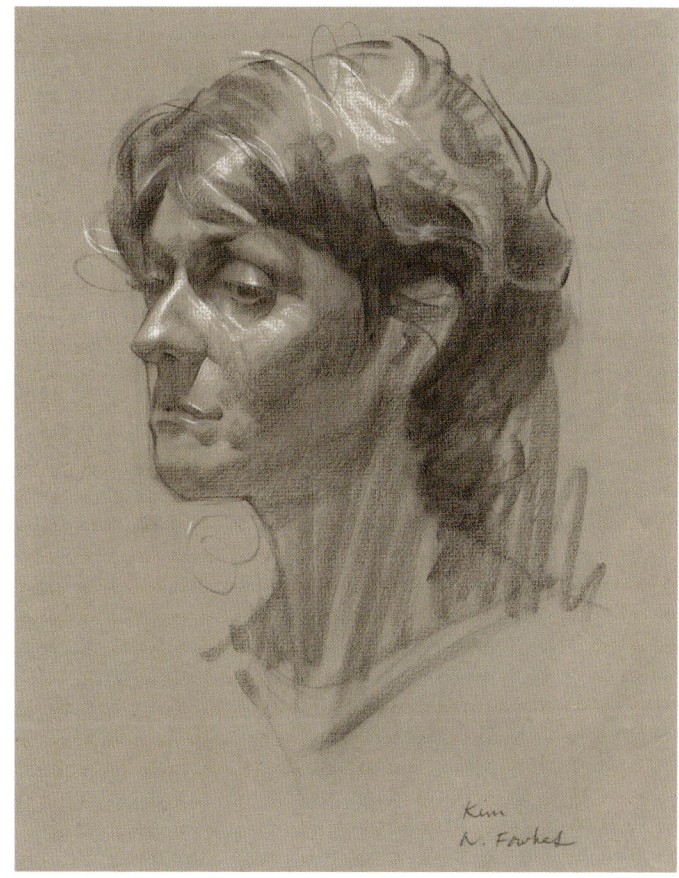

Ritmo charcoal pencil and white CarbOthello
pencil on Strathmore charcoal paper.

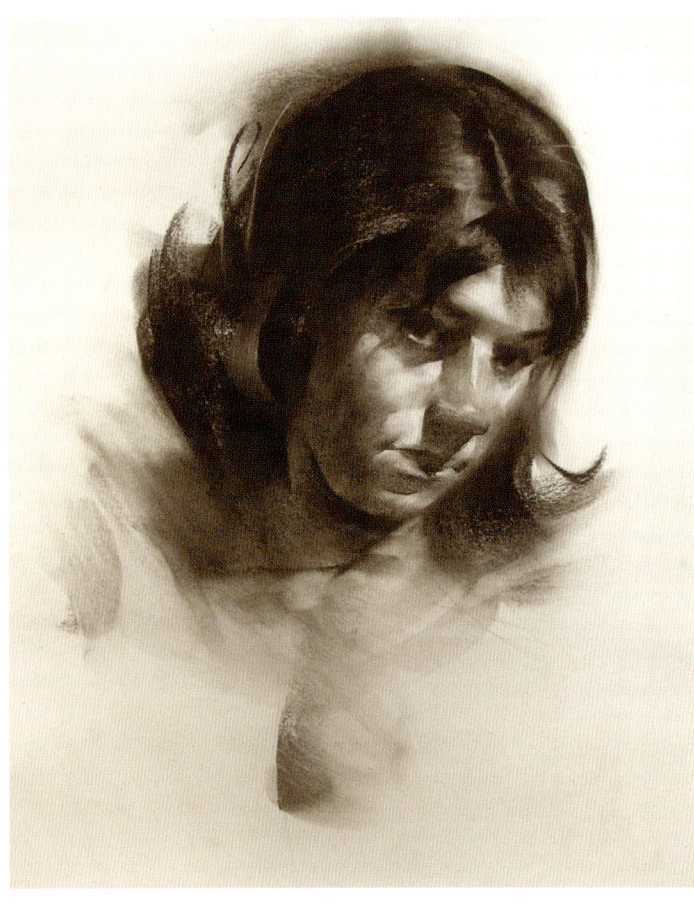

Left: Compressed charcoal on rough newsprint.

Opposite: Compressed charcoal and Pitt charcoal pencil on rough newsprint.

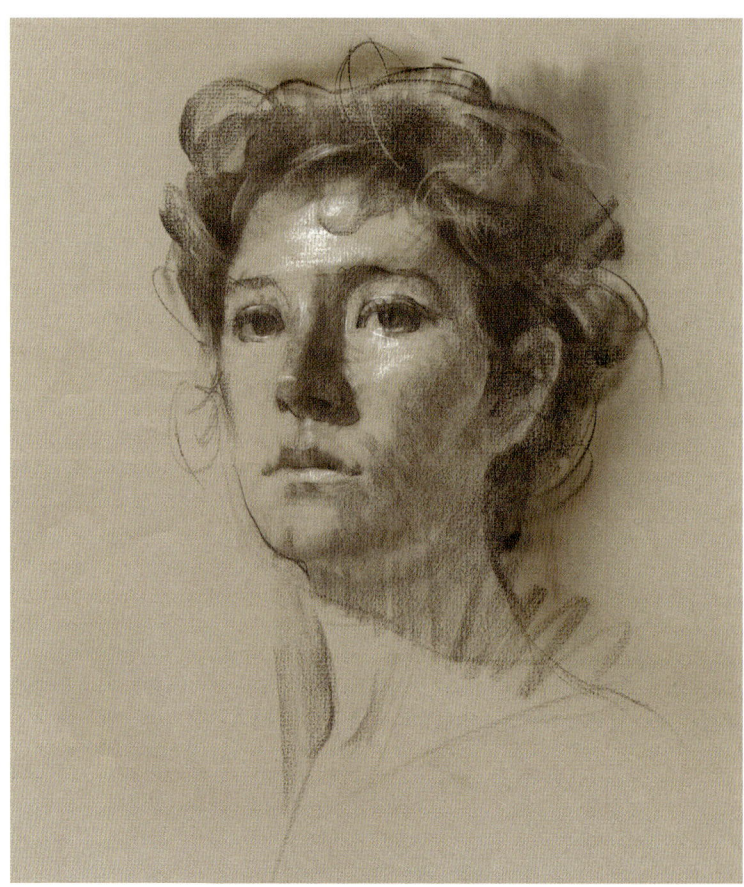

Ritmo charcoal pencil and white CarbOthello
pencil on Strathmore charcoal paper.

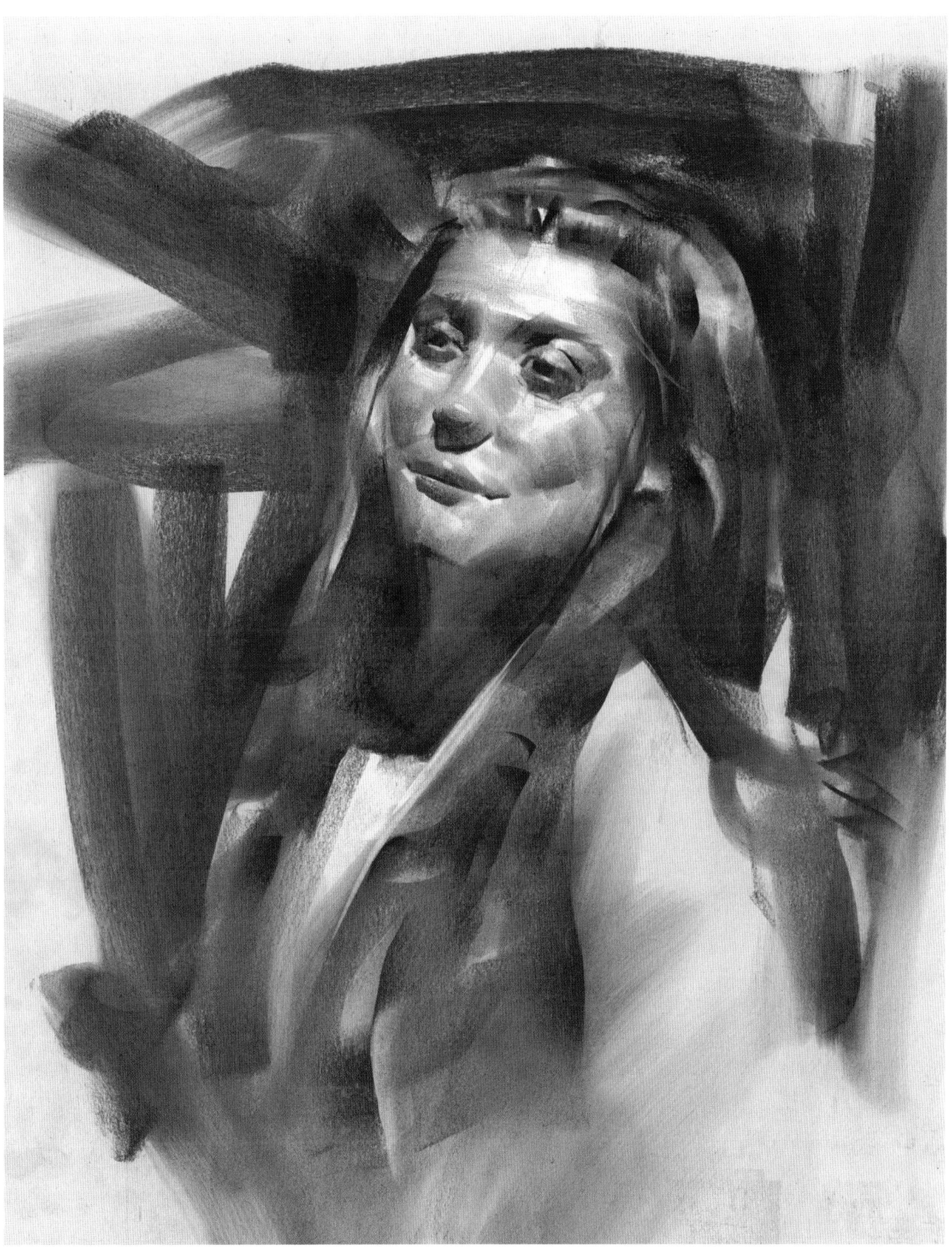

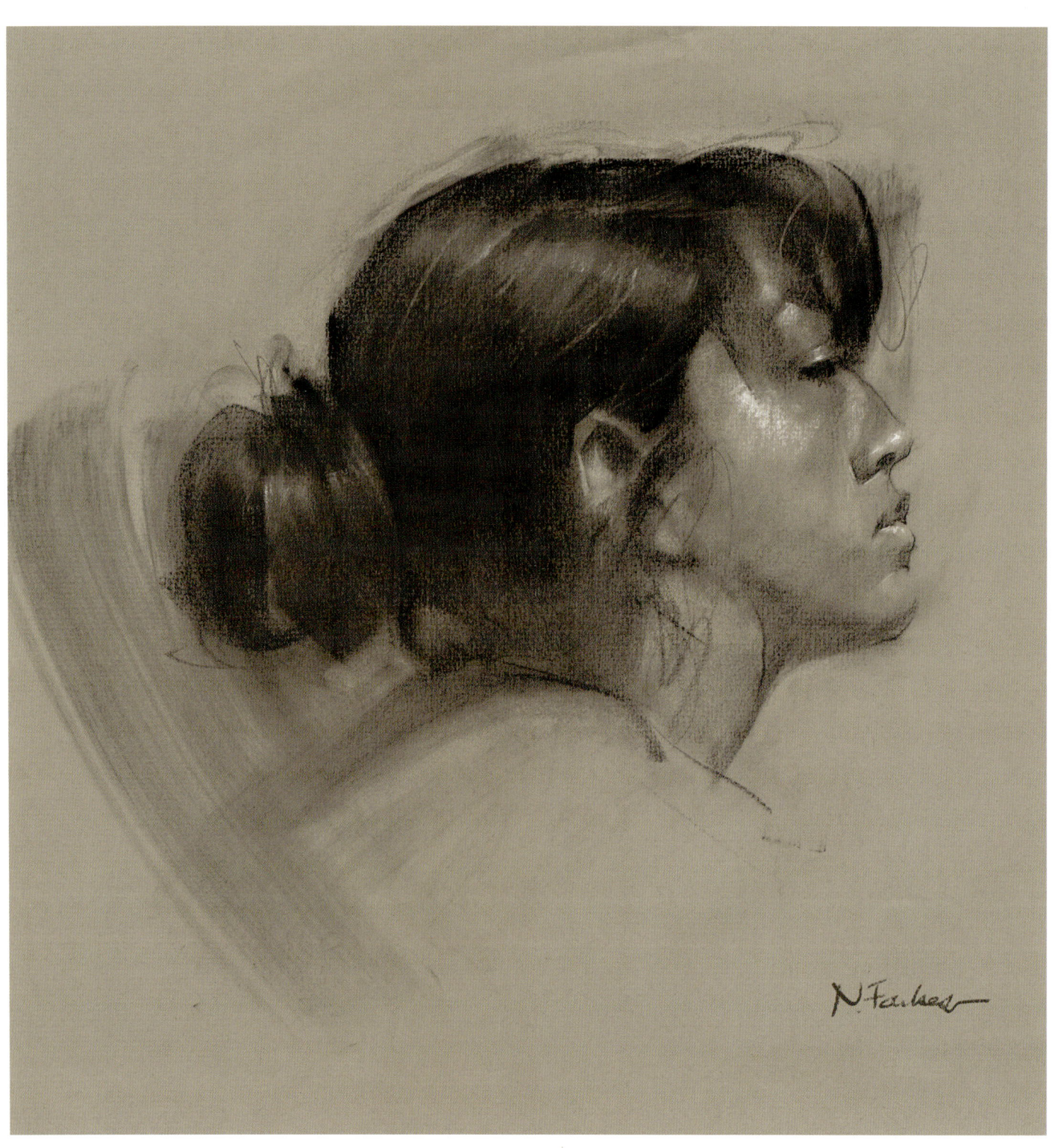

Compressed charcoal, Pitt charcoal pencil, and white CarbOthello
pencil on Canson Ingres Vidalon drawing paper.

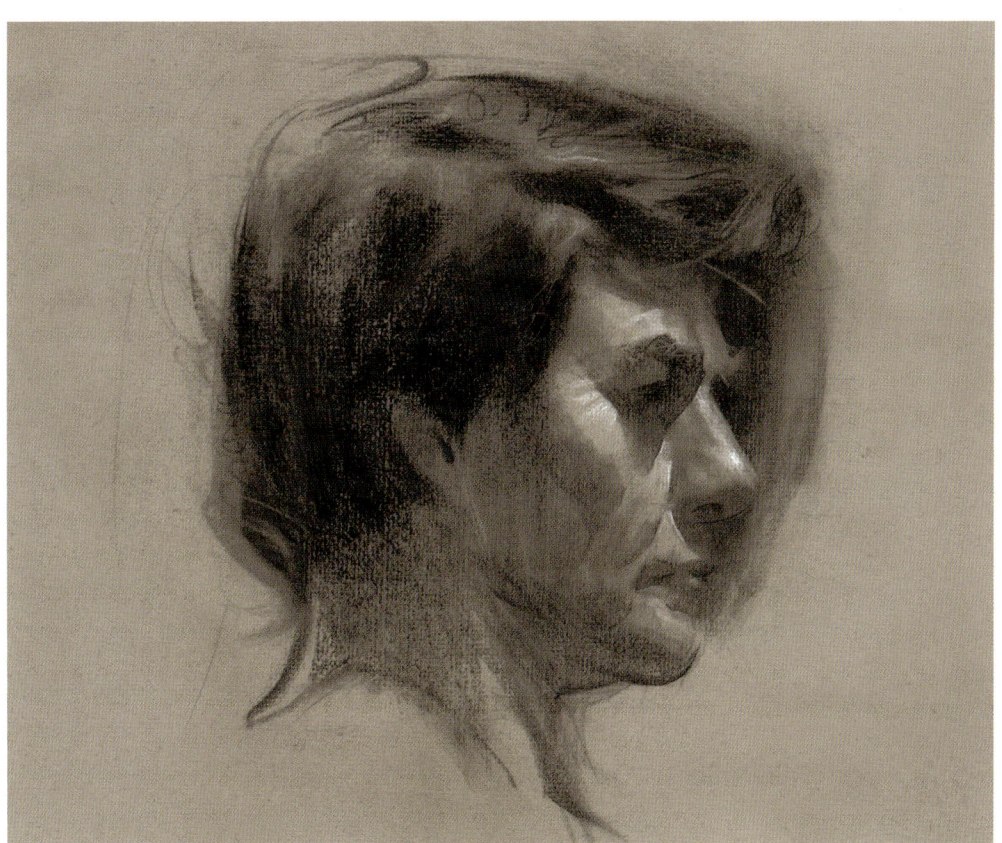

Vine charcoal, Ritmo charcoal pencil,
and white CarbOthello pencil on
Canson Ingres Vidalon drawing paper.

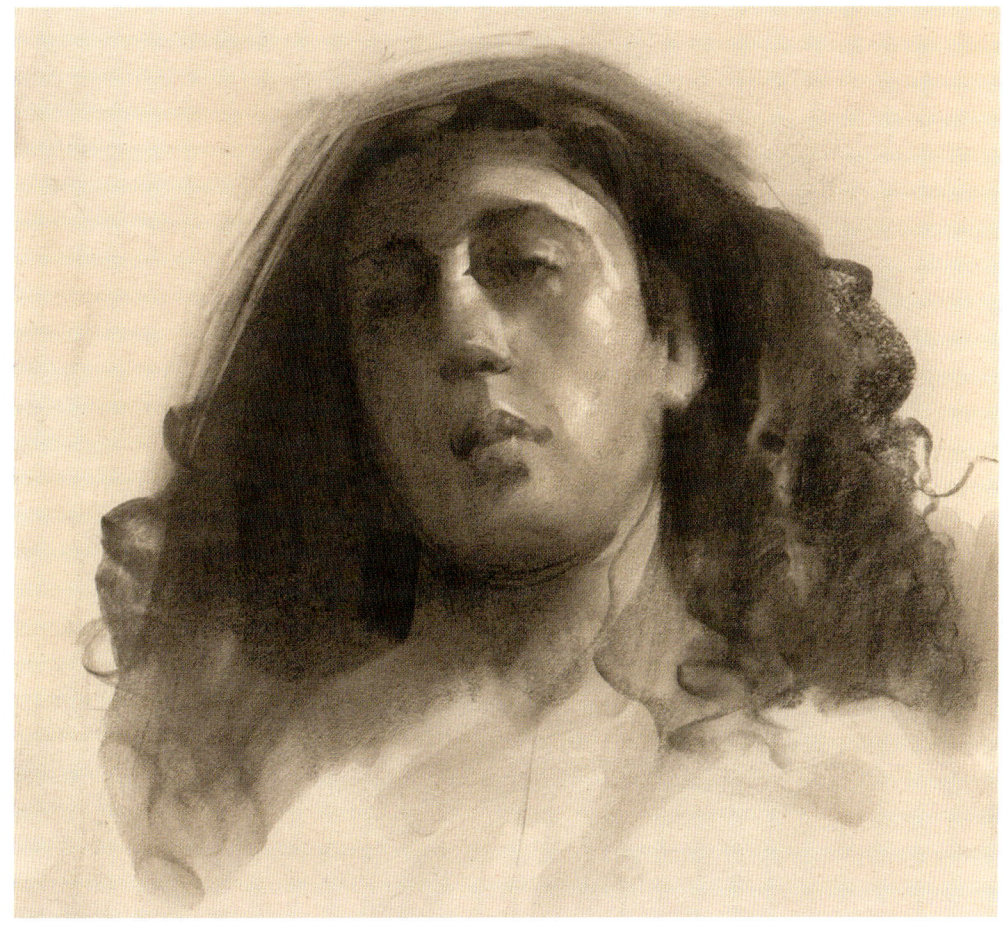

Compressed charcoal on
rough newsprint.

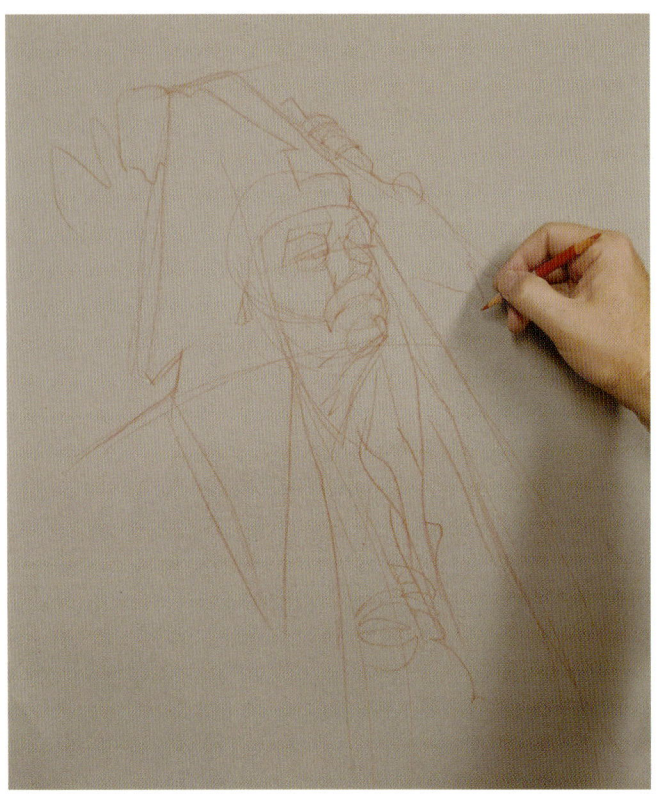

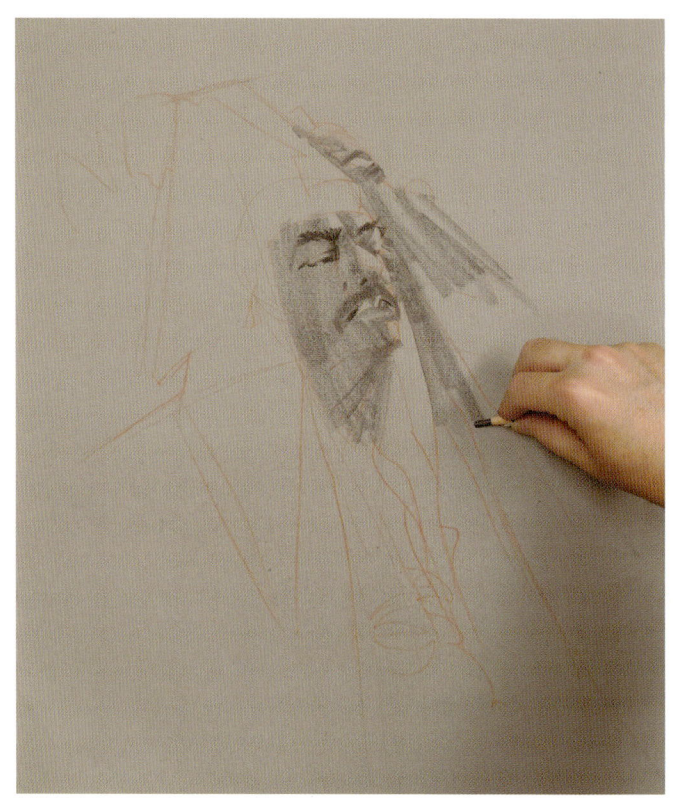

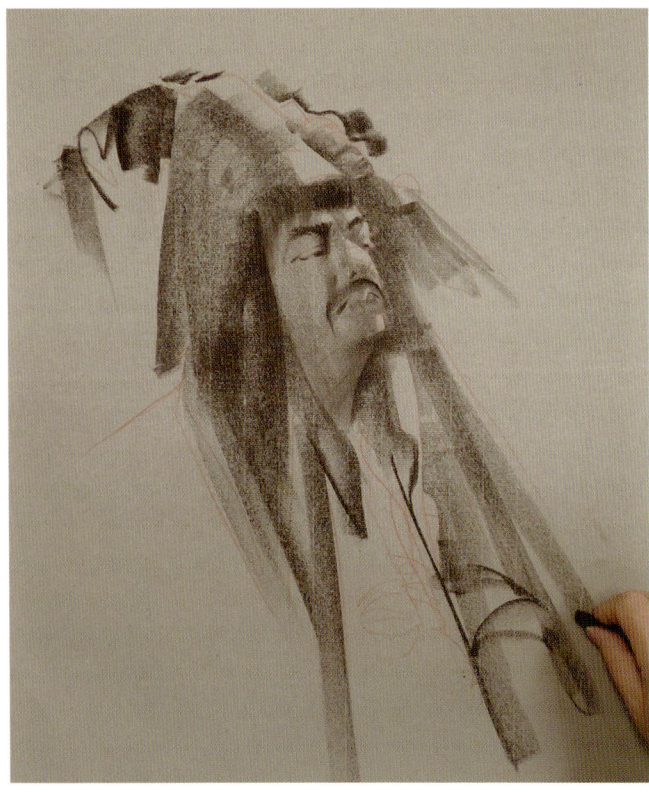

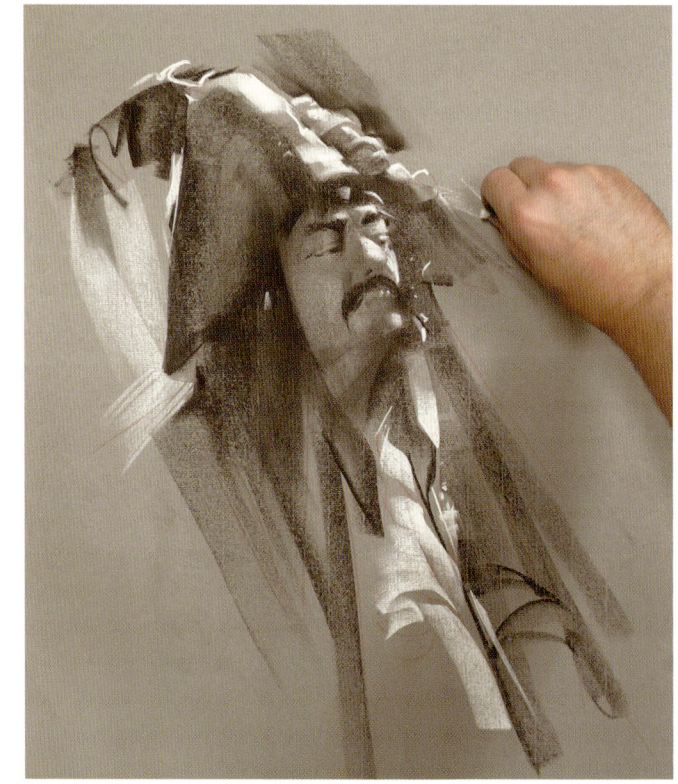

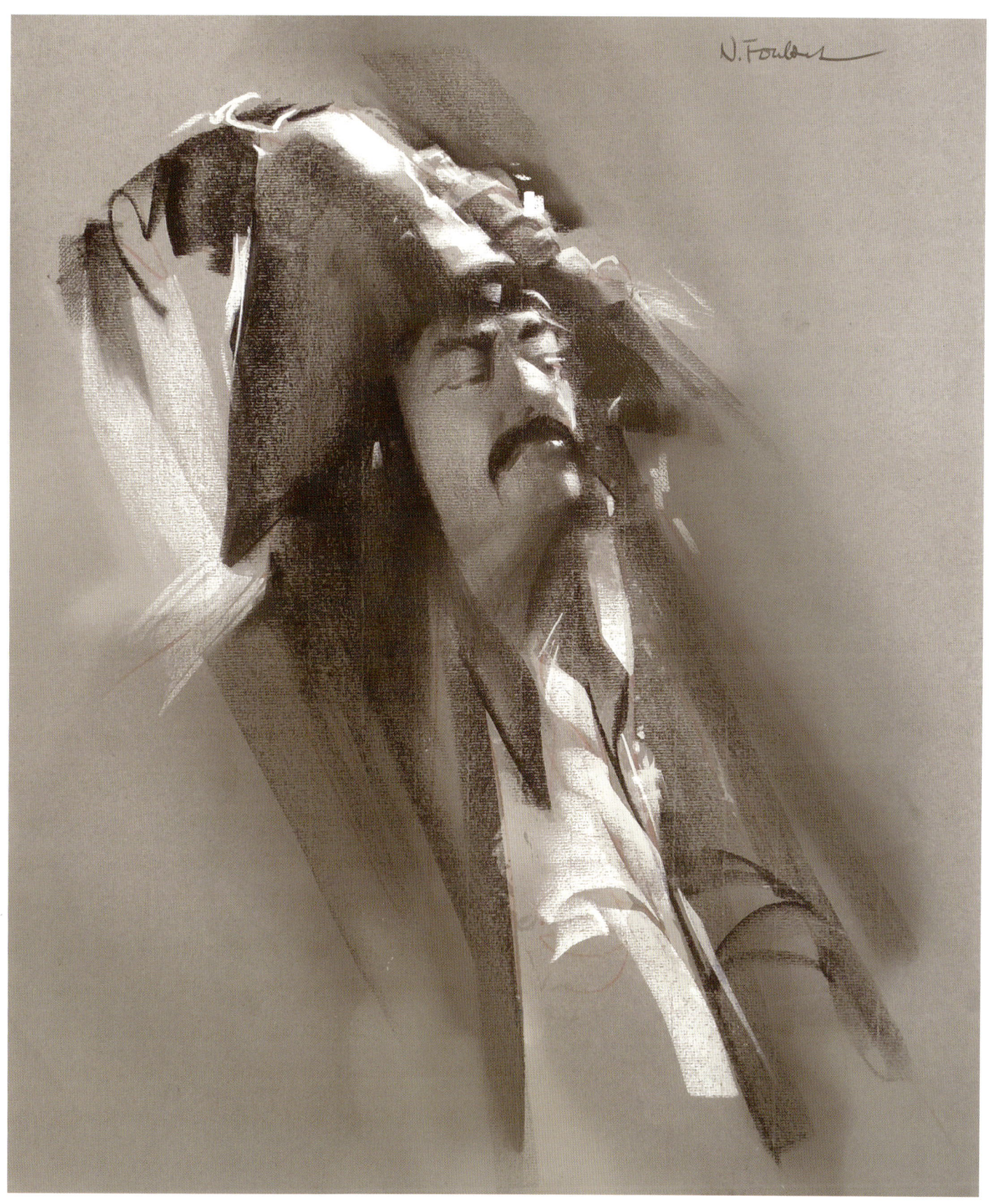

Orange Prismacolor pencil, Ritmo charcoal pencil, compressed charcoal, and white Nupastel on Canson Ingres Vidalon drawing paper.

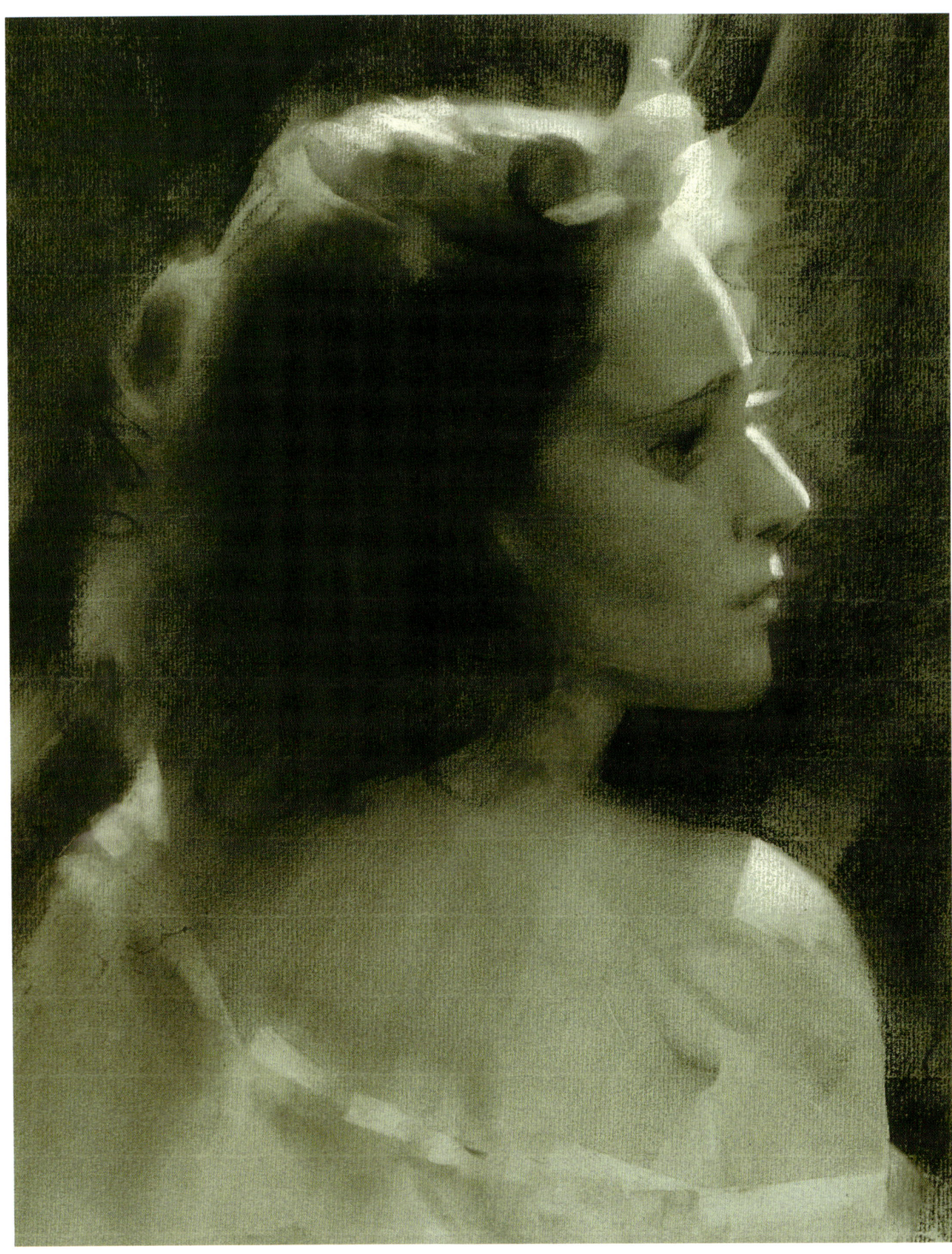

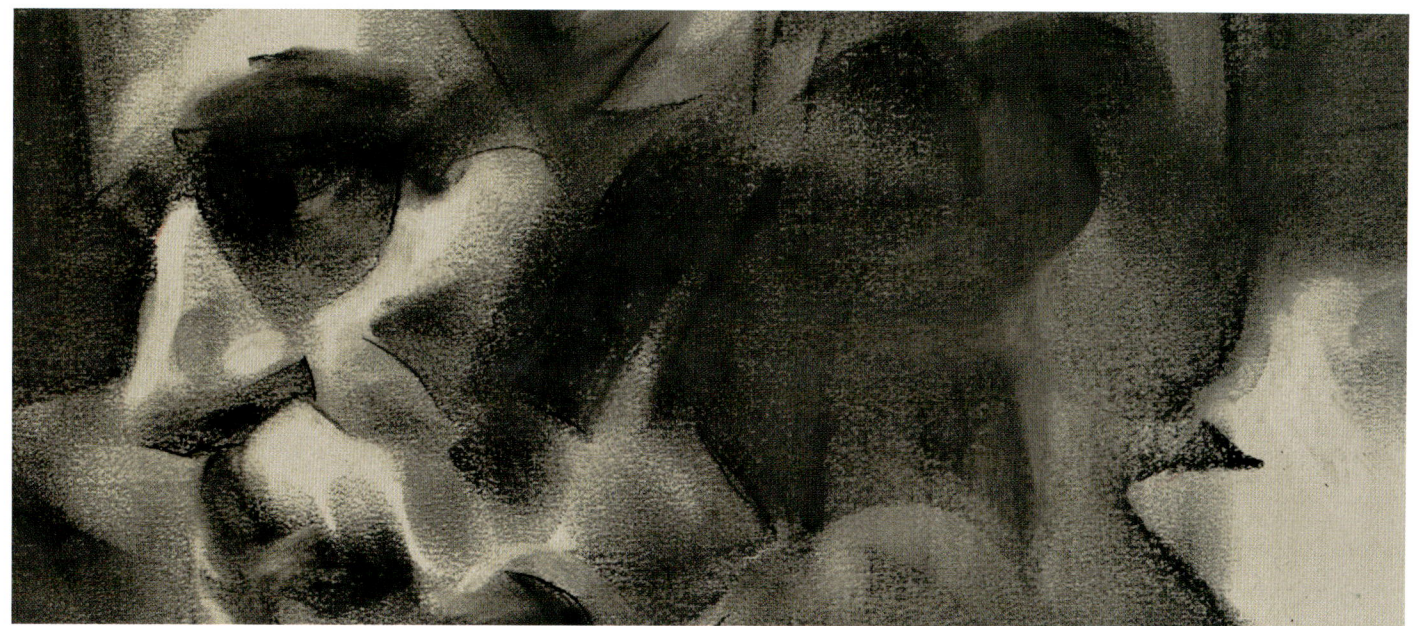

Chapter 12

Gallery of Drawings

And now it's time to look at finished drawings; and in that vein I'd like to share some final tips for posing your subject. Although I believe it's important to just sit down and draw as much as possible, for finished drawings and professional engagements I suggest you take your time until you come up with a pose that you're excited to draw. Your enthusiasm will likely lead you to do your best work. Perhaps chat with the model for a few minutes and do a few sketches to let him or her settle into the pose before you start the final drawing. Even the most professional models will drift a little during the first 10 minutes of the session; let that happen naturally. If you find you are continuously asking the model to move back into position, then you likely have not given him or her a reasonably natural pose. And watch out for the "stern look problem"; your sitter will not necessarily have a natural, relaxed expression during long hours of sitting. Invite him or her to take a break, and then think of something pleasant when they return; do your best to match your sitter's expression during those moments.

And now we're done! No more advice from me; it's simply time for me to do my best to walk my talk. The following gallery of drawings spans the past 15 years of my career; I've tackled them with a variety of materials, techniques, and approaches hoping that each one will do justice to the unique lighting, pose, and character of my sitter.

My finished portraits tend to be drawn slightly smaller than life-size, a scale that feels natural to me since we always see the world in diminishing perspective. I usually spend in the range of two to three hours on each, but I also like to take a fresh look at the drawing the next day and do any additional touch-up that's needed.

Enjoy!

Opposite: Compressed charcoal and ivory Nupastel on Canson Ingres Vidalon drawing paper.

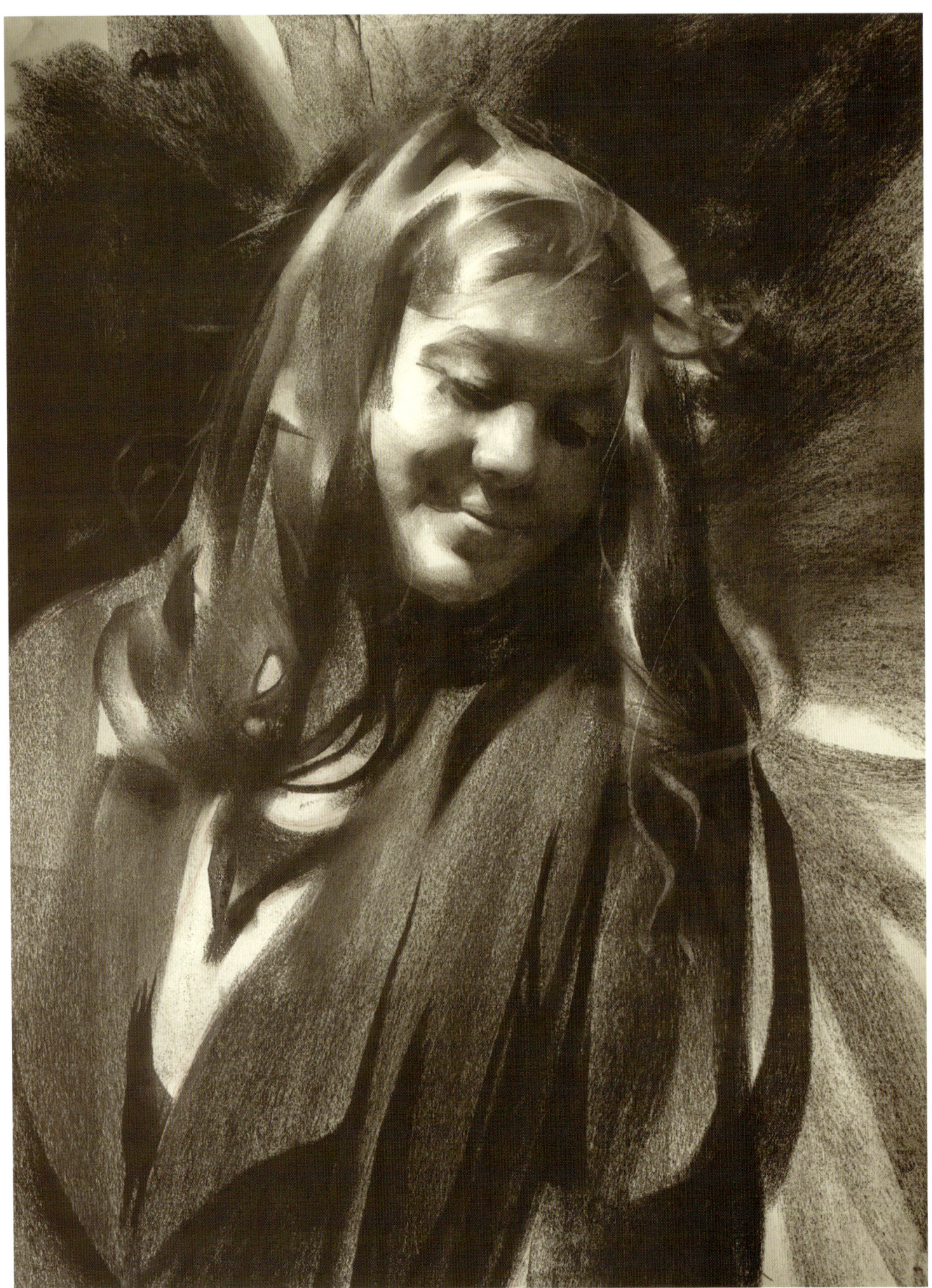

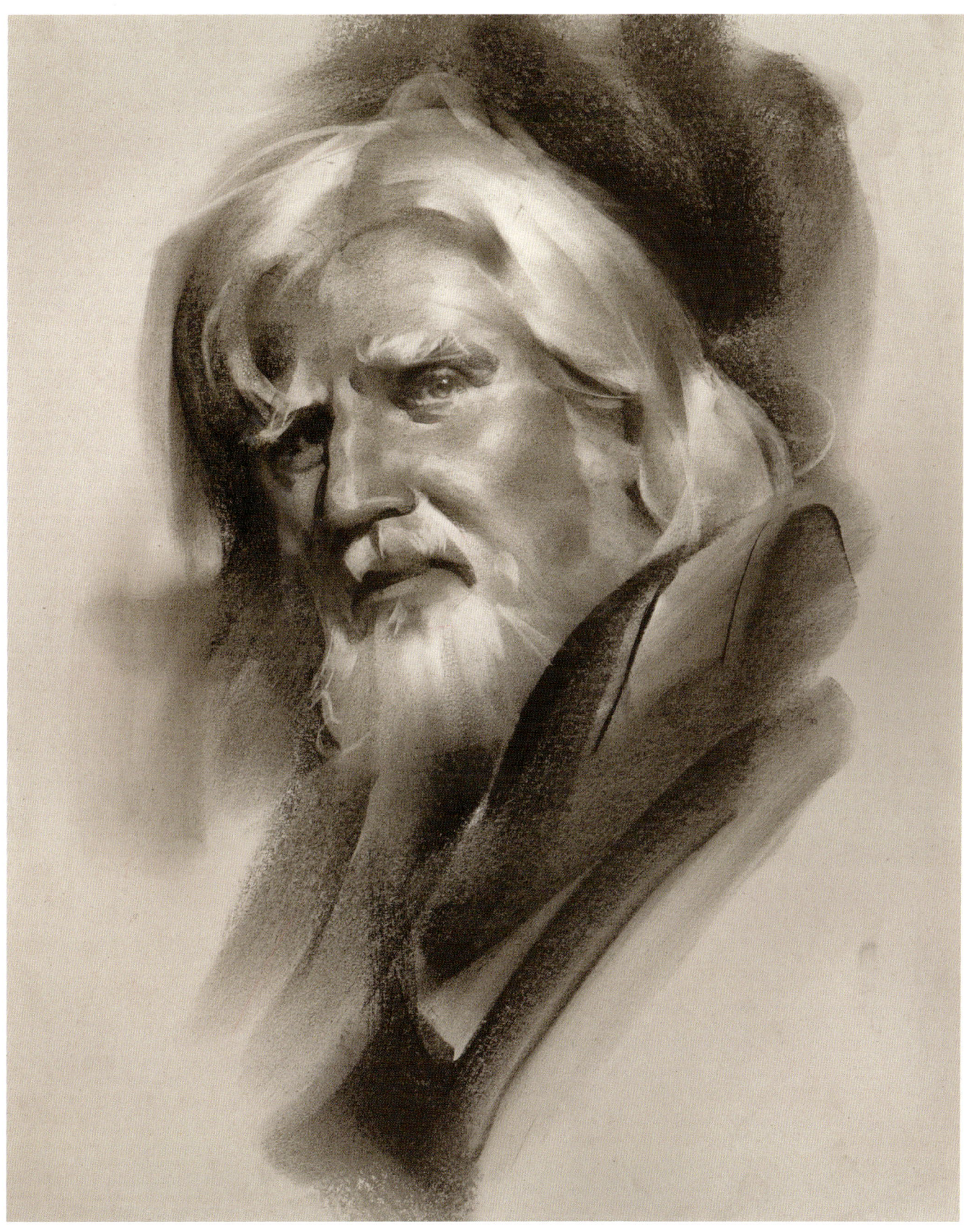

Above: Compressed charcoal and Pitt charcoal pencil on rough newsprint.

Opposite: Compressed charcoal on Rives lightweight white paper.

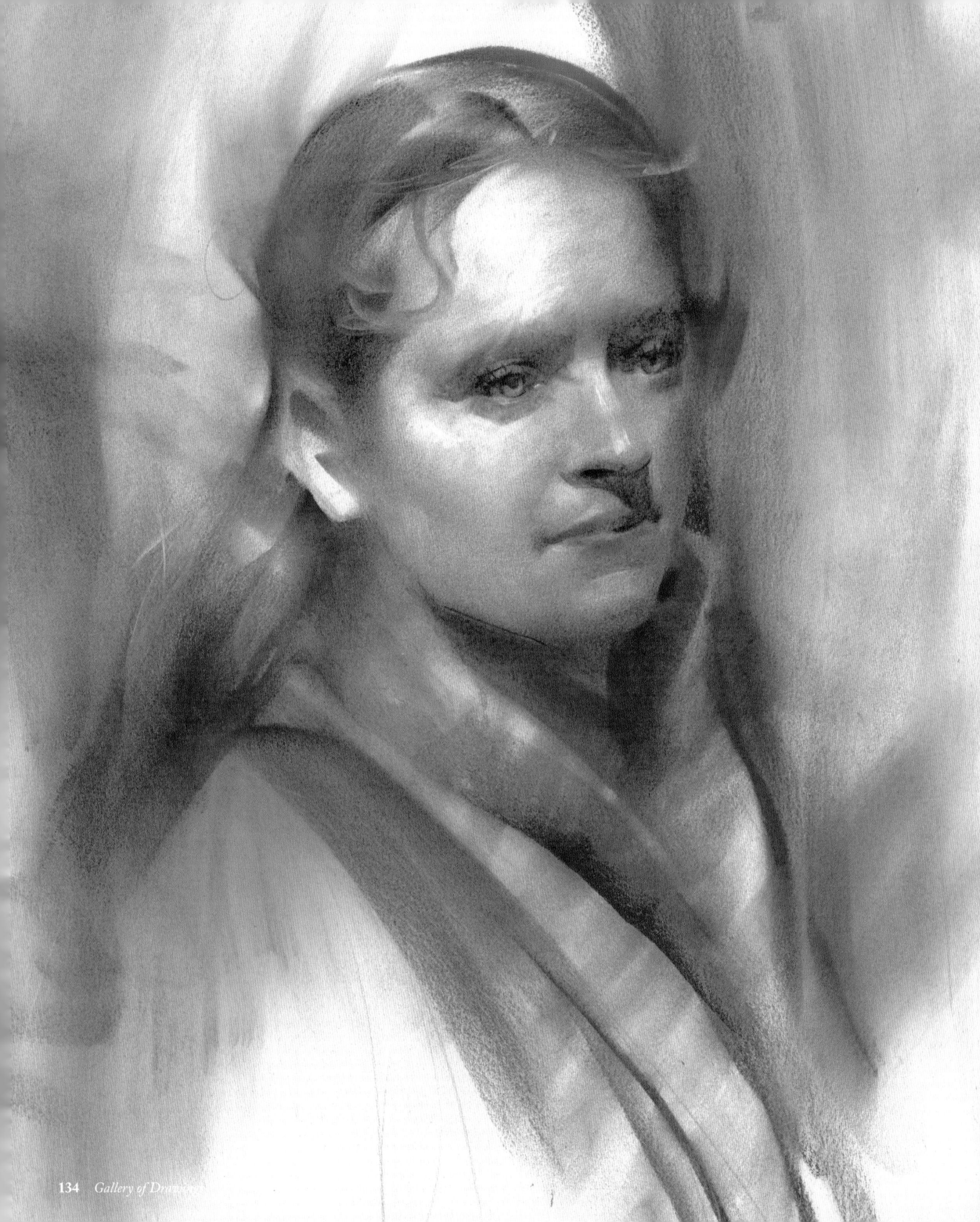

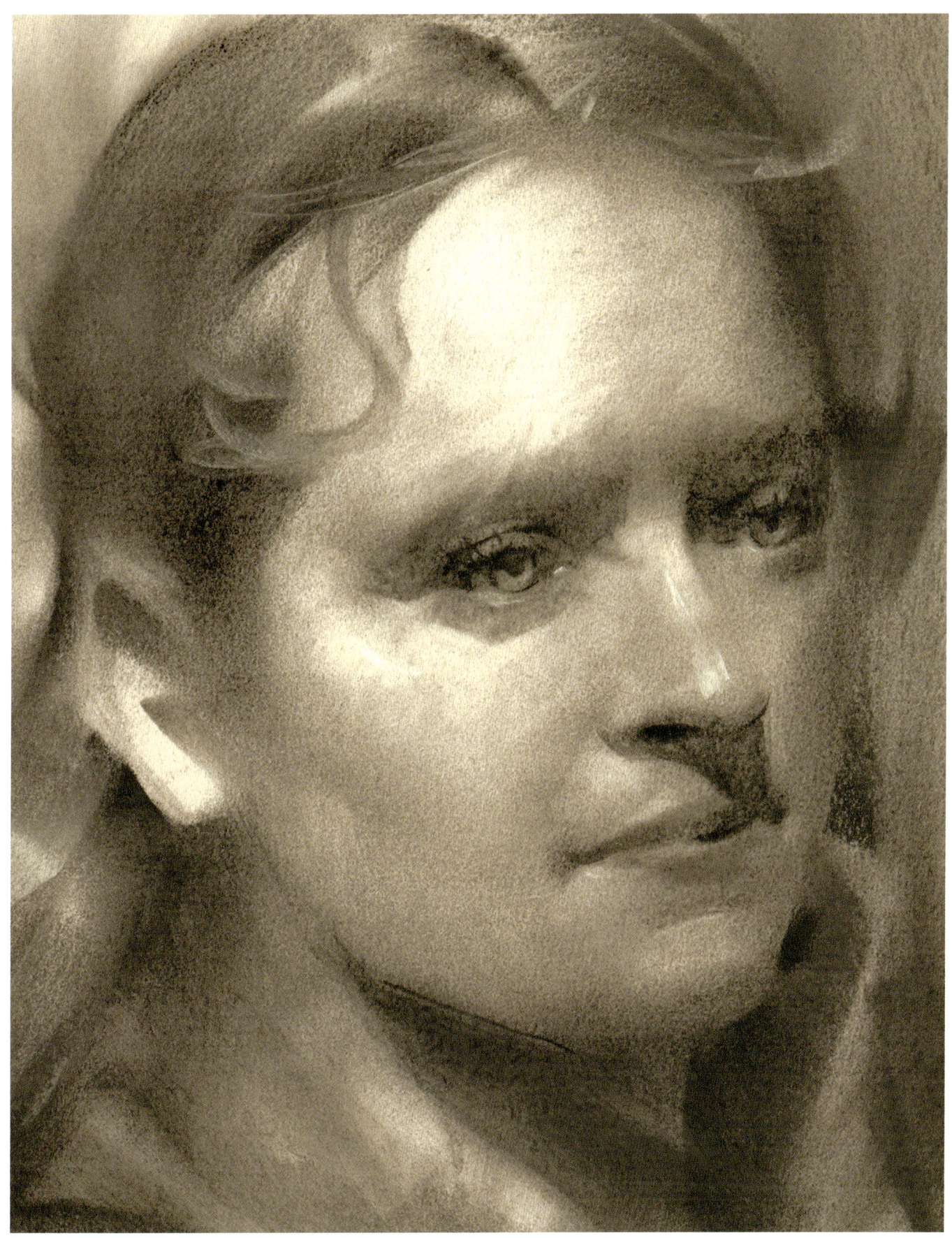

Compressed charcoal, Pitt charcoal pencil, and white CarbOthello pencil on Rives lightweight cream paper.

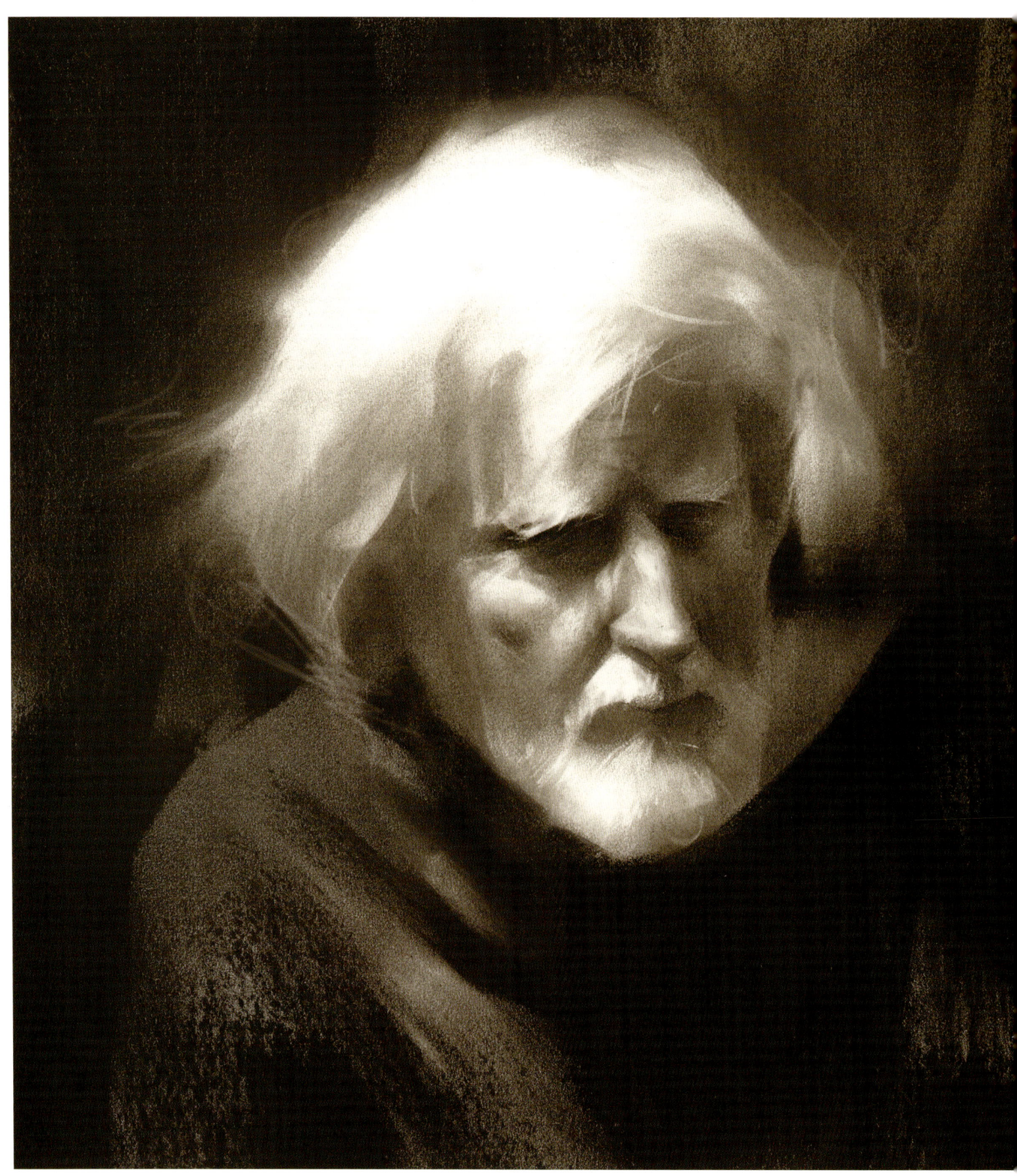

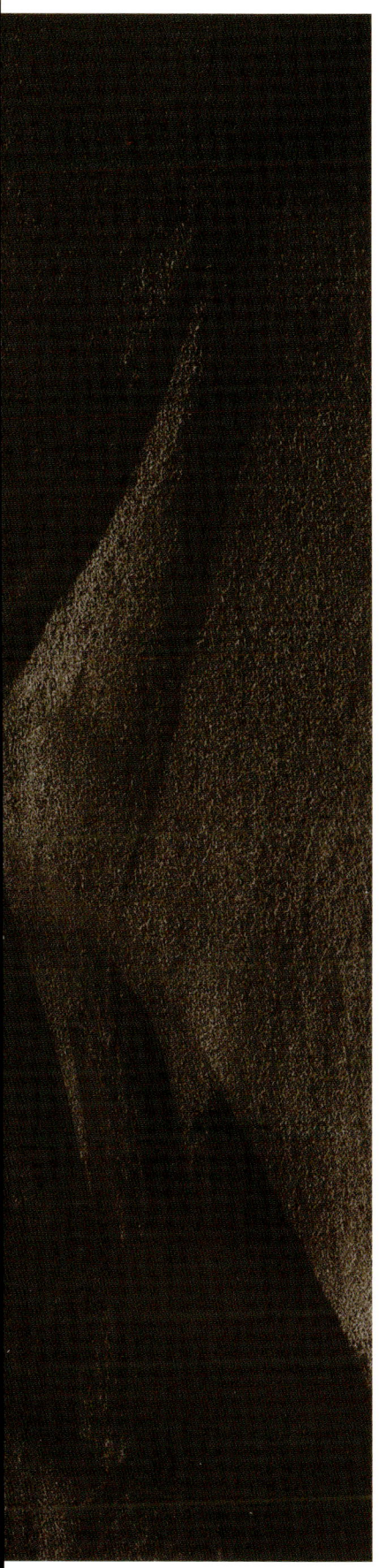

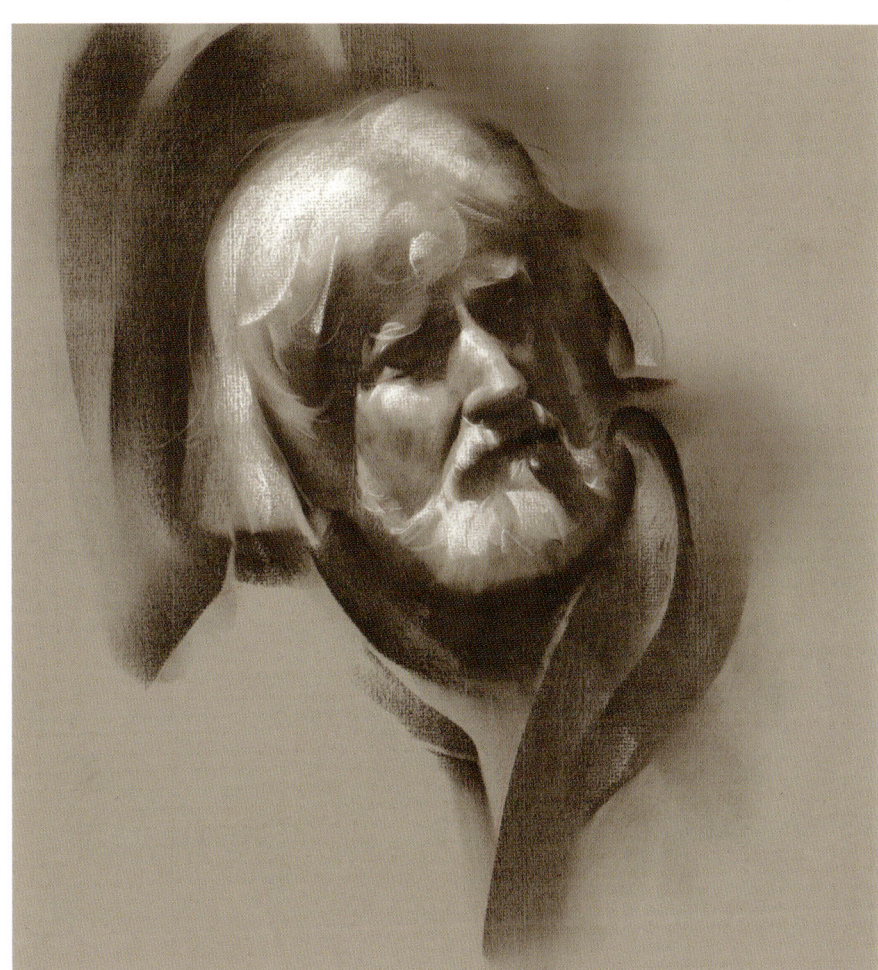

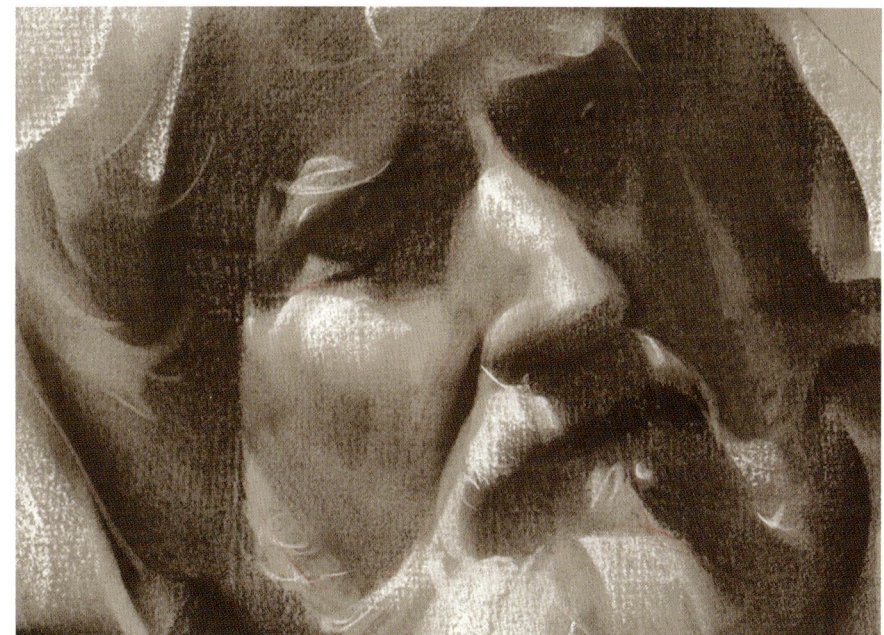

Above: Compressed charcoal and white Nupastel on Canson Ingres Vidalon drawing paper.

Opposite: Compressed charcoal on heavyweight Bristol Paper.

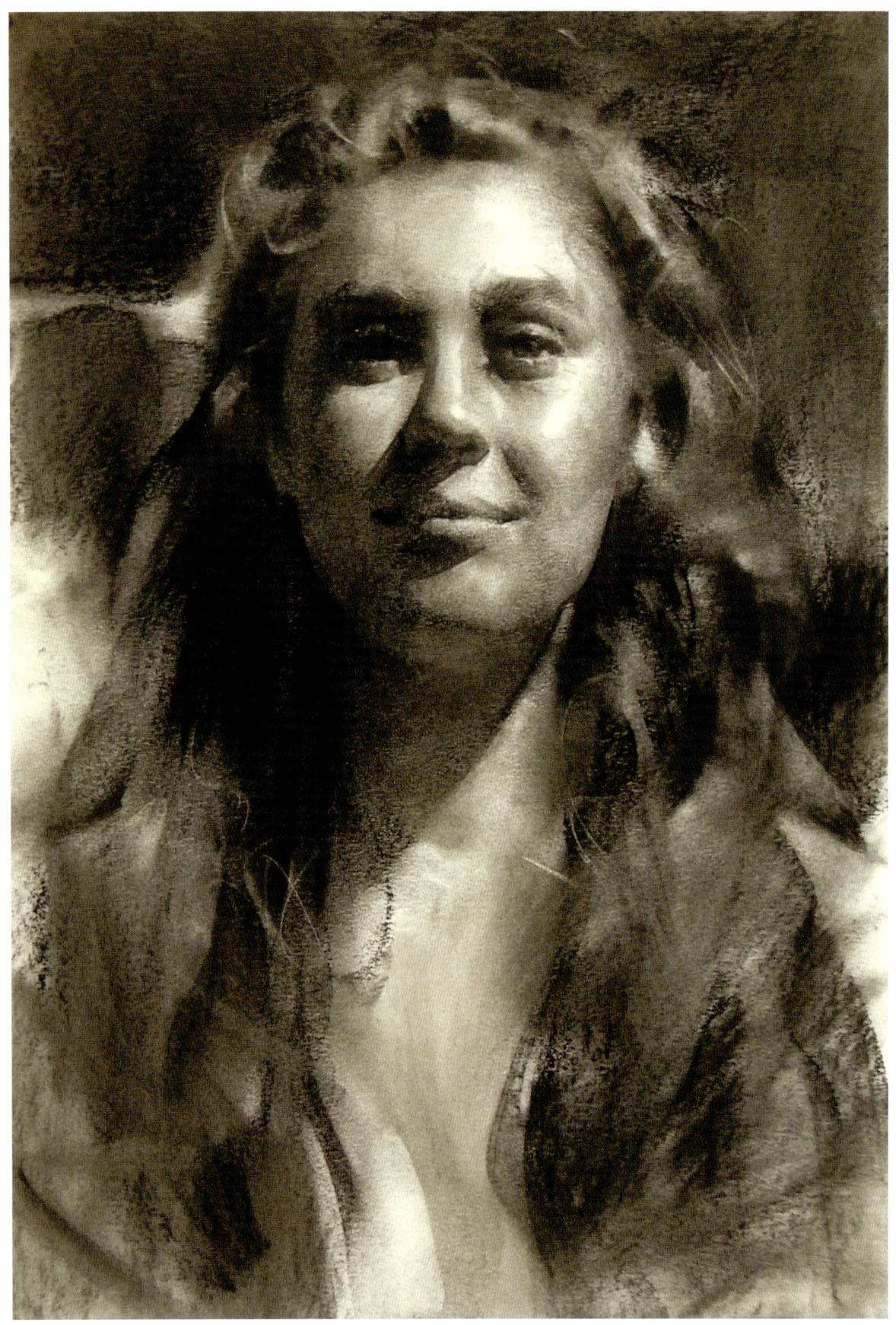

Above: Compressed charcoal and Pitt charcoal pencil on heavyweight Bristol Paper.

Opposite: Compressed charcoal and Pitt charcoal pencil on rough newsprint.

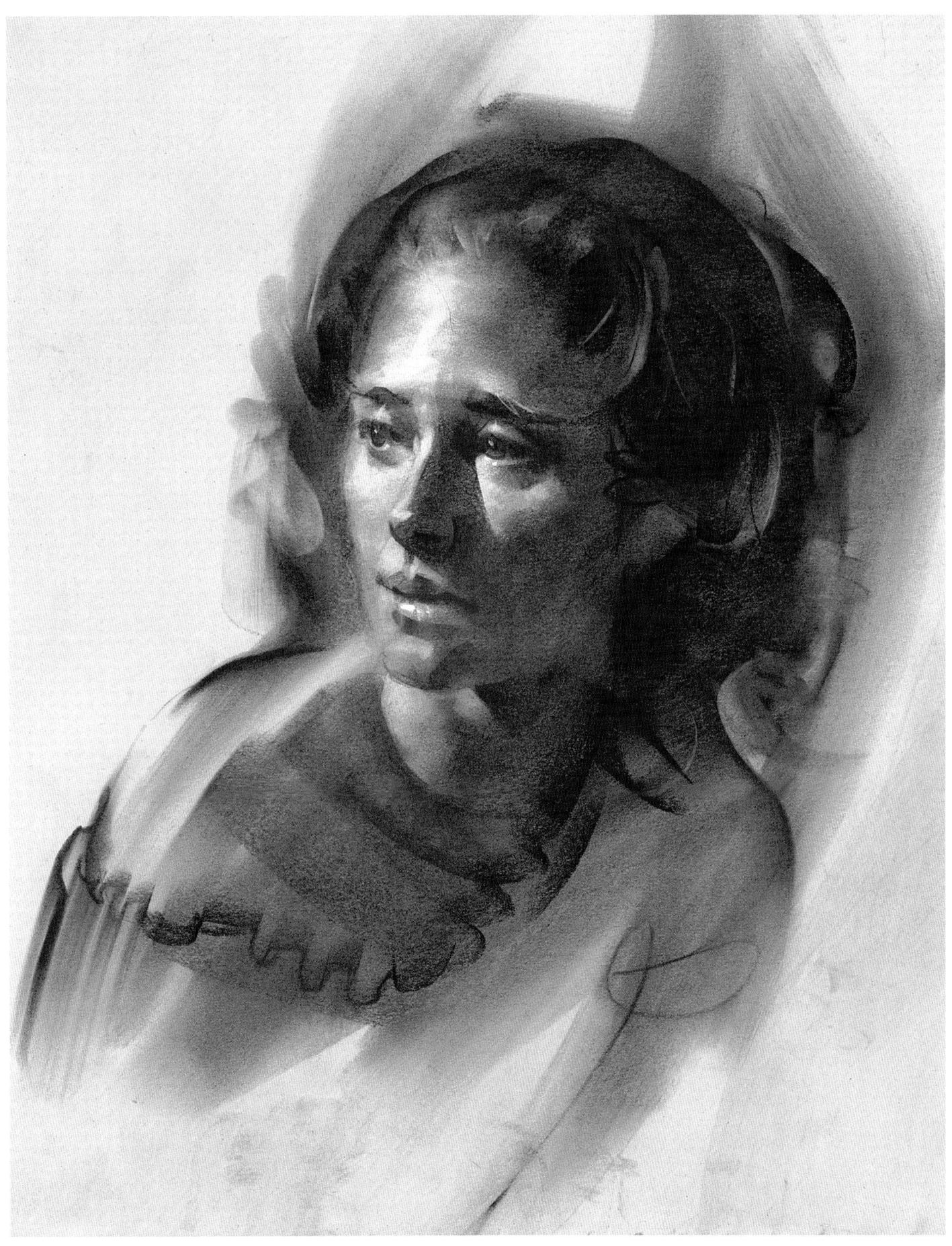

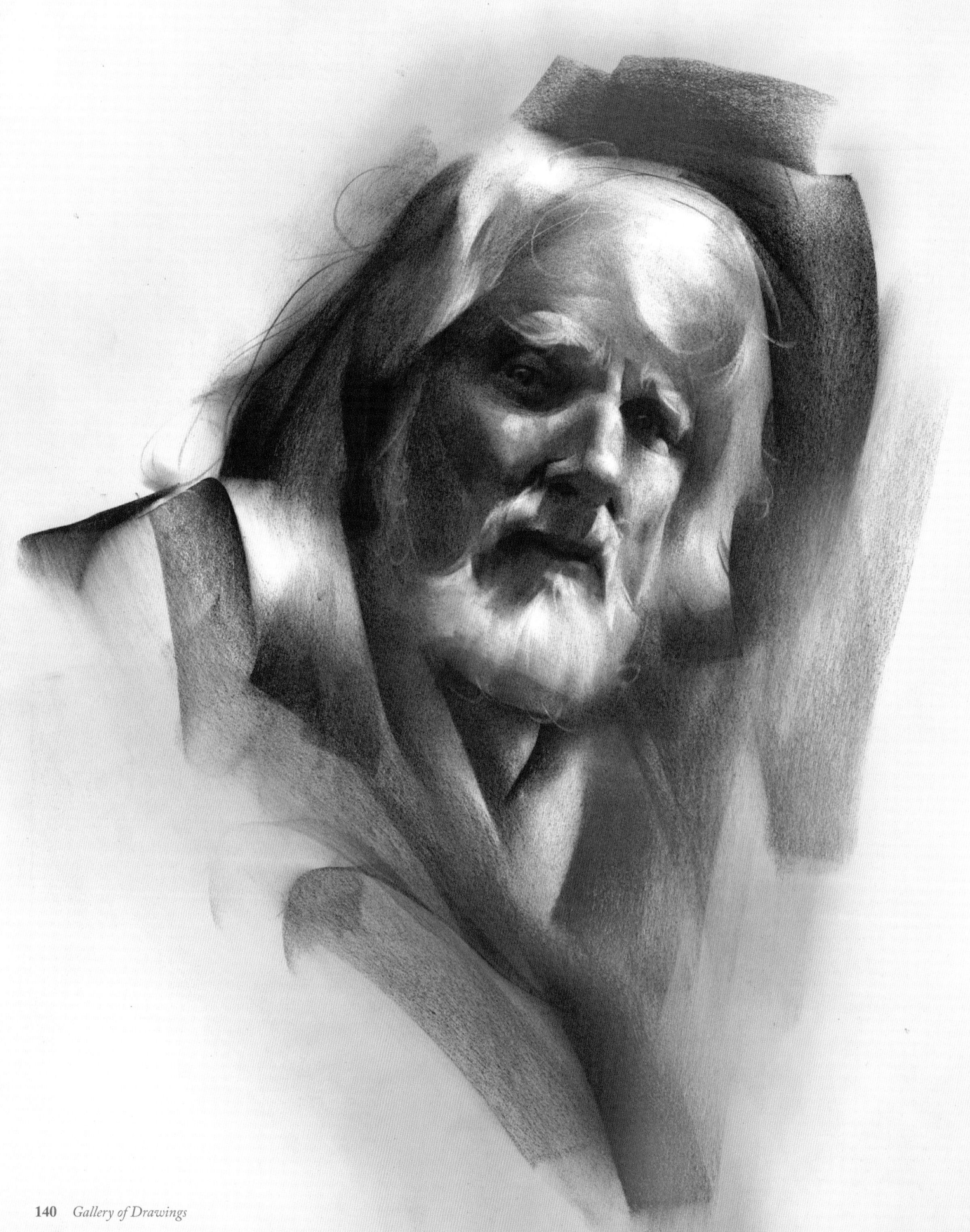

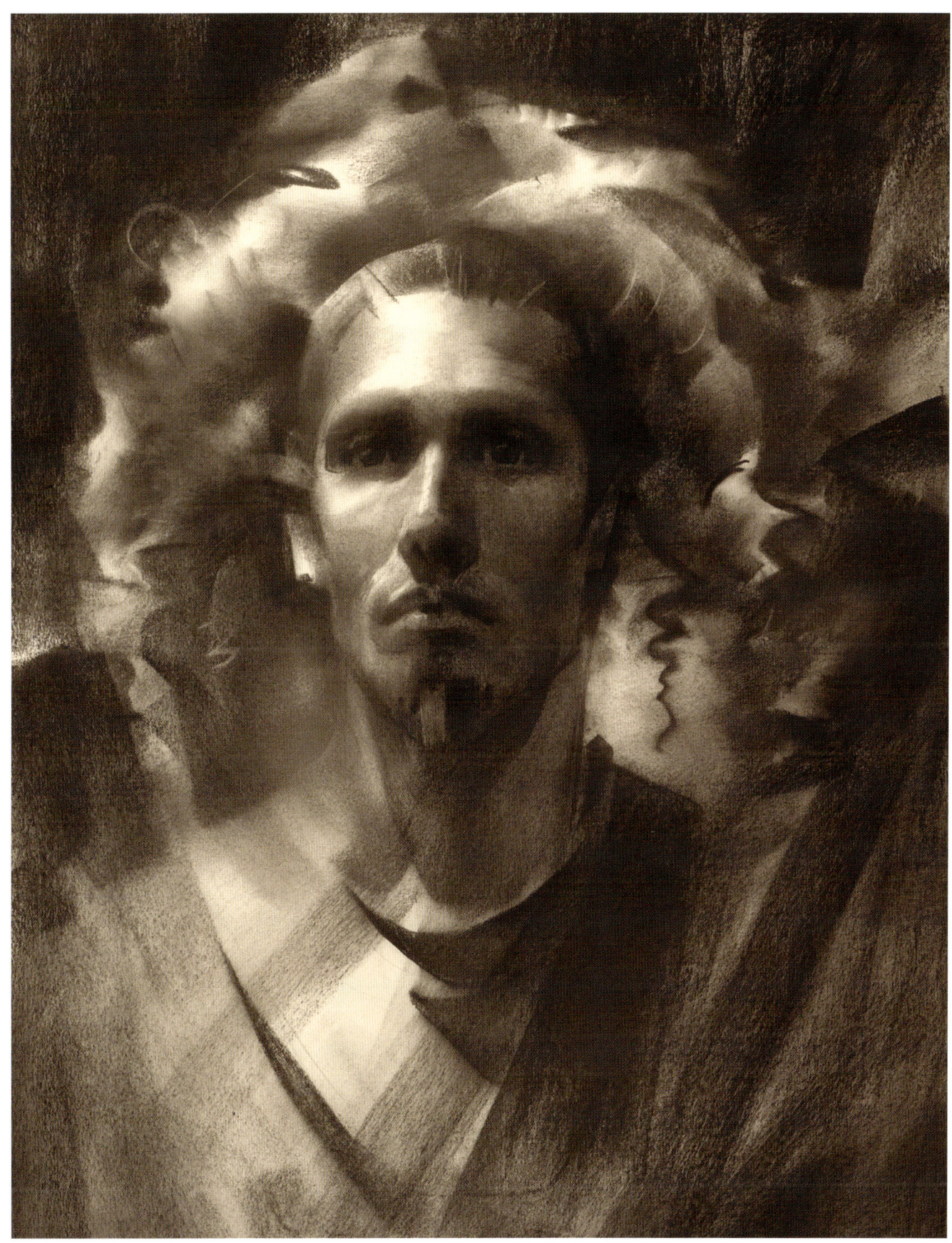

Above: Compressed charcoal on Rives lightweight cream paper.

Opposite: Compressed charcoal on Rives lightweight cream paper.

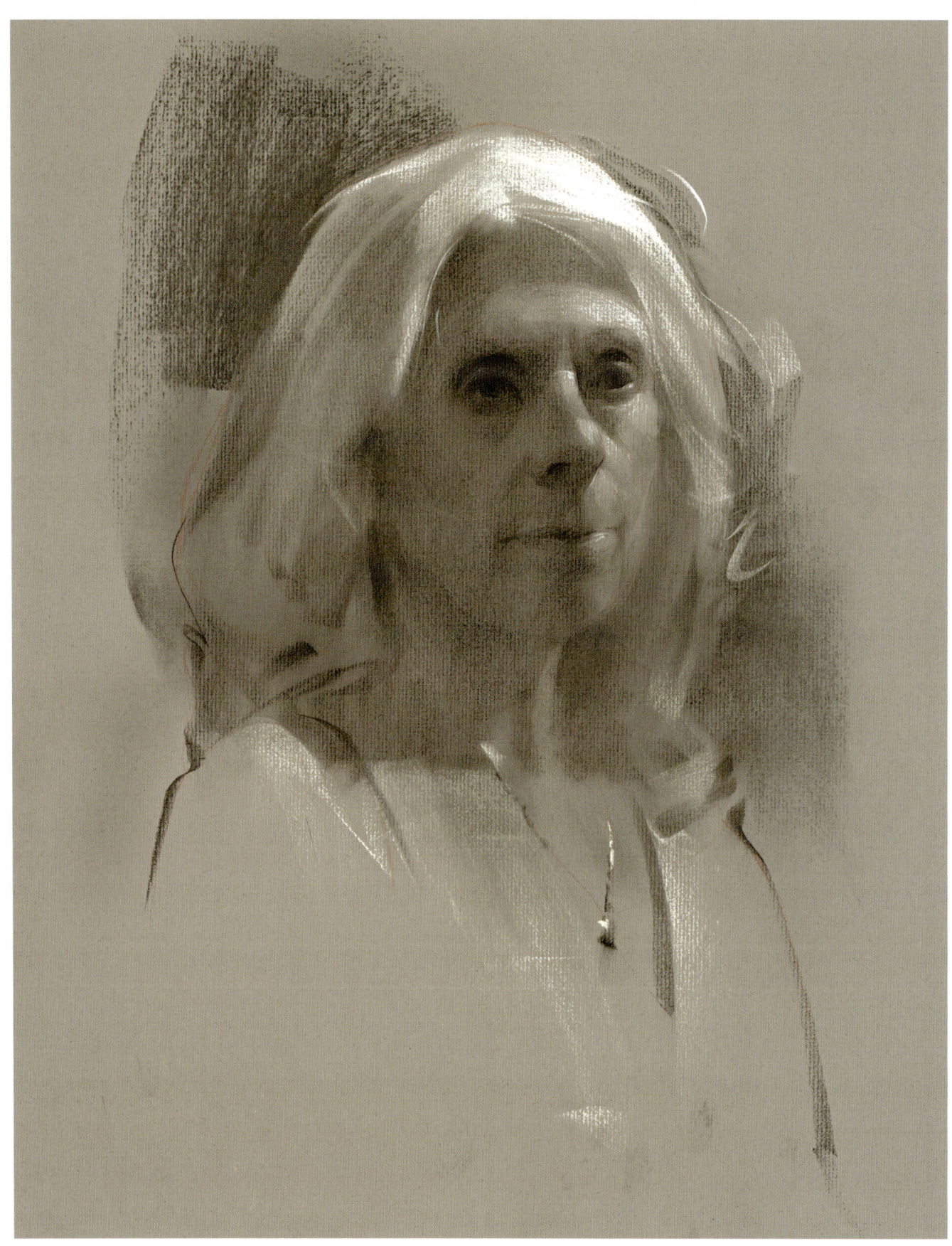

Above: Vine charcoal, Ritmo charcoal pencil, and white Nupastel on Canson Ingres Vidalon drawing paper.

Opposite: Ritmo charcoal pencil and white Nupastel on Strathmore charcoal paper.

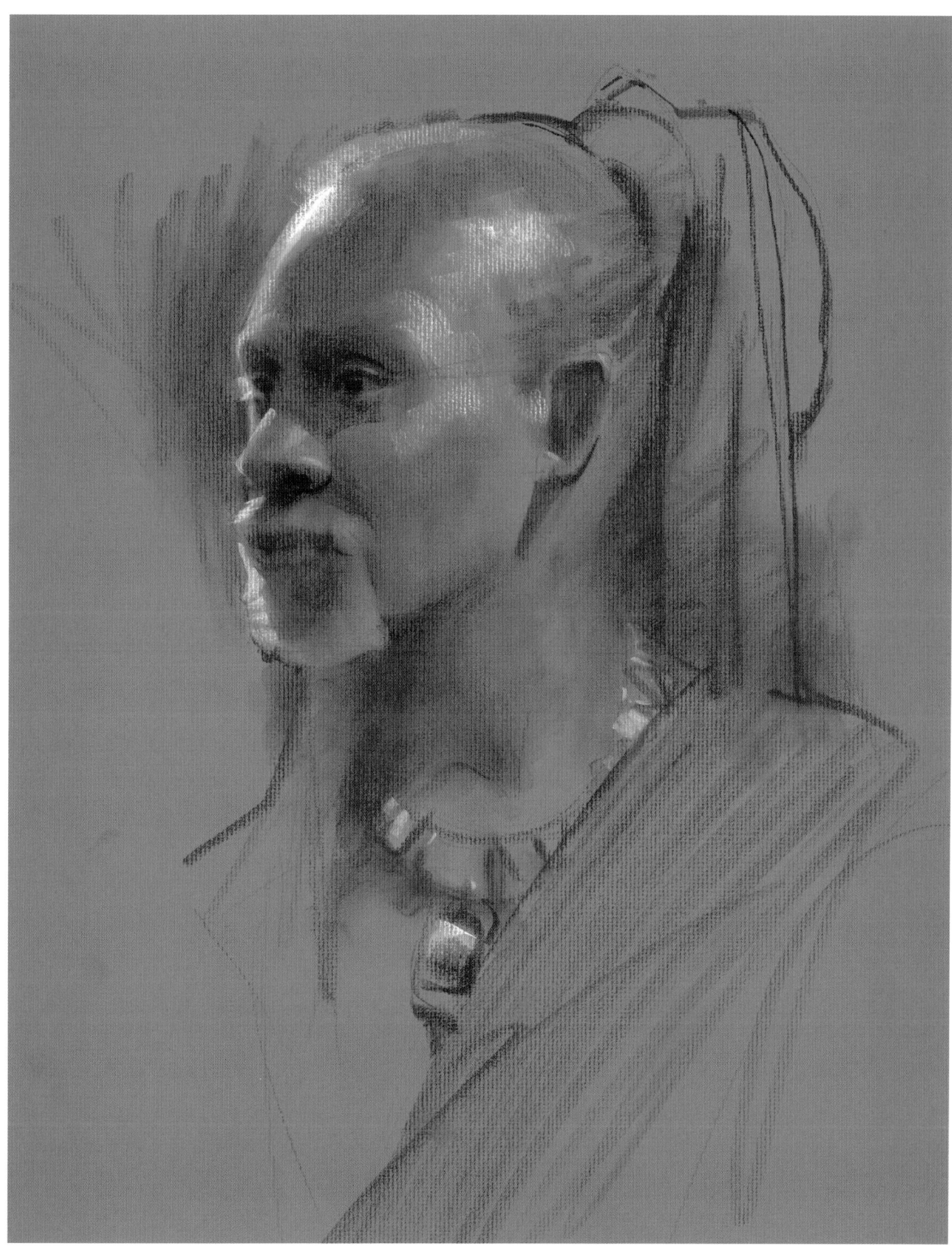

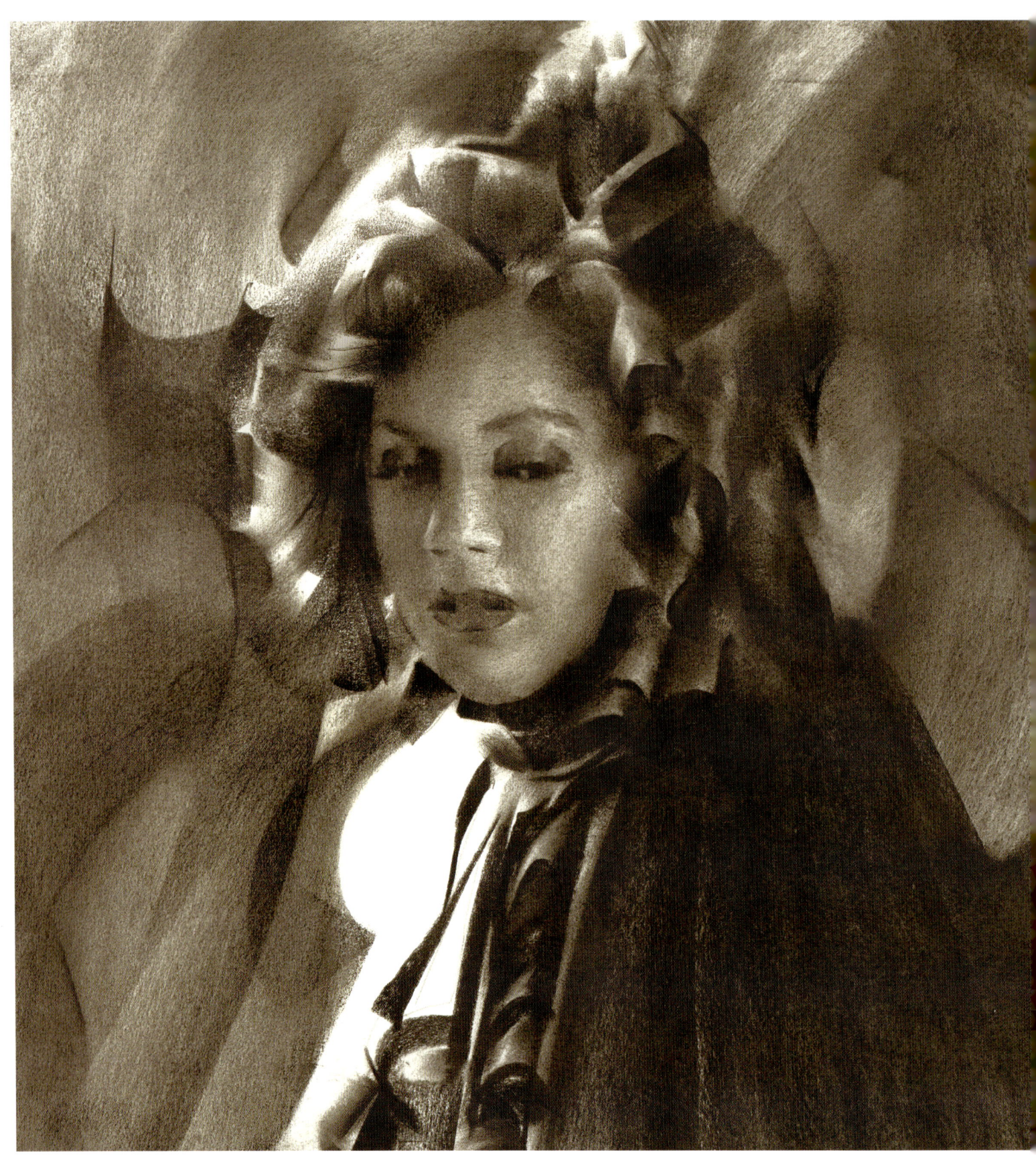

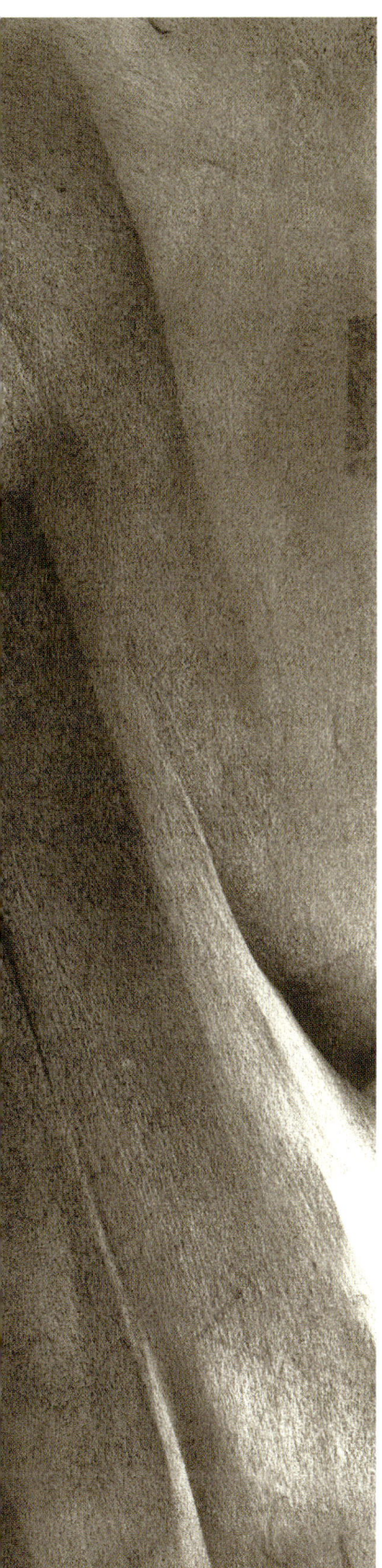

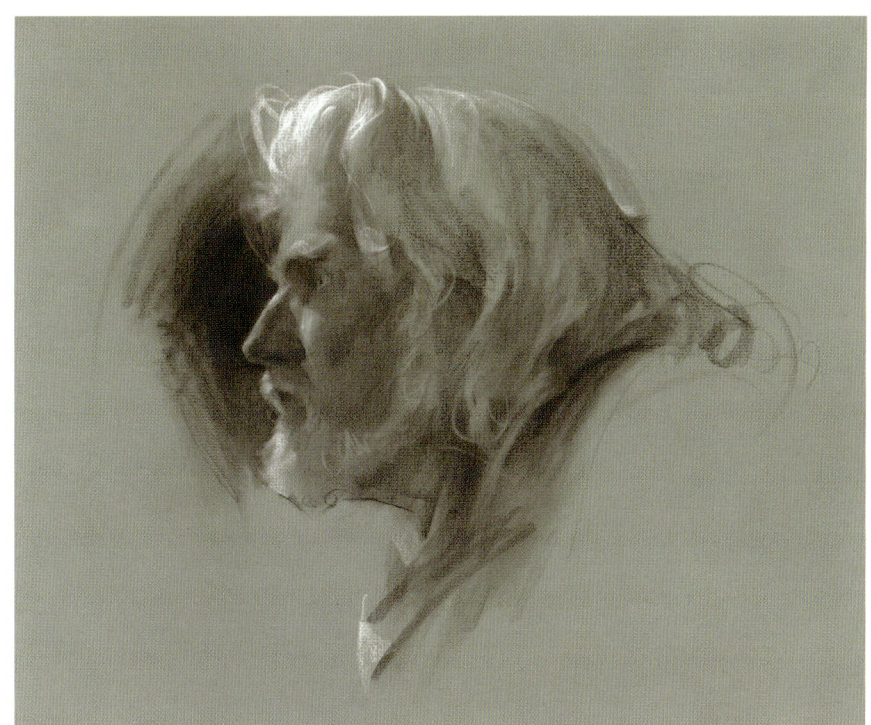

Above: Ritmo charcoal pencil and white CarbOthello pencil on Strathmore charcoal paper.

Opposite: Compressed charcoal and Pitt charcoal pencil on Rives lightweight white paper.

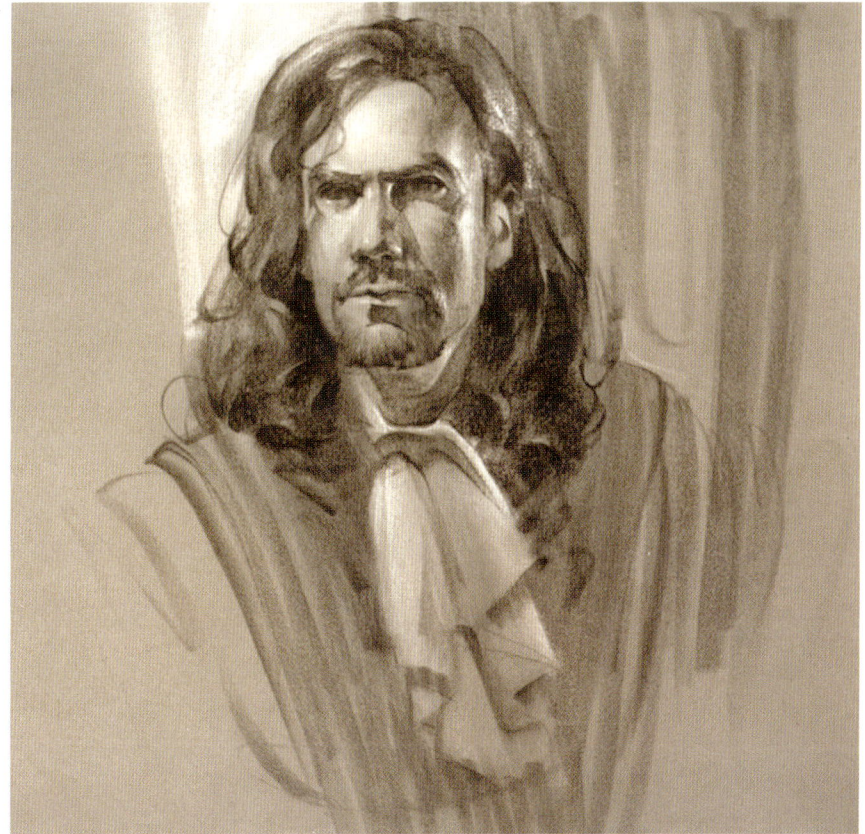

Ritmo charcoal pencil and white Nupastel on Strathmore charcoal paper.

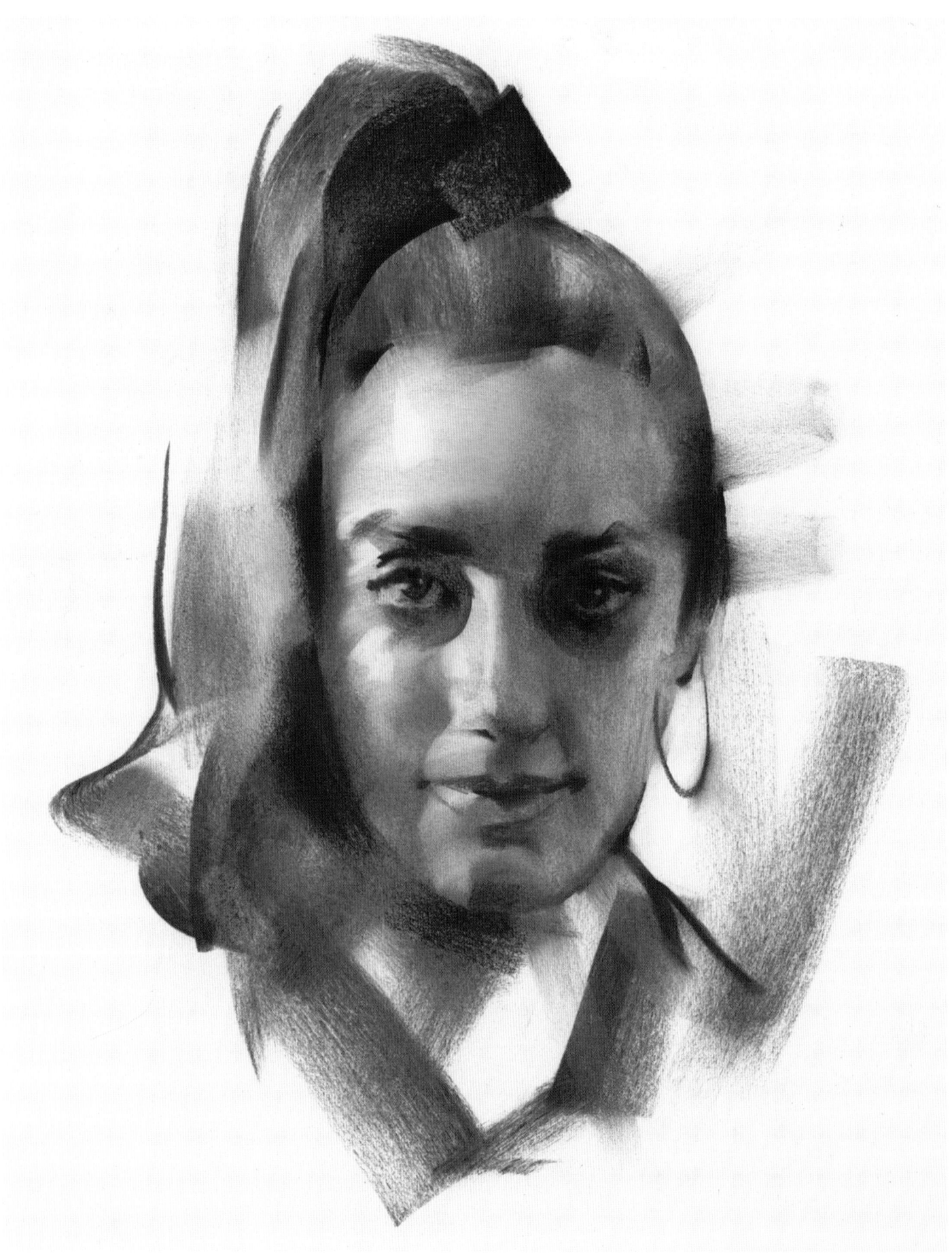

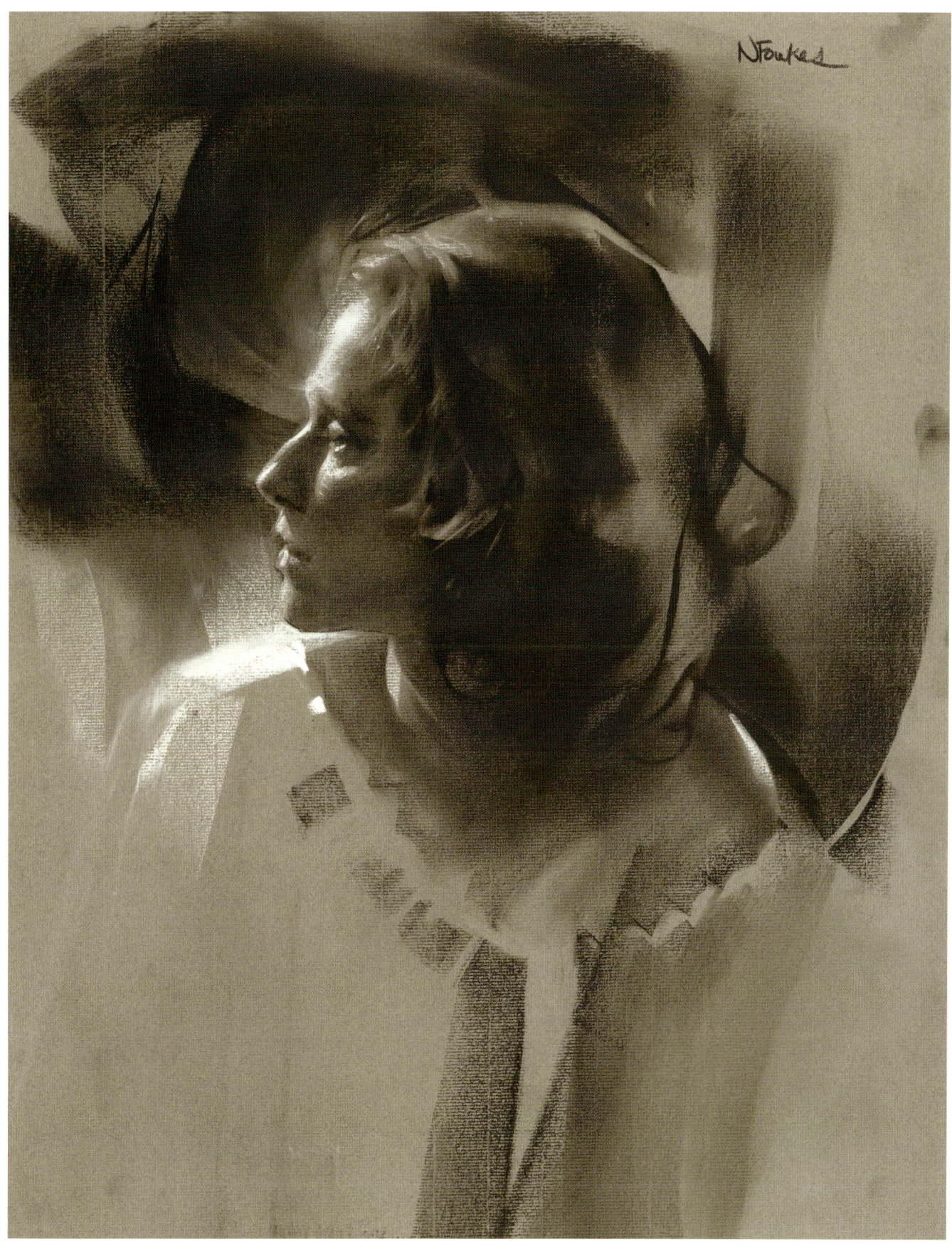

Above: Compressed charcoal and white Nupastel on Canson Ingres Vidalon drawing paper.

Opposite: Vine charcoal on Canson Ingres Vidalon drawing paper.

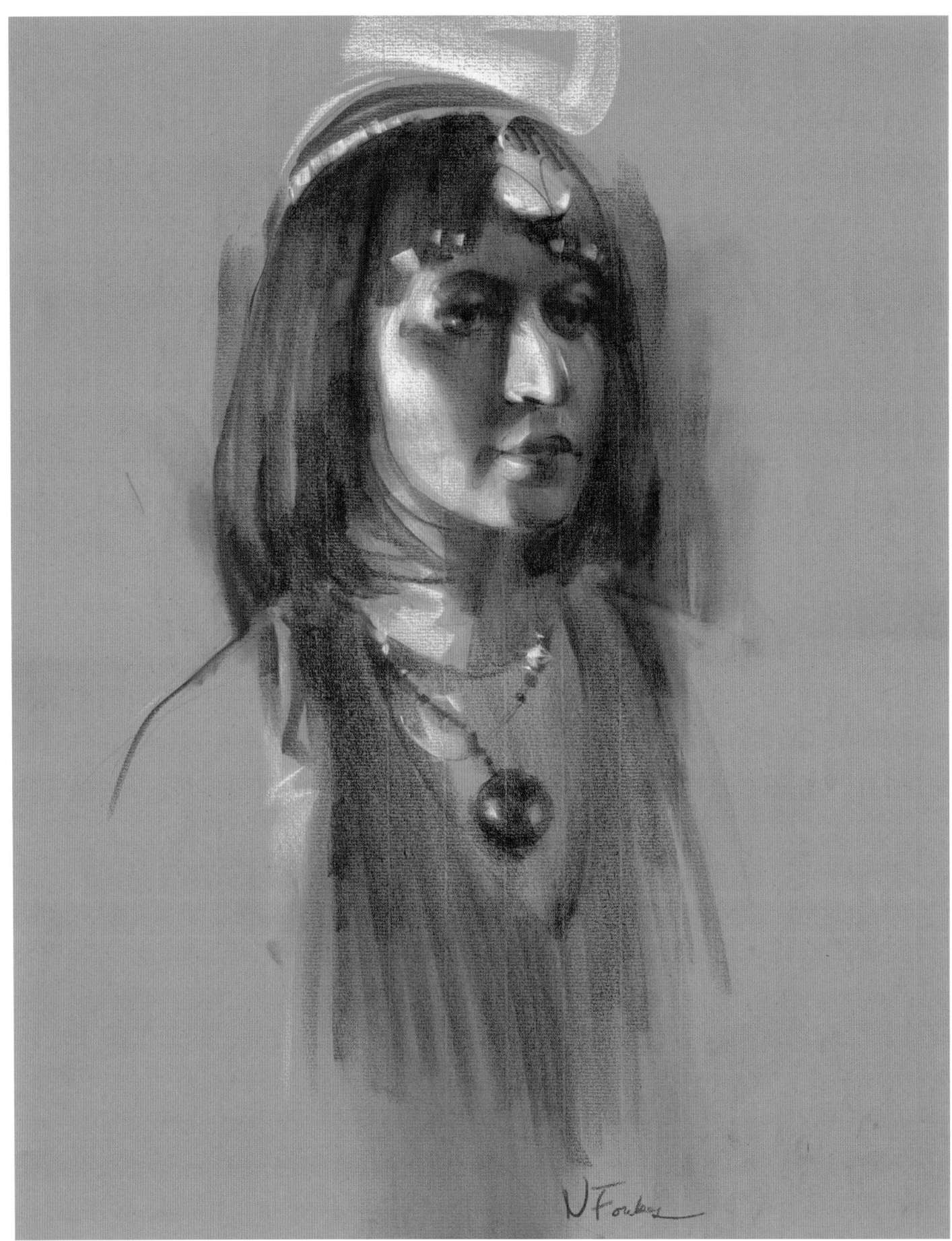

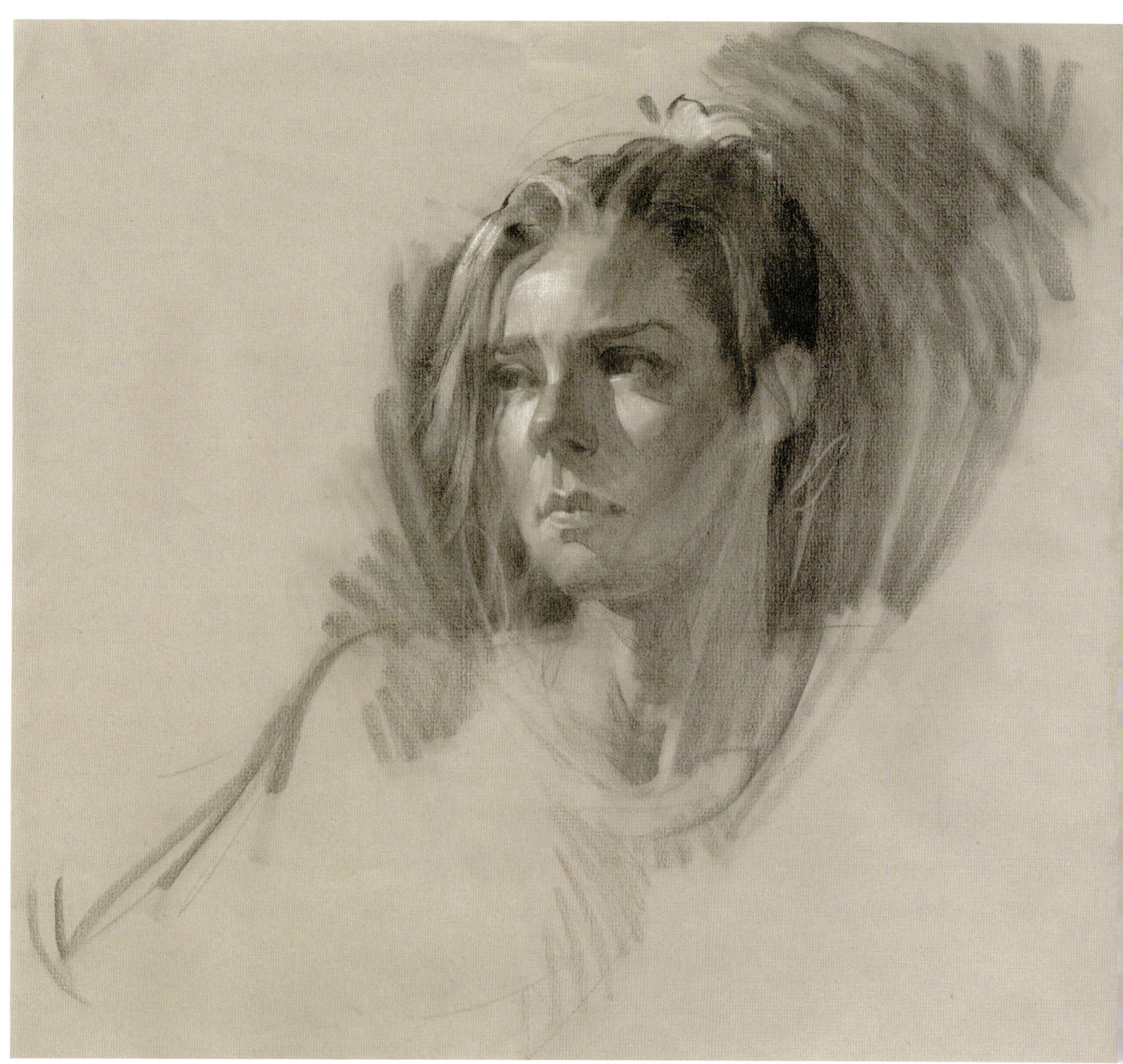

Above: Ritmo charcoal pencil and white CarbOthello pencil on Canson Ingres Vidalon drawing paper.

Opposite: Ritmo charcoal pencil and white Nupastel on Strathmore charcoal paper.

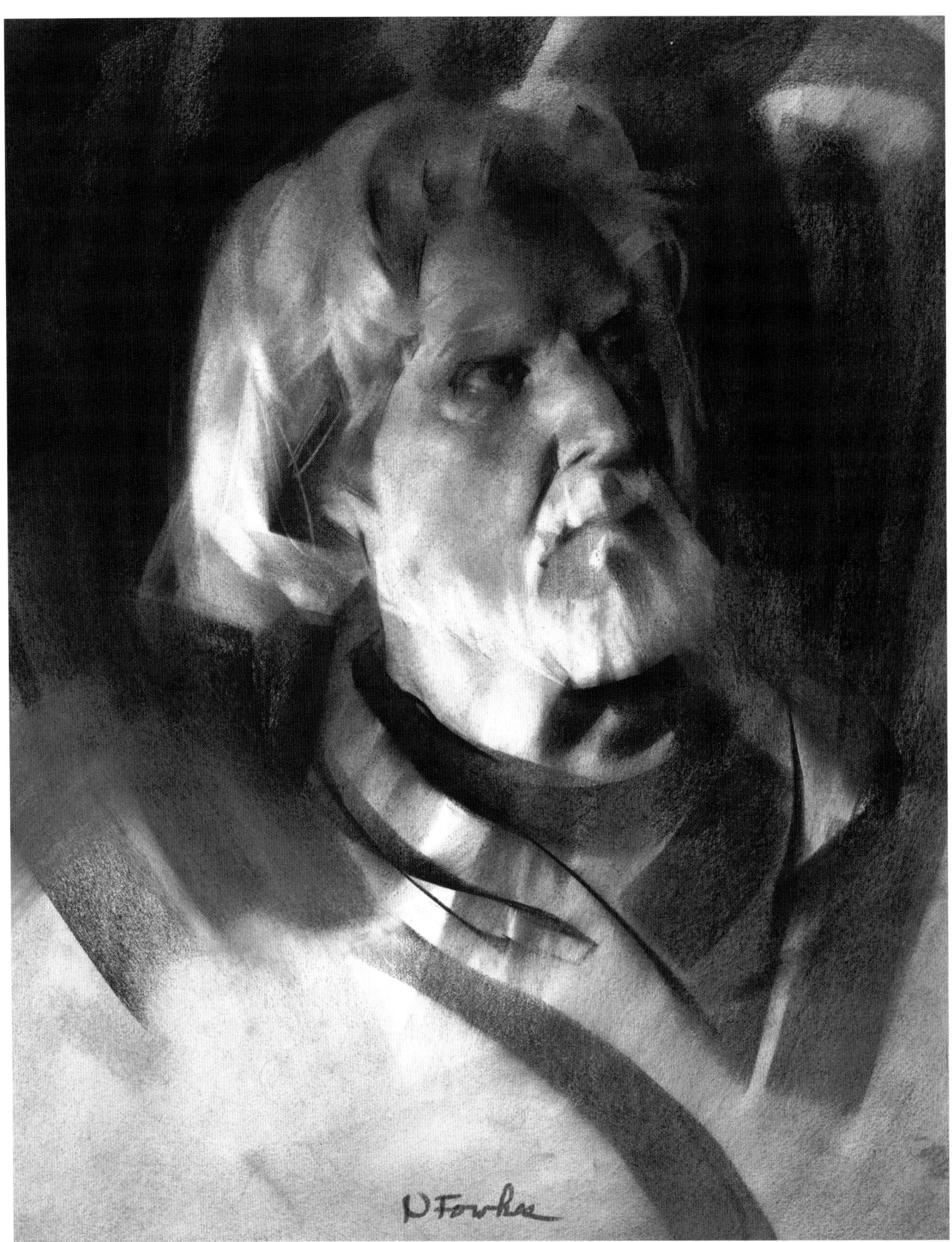

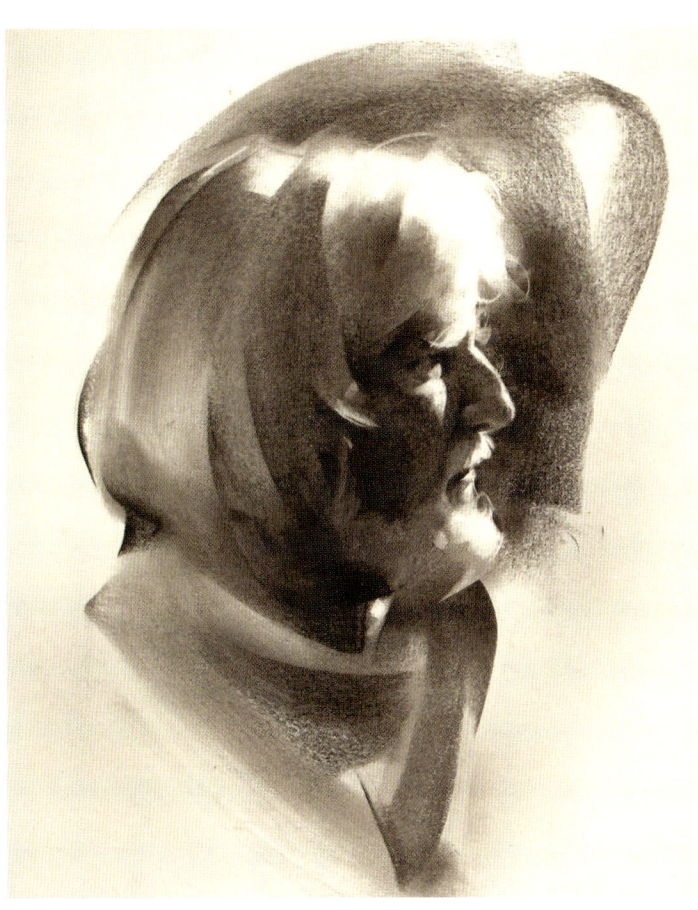

Left: Compressed charcoal on rough newsprint.

Opposite: Compressed charcoal and Pitt charcoal pencil on Rives lightweight cream paper.

Compressed charcoal on rough newsprint.

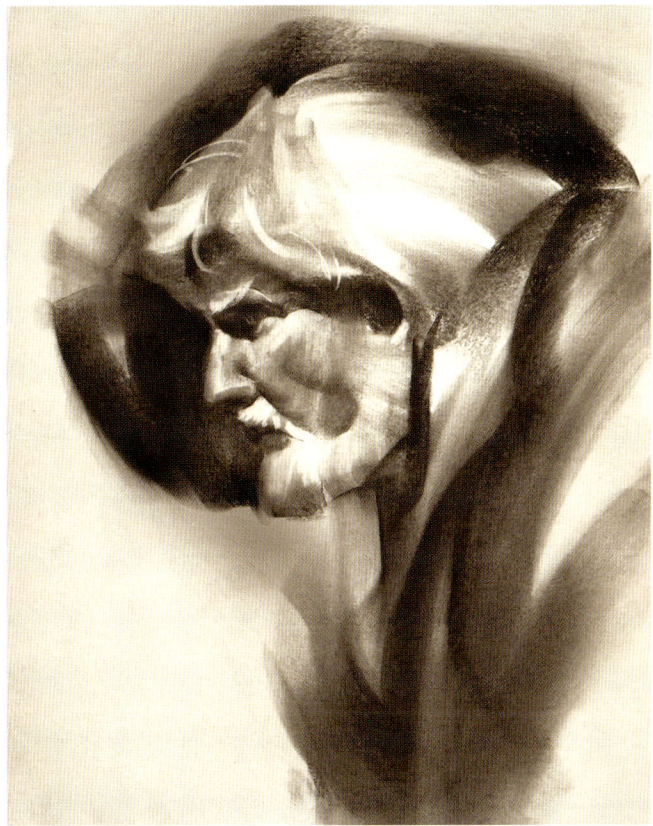

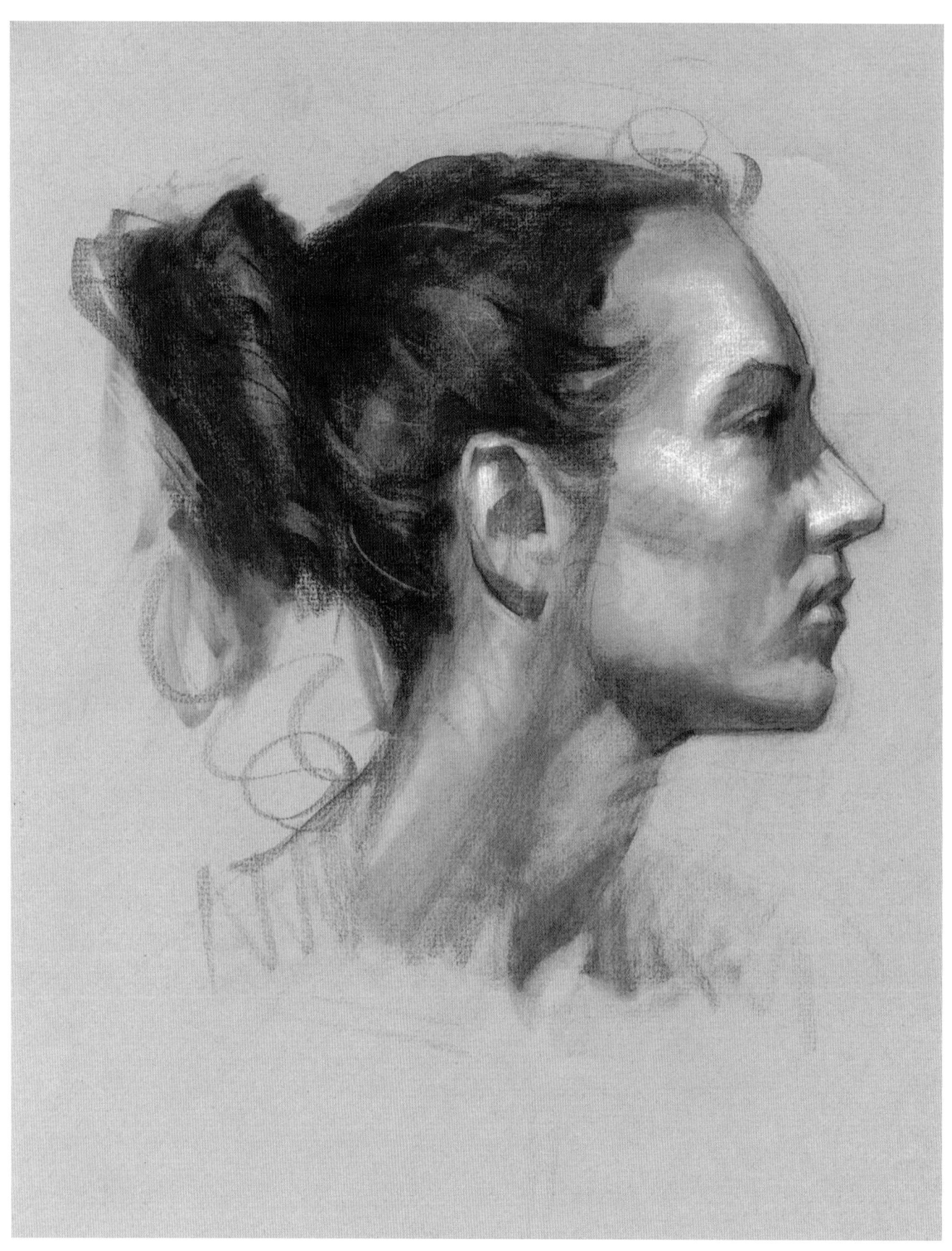

Above: Ritmo charcoal pencil and white CarbOthello pencil on Strathmore charcoal paper.

Opposite: Compressed charcoal on Canson Ingres Vidalon drawing paper.

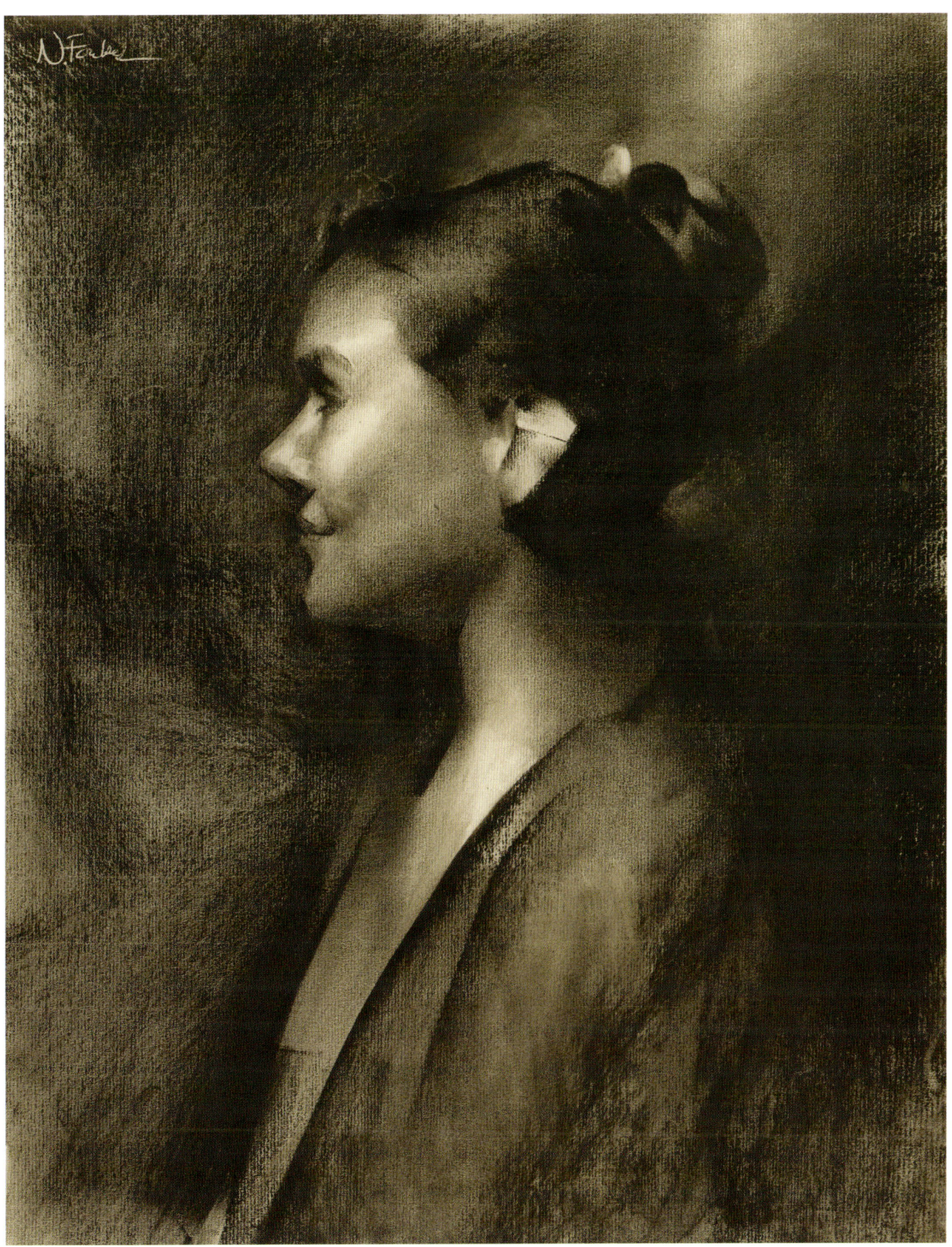

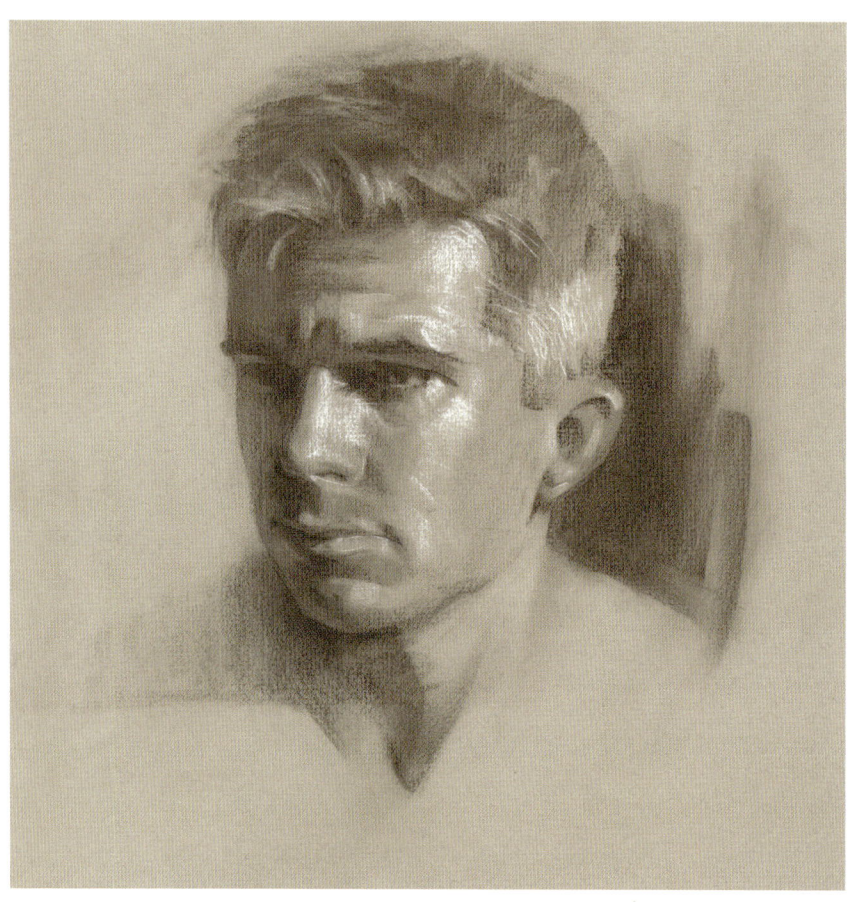

Ritmo charcoal pencil and white CarbOthello pencil on Strathmore charcoal paper.

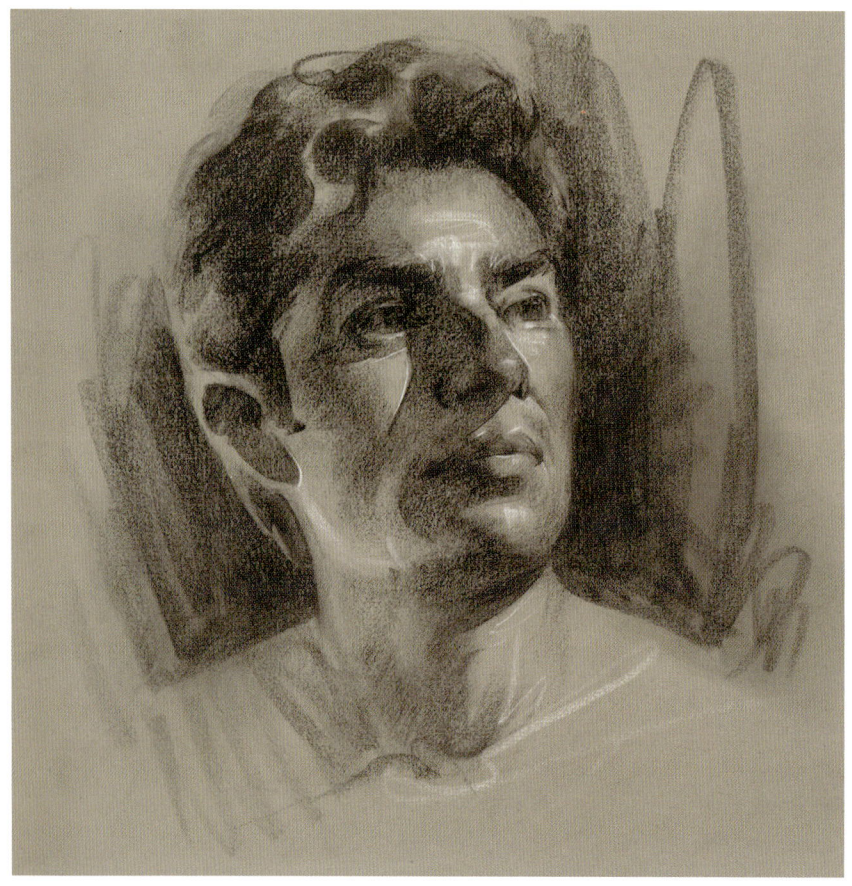

Left: Ritmo charcoal pencil and white CarbOthello pencil on Strathmore charcoal paper.

Opposite: Compressed charcoal and Pitt charcoal pencil on Strathmore charcoal paper.

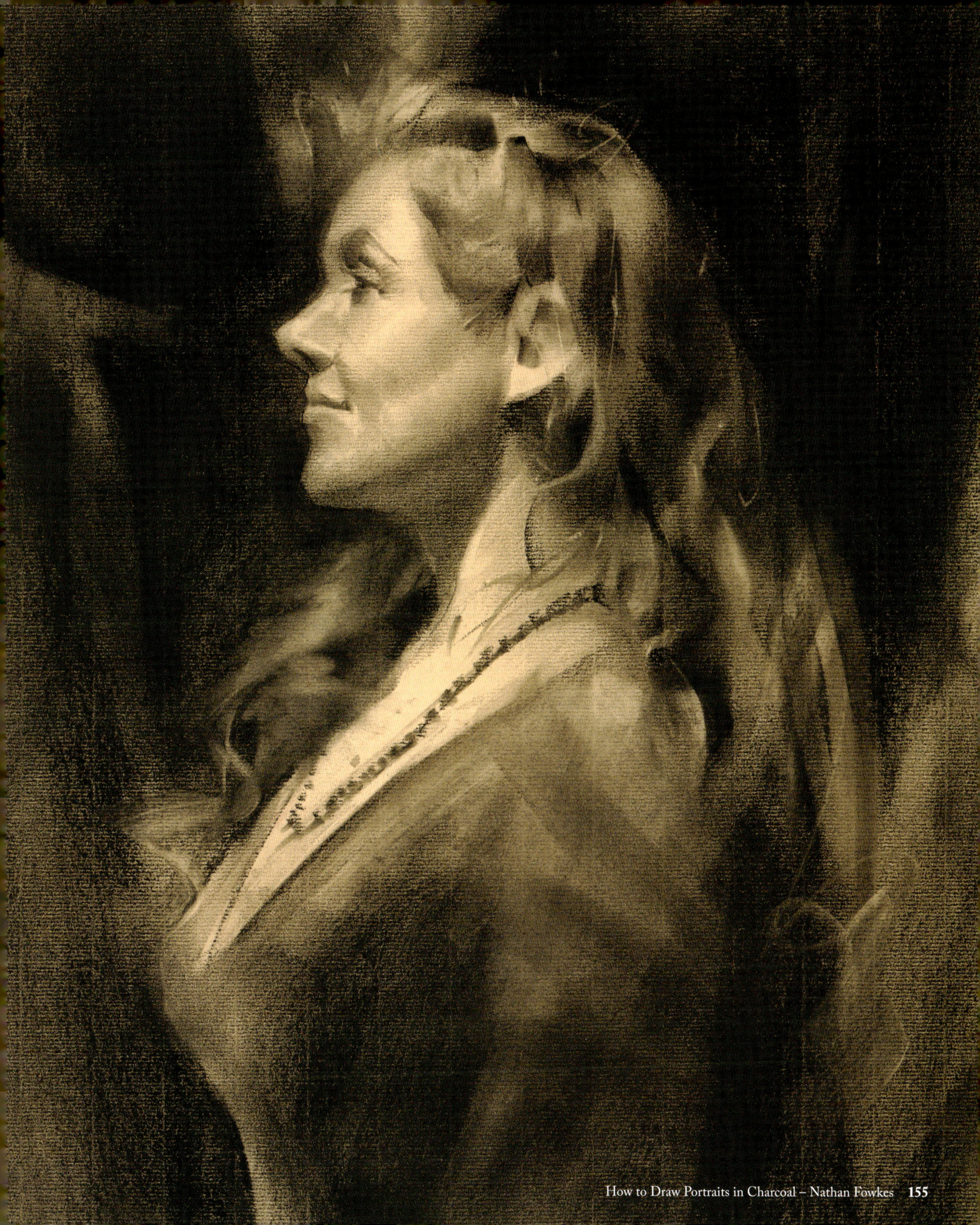

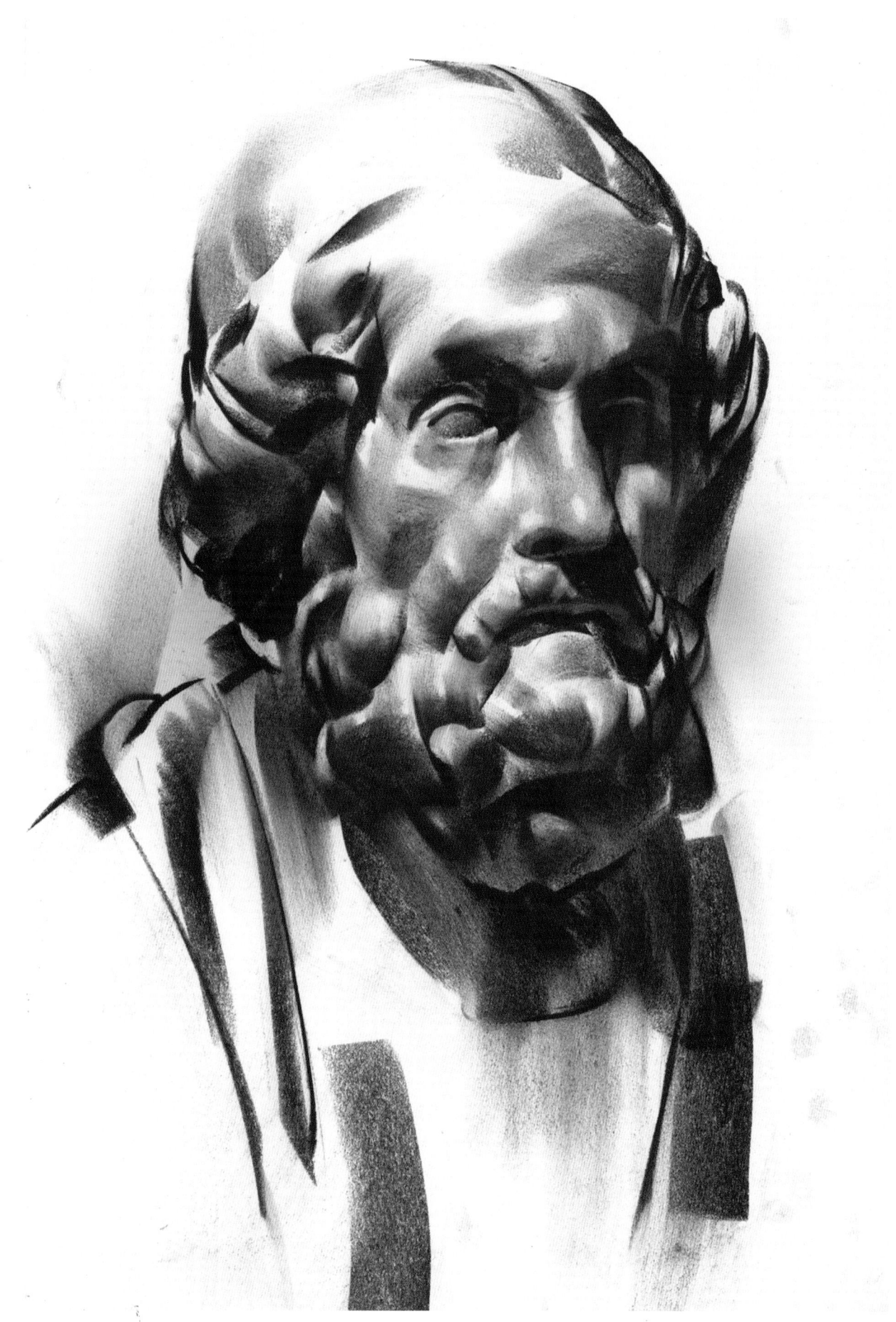

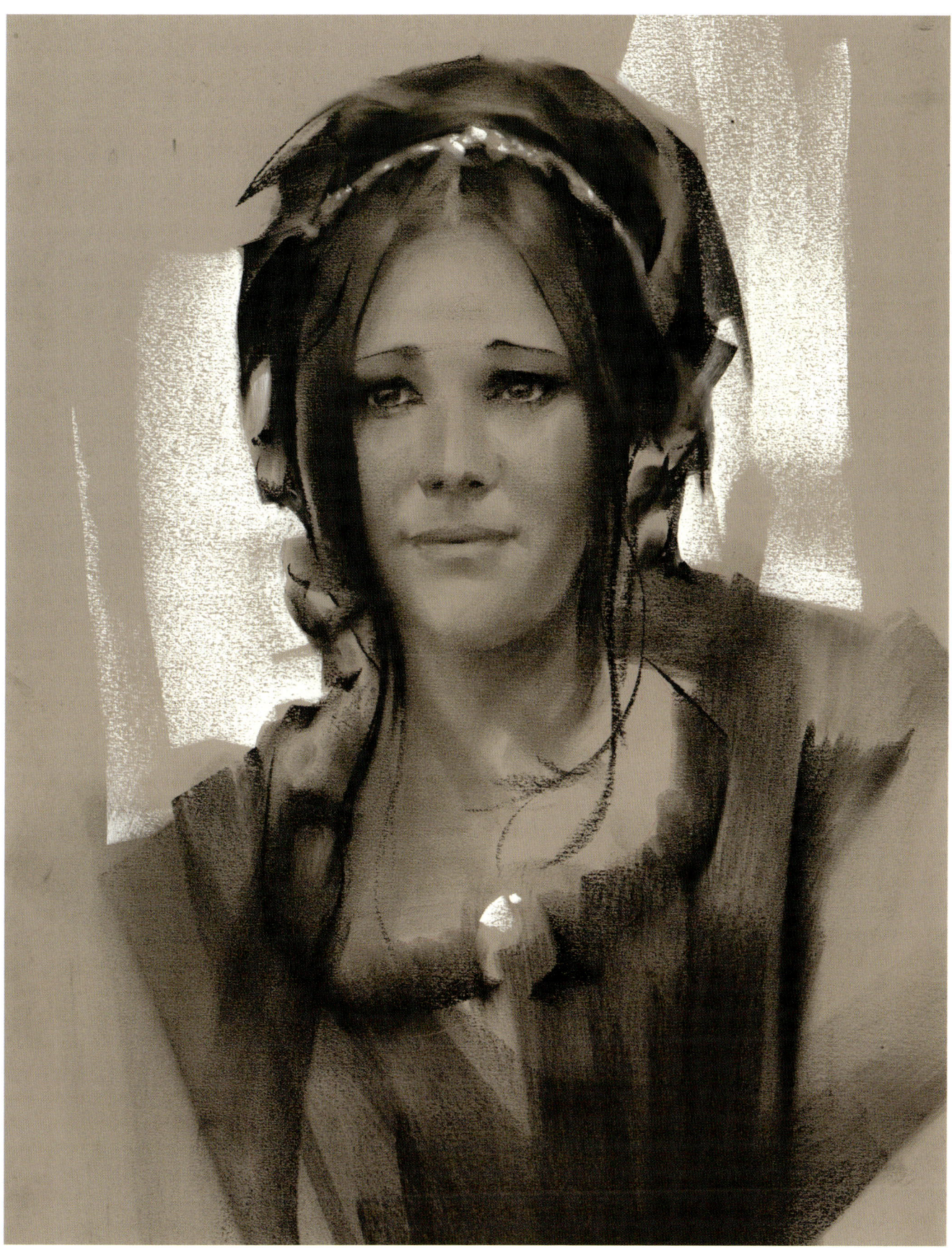

Above: Compressed charcoal and ivory Nupastel on Canson Mi-Teintes paper.

Opposite: Compressed charcoal on Rives lightweight cream paper.

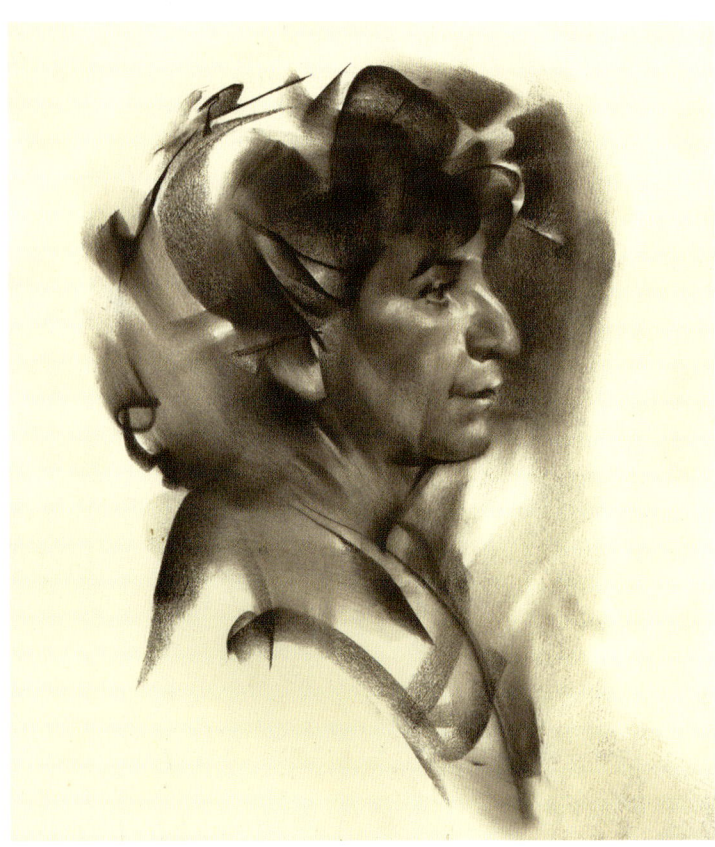

Left: Compressed charcoal on Rives lightweight cream paper.

Opposite: Vine charcoal, Pitt charcoal pencil, and ivory Nupastel on Strathmore charcoal paper.

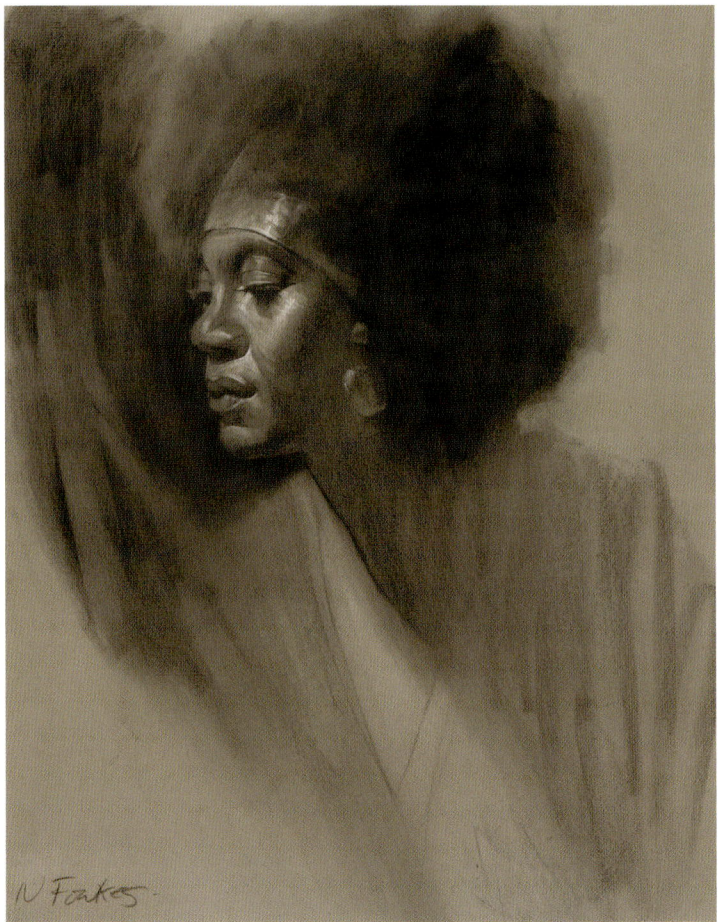

Compressed charcoal, Ritmo charcoal pencil, and white CarbOthello on Canson Mi-Teintes paper.

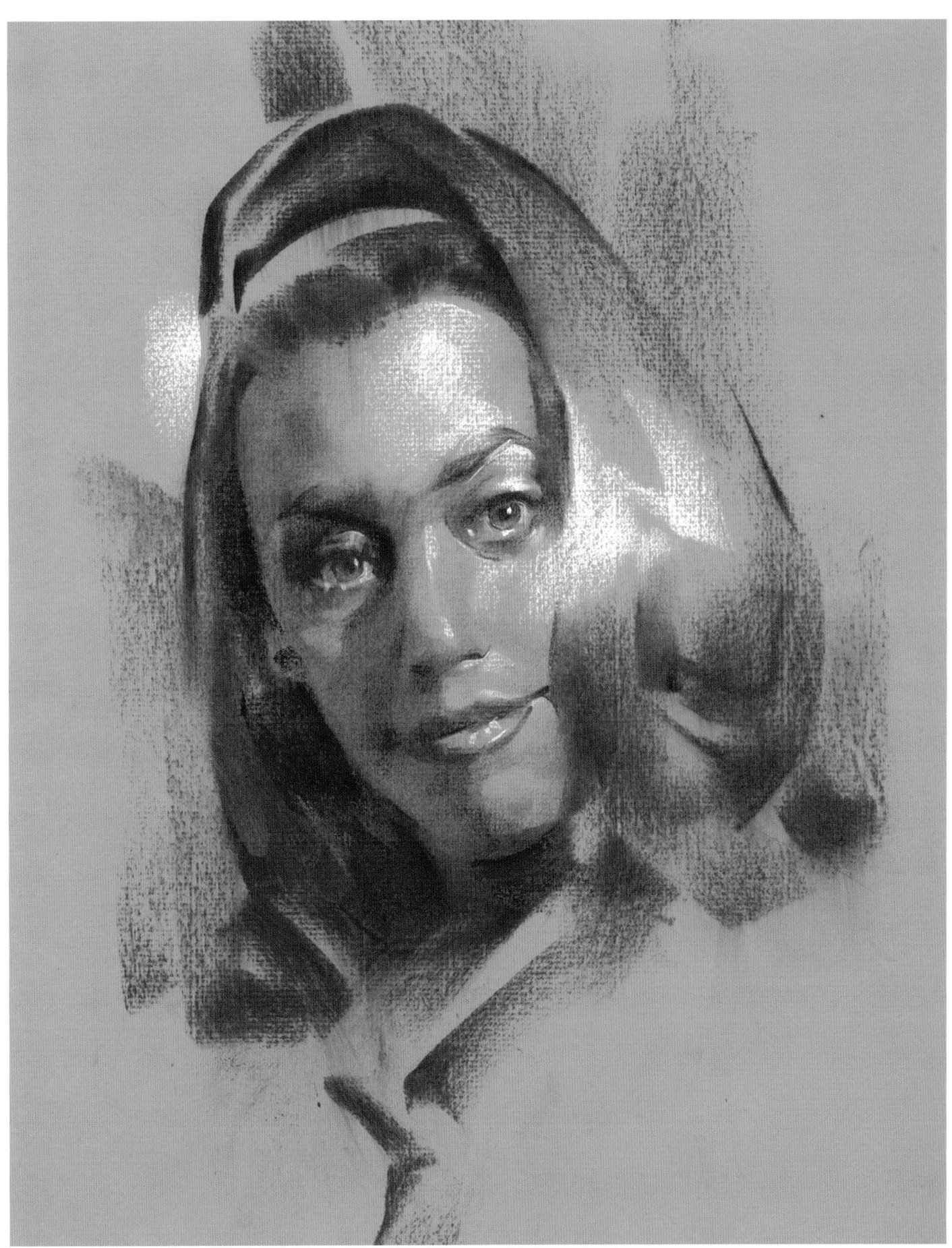

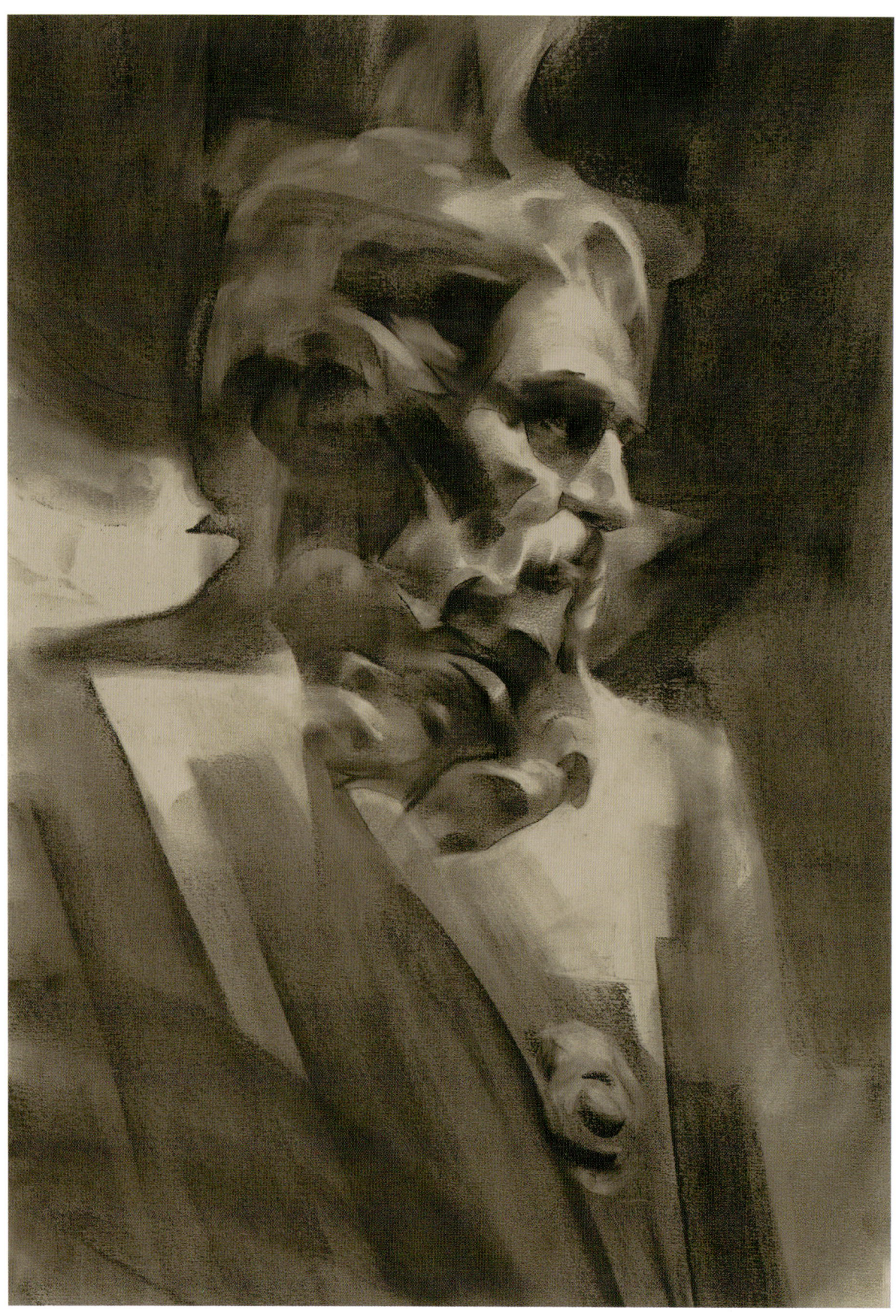

Above: Compressed charcoal on Canson Mi-Teintes paper.

Opposite: Compressed charcoal and ivory Nupastel on Rives lightweight cream paper.

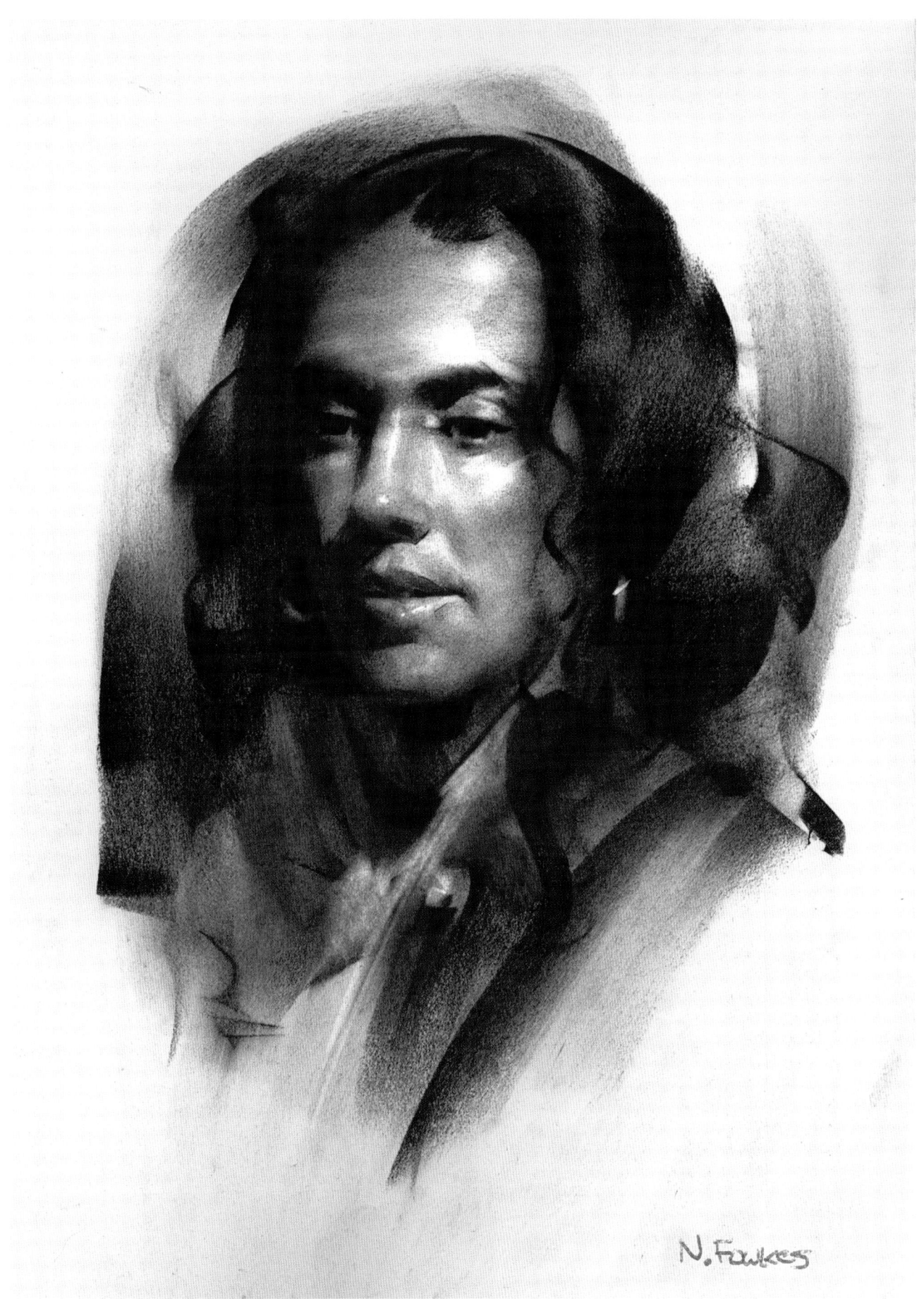

N. Fowkes

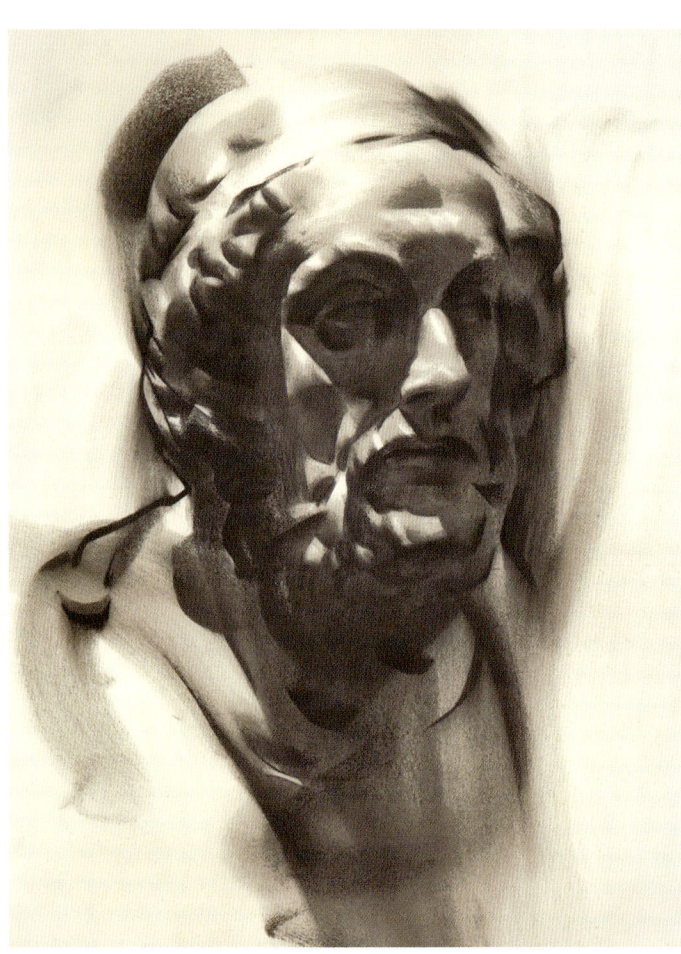

Left: Compressed charcoal on Rives lightweight white paper.

Opposite: Compressed charcoal on Rives lightweight cream paper.

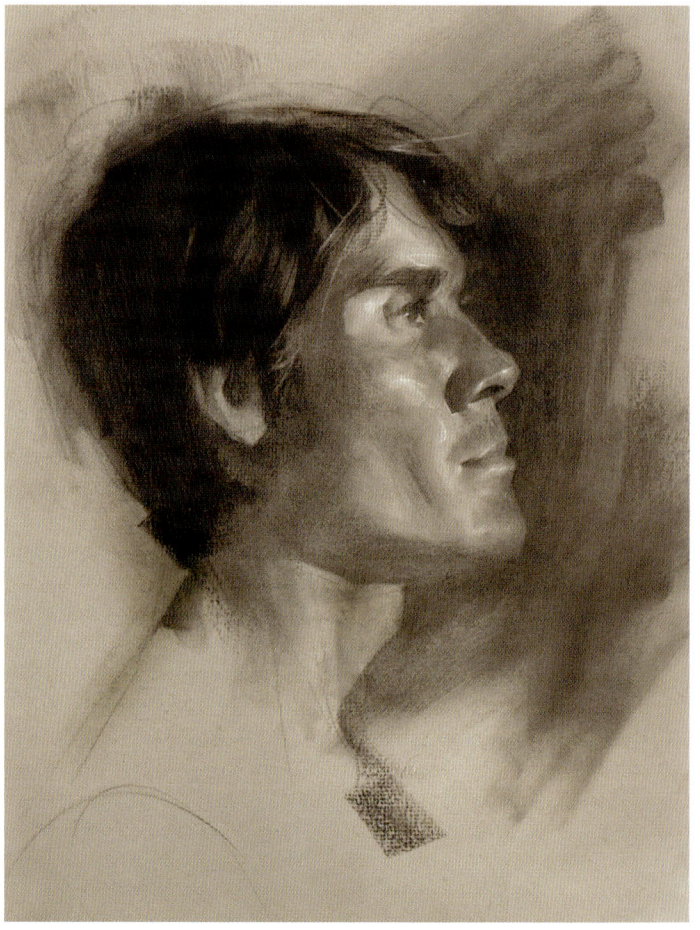

Compressed charcoal, Ritmo charcoal pencil, and white
CarbOthello pencil on Strathmore charcoal paper.

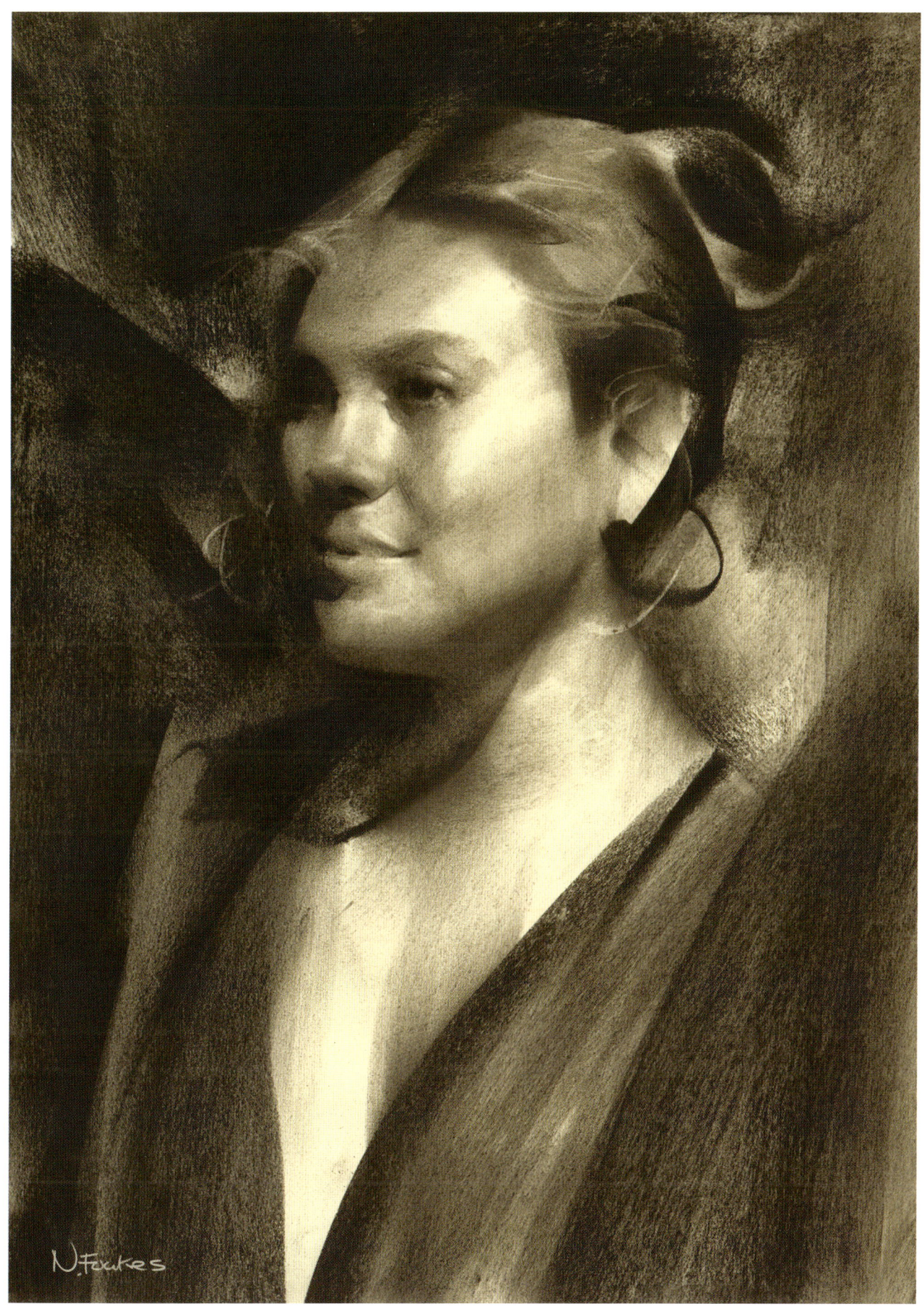

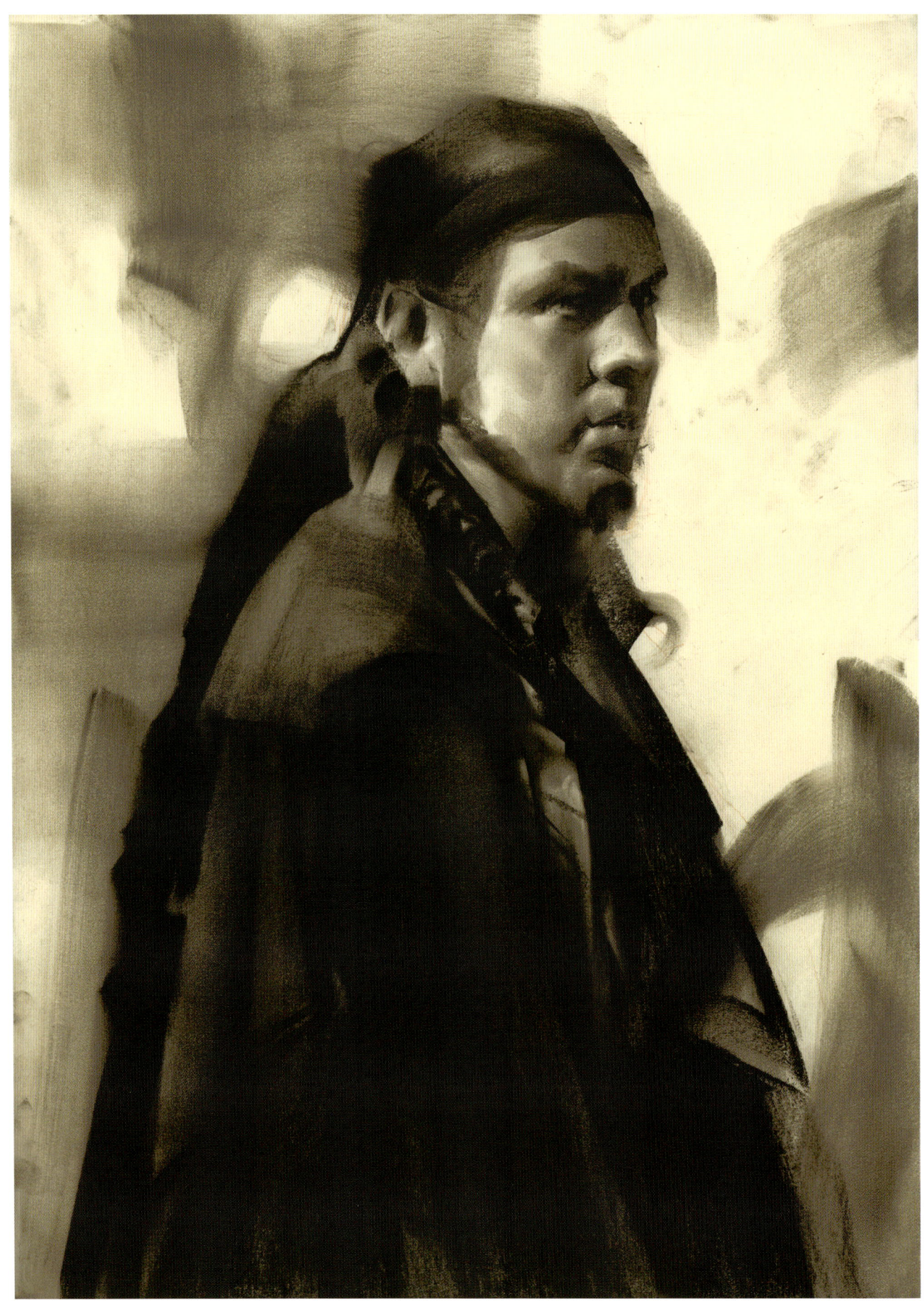

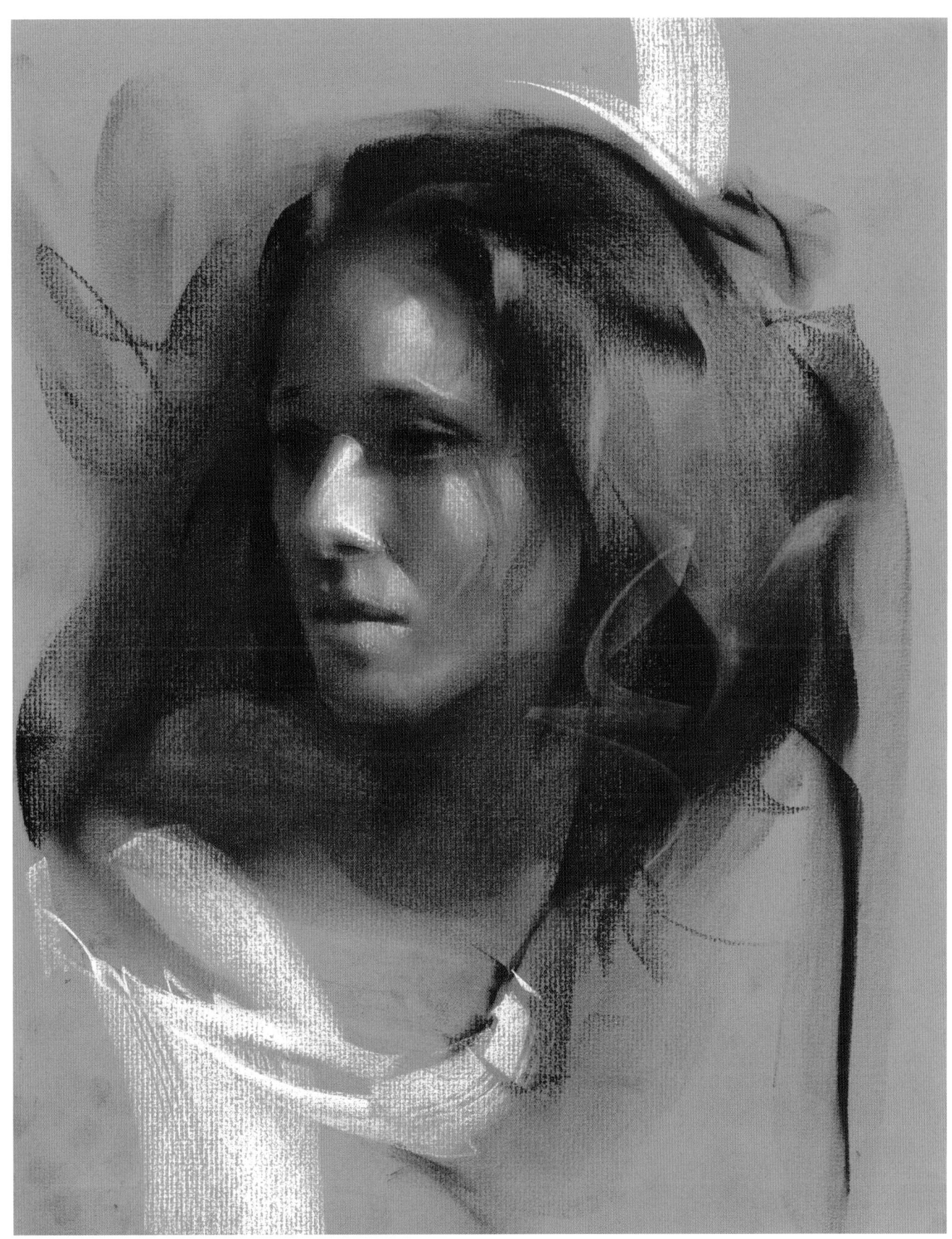

Above: Compressed charcoal and ivory Nupastel on Canson Ingres Vidalon drawing paper.

Opposite: Compressed charcoal on Rives lightweight cream paper.

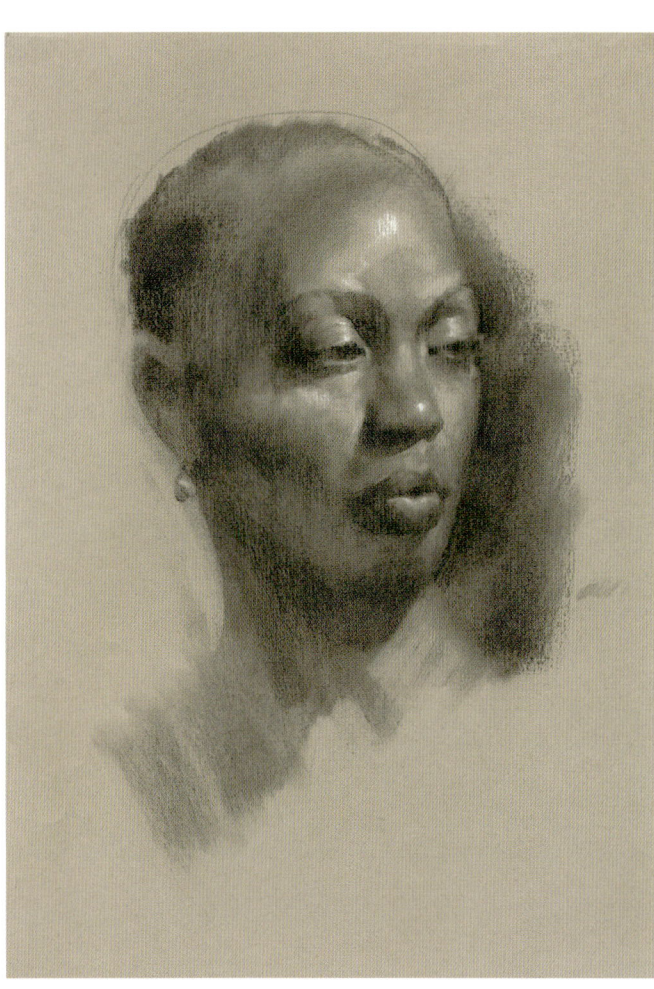

Left: Vine charcoal, Pitt charcoal pencil, and ivory CarbOthello pencil on Canson Ingres Vidalon drawing paper.

Opposite: Compressed charcoal and Pitt charcoal pencil on Canson Ingres Vidalon drawing paper.

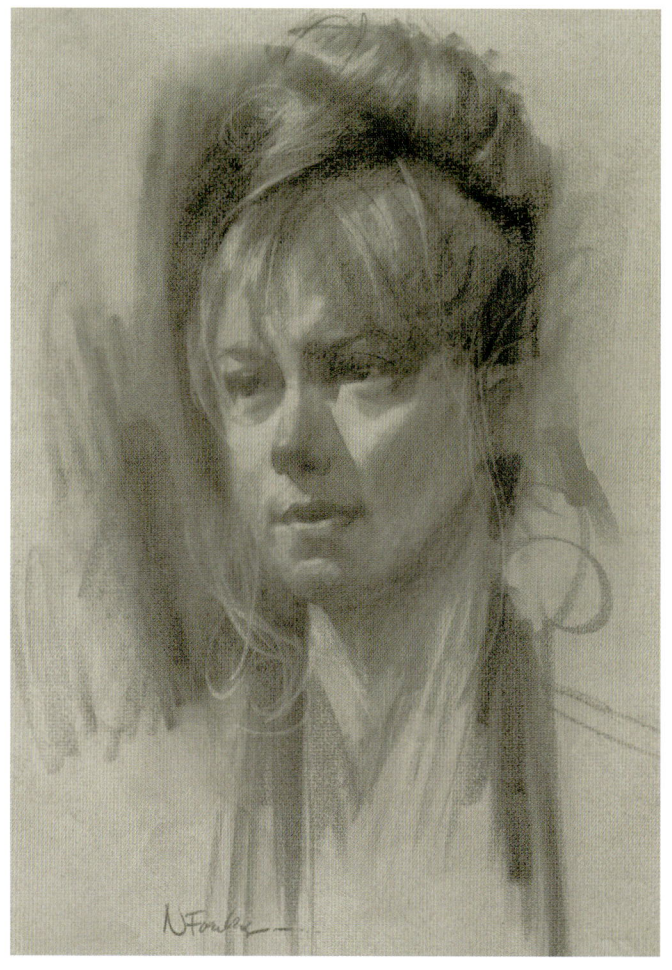

Ritmo charcoal pencil on Canson Ingres Vidalon drawing paper.

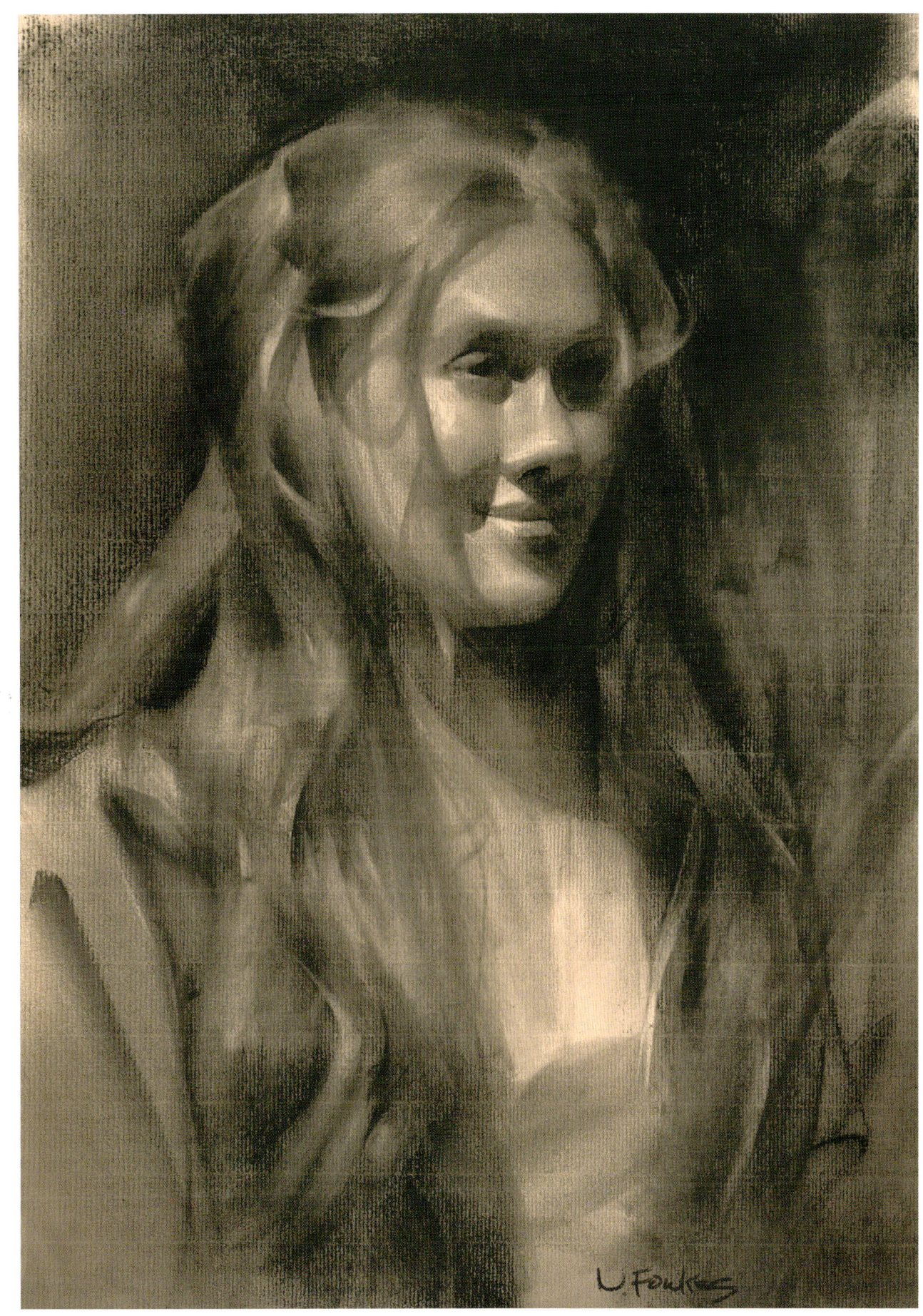

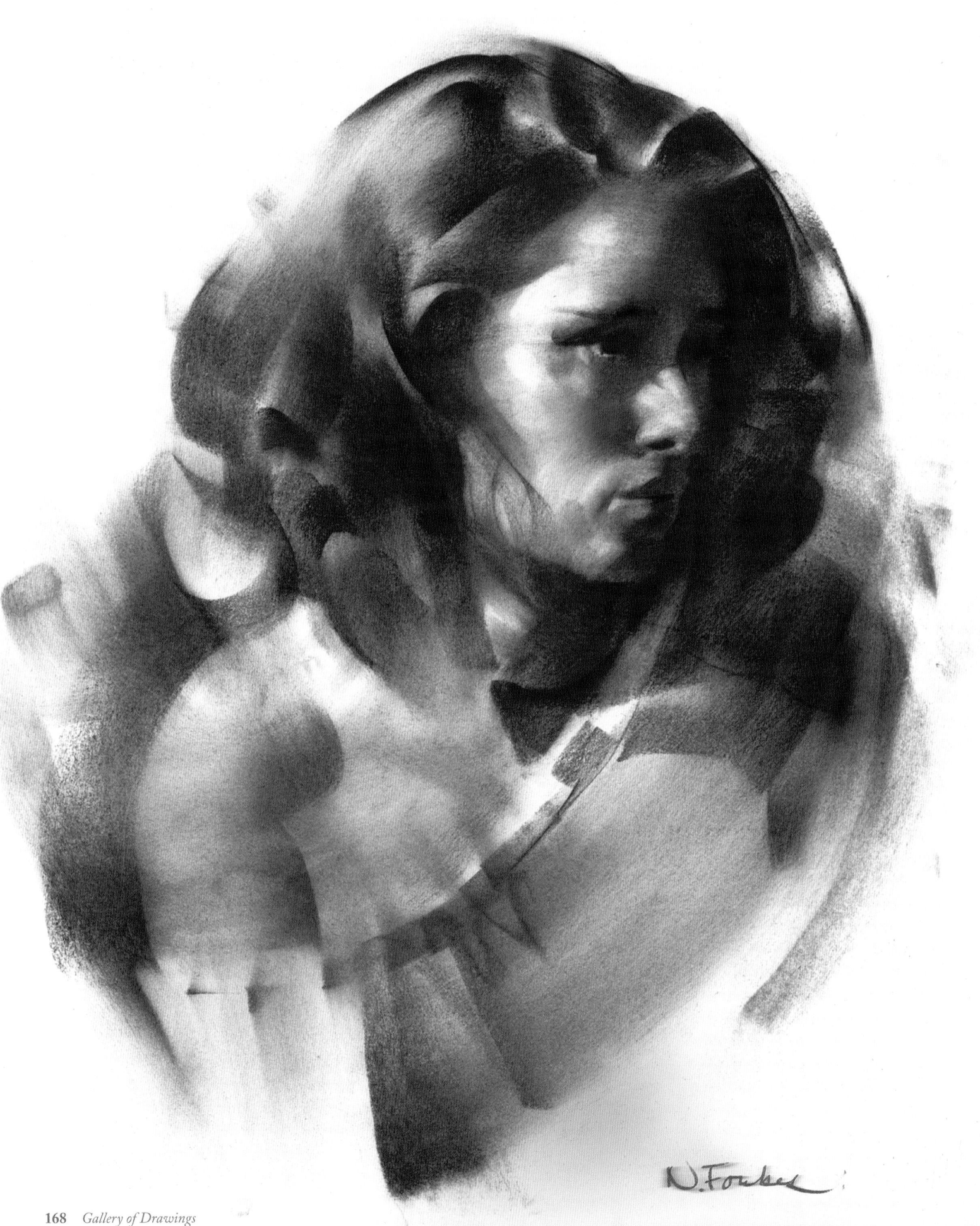

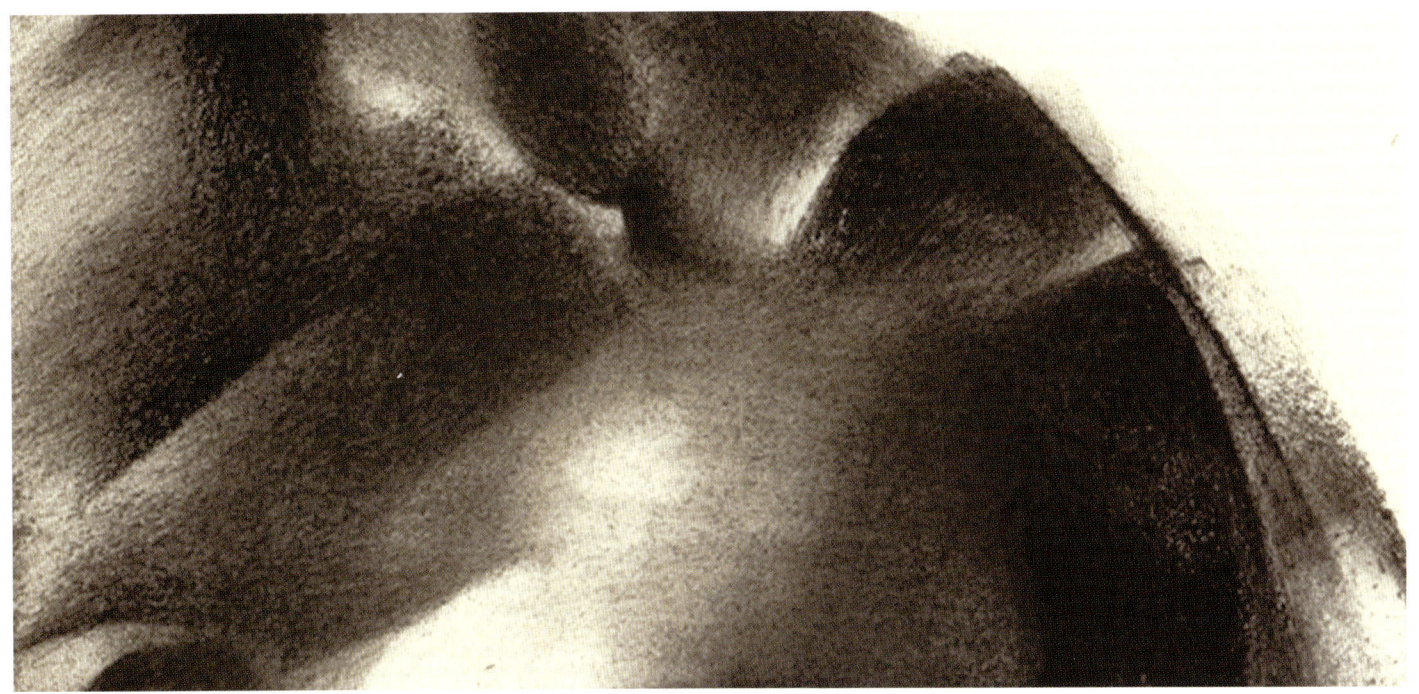

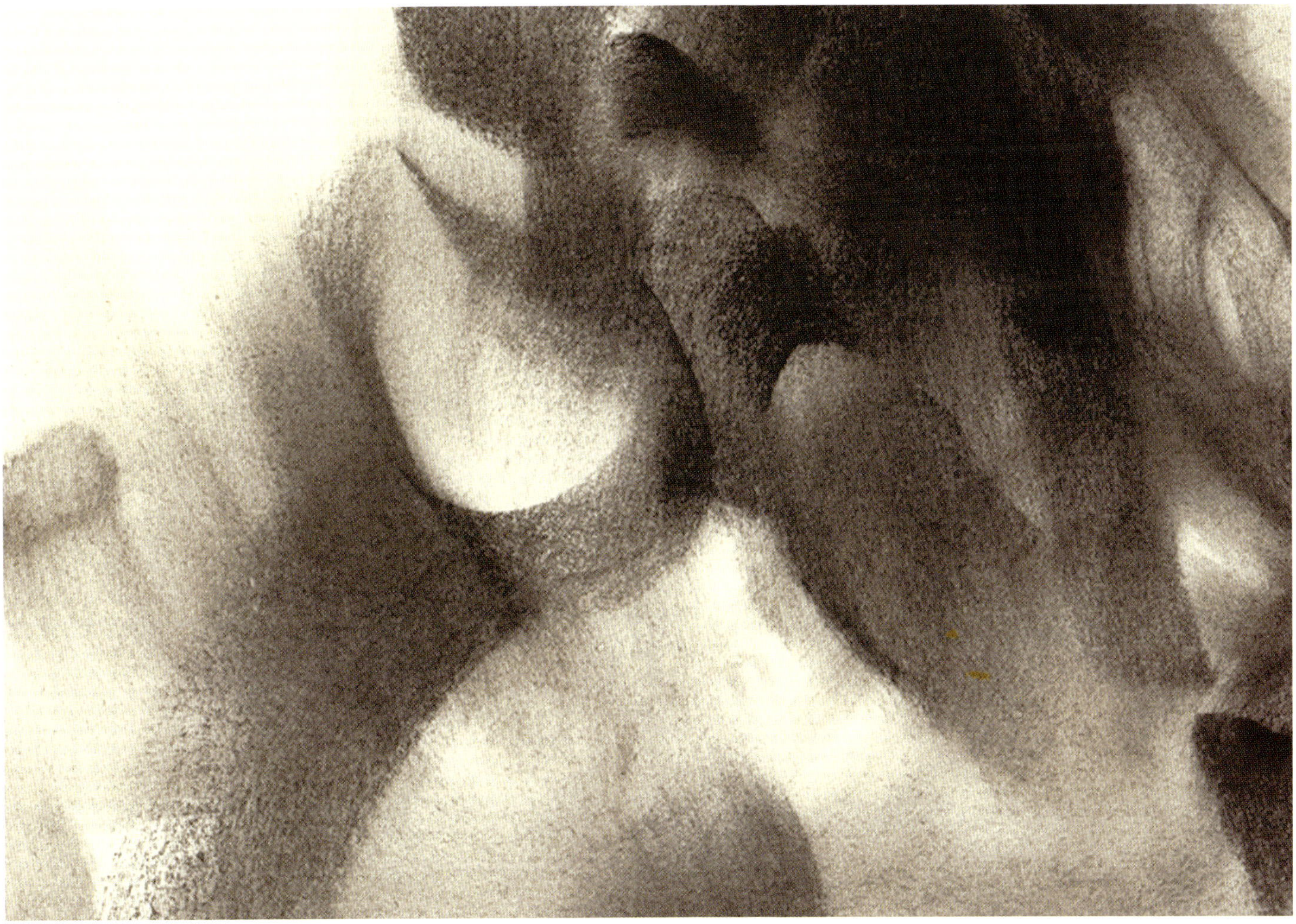

Compressed charcoal on Rives lightweight cream paper.

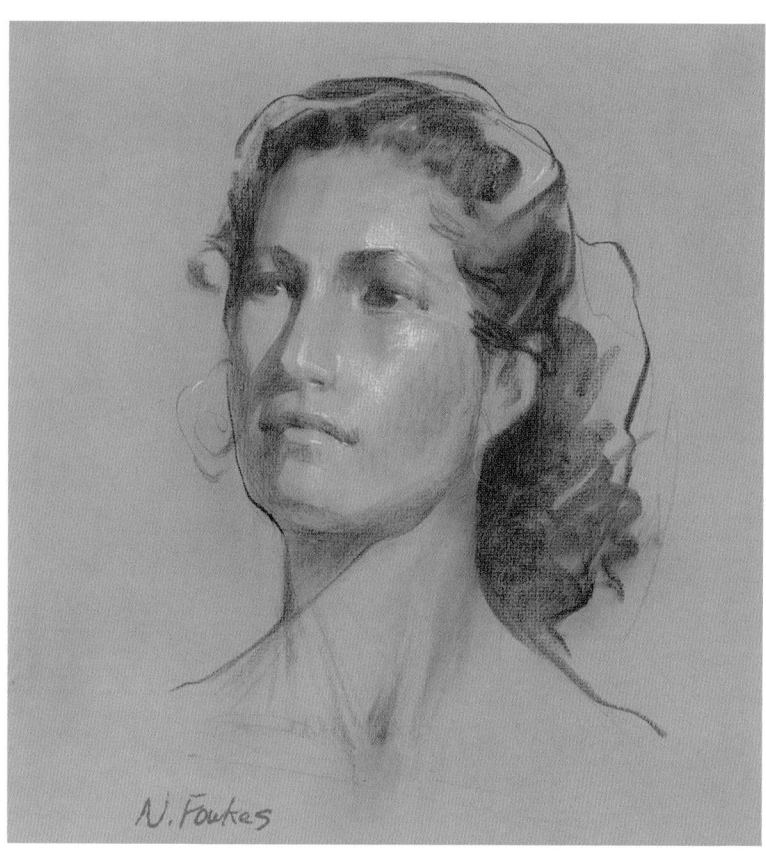

Ritmo charcoal pencil and white CarbOthello pencil on Strathmore charcoal paper.

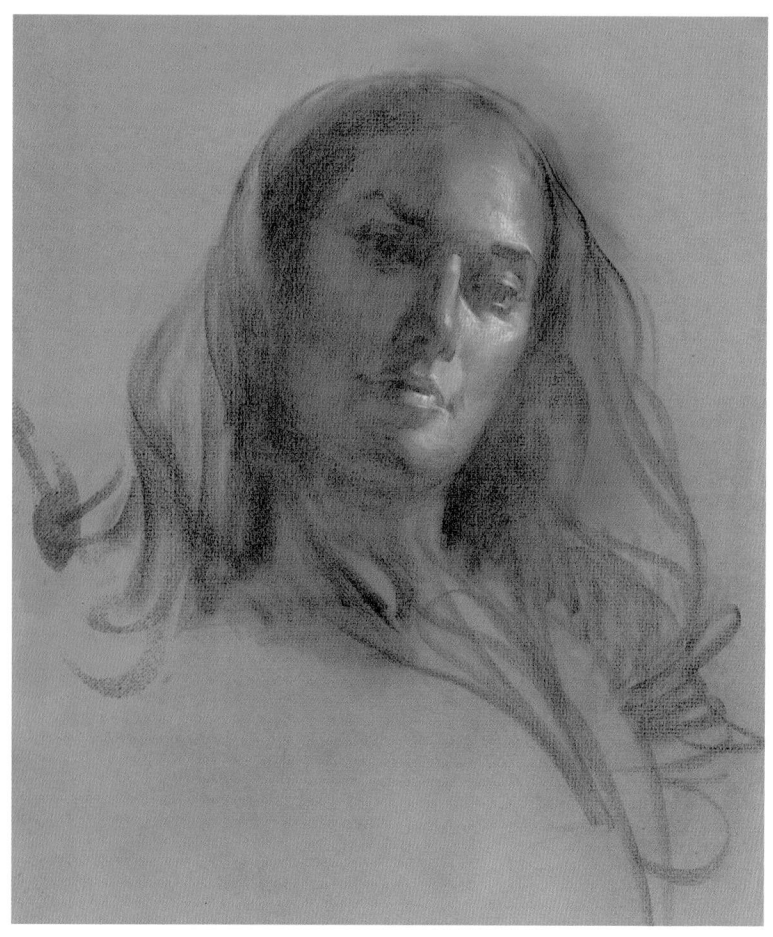

Ritmo charcoal pencil and ivory CarbOthello pencil on Strathmore charcoal paper.

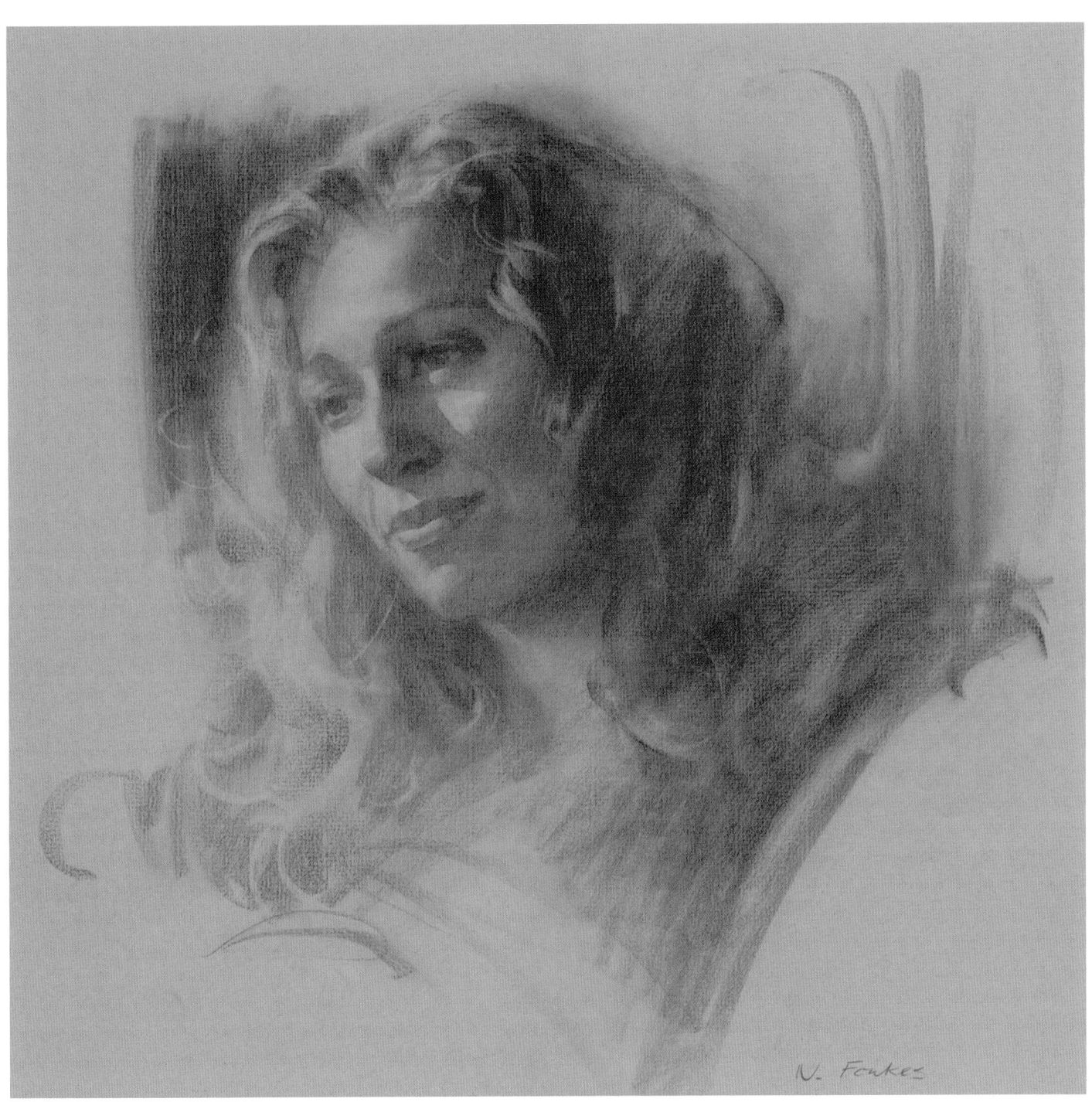

Ritmo charcoal pencil on Canson Ingres
Vidalon drawing paper.

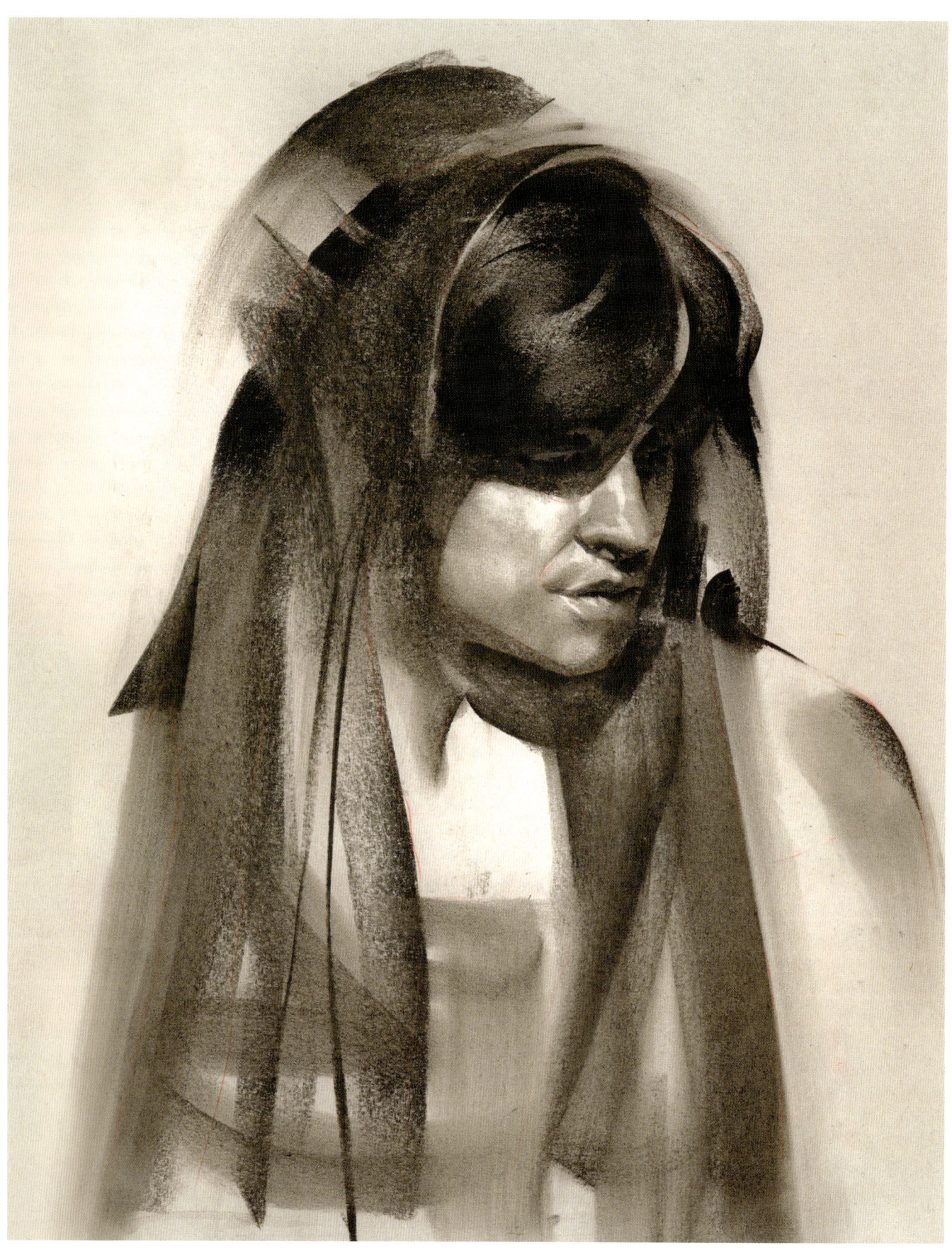

Above: Compressed charcoal and ivory Nupastel on rough newsprint.

Opposite: Compressed charcoal and Pitt charcoal pencil on Rives lightweight cream paper.

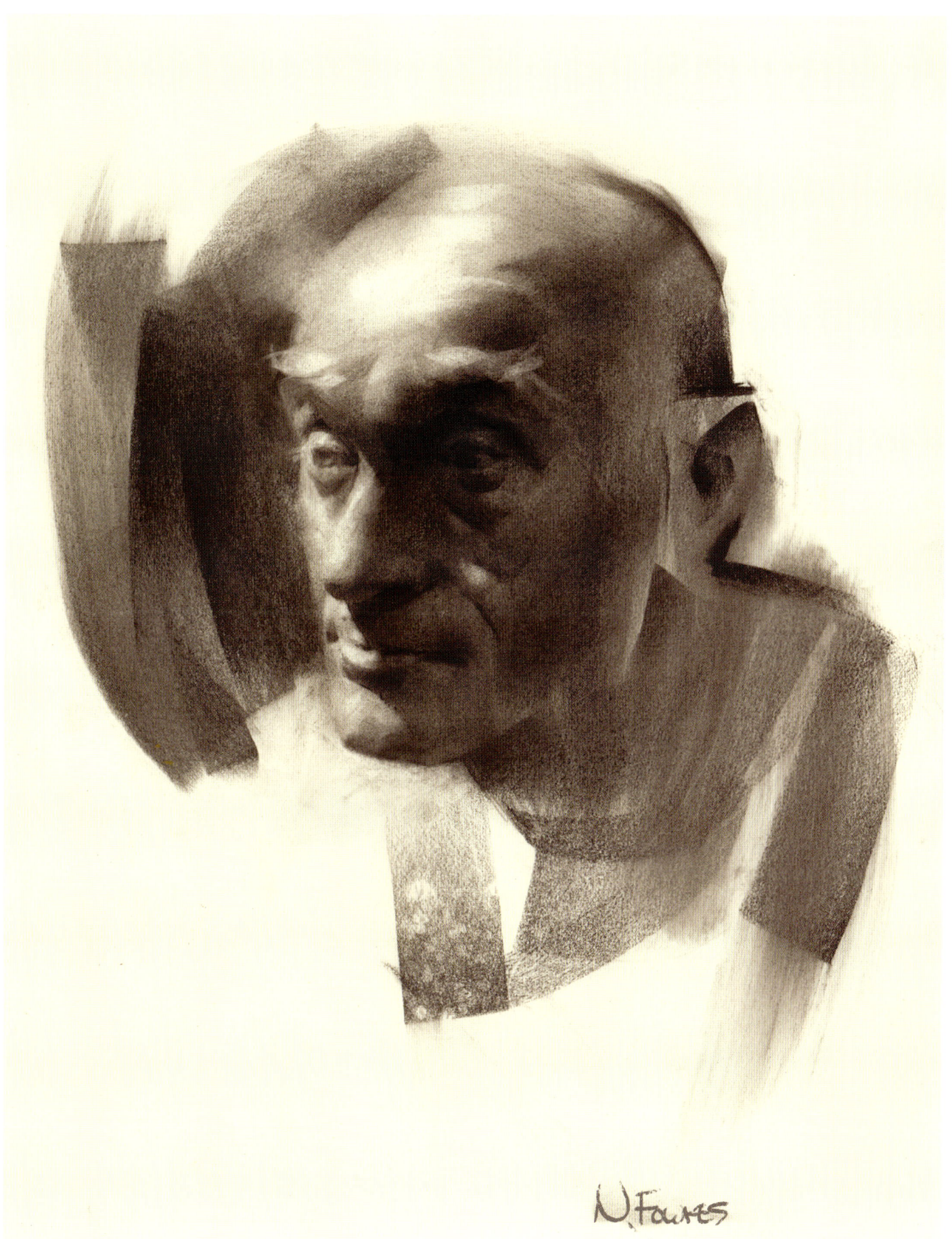

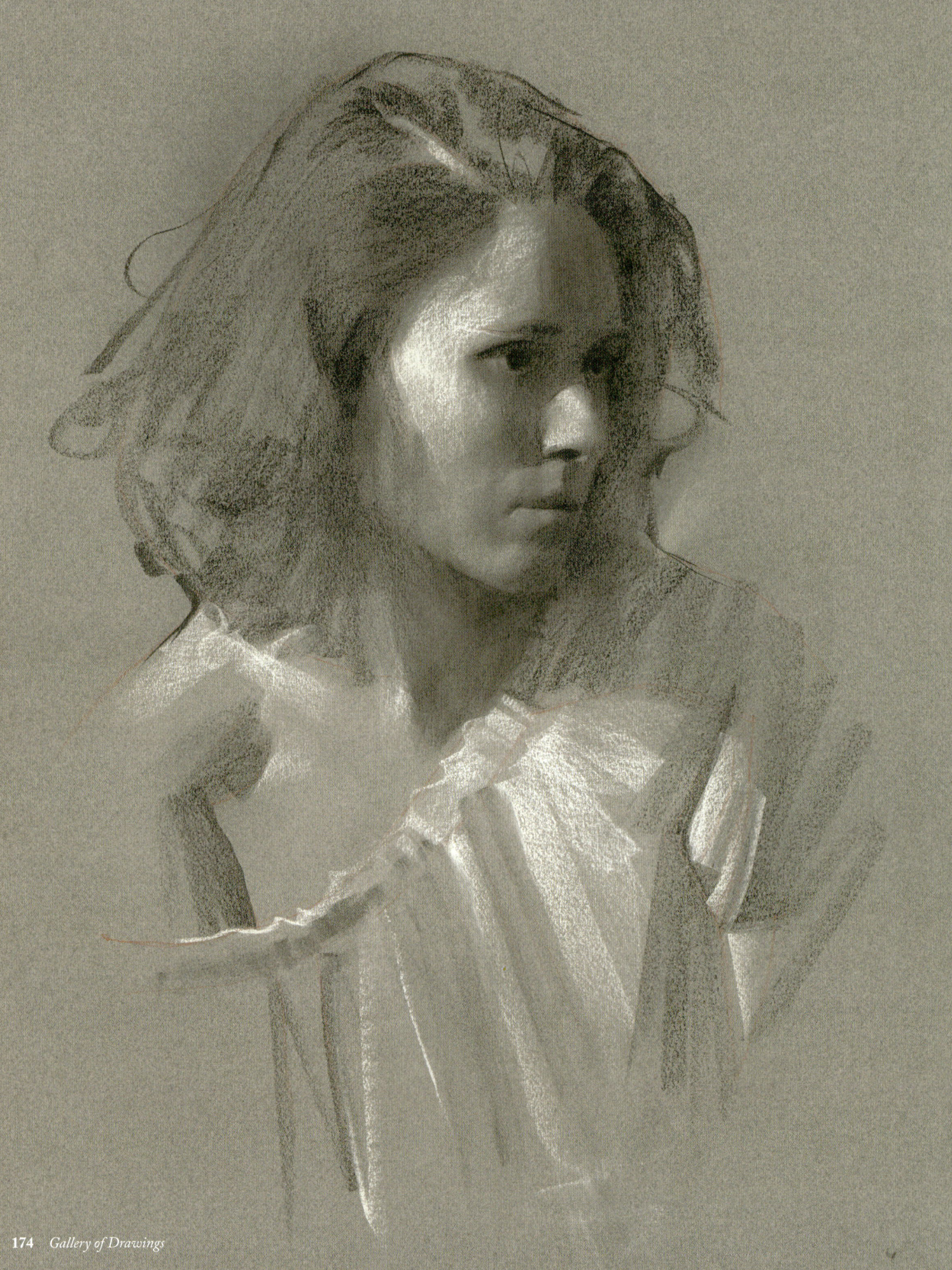

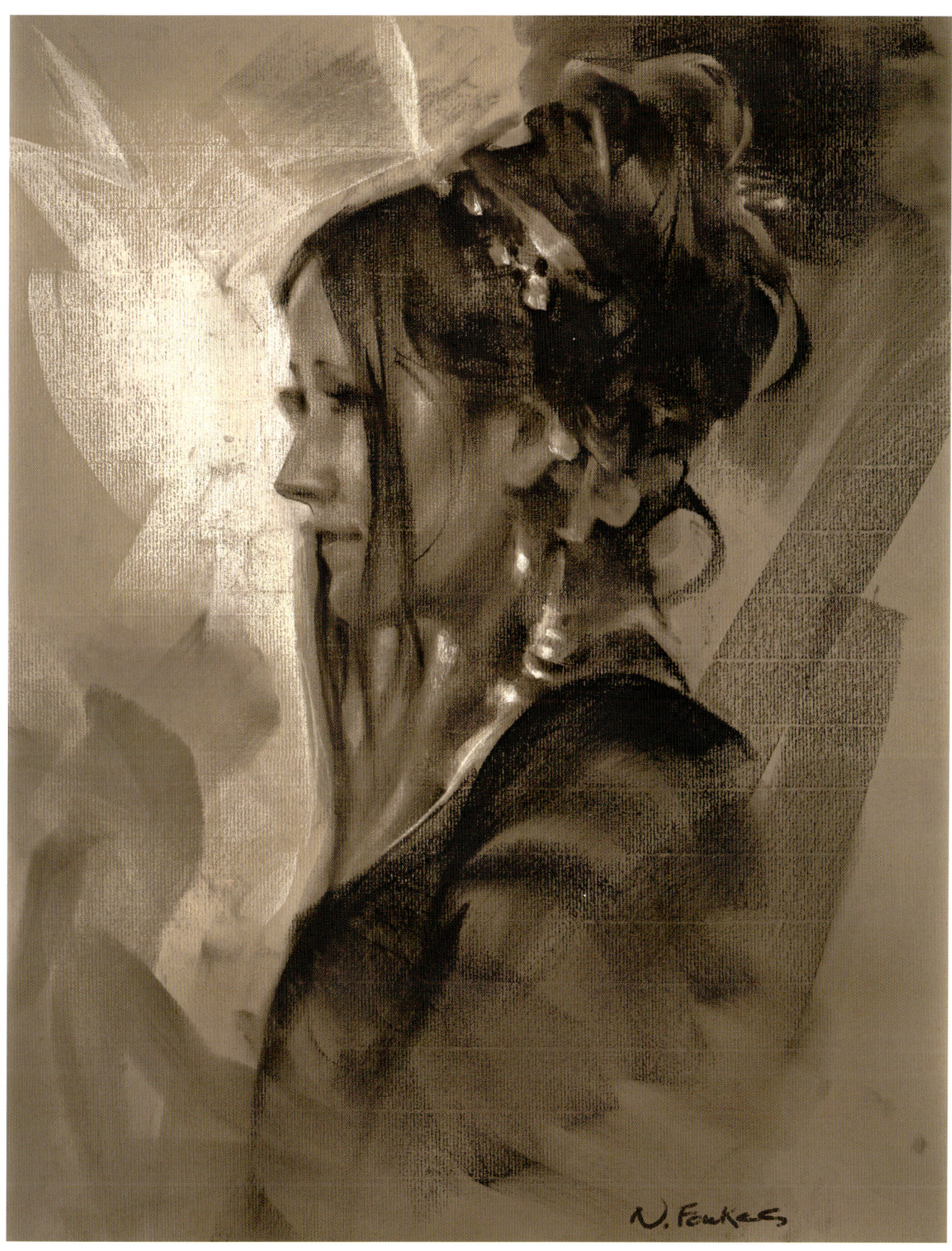

Above: Compressed charcoal and ivory Nupastel on Strathmore charcoal paper.

Opposite: Ritmo charcoal pencil and ivory Nupastel on Canson Ingres Vidalon drawing paper.

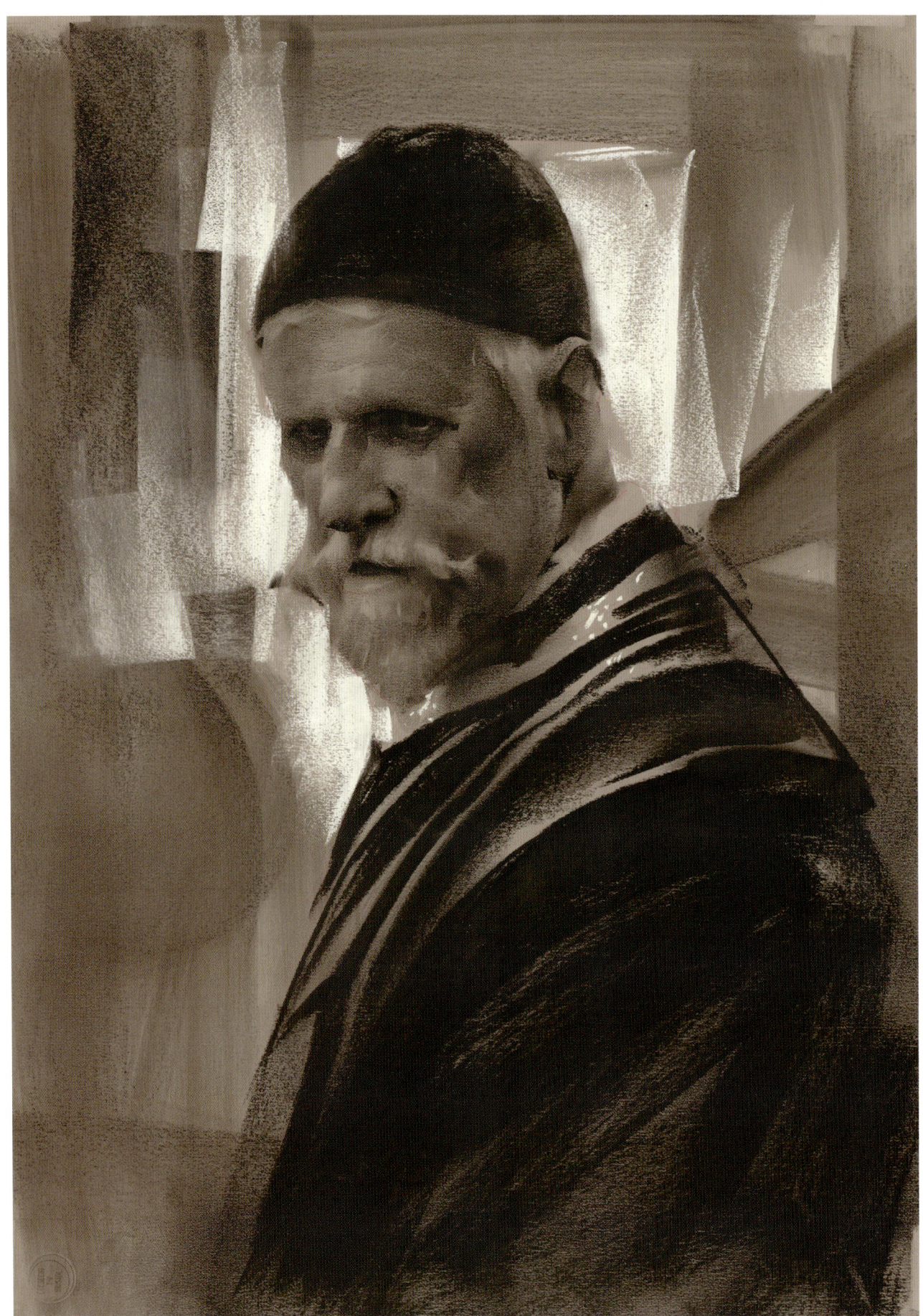

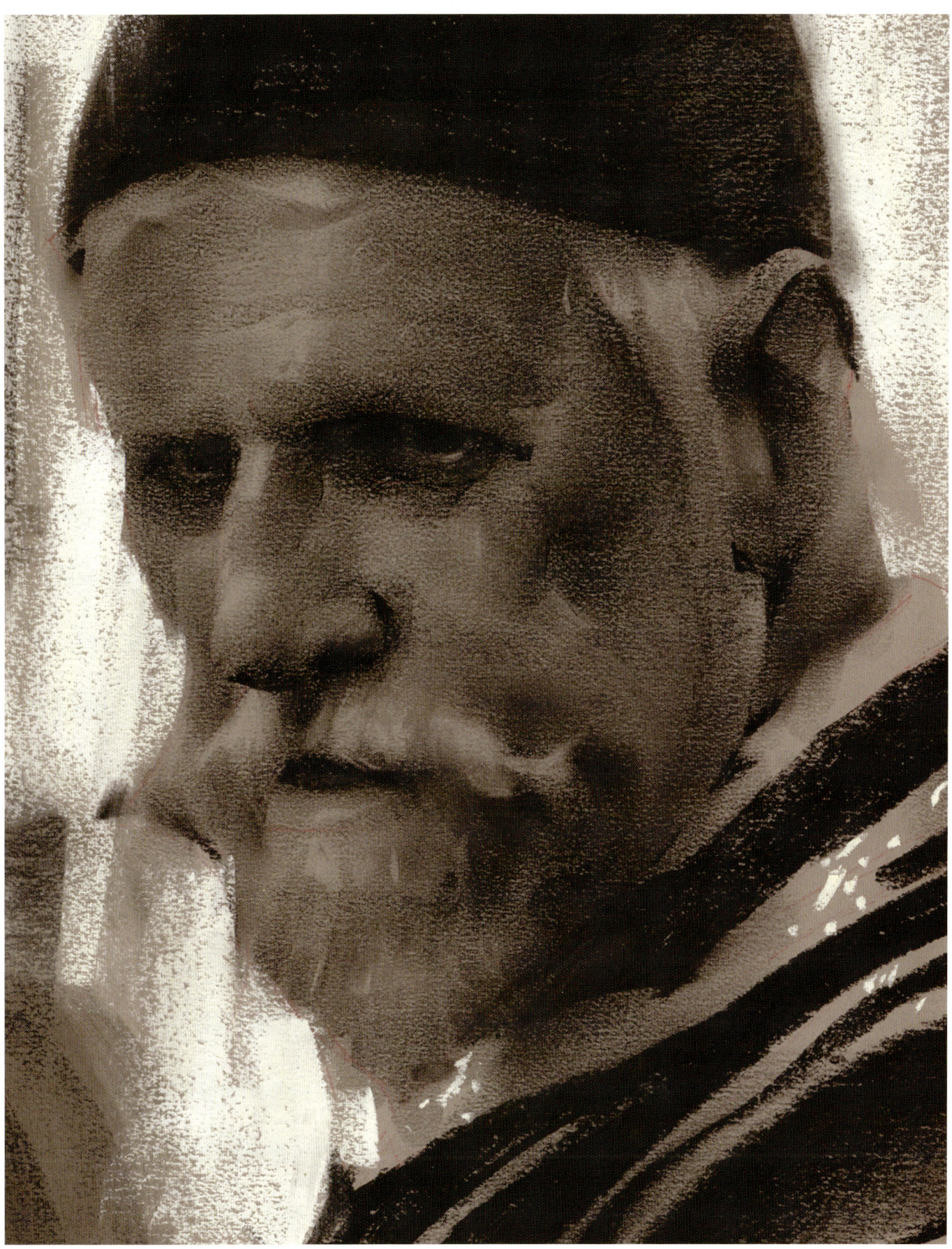

Compressed charcoal and ivory Nupastel on Canson Mi-Teintes paper.

Afterword

Congratulations on making it to the end of the book! I hope you've resisted the temptation to do the thing that I have sometimes been guilty of—to just look at the pictures and not get around to reading the text—because this book is in no way an encyclopedic compendium of all things portrait drawing, but rather the exploration of a useful approach. I do encourage you to expand and complete your knowledge by looking at the other books and resources that are available out there. I also invite you to look at those books (and mine too) with a bit of skepticism. Early on in my drawing career I became distressed by extensive charts and graphs of head measurements, most of which seemed to go out the window the moment that my subject turned his or her head away from a simple front or side view. I started to consider these to be the phrenology of the art world: taking something complex and gaining the satisfaction of forcing it into a box of measurements that in the end does not hold up to real-life practice.

Drawing is very difficult, but each of us is up to the task. Your own brain is the most sophisticated instrument that exists on planet Earth. And with it we are able to parse the vast complexity of living on planet Earth; it gives us the ability to thrive. For most of us, however, translating the complexities of that world onto a two-dimensional sheet of paper with a stick of charcoal is not something that comes to us naturally. But we have the ability to learn new ways of thinking and to overcome challenges through dedicated practice when it comes to the art and craft of drawing. So I invite you to continue looking for good ideas anywhere and everywhere you can find them, and to actively put them into practice. From this point forward my goal is simply to be that angel (or devil) on your shoulder—that nagging voice that's always reminding you to push a little harder and to stand a little taller as an artist. Good luck!

About the Author

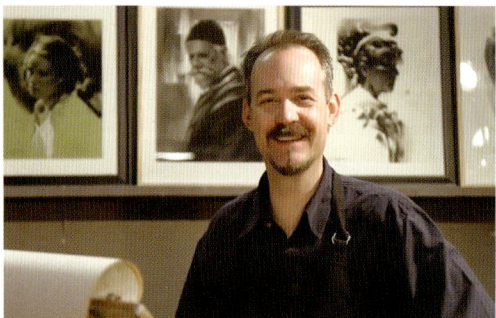

Courtesy of the Los Angeles Academy of Figurative Art

Nathan Fowkes is a world-renowned entertainment and fine artist who has been teaching life drawing, portrait painting, color, and design for the past fifteen years. He studied traditional painting and entertainment design at the prestigious Art Center College of Design and graduated with honors. Currently a conceptual artist for animated films, his clients include DreamWorks, Disney, and Blue Sky; and his film credits include such popular movies as *The Prince of Egypt*, *Spirit*, several projects within the *Shrek Universe*, *How to Train Your Dragon*, and *Puss in Boots*.

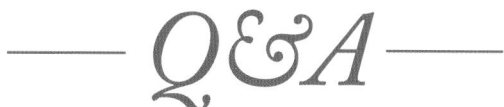

Q&A

What spurred you to write this book?

My day job is as an animation artist, but in my spare time I've been teaching drawing and painting for the past 15 years and putting together my own body of work. So the time seemed right to share what I've learned, as well as present my drawings for anyone who might be interested in having a look.

When were you first introduced to charcoal drawing?

When I was around 15 years old, my folks helped me subscribe to a couple of artists magazines. It was fairly common for the artists to show their finished works in full color and then, as an afterthought, show a few of their drawings that were often done in charcoal. In many cases I found myself most attracted to the charcoal drawings, there was a quality of lost and found in the softness and firmness of the charcoal that I was quite struck with and wanted to learn to do myself.

And why was it not until 2000 that you picked it up again?

I was actually drawing quite actively previous to 2000. I graduated from art school in '95 and began applying my skills toward scene painting for animated films. My employer, DreamWorks Animation, was generous enough to provide life-drawing sessions for the artists three times per week, and during those years I almost never missed a session. My drawings improved but I knew that it would take a greater commitment for my drawings to reach the professional level that I had always hoped for. That's what led to the drawing sabbatical that I took in 2000 as described in the introduction to this book.

How did you select your subjects?

During the aforementioned drawing sessions at DreamWorks, I got to know most of the professional art models around Los Angeles, and when I started teaching I was able to select my favorite ones and work with them directly. They were the ones who brightened the room when they walked in and always gave you the impression that they were thrilled to be there. That enthusiasm rubs off on the artist and my best drawings came out of those sessions.

What is the best and worst reaction you have received from a subject after he or she saw your finished drawing?

Since many of my models are professionals, they respond very politely even if they're not thrilled with the drawing. The most typical negative reaction that I get is from non-artist friends and family. They look at my occasional "flights of fancy" where I'm trying to capture patterns of light and shadow instead of rendering features, and assume that I must not be finished yet.

All the portraits featured in the book are of individuals. Have you ever tried to draw a group, for instance, family portrait? And what kinds of challenges are presented with such a task?

Good question! Because of my work in animation, I'm able to spend my drawing time to please myself rather than pleasing a paying sitter. The biggest challenge for me in doing portrait commissions is that people don't tend to see themselves objectively, this makes commissioned portraits a moving target that is difficult to hit. Group portraits multiply that challenge and I have a great admiration for other artists who do it. Since I have the luxury of drawing what I enjoy, I stick to individual portraits.

Do you find that more students are running to or away from traditional media?

It's a mix. When I first moved to Los Angeles there was one drawing atelier, now 25 years later there are a dozen of them, this is because entertainment-industry artists recognize the importance of understanding form, color, and light. At the same time, too many hopeful art students are running away from it, relying on the quick, easy fixes of digital tools.

Who is someone you've always wanted to draw?

There's actually a particular category that I enjoy drawing rather than a particular individual. I quite enjoy drawing the aged; I like to work at getting all of that character in their faces. It's been a bit difficult to do since there are fewer such professional models available.

Have you ever let someone draw you? And what was that experience like?

Awful, I do not like to sit still . . .

Special Thanks

The Los Angeles Academy of Figurative Art

The crack design and publishing team
at Design Studio Press

"Supermodel" Mark Snyder

My online classes and downloadable drawing demonstrations can be found at schoolism.com and artschoolvideos.com.

For classes, events, workshops, and social media visit nathanfowkesart.com. My portfolio page is nathanfowkes.com.

Also by Nathan Fowkes

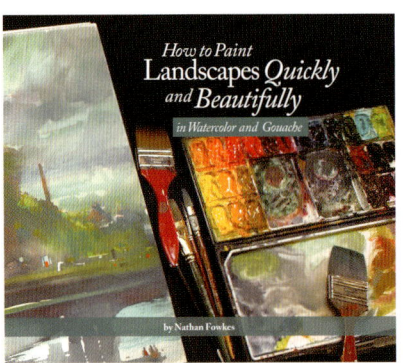

$27.95, 184 pages, 11 x 9 inches, ISBN 9781624650499

To order additional copies of this book, and to view other books we offer, please visit:

www.designstudiopress.com

For volume purchases and resale inquiries, please email:
info@designstudiopress.com

tel 310.836.3116

To be notified of new releases, special discounts, and events, please sign up for our mailing list on our website, like our Facebook page, and follow us on Twitter:

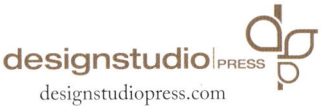

designstudiopress.com

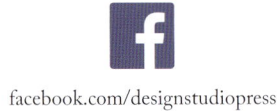

facebook.com/designstudiopress

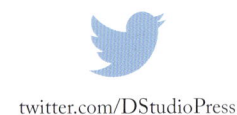

twitter.com/DStudioPress